Signs of Difference

CW01084331

How are people's ideas about languages, ways of speaking, and expressive styles shaped by their social positions and values? How is difference, in language and in social life, made – and unmade? How and why are some differences persuasive as the basis for action, while other differences are ignored or erased? Written by two recognized authorities on language and culture, this book argues that ideological work of all kinds is fundamentally communicative, and that social positions, projects, and historical moments influence, and are influenced by, people's ideas about communicative practices. Neither true nor false, ideologies are positioned and partial visions of the world, relying on comparison and perspective; they exploit differences in expressive features – linguistic and otherwise – to construct convincing stereotypes of people, spaces, and activities. Using detailed ethnographic, historical, and contemporary examples, this outstanding book shows readers how to analyze ideological work semiotically.

SUSAN GAL is Mae and Sidney G. Metzl Distinguished Service Professor of Anthropology and Linguistics at the University of Chicago. She is author of *Language Shift* (1979) and *The Politics of Language* (in Hungarian, 2018) as well as coauthor with Gail Kligman of *Politics of Gender After Socialism* (2000), and coeditor with Kathryn Woolard of *Languages and Publics: The Making of Authority* (2001).

JUDITH T. IRVINE is Edward Sapir Collegiate Professor of Linguistic Anthropology at the University of Michigan. Author of many articles and chapters in linguistic anthropology, she is coeditor with Jane H. Hill of *Responsibility and Evidence in Oral Discourse* (1993), coeditor with Regna Darnell et al. of the *Collected Works of Edward Sapir* (1999), and Associate Editor of the journal *Language in Society*.

Signs of Difference

Language and Ideology in Social Life

Susan Gal

University of Chicago

Judith T. Irvine

University of Michigan, Ann Arbor

CAMBRIDGE
UNIVERSITY PRESS

University Printing House, Cambridge CB2 8BS, United Kingdom

One Liberty Plaza, 20th Floor, New York, NY 10006, USA

477 Williamstown Road, Port Melbourne, VIC 3207, Australia

314–321, 3rd Floor, Plot 3, Splendor Forum, Jasola District Centre, New Delhi – 110025, India

79 Anson Road, #06–04/06, Singapore 079906

Cambridge University Press is part of the University of Cambridge.

It furthers the University's mission by disseminating knowledge in the pursuit of education, learning, and research at the highest international levels of excellence.

www.cambridge.org
Information on this title: www.cambridge.org/9781108491891
DOI: 10.1017/9781108649209

First published 2019

Printed in the United Kingdom by TJ International Ltd. Padstow Cornwall

A catalogue record for this publication is available from the British Library.

ISBN 978-1-108-49189-1 Hardback
ISBN 978-1-108-74129-3 Paperback

Contents

Figures

Tables

Acknowledgments

We thank our colleagues, especially fellow members of the Michicagoan Faculty Seminar, for their commentary and lively discussion: Dick Bauman, Summerson Carr, Hillary Dick, Matt Hull, Webb Keane, Alaina Lemon, Michael Lempert, John Lucy, Bruce Mannheim, Barbra Meek, Lesley Milroy, Costas Nakassis, Sue Philips, Justin Richland, Michael Silverstein, and Kristina Wirtz. In addition, thanks to Andy Abbott, Susan Crane, Victor Friedman, Miyako Inoue, Katalin Kovács, Paul Kroskrity, Rick Parmentier, Kit Woolard, Erzsébet Varga, and Viviana Zelizer – good friends and intellectual partners. The people at our field sites gifted us with their collaboration, for which we are grateful. The graduate students in Judy's Language Ideologies seminars and Sue's Language in Culture seminars contributed with quizzical looks and stimulating discussions, and we thank them, as we do the many audiences that have listened, responded, and challenged us, when we presented versions of our chapters.

Special gratitude goes to the Rockefeller Foundation's Bellagio Center for its unmatched beauty and welcoming calm. The Guggenheim Foundation encouraged each of us with a fellowship; the National Endowment for the Humanities awarded one to Judy, the Social Science Research Council's International Scholar Program to Sue. Further financial support, for which we are grateful, came from the Lichtstern Fund of the Department of Anthropology at the University of Chicago and the University of Michigan's College of Literature, Science and the Arts. It is a pleasure to acknowledge Sue's fellowship at what was once the wonderful Collegium Budapest, and Judy's Mellon Foundation Fellowship at the University of Cape Town.

To our families, we owe special thanks. Judy thanks Becky and Deb Pastner and their families for support and patience; and to the late Steve Pastner, special remembrance, in gratitude for many things. From Sue to Anna Hamburg-Gal, a message just for you: Naturally, one says thanks repeatedly in life. And to Sam Hamburg, thank you, as ever, for musical accompaniment.

Introduction

Statements about language are never only about language – and they are never only statements. This double insight is key to our book. Statements about language always reach beyond the immediate linguistic forms. They implicate knowledge about the rest of social life; they intersect with other communicative means; they give signals about their speakers; and, inevitably, they are social actions embedded in history. To comment on languages, or describe them, or recommend policy with respect to them, is to engage in a metadiscourse, a reflexive activity that is at once a practice and a commentary upon that practice, within a realm of alternative possibilities.

The second part of the insight is equally important. Statements about language are never merely statements. They entail ideological positions that are made evident in multiple sites of social life, often in contradictory and contested ways, and they have wide-ranging consequences in the material world. The communicative signs people use are engaged in social projects, motivating and sometimes transforming their activities – not only commenting upon them.

This book focuses on the ways conceptions of language and linguistic practices – indeed of communication more broadly – depend on *differentiations*: the differentiations among signs, among people's social positions and historical moments, and among the projects people undertake. The same might be said about understandings of social life, which depend in turn on communicative forms and the differentiations they reflect and effect. The questions about language, ideology, and difference that inspired this book have been abiding interests for both of us. How should we understand difference, in language and in social life? How are linguistic differences noticed and their social meaning constructed? How do discourses about difference – even if about mere contrast – naturalize hierarchy and domination? How do some differences become persuasive as the basis for action, while others are ignored? How are scholars involved? Our work, separately and together, has always sought to explore language and linguistic practices ethnographically; to attend to relations of power, politics, and history; and to seek fundamental insights into the nature of signs and sign-relations. In this book we aim to push these approaches further, by focusing on differentiation as ideologized vision – and semiotic process – in a field of linguistic and social possibilities.

In concert with other linguistic anthropologists and some scholars in other fields as well, we take it as fundamental that social action requires a semiotic basis. That is, it requires orientations to the world that rely on signs, which have multiple capacities to represent aspects of our social lives and experiences, not only by labeling them. Those orientations to the world are positioned – that is, they incorporate a point of view – and they are organized in metadiscourses and regimes of value. Such semiotic organizations are aptly called *ideologies* because they are locally and historically specific framings, suffused with the political and moral interests of the social positions and projects in which they are embedded. We will have more to say about our concept of ideology and how our use of this term relates to the enormous literature on it, in later pages. Suffice it to say, for now, that we consider ideologies to be neither true nor false. They are positioned and partial visions of the world. They work via sign relations that entail *comparison* and *perspective*. Ideologized visions link differences in expressive features – linguistic and otherwise – to cultural images, constructing stereotypes of people and activities, and rendering them convincing.

Our topic opens up in multiple directions. It leads us to a foundational discussion of semiotic process, with ethnographic and historical examples drawing mainly on our own research in Africa, Europe, and the United States. We discuss how to compare ethnographic cases; how ideologies can convince even without any linguistic manifestation; how sites of construal and analysis are located and connected in scalings of social activity; and how scholars of language are embedded in social history and ideological projects. Beyond social studies of language, the book shows that ideological work of all kinds – in politics, knowledge-making, embodiment, economics – is fundamentally communicative. So are the social relations and institutions, identities and communities, that ideologies authorize.

In short, the book's goal is to develop a semiotic basis for ideological study and critique of social life. With our approach to ideology as semiotic process and ideological work, we address – and challenge – anthropologists, sociolinguists, and others who study social difference, politics, economics, language, and (meta)discourse in everyday relations of power.

Exhibits: Illustrative Examples

We begin with several brief "exhibits" – examples bearing upon a basic puzzle: How is differentiation in social life manifested or even created by expressive form? How, in turn, are differences in expressive form linked to differentiation in social life? Some examples show the seriousness of the matters involved; others are humorous. With these vignettes, we raise questions that orient the book. Where do we find ideological work? How does it make some construals and evaluations persuasive? How does a focus on differentiation help in understanding ideologized visions? How are details of speech connected to social positions and institutions? In what senses are politics, hierarchy, and social action implicated?

Each of our exhibits focuses on a topic in the social study of language: (1) national language and national character, (2) social types and personalities, (3) social scenes and activities, (4) political stakes in discourses about speech.

Exhibit 1: Wicked French

We often hear someone allege that a language reflects something about its speakers' character – and if national language, then national character. These propositions entail another: that a nation is distinct from other nations in character and in linguistic usage. The practices involved in self-conscious translation and second-language learning reify those oppositions and bring some of them into salience. For a (nonserious) illustration, consider the characteristics attributed to "the French" – and, by way of contrast, to "Americans" – in a passage from a humorous phrasebook, *Wicked French for the Traveler* (Example 0.1):

0.1 MAKING FRENCH NOISES WITH YOUR MOUTH AND NOSE

Americans find French accents charming. This is because they imagine that French people are sophisticated and intelligent.

The French find the accents of Americans speaking French nauseating. This is because they imagine that Americans are boorish and stupid.

... Many of the sounds made by French people are never made by English-speaking mouths. These peculiar noises are therefore difficult to describe and to imitate. Nevertheless, you must attempt to approximate a French accent if you hope to avoid being seen as a creature totally unworthy of respect, *un boucher de la langue sacrée* (a butcher of the holy tongue).

THE U IN STUPIDE

The u in stupide is a tough one, but learning it is crucial. Without it, you will be unable to say such things as:

These stinking truffles are overrated.	Ces truffes puantes sont surfaites.	Say trÿf pÿ-ONT sohn SŸR-fet.
Stop at my petticoat, Luc, you beastly peasant!	Ne te rue pas sur mon jupon, Luc, espèce de rustaud brutal!	Nuh tuh rÿ pah sÿr mohn jÿ-POHN, Lÿk, ess-pess duh RŸS-toh brÿ-TAHL!

> Making the sound requires holding the lips out in an O shape, imitating the look
> of interest sometimes seen on the faces of chimpanzees, while making the sound
> "eee." It does *not* sound like "ooo." The sound, to our ears, suggests sharp disgust
> (Tomb 1989:6–8).

The very sounds of French, it is suggested, express the disgust and disrespect
the author attributes to the whole nation in its attitude toward Americans. "Get
respect in France with the phrasebook that turns the tables," recommends a
blurb on the cover, and sure enough, the book offers insults galore with which
the American traveler can counter the arrogant Gaul who actually insists that
Americans – Americans!! – learn to speak a language other than English.

At the risk of belaboring a text that is not meant to be taken seriously, one
might ask, what relationship between language and speakers is being suggested in this passage? There would be nothing especially humorous about
claiming that people can express their feelings through the way they talk, or
that culturally specific ideas might be reflected in some aspect of language.
But a standardized language's phonological system is not a prime candidate
for these effects. Presumably some of the passage's humor lies, therefore, in its
description of phonological structure as directly reflecting cultural constructs,
and in its proposal that the mouth movements producing those sounds result,
perhaps automatically, from a characteristic feeling-state. No linguist today
would accept such claims, which are indeed treated here as ridiculous. Yet,
what is supposedly more ridiculous is the idea that pronouncing French well
could be so valued that people who fail to do so are objects of contempt, even
if they are Americans. So the humor rests also, and crucially, upon evaluations
of national languages and their speakers. There is also the pseudo-phonetic
transcription that makes French look particularly alien and deprives it of the
appearance of standardness. And there is the content of the example sentences,
about "overrated" French food ingredients and "beastly" amorous behavior.
French language becomes just another "overrated" cultural item.

Other books in the "Wicked" series present German, Italian, and Spanish. We
found the Spanish one conspicuously unfunny, however. As Jane Hill (2008) has
pointed out, there is a lot of mock Spanish in the North American air already, and
its use points to global power arrangements, local inequalities, and references to
language as a stand-in for race. Given the easy slippage from national language
to stereotyped national character, all these books now strike us as more problematic in their implicit ideological work than they at first appeared.

Exhibit 2: The Pirate's Progress

Besides a nation's citizenry, other social types too may be conventionally
imagined as having special linguistic practices and characteristic identifying

signs. Take pirates. Many people who have never met a real pirate know what they should sound like. While teaching an undergraduate Stage Dialects class, Phil Timberlake found that his students were all able to produce pirate speech: "The room immediately filled with swaggering, snarling students saying, 'Make him walk the plank,' 'Aye, matey,' 'More rum, m'boy,' and the rhotic verbal exclamation, 'Arr!'" (Timberlake 2003:85). These are of course English-speaking pirates, and of an earlier century, if the vaguely seventeenth- to eighteenth-century costumes sold as pirate outfits in American stores for Halloween are any guide. They are certainly not the pirates of today, such as those who reputedly ply the seas off the Somali coast. In the absence of real-world models, the likely source of this widespread stereotype is in popular fiction and film.

Timberlake identifies the literary source as Robert Louis Stevenson's (1993 [1883]) *Treasure Island*, which describes its pirate characters' voices as growling, grunting, roaring, raging, barking, hoarse, and full of oaths. It also supplies expressions like "lubbers" and "Shiver me timbers!" The film source is primarily the actor Robert Newton from performances in the 1950s. There were earlier renderings of pirate speech in films, notably Lionel Barrymore's hoarse growling style in *Treasure Island* (1934). But it was Newton who appeared in three widely viewed pirate movies in rapid succession: *Treasure Island* (1950), *Blackbeard the Pirate* (1952), and *Long John Silver* (1954). Newton brought his own native (England's) West Country dialect to these films, while exaggerating its rhotics, frequently inserting "Arrr!" and uttering his lines in a loud, hoarse growl. These films were hugely popular, as was Newton's character, although critics panned his performance as over the top.

The pirate's hoarse, ragged voice, rendered as if damaged by too much rum and shouting, is matched by pirate characters' other mutilations: (variously) scarred faces, missing legs, missing fingers, missing hands, and blinded eyes. The pirates who speak this way wear ragged and patched clothing, their shirts and cloaks damaged just as their bodies are. Their damaged voices, bodies, and apparel seem to mirror a damaged moral compass, for these pirates are represented as cruel, blasphemous, even demonic.

The conventions of pirate speech can be significant only insofar as they are distinctive, contrasting with other ways of speaking. In *Treasure Island* the narrator, Jim Hawkins, speaks and writes in standard English; in many films up through the 1950s, actors playing Hawkins and those playing heroes or innocents speak in a normative voice, usually with American accents (largely unmarked for region). Even their clothing is cleaner and more intact. They, and their standard language, are the voice of moral authority, while pirates are antiauthoritarian and antiestablishment, by definition. Pirates' distinctiveness is something that has emerged over time, however. In an earlier century, the line between privateers (authorized to attack ships of rival governments) and pirates was very thin. Some pirates even gained official posts; Henry Morgan (1635–1688), for example, though at best a privateer, became lieutenant governor of Jamaica. In works by Daniel Defoe (e.g., 1720, 1999 [1724]), pirates, whether real or fictional, are scarcely distinct from other kinds of thieves or, indeed, from other characters. Defoe occasionally contrasts pirates' "roar" and cursing with the "quietness and peace" of people and places ruled by good government (1999 [1724]:182). If a Defoe pirate (like Captain Singleton) sincerely repents, however, he is excused from his crimes and doesn't even have to give back the booty.

To be sure, differences between Defoe's and Stevenson's depictions of pirates are partly due to evolving literary standards and techniques. But they are also due to historical changes in maritime warfare, policing, and criminal careers. By Stevenson's day, privateers were largely a thing of the past. Those who robbed ships on the open sea were presumably pirates.

In the nineteenth century, as pirates become more clearly differentiated from non-pirates, the pirate category itself – in literature, at least – begins to subdivide. The men represented with "pirate speech" and tattered clothing are rank-and-file pirates of peasant or working-class background. Contrasting with these is the Byronic or romantic pirate, exemplified in Byron's 1814 poem *The Corsair* and Walter Scott's 1822 novel *The Pirate*. The romantic pirate comes from a higher social class but questions the status quo. He becomes a pirate because of some betrayal or false accusation that causes him to flee conventional authority. Though engaging in piracy, he is esteemed by his followers, performs many chivalrous acts, and is redeemed by love. In film, *Captain Blood* (1935), starring Errol Flynn in his first major swashbuckling role, represents this kind of pirate. As a "good" pirate, Captain Blood speaks in a cultivated British manner: normative grammar and Received Pronunciation (RP) – apart from a few minor phonetic lapses by the Australian-born Flynn.

Yet, even among higher class pirates differentiations have emerged. If Captain Blood is the good pirate, Captain Hook (in Barrie's 1904 play *Peter Pan*) – educated at Eton – is not. Captain Hook's "elegant diction" is thoroughly RP as well, but he is the evil English aristocrat, a social type available to writers by Barrie's time and certainly available to post–World War II American productions. Differentiations continue; space does not permit considering more recent iterations.

In short, history has played a role in the evolution of pirate social types and the pirate speech register, affording continuing processes of differentiation even while the "pirate accent" – instructions in which are now available on the internet – has become solidified and familiar.

Exhibit 3: Malinowskian Magic

Bronislaw Malinowski's descriptions of life on the Trobriand Islands, where he did fieldwork for two years between 1915 and 1918, are anthropological classics. In one of his books, *Coral Gardens and Their Magic* (1935), he offered a thesis about how and why the language of magic is deemed efficacious by its practitioners. The description emphasizes the opaqueness and irrationality of the language of magic:

All magical verbiage shows a very considerable coefficient of weirdness, strangeness and unusualness. ... We started from the observation that magic in all languages and at all times, and certainly in the Trobriands, almost ostentatiously displays words which are avowedly meaningless. ... The mysterious and sacred words which are supposed to have a direct hold over reality need not conform to the rules of the grammar and word formations of ordinary speech. (Malinowski 1978 [1935]:221, 223–224)

Such language is impossible, he claims, for a European observer to interpret without help:

Unless a competent commentator is secured who, in each specific case, will interpret the elements of weirdness, the allusions, the personal names or the magical pseudonyms, it is impossible to translate magic. Moreover, ... there has developed a body of linguistic practice – use of metaphor, opposition, repetition, negative comparison, imperative and question with answer – which, though not developed into any explicit doctrine makes the language of magic specific, unusual, quaint. (1978 [1935]: 222)

What Malinowski describes, in many passages and textual commentaries in *Coral Gardens*, as the lexicon, grammar, and prosody that distinguish magical language from ordinary language in the Trobriands, a linguist today might call register differentiation. Registers (in this sense) include ways of speaking used by the same speakers but in different social situations – here, the rituals in which magic spells are uttered, as opposed to ordinary conversation. Outside the special scene of spell utterance, he finds, Trobrianders are as rational and pragmatic as anyone else. Moreover, a similar differentiation in registers can be found among Europeans, Malinowski suggests, in the contrast between the language of science and the language of advertising, political oratory, and beauty treatments (1978 [1935]:237). These instances of "modern savagery" show, he argues, that the difference between "native" and European is only a relative matter; it is only a question of how many domains of life evoke "magical verbiage." The differentiation of savage and modern is made into a differentiation internal to a single language and way of life – be it the Trobriand *or* the European.

Malinowski's interest in rationality and in comparisons between "natives" and Europeans led him to look closely at language, to transcribe many texts of spells and formulae, and to discuss register differentiation at some length. But perhaps it drew his attention away from other aspects of Trobriand thinking about language. For example, a Trobriand concept of "hard words" (*biga peula*; Weiner 1984) points to their concern for how language conveys truth or social tactfulness, and for the nature of truth in discourse. Evidently, Trobrianders are much interested in language's involvement in moral evaluation, and in its role in creating or destroying social connectedness. A similar interest is reflected, too, in the ways they mobilize regional linguistic repertoires in inter-island contacts and trading. The distribution of languages in this part of the Pacific differentiates regions; for example, there is a language spoken on the island of Dobu that is distinct from Kiriwinian (the Trobriand language). But multilingualism is widespread, and there are complex intercalations of regional languages in the speeches accompanying the exchange of goods between islands. Even though these language alternations, translations, and mixings seem to play some important part in the *kula* exchanges of ritual goods – exchanges whose significance Malinowski discusses at length – he merely mentions these points about language without developing them in his analysis.

This example shows how differentiations among expressive forms can distinguish among social activities and effects – and how, in Trobrianders' ideologized interpretations anyway, their effectiveness is persuasive. Yet, it also shows that a scholar's intellectual preoccupations, important as they are, can lead him to ignore or downplay observations a later scholar, less invested in broad comparisons between "savages" and Europeans, might find crucial.

Exhibit 4: Speaking Freely of Speech

How do people define "speech" and "speakers"? These seem self-evident concepts, yet there are complex philosophies that argue about them, and the various definitions are involved in international relations. Arguments in a US Supreme Court case differentiated two views of speech and speakers. They contrast on several dimensions: Can speech be a material object or not? Who and what can be a speaker in politics? And need one know the identity of the speaker to detect the truth or falsity of speech? The Court's 2010 decision in *Citizens United v. Federal Election Commission*, like many legal cases, affords an ethnographic opportunity. What do the two parties' presumptions tell us about political imaginaries? How do these presumptions connect historical and international contexts that at first seem quite distinct?

In the *Citizens United* case, the Supreme Court struck down a 2002 bipartisan law that aimed to counteract corruption in campaign financing by restricting some forms of spending in political campaigns. The Constitution's First Amendment guarantees that Congress shall make no law abridging freedom of speech. The Court ruled, in a five to four decision, that this gives business corporations and unions the right to spend as much money as they wish to directly support or target particular candidates. Unlimited spending by corporations and unions through political action committees was already legal. Freedoms of commercial speech were already guaranteed. The *Citizens United* decision lifted constraints on *direct* election spending by corporations and unions, using their general funds. In national polls, people of all political persuasions were overwhelmingly opposed to the decision. Some groups organized protests to dispute this interpretation of the First Amendment, saying, "money is not speech" and "corporations are not people."

Those mottos were clever, but they were not legal argumentation. Let us briefly sketch some of the legal issues on both sides before contrasting the political images they elaborated and relied on for their persuasiveness. The Court's majority argued that "prohibition on corporate ... expenditures is a ban on speech" and it must end because "political spending is protected speech" under the First Amendment. Indeed, an earlier Court decision had established that suppression by a legislature of the financial resources necessary to create or publish political speech is constitutionally equivalent to suppression of speech itself, and the Court tends to accept its own precedents (Post 2014:46). Opponents dissented, responding that as a matter of common sense, money is *not* the same as speech: You cannot pay for a hamburger simply by talking. Money is a material thing, they said, without propositional "content," and without a responsible, identifiable speaker. Thus, it would be better to regulate how speech is paid for, while protecting speech itself, rather than declaring money to be speech. Indeed, before *Citizens United*, campaign contributions were regulated for more than a century with no one worrying about a violation of free speech (Wright 1976; Kairys 2010).

What about defining "speaker"? Government has an interest in safeguarding democracy by support of an engaged and informed electorate. Therefore, the First Amendment specially protects *political* speech. In this case, the Court said, individuals who associate together in a business, "a corporate form," are being treated as "disfavored speakers." They are like victims of a hostile government. "The censorship that we now confront is vast in its reach," said the Court's majority, because by limiting corporate financing of election-related speech, "the government has muffled voices ... of the economy. ... And [so] the electorate has been deprived of information, knowledge and opinion vital to its function" (cited in Toobin 2012). Corporations have not historically had the protection of the First Amendment for political speech. But, the Court argued, making speech available as a source of information for the public is what matters, not the identity of the speaker.

The dissenting justices thundered back that the First Amendment is not a blanket protection of all speech, as such. Its application has always distinguished among speakers, for instance more protection for civilians, less for the military. The First Amendment protects the dignity of individual *opinion*, choice, and political engagement. Although corporations are "legal persons" for some purposes, they do not have human dignity, or individual opinion, or a range of political interests. Corporate opinion is always constrained by the single legal and fiduciary obligation to make a profit. By contrast, the key political speech act of natural persons is choice in voting. Corporations are a different kind of entity: they cannot vote. Dissenters argued that the Court should not protect political speech by corporations under the First Amendment (Dworkin 2010; Winkler 2018).

The contrasts are striking: One view takes speech to be a material thing, equivalent to money, and independent of speakers. The other takes speech to be different from material objects, and freedom of speech to be embodied only in natural persons. Quite different political visions were invoked. For supporters, the decision was a victory over censorship and toward an open, dynamic marketplace of ideas (Abrams 2017). For opponents, the decision's vision was not of active citizens seeking to make their diverse opinions known, but of passive, closed-minded consumers, attending to messages from faceless corporations (Teachout 2014): they worried that disembodied corporate speech, framed as "information," misleads those who don't know that corporations' interest in politics is limited to enhancing profits.

Disagreement among the justices was strong. Yet, they and Americans of all political persuasions unite in support of First Amendment guarantees of free speech when comparing the United States to other countries. An important distinction among people within the country disappears in a wider comparison to other political systems. To see this, let us look at how exactly the justices and their allies characterized speech and speakers.

They used telling terms: "censorship" and "marketplace" and judgments of "openness" and "closedness," "activity" and "passivity." These expressions powerfully echoed the talk of past eras. The First Amendment's history is revealing. Enacted in 1791, it was never invoked in the nineteenth century. The suppression of speech and writing then went unremarked. But in 1918, labor activists and pacifists protesting the First World War were harshly punished, leading several justices to argue for the protection of political dissent. After the Second World War, the free speech clause of the First Amendment was reinterpreted as a general protection of antigovernment opinion (Stone 2004; Weinrib 2016). Free speech became an emblem of the United States, its "brand" in international relations during the Cold War. It stood for an "open" active society and capitalist markets. Communist opponents were charged with being "closed" by censoring speech and restricting markets. But the Cold War is long over;

business corporations are now globally powerful. They have the support of the American government and vast access to the public. Many Americans have learned that truth in speech can be detected only if one knows the social position and interests of the speakers. The distinctions made in the *Citizens United* case echoed Cold War international tensions. They called on old animosities, recontextualizing them in a changed world to influence new domestic disputes.

Ways of talking about speakers and speech are signs that point to speakers' political visions. Differentiations among such signs and the perspectives they entail are potentially present even in the smallest groups. They can be projected to and from larger social contexts, even internationally. By building on and evoking visions and reactions from other times and places, old distinctions can subtly shape present circumstances.

The exhibits we have offered will reappear in this book only sporadically. In the rest of this chapter, we refer back to them in the course of outlining issues and aspects of our approach, which they can serve to illustrate in an elementary way. French language and people will appear – in a very different light from *Wicked French* – in several other chapters too, especially in the context of French colonialism and its afterlife. Malinowski will be mentioned briefly in a discussion of ethnographic method. And American political and legal debates will play many roles in later chapters. Like pirates, some of our examples fit as comfortably in literature as in everyday life. Otherwise, most of the materials we discuss will be drawn from our own research, ethnographic and historical, in West Africa, Eastern Europe, and the United States.

Why "Ideology"?

How is difference made, in language and social life – and to what ends? How and why is it unmade? What difference does difference make? This book asks how we should understand differentiation in language and communication within a world of human social relations and action. We attend to processes of fission and fusion that create and organize difference; how people conceive of it and work with it; and how they relate it to their activities, relations of power, and institutions. Differentiation is a process, not a matter of units. In addressing how people conceive of difference – in linguistic and social practices – we look to the ideological processes that both pervade and inform social action, not to ideologies as doctrines. As our title indicates, we approach these topics through the study of signs, among which linguistic signs are especially important.

Any work concerned with signs, linguistic and otherwise, must also concern itself in some way with ideas and interpretations. As Peirce pointed out long ago, "a sign is something which stands to somebody for something ... in

reference to a sort of idea" (1955a:99). Without some sentient being to interpret it, an object or occurrence in the world is not a sign. A fire will produce
smoke whether or not it is witnessed, but smoke is a sign of fire only if it is
noticed and interpreted as such. Ideas and interpretations, moreover, do not
exist in isolation from other ideas. But why call them "ideologies" – these networks of ideas and interpretive practices, which we discuss in this book? Why
use this term, which comes with a lot of baggage? And when, even within our
own field of linguistic anthropology, which has seen abundant scholarly writing on "language ideology" as pertaining to linguistic practice and analysis, the
term's uses are not entirely agreed upon?

The most conspicuous problem attending the term is probably the common
assumption that "ideology" is false consciousness. As a corollary, the false
ideas are supposed to derive from a reprehensible political program, serving the interests of oppressive dominant, or would-be dominant, sectors of
society. Notice now that if ideology is false consciousness, it can belong only
to somebody else. *We* have a handle on the true state of affairs. Yet, one can
argue (with Terry Eagleton 2007) that an ideology – as a view of the world,
whether it's the world of linguistic practice or anything else – cannot be totally
false, or anyone who held it wouldn't survive very long. Additionally, many
scholars today, including ourselves, do not want to make quite such strong
claims to know the truth, even if truth is what we seek.

Although it is not a simple matter to abandon this familiar assumption, we
do not equate ideology with false consciousness. We see ideologies, instead,
as views of the world that are *partial*, in both senses of that word. They are
partial in that they are incomplete, because someone else, viewing the world
from a different standpoint, would see a different picture; and they are partial
in that they are interested – in the political and legal sense of an interested
party, someone who has a stake in a situation and how it turns out. This point
about stakes in ongoing social action is crucial, not only to our own work but
also to the work of those authors who have looked at "ideology" in a more
positive light than the "false consciousness" interpretation would allow. For
Clifford Geertz (1973 [1964]), ideologies offer road maps for social action
within a cultural framework. Even for Althusser (1994 [1970]), ideologies are
productive, offering subject positions and drawing people in to social activities
and relations. Although the actions and relations at issue might be potentially
disadvantageous to the person drawn in to them, as in Althusser's example of
being hailed by the police and recognizing one's relationship to the forces of
the state, nevertheless the ideologies that govern the situation draw the action
forward.

The concept of ideology might be better thought of as a family of concepts, given all its ups and downs since its inception in the work of Destutt de
Tracy and the French *idéologues* in the late eighteenth century. Other authors

have amply discussed its history;[1] their work releases us from that obligation, although in later pages we will consider some prominent thinkers whose writings have inspired us or whose work we need to compare with our own. One of those authors will be Michael Silverstein, who, writing on "linguistic ideology" (1979), offered a breakthrough by addressing ideology about language itself, not (or not in the first instance) ideology about politics, tracked in political texts. This work inaugurated a new way of thinking about ideology and about language. Research along these lines took off in the 1990s and expanded into a broader concern with semiotics.

What we want from a concept of ideology – what we want to keep from the massive literature on it while discarding the necessity of equating it with false consciousness – is the connection with power, politics, interest, and social action. We also want, perhaps most of all, to retain the sense of difference, positioning, and perspective. To speak of an "ideology" always implies that there is an alternative one that somebody else, differently positioned, might hold. An ideology, then, is something contestable. This is the case even though the ideology itself, viewed from inside, as it were, may be a totalizing vision, purporting to account for everything and everyone in the world. It is generally the outsider, the "unbeliever," who calls this vision an ideology. But even among insiders, there is usually the recognition that unbelievers exist. Implicitly, there is some sense of contestation.

Another reason we retain this term is the lack of a better one for what we want to explore. "Culture," in particular, even in its ideational versions, tends to connote wholeness and homogeneity, and perhaps stasis, given its emphasis on tradition; it does not easily suggest future-oriented political projects. Nor does it readily connect with point of view or with power relations. We do take from "culture" the notion that background knowledge and values vary among local settings around the world, and that the variation has something to do with local history and circumstance. Yet, the people who participate in those settings come to them with different points of view and different agendas. Because the connection with power is important – although what power consists in needs to be specified – we prefer "ideology," which can be thought of as a *regime of value*, since the values are anchored to political relations.

Still, our approach to ideology has its own particularities and emphases. Many scholars, especially those whose disciplinary backgrounds lie in political science or political philosophy, identify "ideology" with major political programs and "isms" whose doctrines, even when contested, are laid out in texts: communism, liberalism, feminism, "Islamism," and the like. For us, ideology is not limited to these, and need not even be self-consciously articulated. What is most interesting to us is the way regimes of value operate in everyday life, penetrating ordinary practices and actions. Since our approach is fundamentally semiotic, it concerns the most intimate, experience-near apprehensions of signs as well as their widely proliferating connections. Moreover, we do not insist that the values undergirding people's actions be completely consistent. Indeed, our approach will offer some account of inconsistencies and apparent contradictions. Finally, because our emphasis is on process and the ongoing, ever-evolving flow of social life, any conceptions of ideology that treat it as a static system, or as a doctrine that exists in some realm separate from its applications, are not for us. Ideology, for us, is not like a miasma that hovers over a community, or like a rock that hits someone on the head. Instead, we understand it as productive – as part of people's creative interpretations of their situation and part of their consequent social action. In much of our analysis, therefore, we will speak not of "ideology" but of *ideologizing* and *ideological work*: the active making of social life.

What Kind of Semiotics?

As a semiotic approach to ideological work, our account relies on signs and meaning-making. But there are many kinds of semiotics. All start with an understanding of contrast, which is widely recognized as a basis of human perception, in engagement with its environmental surround. Cognitive scientists agree that there is no concept so elementary that it can be held in and of itself without contrast to its alternative or its absence (Keil and Wilson 2000). The key role of contrast is further attested by its ubiquity in every aspect of linguistic structure. Also, contrast has long been recognized by literary and philosophical thinkers, in the ever-present possibility of ambiguity, double entendre, and punning, even in a single utterance.

Yet, that does not take us far enough. A fuller theory of signs goes beyond perception and utterances, developing a more thorough understanding of contrast and its implications. What are the issues we would like such a theory to address? First, that the role of ideological meaning-making in action, situated in history, is as important as interpretation in the more usual sense of contemplation. Second, as regimes of value, ideologies are as involved in knowledge-making – for instance about the specifics of those values – as in evoking that knowledge and communicating it. Finally, the ideologized workings of power and politics are as significant in the details of everyday life as in wider realms, to which ideologies link daily life. We wish to engage both action and thought, the combination of knowledge-making and communicating, and the connections of daily life with far-reaching politics. Moreover, the prospect of connecting these three apparent distinctions is of the greatest interest.

The writings of Charles Sanders Peirce are particularly apposite for the first two goals. We draw on other philosophers too, and throughout we build on the writings of our colleagues, joining the many who work with Peircean semiotics.

But first, let us clarify how Peirce's voluminous and often difficult writings are inspiring, yet why and how – especially in approaching power and politics – we part ways with him.

Action and meaning are two sides of a coin in the Peircean view. Through acts of attention people notice phenomena, in contrast to a background, by taking them to be signs. They make guesses (hypotheses) about what these posited signs might mean. Peirce called such guesses abductions. A guess is both a communication (sometimes only with oneself) and a route to further guesses that comment on the first, as a metasemiotic reaction, by extending the previous guess, or revising it. Each act of conjecture implicates further uptakes, that is, more hypotheses, leading to cumulative growth and change in knowledge about the encountered world. Even this brief glimpse shows how Peirce's analysis is open-ended, embracing change in knowledge through continuing action with signs. For us, this has implications for thinking about historical contingency. On the one hand, it suggests action and thus that an active intervention in historical process is possible. Yet, the potential of recalcitrant circumstances is very much present, contingencies that cannot be controlled but only grasped with the meaning-making tools available. This approach brings together knowledge, social action, and communication not to emphasize their differences but to characterize their interdependence.[2]

For Peirce, the continuous chains of abduction that constitute both communication and knowledge do not distinguish linguistic signs from any other types of signs. This is because, as we have noted, signs are made by human beings and humans may do so out of all the many kinds of phenomena in their worldly surroundings. To separate the linguistic from other signs preempts the possibly quite various assumptions about communication around the globe. It favors, instead, a Western philosophical position that distinguishes between materiality and ideation, between the physical and the mental, and places language in an ideational-mental realm. A separation between linguistic ideology and semiotic ideology presumes this same problematic view. It posits a border between language and nonlanguage that many non-Western traditions reject. Even in the Western world, these distinctions do not always hold, as is illustrated in some of the exhibits we presented. In the Pirate Exhibit, the pirate's clothing is as much a sign to be interpreted as qualities of speech; in the Free Speech Exhibit, there is a debate questioning whether speech is ideation or money. By contrast, a great value of Peirce's view of signs is that it does not make these distinctions. He proposes other, intriguing ones that we will discuss throughout this book. They enable us to embrace all kinds of signs within a single semiotic logic, while making room to recognize – within this larger frame – the particularities of linguistic form and its special place in social life.[3]

The continuous process of taking up signs, in the Peircean sense, has still other implications for us. Since knowledge is constructed through repeated conjectures that build on each other, the connections among signs may extend over vast and unexpected reticulations of time, space, and social distance. Where and by what paths signs may "travel" depend on when, where, and for what purposes they are taken up. There are no inherent boundaries to their connections. Peirce implicitly urges us to follow the sign, not only the signer. We should watch changes that occur in successive uptakes, not only the presumed source. This shifts the focus somewhat, away from individual intentionality and toward the innumerable guesses – not necessarily consistent – that sentient, biographical beings inevitably make. The unified subject is not the center of his philosophy, which is built on acts of conjecture, not on persons.

These philosophical views contribute significantly to the first two of our desiderata for a theory of signs. Yet our agenda also leads in other directions, especially to engage with questions of power and politics. Peirce hoped his approach would ultimately produce agreements among investigators about the makeup of the world, reaching truth through convergence. Instead, we are at least as much interested in the divergence of conjectures and the different knowledges they rely on and build. Everywhere evident around us are contestations about meanings, values, and ideologies. We note that quite various hypotheses about signs are possible, even with the same semiotic logic, but depending on differences in earlier presumptions and present circumstances. Peirce was well aware of the importance of circumstances in the uptake of signs. His examples for concepts are often concrete moments of socially located individuals in the midst of scenes: two friends pointing out at the sea; the driver of a carriage signaling to pedestrians. Peirce's dictum is said to have been that in philosophy, one must start in the middle of things, not at beginnings (Scheffler 2001:666). This acknowledges that the use and uptake of signs is embedded in the flow of social life. Yet, Peirce's interest was in the logic of semiosis, not its social surround.

By contrast, we seek to understand – in addition to the semiotic logic – how existing regimes of value (ideologies) organize and direct even the simplest noticing of any phenomenon as a sign. Social actors, in taking something as a sign, always have projects, interests, motivations. They always already have background knowledge, experiences, assumptions, forms of attention, expectations; in short, ideologies. And the phenomena of the world are not construed as signs de novo. On the contrary, as Peirce emphasized, signs are usually typified and conventionalized. For us, this conventionality makes them socially embedded and thus a complex arena of analysis that we approach in ways distinct from Peirce.

Convention and typification are multilayered and historically variable. We ask how the construal of signs is shaped by the situatedness of action in recognizable (typified) social scenes. Calling on the tradition of Erving Goffman (1981), and refinements in the tradition of interactional analysis in linguistic anthropology, we attend to typified social roles that participants evoke in scenes.[4] And beyond scenes, how are participants located vis-à-vis historically variable person types and their characteristic "voices" that, as Bakhtin (1981) emphasized, appear with presumed interests, projects, and expectations attached? Thus, indexicality, enregisterment, metapragmatics, and alignment are fundamental to our analysis of scenes, as they now are to any work in the social study of linguistic practices.[5] By selectively engaging with forms of convention and typification, individual persons construct and embody interests, craft projects, and adopt vantage points. They also evoke (index) and instantiate conventional discourses as explanatory narratives.[6] These matters of knowledge are differentially available, and with these as background assumptions, socially positioned participants approach scenes of action that are always also scenes of communication.

Relying on these analytical tools, we rethink two familiar-sounding concepts, keeping semiosis in mind. One is *perspective*; the other is *comparison*. Perspective is the point of view or line of sight that biographical persons can take up and bring to bear on a situation. Perspectives are typified and are changeable over time and across situations. A person need not take up the same one at all times; people construct and deploy their own versions with materials that are socially available. And the social-conventional aspects also change. In semiotic terms, perspectives are clusters of conventional conjectures that are presumed by ideological work to go together, in some sense, in a particular time-place. They are related to a person's social position – but never simply a reflex of that position. One of our goals in this book is to demonstrate the logic and dynamics of perspectives as inherent in ideologies. We show how one finds them empirically and tracks them in ethnographic and historical materials.

Perspectives are always partial views and so imply the existence of other vantage points. Therefore, *comparison* is equally important. It is in particular scenes that comparisons are evoked and have their effects. As we will see in later chapters, comparison has many kinds of effects, all of which interest us. But one particular effect worth highlighting now is exemplified by scholars working in the Marxian tradition – Antonio Gramsci (1985) and Raymond Williams (1977) – and in ethnography by cultural critic Dick Hebdige (1979). Their early work showed nicely how situated comparisons of cultural materials can create and reproduce politically powerful differentials. Their writings, though not specifically semiotic, nevertheless demonstrated how domination may operate through the comparison and hierarchical valuation of *qualities* as potentially embodied in a wide range of phenomena. This included "structures of feeling," aesthetic judgments, artistic styles, forms of speech, music, and other diverse products of popular culture.[7]

Dynamics of Comparison, Process of Differentiation

Given its centrality in our definition of ideological work, the dynamics of comparison deserve conceptualization in semiotic terms. Part II explicates the process in detail, but here we offer a preliminary outline. Consider index-icality, which has been well developed in the scholarly work drawing on a Peircean framework in the analysis of linguistic practices. To construe something as an index is already to focus attention on it and, in doing so, to distinguish it from its surround. That is, there are processes that are presupposed in the construal. To posit something as an index (or any other kind of sign) one needs the fundamental notions of *attention* and *contrast*: to grasp the sign as figure-against-background. Indeed, for any sign, one recruits ideologized assumptions about what might conceivably be a sign in the world. To construe it as an *index*, one takes further notice of some aspect of the conditions that may have created the sign; what one may suppose or guess it points to by being in contiguity or co-occurrence with it. But indexes reveal nothing more. To see the sign as part of a comparison, it is necessary to hypothesize further about those conditions of production, to make more guesses about aspects of the sign itself, what it might be pointing to, what it perhaps contrasts with.

How might these further conjectures work? Here we can draw on the kinds of signs Peirce called icons: signs that depict what they represent by some kind of similarity with it. Peirce's presentation of sign relations has icons already incorporated within indexes (as, for example, the weather vane depicts the direction of the wind it points to, by turning in a similar direction). Icons also do more: they figure in relations of contrast and comparison, developing how the index works. Indexical and iconic signs operate together, not only in examples like the weather vane, but in ways that go beyond incorporation. We must also notice, however, that similarity is not always so simple, as Nelson Goodman's (1972) philosophy argues; and for Peirce too, iconic signs come in more complex forms.

The first exhibit is a handy example of how indexical and iconic signs are taken up together. The book *Wicked French* mentions that pronouncing *ü*, a linguistic sign, points to the speaker as its condition of production. Speech is often taken to index the speaker. But to hear it as a specifically *French* *"ü"* one needs some contrast, and indeed, the book contrasts this sound with English sounds. Ideological work equates each kind of sound and its qualities with the qualities of the speakers who typically produce it. The relation of contrast between qualities of the signs (the sounds) depicts the relations of contrast in qualities of what the signs represent (national stereotypes). A map works in the same way, depicting territory. Peirce called such a configuration a diagrammatic icon. A diagrammatic icon of contrast, then, uses contrasts to differentiate and compare signs; it organizes them through what we call an *axis of differentiation.*

With this background, and taking into account the *attention-focusing* and *contrast* that are presupposed by any identification of a sign, we propose that ideologizing difference works through comparison, in a semiotic process that has the following aspects: *rhematization, axis of differentiation, fractal recursivity*, and *erasure.*

In *rhematization,* a contrast of indexes is interpreted as a contrast in depictions: A conjecture focuses on some perceptible contrast of quality in indexical signs and takes that contrast to depict – not only to index – a contrast in the conditions under which the signs were produced; some contrast of quality in what was indexed. That is, a conjecture posits an *axis of differentiation,* creating a schema of qualitative contrast both for indexical signs and for what they are taken to represent. The contrasting qualities in the signs are "found" or projected onto the contrasting phenomena that the signs are taken to index. The specific qualities presumed to be in contrast depend on the ideologies – background knowledge, interests and projects – that social actors bring to the scene of comparison. Often the contrast itself is erased from attention, making it seem as though the qualities inhere in each entity by itself.

Thus, in the *Wicked French* exhibit, the ideological work of rhematization conjectures that the *ü* sound of French, and the mouth position necessary to make it, derive from (ideologized) stereotypes about French people's national character, *in contrast* to American speech and character. If the sound is deemed alien and the expression sneering, then the people are alien and sneering too, while Americans and their speech are characterized in some contrasting way. Importantly, rhematization also works conversely: if one assumed that French people were inherently alien and arrogant, compared to Americans, then one could "find" those qualities in their speech. Similarly, in the Pirate Exhibit, if a loud, harsh voice with strong rhotic consonants is associated with – points to – the pirate as social type, it is in contrast with some other stereotype that such qualities become evident. If the qualities of the voice, as harsh and damaged, are taken to be an auditory depiction of the pirate's moral defects, in contrast to the moral goodness of the contrasting stereotype, then that interpretation is a rhematization. Conjectures pick out indexes that call attention to something; axes of differentiation set up a qualitative comparison. By rhematization, contrasting qualities perceived in the signs are taken to be like, to resemble, qualitative contrasts in what the signs are taken to index.

We emphasize *taken to be* like, not *are* like. Conjectures are not observations, nor are they conclusions based on evidence. Rhematization is most powerful when it attributes perceptible qualities to something that is not directly observable, such as the (putative) French national character. In later chapters we investigate how further ideological work develops these effects. Often, narratives of rhematization interpret the quality as cause – as if the (invisible) national character imputed to French people caused the linguistic phenomena that are taken to resemble it. The similarity that rhematization conjectures – and the difference it posits with the compared entity – may be a misrecognition. Or it may rest on picking out qualities that are merely contingent and construing them as necessary. Or people noticing the sign may be so accustomed to picking out a particular quality that they see it everywhere and invest it with much importance.

Fractal recursivity is that aspect of ideological work that reiterates the comparison created by the axis of differentiation, altering the sets of objects that are compared, under contrast. Ideological work expands or contracts the scope of those sets. The qualities in which the sets of objects contrast are drawn upon again, to differentiate subsets. Alternatively, they are projected onto more encompassing sets, thus bringing the original sets together as against something else. Although the result may seem to resemble a nested hierarchy, the process is not a typology. The systematicity of the process comes from the reiteration of the comparison, not from the nesting of sets. In fractals, it is always the same distinction – the same contrast – that organizes the relations among units, at whatever degree of inclusiveness or differentiation.[8] Presumably an American speaker who followed the instructions in *Wicked French* would "sound French" to some French people, to some extent, and so the distinction between Americans and the French would be reiterated among Americans, distinguishing those who wisely followed the book's (ironic) advice from others who failed to do so. In the Pirate Exhibit, the "romantic pirate" reiterates the contrast of moral damage within the pirate social category itself. The romantic pirate and his voice and clothing are less damaged, hence redeemable, in contrast to the wicked pirate such as Blackbeard, who is more damaged. In the Free Speech Exhibit, an encompassing fractal is created. Despite their differences about campaign financing, Americans are united in the great value placed on the principle of free speech, when contrasted to other countries' politics of speaking. Fractal recursivity depends on axes of differentiation and rhematization; these are not separate processes. Axes change under historical pressure, and sometimes several are simultaneously active. Fractal recursivity makes axes of differentiation iterative.

Erasure is that aspect of ideological work through which some phenomena (linguistic forms, or types of persons, or activities) are rendered invisible. Whatever is inconsistent with the ideologized schema either goes unnoticed or is explained away. Notice that erasure is the inevitable concomitant of the other parts of the process. We have already seen that axes of differentiation often get reduced by erasure to simple icons in rhematization. And creating an axis of differentiation requires selecting some qualities and ignoring or downplaying others. As another example, the distinction applied in fractal recursivity is deemed the same, even though the qualities compared inevitably shift somewhat as the scope of comparison changes.[9] Thus, erasure is not a separate process. For instance, in the Malinowski Exhibit, his comparison of Trobriand magic with the forms of talk in Europe that he finds similar depends on ignoring the Trobrianders' yams, since the European talk, unsurprisingly, does not concern tropical plants. In the Free Speech Exhibit, when the United States is compared to other countries, the zealous struggle within the United States about speech in political campaigns and the details of campaigns are erased, if only temporarily.

Erasure is a way of simplifying ideological work. Since ideologies are totalizing visions, elements that cannot be seen to fit the ideological schema are ignored or transformed. Erasure in ideological representation does not necessarily mean, however, actual eradication of the awkward element, whose very existence may be unobserved or unattended to. Erasure simply implies an explanation or explaining away the phenomenon that does not fit, leaving the observer's vision of the world intact. But in some cases ideological work may motivate action to alleviate, remove, or transform what is seen as a divergence from the schema. It is when the "problematic" element is seen as fitting some alternative, threatening picture that the semiotic process involved in erasure might become some kind of practical action to remove the threat, if circumstances permit. In sum, the parts of our semiotic process implicate each other. They are aspects of one semiotic process of differentiation.

Analytical Strategies

As with any serious conceptual proposal, this one has implications for doing research, for the analytical strategies that one adopts in facing empirical materials. Questions of research strategy are discussed in detail in Part III, but here we offer a simplified outline. And in mentioning research strategy we do not imply a qualitative gulf between researcher and those social actors who are – for the moment – the objects of research. We argue, instead, that the researcher is engaged in similar practices of construal and comparison as the social actors observed. Indeed, the participants in any system of social relations are, necessarily, investigators in their own right. In this sense researcher status does not confer inherently privileged understanding. Both researchers and participants, in short all social actors, must seek to interpret semiotic forms and to find the ingredients and steps that will allow them to interpret and act. The research we envision targets social actors' ideological work; yet, research is itself a similar kind of practice.

In the spirit of Peircean semiotics, we conceive of ideological work starting with a *gaze*, an uptake – from some vantage point – that creates a sign relation worthy of notice. A *site of ideological work* is then a *focus of joint attention,* for making construals and conjectures. Whatever the immediate participants make of this site, the investigator's gaze differs only insofar as it is a metasemiotic move, paying attention to the uptake – the gaze and its conjecture – of those being observed. To be sure, researchers may see different relevances than the people studied do, and researchers likely also have different social positions, different perspectives and commitments, differing background knowledge and often differential access to modes of power and authority. But differentiations of all these kinds are to be found everywhere, and everywhere they are the stuff of construal and conjecture. There is always a plurality of gazes and perspectives on any site. A methodological imperative is to find as many of these gazes as possible and pertinent, and to investigate their differing construals. Evidence is limitless: linguistic, metapragmatic, nonverbal, patterned activity and display of all kinds, sociological arrangements, and much more. What does the evidence show about what the various gazes pick out about the site? What differentiations and similarities among the gazes are thus revealed? What do they project onto the site? And with what further uptakes do they connect any particular site to other sites?

When one takes seriously the Peircean notion of ongoing semiosis and the potential for chains of abduction, it becomes clear that there can be no boundary around a site and its construals. The succession of uptakes is endless and their discovery depends on the creative efforts of researchers (as does the decision about where to stop). These connections potentially radiate outward from the site in many directions. Even if participants themselves assume or create a boundary, the boundary presupposes that there is something outside it – therefore, a kind of connection to other site(s). Moreover, connections among sites made of successive uptakes by participants may be ideologically understood in many different ways. For instance, one site may be a model for action in another, or explain another, or authorize it, or take it as precedent; or, one site may be understood as containing (or being contained by) another. The ideological work that links sites may involve processes of institutionalization, imposing complex and perduring connections, and regimenting the sites and the practices involved in them.

Analyzing the connections across and among sites is a different and complementary analytical strategy to observing a comparison or a differentiating process. In particular, some kinds of connections among sites reflect the ideological work of organizing the differentiations, created by the process of differentiation outlined above, into systems of comparison. The projections created in fractal recursivity result in one such system; there are others, and researchers need to consider what systems of comparison they bring with them, as opposed to those they find. The analytical strategies we propose in this book enable us to rethink scales and scaling as a mode of comparison. To do so has consequences for understanding social life: a semiotic lens explicates, for instance, just how qualities seen as "personal" are also "political," how the intimate is linked to institutional forms, how capillary power works.

Comparison in Anthropology

Comparison has been, of course, a major analytical strategy of our discipline. The work of our teachers in the 1960s, in the emerging fields of sociolinguistics and the ethnography of speaking (Gumperz and Hymes 1972), was premised on the idea that ways of speaking and their relation to social settings differed across the globe and that this variation was worthy of comparative investigation. More broadly, anthropology and linguistics, since their formal beginnings in the nineteenth century, have had global ambitions, as we discuss in Part IV. They have aimed for universal comparisons that would incorporate all of the sociocultural and linguistic variation across the globe and across historical eras as well. But not all comparisons are alike. Many comparative projects in the history of anthropology have been attempts we consider ill-conceived. They have made a single grid or several grids on which scholars would place their assessments of the practices of others. This presumes a form of "objectivism," in which the scholar, merely by virtue of being a scholar and an outsider, has a view that is stable and not perspectival.

Other kinds of comparison have existed side by side with these, as striking exceptions. They have been experiments in what one might call situated relationality: scholars presumed their own perspective and comparison were positioned, even as they documented the play with perspective and comparison of a comparable kind that they encountered in the field. These were sometimes exceptions even in the writings of the particular scholars, but they have been inspiring for our work. For instance, Max Gluckman (1940) refused the then-current mode of analyzing single, unified social structures. In his analysis of a bridge-building project in Zululand, he sought instead to characterize an event by specifying the many distinct perspectives on it and tracking the implications as one moved away from it in time and space. Sapir (1949 [1938]) too, in discussing an older ethnography's throwaway line "Two Crows denies this," pointed to the contestations evident in sociocultural scenes. Other scholars wrote works of comparative insight that included their own perspective. For instance, Evans-Pritchard (1976 [1936]), documenting Azande understanding of causation as witchcraft, was able to note parallel logics in the west. Malinowski (1978 [1935]), in our exhibit, discussing the "weirdness" of garden magic in the Trobriands, was doing much the same. Gregory

Bateson (1958 [1936]) puzzled over the oppositions enacted in the Naven ceremony among the Iatmul, and realized it mirrored the escalating antagonisms of Western nationalisms, just then threatening to explode into war in Europe.[10]

Comparison has also been the basis of our own project, which started when we spotted interesting and surprising similarities between ethnographic cases we had separately described, ones far removed from each other. We realized, in comparing our cases in Senegal and Hungary, that the differentiation in them – differentiation among ways of speaking, social sectors and roles, and other aspects of conduct – was similarly organized, despite our field sites' obvious differences in geographical locale, language, and history. Exploring the differentiations as a matter of semiotic organization allowed the comparability – and similarity – of the two field sites to emerge. The semiotic framework that developed from our alignment and comparison of these two very separate cases is itself based on the kinds of comparisons that the social actors in our field sites – and everywhere – are always making in the conduct of their social lives. Comparison is inescapable. We wish to see our own comparative efforts and their results as engaged with the distant scholars of the past as well as with the townspeople we have each described and the colleagues whose areally diverse, semiotically inspired ethnographic work we build on. Indeed, our book rests on the notion that a semiotic analysis enables and will illuminate comparison among cases widely different in space and time.

Outline of the Book

The rest of the book consists of four parts, and ethnographic description is the first problem to which we turn our attention. Part I presents our ethnographic cases, in Senegal and Hungary, exploring the way ideological work and the enactment of difference look from "inside" each ethnographic site. How do they organize and shape social relations and linguistic practices? The three chapters of Part II are quite different, since they delve into the details of the semiotic process of differentiation briefly outlined in this introduction. The chapters explicate step-by-step how differentiation and similarity are made and illustrate this with examples from regional stereotypes of people, spaces, and linguistic practices in nineteenth-century America. These chapters also focus on changes in the representation of difference and its political consequences. The three chapters of Part III offer yet another angle of approach to ideologies of differentiation. They develop ways of analyzing sites of ideological work, including research sites; they reveal connections among those sites. Here we take up issues such as institutionalization and scaling, both of which are illuminated by our approach. Finally, Part IV is a discussion of the past of research on linguistic practices. We describe how linguistics went global at the end of the nineteenth century, incorporating materials from unwritten languages. What difference did this make, for language, for speakers, for scholars? This was a scalar step, and, as we show, our approach to differentiation provides a novel slant on this historical development. For the convenience of readers, each part is introduced by a brief overview. The coda follows with suggestions for expanding inquiry in new directions through the use of the semiotic tools presented in this book.

Part I

Ethnography

How is ethnographic analysis illuminated by the semiotic process we have just outlined? These two chapters describe settings we know very well and can portray in some richness of detail. Drawing on our own fieldwork and related materials, we show how attention to semiotic process helps bring out important aspects of the ethnography. In fact, examining our field materials convinced us that this approach revealed aspects of social life and ideology we might not otherwise have seen. We draw on these cases in later chapters as well.

Another goal of Part I is to point toward comparison. The ethnographic cases we discuss come from places very distant from one another geographically and in many other ways. Neither the linguistic resources (languages, registers, repertoires) nor the social and historical forms (specifics of town organization, social categories, religious affiliations) had any close historical relationship. Indeed, none of the conventional units or dimensions of comparison seemed adequate starting points. Only when we looked at the cases in a new light – not at the specifics of social forms, language forms, or histories, but instead focusing on semiotic, ideological processes – were we able to see how and why there were parallels. In each case, similar processes of differentiation organized important forms of social action and linguistic variation. Moreover, the differentiation in both cases happened to engage similar cultural themes.

Comparison is a foundational characteristic of anthropology as a discipline. Yet, we are well aware that it can be problematic to compare Africans and Europeans. What populations, what practices can be appropriately extracted from the global history of colonial and postcolonial relations between North and South, the West and the Rest? Our goal here is simpler: to offer localized perspectives, the "inside" view of how immediate participants in a social scene envision and display cultural and linguistic distinctions, and how they act on them. Juxtaposing the two cases reveals the similarity between the differentiating processes in them, at the same time highlighting the very different ways they handle hierarchy. It is equally noteworthy that our own comparative impulse was mirrored in what the people we had observed were doing: how the social actors in each case compared things and people, made relative judgments, invoked contrasts, and expressed (and sometimes switched) points of view.

Chapter 1 focuses on Wolof society in a small town in Senegal, which was similar in population to the town of German-Hungarian bilinguals in Hungary described in Chapter 2. Both chapters draw on fieldwork as well as on published and archival sources. In both cases, an ideological theme of expressive restraint versus elaboration organized differentiations among social types and practices. The two chapters explore how those differentiations, and the ideological work of comparing, evaluating, and assessing the stakes of a situation, are revealed in actions, interactions, and statements. Our discussion addresses how people "explained" the differences they saw, how they expressed their own points of view, and how they negotiated difference in their own practices. Although these two chapters devote most of their attention to everyday life, each chapter also situates the town and the farmers and artisans who live in it within broader social and historical contexts.

1   Wolof in Senegal

While working on acquiring Wolof language for her upcoming fieldwork in Senegal, Irvine – still in the United States – played a recording of a public performance by a griot (bard, praise singer) for a Wolof-speaking tutor's commentary.[1] To her surprise, the tutor remarked that he wasn't sure whether the performance was in Wolof at all. He requested several replays before he could confirm that it was, and his comments were vague. Why should this be?

One possible answer could be that the griot came from a different region, so that the difficulty stemmed from geographical dialect differences between the performance and the tutor's own Wolof. (He was from a region farther south.) Other possible answers could concern social dialectology and/or the special linguistic characteristics of the performance genre, which might include esoteric lexicon unfamiliar to the tutor. Yet another answer might concern the notion of "Wolof language" and under what circumstances a stretch of discourse is assigned to it. Since these possible answers are not mutually exclusive, a final possibility might be "all of the above."

The geographical difference is probably the least important. Most linguists agree that geographical dialect differentiation in Wolof is relatively minor. Although Wolof-speakers notice a few regional differences in speech and comment on them, there is little reason to think that these differences would lead to massive incomprehension.[2] What is more relevant to the tutor's uncertainty is the particular performance genre on the tape: genealogical praise oratory. This genre's conventions include extremely rapid delivery, certain kinds of esoteric expressions, and detailed genealogies, recited in the form of long lists of names (see Irvine 1978a). Since many of the same names are found over a wide region of the western Sahel, long passages of praise oratory cannot always be identified easily with one local language rather than another, even if the listener can follow the delivery.

Yet, important questions remain. What understandings of language and social relations might underlie these performance conventions? Who commands these verbal skills, what is their social positioning, and how are they distributed in the Wolof-speaking population?

We begin by sketching an ideology of language that Irvine identified in her early fieldwork in a rural community, a small town – or large village – of some twelve to thirteen hundred people when she first lived there in 1970–1971 (grown to more than four thousand by the time of her visit in 2006).[3] Because the fieldwork on which our discussion of Wolof rural life is based was carried out mainly in the 1970s and 1980s, we describe it using past tenses. However, more recent research, including Irvine's own visits, suggests that the main outlines of rural social practice as sketched here remain important on the rural scene.

An Ideology of Differentiation

In this rural Wolof community, townspeople identified ways of speaking – registers – that they identified with opposite social groups: the high-ranking *géer* 'nobles,' and the low-ranking bardic category, the *gewel* 'griots.' The labels for these registers were simply descriptive. *Waxu géer* is 'noble talk' and *waxu gewel* is 'griot talk' (*wax*, 'talk,' is a stem that can take either nominal or verbal morphology).[4] Performances such as the one Irvine's US-based tutor listened to displayed an extreme version of the "griot register" of speaking, and such performances differed from the "noble register" in many linguistic features, as we shall show. Among other characteristics, the "griot register" is rapid, loud, verbose, and elaborate, even hyperbolic, and includes esoteric vocabulary and epithets, while the "noble register" is plain, quiet, and terse. The extremes of both registers fell well outside the range of variation found in ordinary talk. Yet, it is on those extremes that the metapragmatic terms focus: the poles of a linguistic differentiation that is observably gradient. The labels identify those poles with two saliently contrasting social categories, picked out of the larger set of categories in Wolof society.

As Irvine has argued elsewhere (for more detail see Irvine 1990 and other papers), the linguistic differences between these registers were ideologically motivated in a rural Wolof schema connecting social identities with verbal conduct. Social organization was understood as depending upon the differentiation of persons who contrasted – in their behaviors, their talk, and supposedly in their very essences – between gravity and exuberance. That contrast, also understood as between the austere and the elaborated, was conceived as morally loaded and bearing implications of social rank. It organized social interaction and the behaviors, including speech, that were considered typical of persons belonging to opposite social categories. As a kind of *master metaphor*, the contrast between the austere and the elaborated organized differences between ranked persons in many aspects of behavior – from bodily movements to food preferences and professional specializations – including differences in registers of speaking.

Commenting on the broad contrast they drew between gravity and exuberance in speech and other behavior, Wolof townspeople located it in a difference between laconic and impulsive temperaments. The central assumption was that people were inherently dissimilar, having different constitutions – even, in some relatively detailed versions, different physical ingredients, or perhaps the same ingredients but in different proportions and relationships – which were sometimes described in terms of the viscosity of bodily fluids. (Thus, viscous fluids are substantial yet sluggish in flow, while thinner fluids are more volatile and more subject to agitation.) Alternatively, the differences might be explained with recourse to a concept of weight: higher ranks are "heavier," lower ranks "lighter" – not in body fat, but in moral weight, as opposed to impulsivity or flightiness. Or again, the differences might be explained as located in variable types of *xel*, a term sometimes translatable as 'mind,' 'temper,' or 'temperament,' even 'conscience,' yet implying a referent more material than glosses like 'mind' might suggest. *Xel* can be heated (like coals); it should circulate; it can have holes; it is like a boat on water; or it is itself liquid (Marone 1969). Perhaps the best analogy is with the Galenic concept of humors, bodily fluids whose particular balance was supposed to determine a person's temperament, emotions, and physical health. At any rate, for these rural Wolof, the supposedly different constitutions governed their possessors' affectivity, motivations, and activity, making people behave in dissimilar ways. Whether explicitly stated or not, these assumptions amounted to a theory of social relations. That theory underwrote social inequality, since conduct had moral implications and the social hierarchy was based on supposed moral distinctions.

Clearly, the ideology that is operative here is an ideology of much more than language. It is a structure of symbolism and precepts that organize, and in that sense "explain" or rationalize, differences of social rank. The principle of difference and inequality was an acknowledged value that organized many kinds of social activities and interactions, ranging from economic specializations and exchange to the regulation of marriage, and including social contact and conversation.[5] The social categories that are thus ranked are generally called "castes" in the literature on the region because of the association between rank (including certain ritual constraints on contact), endogamy, and professional occupation.[6]

Rural discussions of these principles of social relations articulated their basis in differentiation, segregation, and inequality in moral and essentializing terms. The following excerpt (Example 1.1) from an interview with a local man (of medium rank within the high "noble" caste) is but one expression of these principles out of many Irvine encountered.

He was discussing *xel*, the mind or temperament that governs a person's behavior:

(1.1)   SaliT, T20-1A (1975)

Yalla, bi mu bindee, yaar rek la bind.	When God was creating the world, he created it just in pairs [of opposites].
Dégg ngga, bi mu bindee – góor, bind jigéen; dafa binde, xel mu baax, am xel mu bon. Bind ku baax, bind ku bon.	You see, when he created – man, he created woman; because he created good temperament, there's [also] bad temperament. He created who's good, he created who's bad.
Xel yi, yému nyu, nit nyi yému nyu.	Temperaments are not identical; human beings are not identical.
Nit nyi – su – bu nyett dajé, bu nyaar dajé rek, ay woroowaangga am na ca.	Human beings – if – when three [people] get together, even when just two get together, there are differentiations.
Kër gi, am na lu ko yor. Le ko yor, lëpp, ci jikko yi, man ngga dem ba ci wañ wi, fa SG di toggé, la nyu woroo, la mu woroo.	The house has what produces/ maintains it. What produces it, everything about people's characters, you can just go to the kitchen here, where SG is cooking, that's [where] they are distinguished, that's what she differentiates.

As he expresses it in this bit of talk, differentiation is key, both to God's plan in creating the world and to the way human beings maintain that order. Continuing, he explained that minds (*xel*) are like the different kitchen utensils a respectable high-caste woman (SG) uses, which she arranges carefully in different places in the kitchen. The arrangement is not just a simile, since it is also the kitchen and the food prepared in it that produces the family's *xel*.

Example 1.2, from a conversation between two middle-aged high-caste men, links the principle of differentiation to inequality, caste endogamy (barriers to intercaste marriage), and high-caste rejection of low-caste behavior:

(1.2)   ST and MK, T32-1

ST: Yalla sàkk fëpp, waay ay worowaro am na ca.

ST: God established everyplace/ everything, but there are differentiations in it.

[unintelligible; ginnaaw ya?] worowaro am na ci nak, te woroworom it la banggi. [...]

[... ? In the past] there were differences, and there are differences now too.
[He gives examples: dark-skinned and fair-skinned; tall and short. Go in the kitchen, study what's there, see how the head wife arranges it.]

Yalla sàkke na benn baraas, defar yi berang' kilé, defanggi [lu?] mere nit.
Alors ni ku ruusee, nya xajiléku, te demtowula wujj 'k sa moroom, mbaaraanggi.

God established a barrier, setting apart the person doing things that angered people.
So, whoever was ashamed, they set themselves apart, so that they would only marry with their peers; that's the shelter they arranged.

MK: Mbaaraanggi dall, mu né da nyu xajiléko, kenn ku ne di fa am partam.
Teetowaaté itam, maaséwu nyu. Maaséwu nyu ; bii moo gënn gatt ; bi itam, moo sut bi. Bi itam, moo sut bii. Mu né, tolluwu nyu.

MK: This is the shelter – he says, it's because they set themselves apart. Each person had a place. And it didn't prevent the fact that they are not equal. They are not equal: this one is shorter, that one is long (tall and strong). That one is long. He says, they are not equal.

ST: Noonu nak, lee la xel yi dafa am ...

ST: Likewise, there are the minds/ temperaments ...

As another man put it, "Separating people is very important to Wolof." He was explaining why griots are buried separately from people of other castes.

The social categories that are differentiated in this system include "nobles" (*géer*) and griots, but not only these. Like many other peoples of the West African Sahel region, Wolof have traditionally divided themselves into three principal social categories: high-ranking persons (*géer*, 'nobles') and two sets of low-ranking categories, *jaam* ('slaves') and *nyenyo* (the various artisan categories). Among the low-ranking artisan castes, the griots – artisans of the word – were the most numerous and conspicuous on the local scene in the region of Irvine's Senegalese fieldwork. The griots' occupational specializations mainly lay in rhetoric and the arts of communication, such as public oratory, praise singing, secular music, and message relaying (also – and this is related to their other aesthetic skills – beauty treatments such as hairdressing). Besides griots, the nyenyo artisan category included blacksmiths, leatherworkers, and weavers, among others. The "slaves" (*jaam*) – formerly a legal status, now only a social one – were mostly menial laborers owing part-time service to higher ranking persons who helped to support them.

Within each category there were further distinctions of rank, according to more detailed criteria of occupation, lineage, seniority, ritual niceties, and the like. For example, the local gold- and silversmiths distinguished themselves from blacksmiths; and there were different kinds of griots, as we will mention later in this chapter. Meanwhile, even *jaam* could have "slaves" of their own, and so could members of any other category. The system of ranks permitted elaborations and emergent distinctions, although practical considerations (such as demographic constraints on availability of marriage partners) limited the extent to which narrowly distinguished subcategories could become segregated social groupings over the long term.

Since the "noble" (*géer*) category is quite large, including common farmers as well as royalty and most Muslim clerics, distinctions within it are especially important on the rural scene. A reader unfamiliar with Sahelian social ranks should think of the term "noble" as implying a sense of moral normativity, rather than equating it with an elite minority. Although the traditional aristocracy – royalty and large landholding families – was a key component of the "noble" caste, there are other components as well.[7] Distinctions of rank could be drawn on various grounds: for example, on genealogical seniority and connection to princely lineages; on the relative rank of co-wives in a polygynous marriage; on relative age; on landholding title and political office; and, to a lesser extent, on important achievements, usually involving the control of sufficient wealth to support a large following of dependents.

Among the lower-ranking castes, the griots in particular were culturally stereotyped as persons of high affectivity and excitability. They were seen – by themselves as well as by others – as active and theatrical personalities, endowed with the energy and rhetorical skills enabling them to excite other people with whom they interacted. The highest-ranking nobles, meanwhile, were conventionally associated with stability and restraint, but also with lethargy and blandness. Their self-control (*sago*) and restraint (*kersa*) might "make them reluctant to say bad things," as some people noted, but (they continued) it also made high nobles reluctant to say or do much of anything. It took a griot to make life interesting and attractive and to keep the high nobles awake. Once roused, kings and chiefs might be moved to great deeds – the greater because of the seriousness and weightiness of their personalities, and the many dependents they commanded – but griots were needed to stir them to that point. The griots' main services, therefore, lay in their ability to stir others, including their ability to convey a noble patron's ideas energetically and persuasively to his or her public. High nobles were considered to be too torpid, too removed, too conscious of their dignity, or too cautious of the effects of their acts to address a public themselves.

These principles of comportment, and the contrast between restraint and flamboyance, have often been described in the literature on Wolof and their West African neighbors. The structure and ideology of caste and caste-linked behaviors are found widely in the western Sahel, not just in Senegal. Senegalese scholars have pointed out these regional continuities; for example, in discussing Wolof moral philosophy, Assane Sylla (1978:198) approvingly quotes a passage from Dominique Zahan's work on the Bambara of Mali (Zahan 1970:189) as equally true of Wolof. Zahan's text asserts that the Bambara farmers (nobles) are reserved and sober in words and actions, silencing their feelings; their ethic is sober and severe; meanwhile the low-ranking artisan castes are uninhibited in their behavior, especially the griots, with their fluid, forceful, and elegant speech. Similarly, Boubacar Ly (1967:50) describes the dignified comportment of the noble – the "man of honor" – among both the Wolof and the neighboring Tukulor:

What is characteristic of this dignity is that it is based on a certain *slowness*. Gestures are thus slow, deliberate, never gratuitous; elocution is slow and affirmed by certain "techniques of the body." The entire person thus reflects dignity and nobility. At a *deeper* level dignity manifests itself in the form of *self-control (sang-froid)*. To evidence one's dignity is to show calm, tranquility, confidence, and never abandon them. At all times it is appropriate, for the Wolof, to maintain his self-control (*sago* in Wolof) and not to "lose himself" (*sâlit* in Wolof). (emphasis original, translation ours)

Locally, explaining the noble's *kersa* (restraint), a high-caste person told Irvine (Example 1.3):

(1.3)   MK T15 (French insertions in the Wolof text, and their translations in the English version, are in italics)

Waaw, ndàngk ngga-i wax. *C'est ça. Parce que* wax ndàngk, moo gënn baax.	Yes, you [should] speak slowly. *That's it. Because* speaking slowly, it's better.
E, waay, wax ci kaw! Yaangga tànggal kër gële. Walla ngga tànggal ni ceete[??] bi.	Eh, but please! speaking high/loud! You're heating up/stirring up the house. Or you're heating up the event [assemblage?]
Nyu-i né, a, waay, diw moom, bari wax, kon ku [kooku?] munggi wax rek !	They're saying, Oh hey! [Gimme a break!], that person, so much talk, all he does is talk!
Xamu-loo ku miraatengge [meretangge??] foofu, xamu-loo.	You don't know who is bleeding from just giving birth there, you don't know.
Xamu-loo jigéen ji-uw mat-angga foofu, xamu-loo.	You don't know, a woman in labor is there, you don't know. [OR: jigéen ju mat, "a worthy woman"?]
Xamu-loo – góor gi ngga-i waxante fë bëggënt', am, dafa përt, *mais pressé*, ku am bëgg dem.	You don't know – the man you're chatting with there, maybe there's somebody who has suffered a loss, or who's *in a hurry*, maybe there's somebody who wants to leave.
Ngga nekk fi, wax rek.	There you are, just talking.
Mu am soxlo bëgg dem, ngga teye ko wax rek, kooku baaxul	He has some need and wants to leave, and you're holding him back just talking – that's not good.
War ngga wax ndàngk rek, tuuti.	You ought to speak just slowly/ softly, [and] just a little.
Noonu, kersa, baax na torob ci nit.	Like that, *kersa* [restraint], it's very good in a person.

Even though the noble was supposed to be brave in battle, for the highest-ranking men bravery meant steadfastness in the face of assault – "lunching on bullets and dining on cannons," as a local griot put it, describing his noble patron's princely behavior – more than energetic assaulting itself. Assault – as opposed to defensive action – was left to ordinary men and to the *ceddo*, crown slaves. It was mentioned locally only with disapproval, as incompatible with high dignity. The noble woman, meanwhile, should show patience and restraint even when in pain, such as in childbirth; she should not cry out. In fact, one night while a *géer* neighbor gave birth, Irvine was sitting in the courtyard just outside the house and heard nothing. And another example: one afternoon a noble woman who felt her dignity had been gravely insulted ran to one of the town wells and threw herself down it, attempting suicide. A group of women, both nobles and griots, were standing near the well at the time, some washing clothes. Such was the austerity of expression among noble women, and freedom of expression among griot women, that only the griot women screamed.

The system of ranks among Wolof includes many more categories than just these two, but the contrast between (high) noble and (low) griot epitomized the principle of hierarchical differentiation as it related to language and linguistic practices. Professional expertise in the arts of rhetoric and communication was the griots' prerogative, and the occasional high-caste child or youth who showed too much interest in performance was teased or scolded by his or her family. It was not just the professional specializations and specific caste identities that were at issue. Differences of rank, and the obligations those differences entail – service and deference on the one hand, and largesse on the other – pertained to any and all social relationships. Younger siblings owed service to older siblings and could expect material aid in return. Similarly, children owed service to parents, the patrilateral cross-cousin to the matrilateral cross-cousin, debtors to lenders, nyenyo to *géer*.[8]

The obligations of service and deference, exchanged for material support or payment, pervade this system and undergird the relationship between high and low ranks. It is not only a matter of different essential qualities, but also of roles in a transaction. This point arose early in Irvine's Wolof fieldwork, when she did not yet know who was who. As she stood at the edge of a gathering in the town plaza, observing what was evidently a political meeting, she noticed that two men were the main focus of attention: one seated, and one standing. They alternated speaking turns, the seated man's talk being practically inaudible but followed by loud speech from the standing man, who appeared to address the crowd. A companionable local man offered the following explanation of the standing man's behavior (Example 1.4):

(1.4)   N1 (1970) (French insertions in Wolof are in italics, in both the Wolof and the English versions)

Munggi jotilé waxu *seef d'arrondissement*, ba nak waa dëkk bi dégg bu baax.	He is transmitting [jotilé] the speech of the *chef d'arrondissement* [regional official], so that the townspeople will understand it well.
Ndax moom, gewel la. Dafa mëna wax ci kaw.	Because he is a griot, so he knows how to speak loud/high-pitched.

The concept of *jotilé,* 'transmission' (or relaying), on which this excerpt focuses is central to the griot's role and, by analogy, to all communicative services lower-ranking people perform for the higher-ranking. The griot relays a message from one high-ranking person – who, out of dignity and restraint, cannot speak loudly or at length – to another high-ranking person or persons, whose essential torpor might otherwise prevent them from hearing it. The griot's transmission is loud and energetic, pitched high above any chatter in the crowd, often accompanied by theatrical gestures, and elaborating, perhaps clarifying, the original message, supporting it in repetition. It is not only at political meetings that griot "transmission" is necessary. Any important gathering – funerals, naming-day ceremonies and other life-passage events, local religious pilgrimages – calls for transmitters.[9] Irvine observed this practice even when the gathering was very small, such as when two town chiefs, inside a room, conferred with each other on a matter of importance. Each brought his griot to carry on the meeting on his behalf; and each chief whispered in his griot's ear. It was the griots who spoke aloud, gazing at one another.

Communication services, whether they were formal performances of eulogy and genealogical history, or relaying a patron's address to a group, or simple acts of message-bearing and speaking for others, were to be rewarded with gifts and payment in cash or in kind. Some of these services required a professional, that is, a griot. But apart from the most technically demanding kinds of performances – those that required long-term study and practice to acquire the knowledge and skills necessary for successful performance – other non-noble castes could substitute for griots or participate along with griots if too few actual griots happened to be present. In fact, some minor griot-like roles might even be taken on by low-ranking nobles or children, if no person of lower caste was available. In short, rhetorical elaboration and message bearing were services lower-ranking people might provide in exchange for economic aid from the higher ranks, and this principle governed not only the professional specialties of griots but also the broader patterns of communicative conduct and display.

Although many nobles claimed that griots were greedy and cared only for what they could extract from their patrons, griots themselves presented a different perspective. They emphasized the aesthetics of performance, and the ethics of supporting one's patron and being energetic in carrying out one's obligations. As one griot told Irvine, "The presentation is everything. The old griots, like my father, tell us that the presentation is what is important, and if someone gives you five thousand francs but then says 'Get out' and doesn't want you to present anything, you will never go back there again." Another griot talked about politeness, recognizing the nobility of one's patron, and not ignoring one's traditional patrons in favor of someone who might offer more money. Of course, griots were aware that their caste was stigmatized. For example, a griot with whom Irvine often conversed told her he was reluctant to bring his wife over to meet her, lest the high-caste family in whose household Irvine lived would say – he voiced them in sneering tones – "*Qu'est-ce que c'est que ces griots?*" ('What is it with these griots?').[10] That griots themselves shared much of the ideology that stigmatized them, however – or were willing to sound as if they shared it – is suggested by how common it was for a griot to make the same disparaging comments about other griots as nobles might make about the caste as a whole.

In sum, the image of the griot publicly eulogizing, persuading, and entertaining the noble was a cultural stereotype – the crystallization, on the level of caste differences, of a cultural convention associating certain kinds of dramatic verbal performances, elaborated verbal activity, and requests, with rank differences, be they small or great. Yet, the differentiation of verbal behavior associated with griots and nobles pertained not only to persons actually born into those categories. Instead, the relationship served as a cultural model – a prototype – for the organization of talk among any interactants when differences in rank became relevant.

The ideology that contrasts these social images is what motivates the particular linguistic contrasts distinguishing the two registers of speaking mentioned earlier, identified by local consultants: 'griot speech' (*waxu gewel*) and 'noble speech' (*waxu géer*). The workings of this ideological construction, along with the distribution of speech registers and their variation, are illuminated by a consideration of semiotic process, as we will show.

Semiotic Aspects of Register Differentiation

The semiotic process that constructs ideology can be understood, in the Senegalese case and elsewhere, in terms of the aspects we have proposed: rhematization, fractal recursivity, and erasure, with the axis of differentiation organizing these.

Speech Registers as Rhematizations

Let us first explore the ideological construct in regard to rhematization, in which verbal conduct is understood as if its particular qualities iconically displayed some underlying social quality. The "griot" register can be summarized as involving affectively charged, elaborated, aesthetically polished, supportive repetition. (The idea of repetition derives from the griot's role as "transmitter" of the high-ranking patron's ideas, which were sometimes initially whispered or conveyed to the griot in private, then repeated elaborately by the griot in public.) The "noble" register, in contrast, is the register of the laconic, restrained, stoic, or cautious speaker who lacks – or performs as if lacking – special rhetorical skills or fluency. Linguistically, the relevant contrasts are found in all aspects of verbal performance, from prosody, phonetics, morphology, and sentence structure to turn-taking and the management of conversational discourse (see Tables 1.1, 1.2, 1.3; for more discussion, see Irvine 1990).

Table 1.1 *Wolof register contrasts in prosody*

	waxu géer 'Noble speech'	*waxu gewel* 'Griot speech'
Pitch	Low	High
Volume	Soft	Loud
Tempo	Slow	Fast
Voice	Breathy	Clear
Contour	Pitch nucleus last	Pitch nucleus first
Dynamic range	Narrow	Wide

Table 1.2 *Wolof register contrasts in phonology*

Register	Noble speech	Griot speech
Feature contrasts	Contrasts in vowel length and consonant length not clearly maintained	Contrasts in vowel length and consonant length clearly maintained
	Nonnasal stops affricated and/or prenasalized, e.g., [p] → [pφ] or [φ], [b] → [β], [mb], [mβ]	Stops in stressed syllables, and all "fortis" stops, energetically articulated
	"Breathy" or "creaky" (laryngealized) articulation of voiced stops	Voicing contrasts in syllable-initial consonants, and all "fortis" stops, clearly maintained
Stressed/unstressed syllables and elisions	Stresses not clearly marked (little difference between stressed and unstressed syllables)	Stressed syllables clearly articulated; elisions in unstressed syllables: (1) "Lenis" final stop elided (2) Unstressed CV# → C# (3) Initial [k] → [ʔ]
Vowel height	Some lowering of vowels	Some fronting and raising of vowels, especially before palatal glides

A few comments on the prosodic contrasts in Table 1.1 may be useful. To quantify the differences in tempo, Irvine constructed a sample (twenty excerpts

Table 1.3 *Wolof register contrasts in morphology and syntax*

Register features	'Noble speech'	'Griot speech'
Emphatic devices	Unmarked order of basic constituents (SVO); sparse use of focus markers	Left dislocations; cleft sentences; heavy use of focus markers (subject focus, object focus, and "explicative" verbal auxiliary)
	Sparse use of spatial deictics and determinants	Frequent use of spatial deictics, especially their "emphatic" forms
	Sparse use of modifiers	Heavier use of modifiers; ideophones (intensifiers); more use of verb-complement construction *né* ___, which often conveys details of sound and motion
Parallelisms	Little use of parallelism	Repetitive and parallel constructions (e.g., parallel clauses)
	Few reduplicated forms, especially in verbs; no novel constructions using morphological reduplication	Frequent use of morphological reduplication, especially in verbs, including novel word formations
Disfluencies – morphology (see Irvine 1978b)	(1) Choice of noun class marker "wrong" or semantically neutral (2) Avoidance of class markers when possible (3) Incomplete or inconsistent concord	(1) "Correct" class markers, following principles of consonant harmony and/or semantic subtlety (2) Inclusion of class markers, when optional (3) Complete and consistent concord
Disfluencies – syntax	Incomplete sentence structures; false starts	Well-formed sentence structures

of talk) of nobles and griots speaking in various circumstances and genres, all "naturally occurring" in that she did not stage them herself; they did not include interviews. Speed of talk was calculated in terms of syllables per minute. Since nobles' turns at talk were usually brief, much less than a minute, their speed was calculated proportionally. Thus a noble who produced only an eight-syllable utterance but took ten seconds to do it was speaking at a rate of 48 syllables/minute. The calculation is very rough, and it does not account well for the brevity of some nobles' talk, or the necessary pauses for breath in the griots' longer discourse. It is not obvious anyway how one should construct an

appropriate sample of speech for this purpose. Still, in a range of genres ranging from conversation through more formal speeches (enabled by microphones
or griot transmitters), nobles' rate of speaking ranged from 48 to 264 syllables per minute. Griots, again in a range of genres from conversation through
transmissions and public performances, clocked in at between 138 and 386
syllables per minute. Although the ranges overlap, the registers became more
sharply differentiated as the occasion and genre were more public and/or more
focused on matters that concern caste relations. The more public and rank-
relevant the occasion, too, the more likely it was that the speaking roles would
be inhabited by actual members of the relevant castes, not by substitutes.

Regarding loudness, the physical setting of the talk – indoors or outdoors –
was an additional factor, though always trumped by differences in rank. Thus
if a griot visited a noble's house and entered into conversation indoors, the conversation as a whole might be quieter than if the same conversation took place
outdoors; but the griot's talk would still be louder than the noble's.

The most extreme version of "griot talk" was displayed in the griot's public
(outdoor) performances: loud, rapid oratory accompanied by emphatic gestures;
pitch mostly high, but including sharp pitch contours; sentence constructions
that contained many morphological and syntactic devices for emphasis, intensification, and repetitive parallelisms; and vivid vocabulary, especially regarding
details of sound, motion, and feeling. The extreme of "noble talk," meanwhile,
is no talk at all, and indeed on many occasions where griots performed, nobles
were silent. Sometimes a noble who was the focal interlocutor of a griot (either as
sponsor or as addressee) remained offstage, invisible behind a wall or curtain.
But if the noble did speak, and in more than a brief whisper, then "noble talk"
would emerge as a laconic, slow, low-pitched drawl or mumbling, with simple
or even incomplete sentence structures. Prosodic contrasts between the registers (shown in Table 1.1) were conspicuous and salient to consultants, while
phonological aspects of register differentiation were less available to conscious
contemplation. Yet the two kinds of contrast (prosodic and phonological) are
closely linked. The "noble" register's mumbled drawl neutralized features of
vowel and consonant length and some distinctions between stops and contin-
uants, as opposed to the "griot" register's shotgun articulation that preserved
those feature distinctions but highlighted consonants at the expense of vowels
(see Table 1.2).

Similar contrasts distinguish the morphology, syntax, and lexicon of the two
registers – the emphatic, vivid, elaborate register of *waxu gewel* and the bland,
laconic, sometimes even disfluent register of *waxu géer* (see Table 1.3).

Notice how an ideology of language "explains" the form of linguistic differentiation of these registers by associating speech registers with essential-
ized social differences, via particular *qualia*. The linguistic contrasts that

differentiate the registers are not arbitrary; instead, they are motivated by a language ideology contrasting the laconic and austere with the impulsive and elaborated, and deriving these qualities from the supposedly differentiated temperaments of their speakers. This is what we mean by rhematization. The rural Wolof ideological construction takes the contrasting linguistic behaviors as iconic representations – depicting the social relations they index. Linguistic features occurring at many levels of linguistic organization, along with their associated social images, are vertically integrated along an ideological axis that contrasts them with opposed features and images, according to the temperaments that supposedly "cause" the differentiation. And the linguistic differentiae themselves offer linguistic images that (iconically) share qualities such as slowness versus dynamism with the social images they represent.

Speech Registers as Fractal Recursivity

In addition to rhematization, these Wolof materials also illustrate another common consequence of an ideology of contrasts: the fractal replication of the same axis of contrast at different levels of inclusiveness. That is, the principles of register differentiation operate recursively at many different magnitudes, from gross contrasts to subtle ones. Linguistic differences as well as social differences can be great (gross contrasts) or small (subtle contrasts). Despite the labels Wolof townspeople assigned to these ways of speaking, actual speech in this Wolof community sorted out linguistically – from an observer's perspective – not into two utterly distinct types, but rather into a continually reproduced relation of difference.

One way recursivity can work is in projection of a contrast inward, producing narrower categories. We have noted that the poles of the contrast, that is, the most extreme versions of the registers, were to be found in the utterances of griots and high nobles in large-scale public occasions. Apart from those polarizing scenes and extreme versions, however, *any* speaker, no matter what his or her caste, could use either a noble-like or a griot-like register, depending on the circumstances. So while a local ideology of language linked these registers with the social categories of noble and griot – caste categories whose membership was permanent, nonoverlapping, and ranked on an absolute scale – in practice the registers, in less extreme versions, were drawn upon by everyone as a way of organizing the social relations and speech activities at hand. Two persons belonging to the same caste differentiated their speech according to the same axis of contrast that differentiated the castes' registers from each other. In so doing these same-caste speakers would represent subtler differences of rank (such as lineage seniority), or they would define an activity, such as petitioning, that was reminiscent of intercaste relations. The linguistic differentiae they deployed to do this echoed the differentiae of caste-linked registers, but to a lesser degree; the differences of pitch, tempo, fluency, and so on were somewhat narrower.

Example 1.5 illustrates this process in a transcript segment in which subtle differences of rank among nobles were reflected in subtly differentiated discursive practices. The setting is a warm summer evening in the courtyard of the town chief's compound. A half dozen family members, a couple of neighbors, and Irvine are casually chatting; the chief himself has joined the group, a somewhat unusual occurrence since he often remained inside his room reading or advising a visitor on some private matter. At some point a truck is heard in the distance, probably delivering supplies for a shop. The talk, a moment of which is transcribed in Example 1.5, turns to how the truck drivers at a phosphate mine some distance away have been trained in France and really know how to drive. They can drive as far as between the cities of Rufisque and Saint-Louis (some two hundred miles), no matter what the conditions:

(1.5)   T31.2 (1975) Transcription conventions: // represents an overlapped transition – the end of a prior turn overlaps with the start of the next bit of talk. Large brackets represent overlap of more than just the transitions between turns. Text layout represents the temporal organization of the talk. Italics (in English translation) represent stress. This Wolof text has no French insertions.

1   MT: Xamxam   ci   li   nyu xam né, nyoonyu!
            Knowledge about what they know   they (emphatic)
            The knowledge they have, *those* people! [the drivers]

2   MF: E – Tingééj [? Indistinct]
                [name of town, also known as Rufisque]
            Eh – [the ones in] Rufisque. [?]

3   MT: Xamxam,   xamxam   dàll la nyu ko am, ba m'ko doylé
            Knowledge knowledge really they it have till it   suffices
            They *really* have enough *knowledge*

4   Ci diggïnte, diggïnte, aa//
            Between   between
            [to drive] between – ah –

5   Chief: // [indistinguishable] Mariama, yów fi
                                    [JTI]   you here
                                    Mariama [JTI], you

6   de   woon sax.   [pause]   ⌐Fekk fu kenn   du   nyui   xam   fu –
                     Emph past even   find where anyone neg they-contin know where
                     were *here* then.   Turns out nobody knows where –

7   MT: diggïnte Tingéej ak   Ndar.
                                                  between [town] and [town]
                                                  between Rufisque and Saint-Louis.   ⌐

8   Chief: li   ca – li   nyui   ci –   jogé ba xam – [pause]
                    what at   what they-cont. about set out till know
                    about what – about what they – get to know – [pause]

9   ⌐li   ci de   wonee –
                        what at emph was shown
                        what was indeed shown about –   ⌐

10   MT: │ A!   A –   a –   │ am ngoonent, da   nyu fi musa am
                                             │ an afternoon expl they here once have
                        Ah! w-   w-   [because] one afternoon, they once had here

11   benn, benn, benn kii   bu fu –   bu ko musa riix ci
                    one   one   one *machine* rel. where rel it   once stick in
                    a, a *machine* where – that got stuck in

12   genn   kekk. [pause; then rapid:] kaay topp ko, topp-topp-topp-topp-
                    one(aug.) pothole   come push it   push continually
                    a big *pothole*. [pause; then rapid:] [They] come and push it, pushing pushing

13   topp-topp – mu nyàngg –   mu nyimé   tabasiku!
                    pushing   it suddenly active it manage suddenly disengage
                    pushing – it suddenly moves – it manages to burst out!

14   KN: A bon   nak –
                    well   thus
                    Well then –

15   MT: Bon nak, bu   nyu jubuló,   demal   ci biir   nger,
           well thus when they straighten go-caus. in middle highway
           Well then, when they straighten up, they make it go in the middle of the highway,

16   kii   bu nyui   law!
           machine rel they-cont touch
           the machine they were handling!

In the conversation excerpted here, everyone present is *géer* (noble), but MT, a neighbor, ranks lower than others. He is a junior member of a lineage segment that owns no land locally and is dependent on the chief's patronage. Notice the features of his talk that look relatively griot-like: the presentation of a narrative with dramatic action; emphatics (*nyoonyu*, *dàll*, and emphatic deictics); repetitions and reduplications; also (though not easily represented in transcript except by exclamation points) relatively rapid, loud, and exclamatory prosody. Meanwhile the chief, in Lines 6 and 8–9, pauses and becomes disfluent, just as the narrative gets going.

As the example illustrates, even though the metapragmatic labels for these registers of speaking identify them with permanent social identities (castes) occupying opposite positions in a social system, the distribution of these linguistic varieties was not actually that of social dialects, but actually like the distribution of situation-linked registers. The metapragmatic labels represent a local ideological appraisal, belied in field observation. Yet, a better way for a linguist to think of the patterning of behaviors in this case is not in terms of a set of "things" (whether dialects or registers) but in terms of a relational enregisterment – a process that differentiates the emergent forms of talk according to the particular ingredients and dynamics of a social situation.

In short, there is not just one social boundary or relevant distinction here, but, instead, a scheme of sociolinguistic differentiation that semiotically organizes relationships at many degrees of encompassment. This is what we mean by fractal recursivity. The recursive structure organizes many situations, and many aspects of talk, even when the register contrasts are subtle. There is an axis of differentiation around which forms of talk contrast, in all sorts of settings.

The transcript in Example 1.5 illustrates the recursive differentiation of speech registers within the *géer* ('noble') caste category. The same kind of recursivity applied within the griot category as well. For example, when a griot family had a celebration requiring praise oratory, such as a naming-day ceremony, the oratory had to be performed by lower-ranking griots, while the host family remained quietly seated. In these events, the system of kinship relations provided the contrasting ranks: the performers were the patrilateral cross-cousins of the male head of household. This is because of a relationship that pertained in any caste, griots included: the patrilateral cross-cousin was considered lower-ranking than the matrilateral cross-cousin. (In fact, even the terms for these kin represented the difference in rank. The patrilateral cross-cousin was metaphorically termed *jaam* 'slave,' the matrilateral cross-cousin *sanga* 'master.') Thus the categorical status relationship described in earlier pages as stereotypically conceived in the praise performances griots address to nobles was, among griots, fractally repeated in the realm of kinship.

What about griots' informal talk among themselves, in situations comparable to that represented in Example 1.5? We cannot supply direct evidence of fractal recursivity in such talk because of an observer effect. Residing in the deputy chief's household, Irvine counted as noble, as did her initial assistants, so her presence turned any griot gathering into a mixed-caste setting.

So far, we have considered how fractal principles can replicate a structure of difference internally, producing contrasts of ever smaller magnitude. But the replication can also move in the other direction, projecting outward onto larger, more encompassing categories. In this kind of recursive process, opposed categories fuse when they are jointly contrasted with something external to them both. A process of ideological projection can be seen, for example, in the way some Wolof townspeople viewed the relationship between Wolof language and French, the language of the former colonial power. The same *axis of differentiation* applies; but notice that (in this view) the linguistic contrasts between French and Wolof lined French up with *waxu gewel* as high-pitched, rapid, verbose talk by volatile people, contrasting with the slow, serious, more deeply meaningful talk of Wolof nobles. This did not mean that anyone thought French people actually *were* griots, although they thought the caste background of Africans who spoke a lot of French might well be low or questionable if it was not locally known to be high. Regarding French people themselves, it was simply that to speak French was considered as speaking in a griot-like manner. Table 1.4 illustrates this point about Wolof and French. It also maps the recursive structure according to which the contrast between nobles and griots – the level at which speech registers are metapragmatically labeled – provides the registers' primary social index; other social contrasts are derived, recursions of the primary one.

There are some interesting questions about social positioning and point of view in regard to this outward projection onto the contrast between Wolof and French. Most of the evidence for this recursion came from noble consultants, so it is not entirely clear whether griots thought of French the same way, although they were certainly more willing to speak foreign languages than nobles were. In any case, a view of French that aligns it with "griot speech" does not exactly correspond to the colonizers' own ideology of language, nor does it support French claims to moral authority or political legitimacy.

Table 1.4 *Wolof sociolinguistic recursions*

	← Register contrasts →	
Prosody	Slow	Fast
	Soft	Loud
	Low pitch	High pitch
Style	Laconic	Verbose
	Plain, simple (lexis, syntax)	Ornate, hyperbolic (lexis, syntax)
Social distinction	Senior	Junior
	Higher rank (within caste)	Lower rank (within caste)
	Géer ('nobles')	Gewel ('griots')
Language stereotype	Wolof	Pulaar (another Senegalese language)
	Wolof, English	French
	Axis of Differentiation ↑	

The Wolof conception of "griot speech" as filled with elaborate rhetorical flourishes and drama, emphasizing aesthetics and persuasion over referential transparency, scarcely coincides with the long-standing French claims to exactness and clarity. Compare, for example, a passage from an often-cited work by Antoine de Rivarol (1784, cited in Swiggers 1990:123, his translation): "In vain do passions excite us and invite us to follow the order of the sensations: French syntax is incorruptible. Whence that admirable clarity, the eternal foundation of our language: what is not clear is not French." On this basis French language lay at the heart of the colonizers' *mission civilisatrice* and the colonizers' authority over "primitive" populations supposedly mired in ignorance, fanaticism, and ungoverned passions.

Speech Registers and Erasure

Notice now that the rural Wolof ideological construct, with its fractal structure, entails several kinds of erasure. One kind obtains when one moves outward from narrower scales of contrast to broader ones. Distinctions that have been salient in contrasting (say) the talk of low- and high-ranking nobles within an informal conversation, as in Example 1.5, are ignored when one turns to the broader contrast between griots' public declamatory speechmaking and the brief whispers of their noble sponsors. A related kind of erasure is manifest in the metapragmatic labels for these ways of speaking, which, in attributing them to permanent and exclusive social categories – the noble and griot castes – disregard the recursive practices that distribute their use throughout Wolof society. Finally, in emphasizing a binary opposition, this ideology of language ignored the social relationships and categories that did not fit a binary model. Wolof society included not only nobles and griots, but also other "artisan" castes and, especially, the descendants of persons of slave status (*jaam*). Yet, the linguistic ideology described here erased slaves from the picture, ignoring their differences from griots (and nobles). There was no comparable notion of "*jaam* speech" as a recognizable register of talk coordinate with the other registers.

These disregardings are an important form of erasure. A linguistic ideology is a totalizing vision in which some groups (or activities, or varieties) become invisible and inaudible. In the ideologized vision we have described, the descendants of slaves were accorded no voice.[11] Of course, the silence of *jaam*, who lacked the authority to speak in public (except insofar as they sometimes joined in with griots), differs enormously from the silence of high nobles, who had all the authority but also the caution and restraint that inhibit verbosity and loudness. A binary metapragmatics of speaking, in labeling speech registers and organizing their distribution, belied the fact of a tripartite social categorization. Sahelian triadic categorizations are evident not only in the major distinction among *géer*, *nyenyo*, and *jaam*, but also in triadic fractal replications within each of these: for example, the subcategories of griots, namely *ràbb* (locally, these are morally upgraded griots who sing praises only of God), *gewel* (ordinary griots, who praise humans), and *jaamu gewel* ('slaves of [other] griots').

Processes of erasure are one reason why a language ideology, whether discovered in informants' explicit statements and explanations or otherwise deduced, is not identical with an outside observer's analysis. The language ideology offers only a partial picture (or explanation) of a sociolinguistic scene, even while motivating important portions of it.

Two Individuals and Their Talk

Let us illustrate the workings of this ideological schema in a different way: in case studies of two individuals. We first track the shifting speech registers of MF, a mid-ranking noble man (*géer*) in his early thirties in 1975. As MF converses with different people, his speech can be seen to change depending on his relationship with his addressee.

Why call him "mid-ranking"? His age, neither an elder nor very young, is a contributing factor. The eldest son of a local notable who, by 1975, had become frail, MF stood to inherit land and position, and he already represented the family at most meetings of the chief's council. His education, which had taken him at least through primary school and perhaps a little further, had given him enough literacy skills and basic competence in French to be useful in dealing with bureaucratic institutions. His lineage rank was ambiguous. On the one hand, his lineage was distantly related to precolonial kings, suggesting a claim to particularly high status. On the other hand, his local family was not related to the local chiefs; his family's local land holdings were not especially large; and in age MF was junior to most of the local persons of consequence. He could claim to rank higher than some people, therefore, but not others. And there were persons to whom he stood in a relationship of dependence: his father; the chief; a wealthy friend in Dakar who worked for the civil service.

The friend from Dakar, S-, passed through town one day and stopped by to say hello while MF was talking with Irvine in her workroom. When S- entered the room, MF immediately rose and initiated a greeting routine (see Irvine 1974; greetings are normally initiated by persons of lower rank or who want to ask a favor). As the conversation proceeded, MF asked S- many questions. Many of the questions were about work and family, but also, after any pause in the talk, MF recycled the questions that are part of the greeting routine. Examples 1.6 to 1.8 show excerpts from the conversation, drawn from moments well after the initial greeting routines had been completed, and illustrating this recycling of the conventional greeting questions:

(1.6)   N9:90 (1975) French insertions in Wolof are in italics, in both the Wolof and English versions:

S-.	[pause]	
MF.	Na ngga def?	How are you?
	...	... [several lines of talk omitted]
S-.	[pause]	
MF.	Ana waa *service* bi?	How are your colleagues?
		[literally: How/where are the people of the *agency*?]

S- asked only one question of MF, a request for clarification when MF mentioned something about corn (Example 1.7):

(1.7)   N9:90 (1975)

| MF. | ... mboq. | ... corn. |
| S-. | mboqu lan? | What corn? |

Throughout the interaction, MF spoke loudly and with sharply rising pitch, ascending nearly to falsetto. S-'s voice, meanwhile, though sometimes high-pitched, was soft and with falling intonational contour. After about ten minutes of conversation, MF asked for a gift of cement. He was building a new house and was running out of materials. S-, speaking slowly and with pauses, was evasive:

(1.8) MF, N9:90 (1975) French insertions in Wolof are in italics, in both the Wolof and English versions

MF.	[rapid] *Il faut* ngga jaaral ma ay sàki *cimã*.	MF. [rapid] You *must* pass on to some bags of *cement*.
S-.	A? [pause] – Xaw ma. [pause]	S-. Ah [pause] – I don't know. [pause]
	Xaij na ma mana am waaye – [pause]	Maybe I can have (some) but – [pause]
	Ma seet ba xam. [pause]	I'll find out. [pause]
	Sa tabax booba di na xawa agg.	That building of yours must be almost finished.

At this point, another man enters the room; MF introduces S- to him, and the topic changes.

In this conversation we can see MF, noble though he is, speaking in a version of the griot-like register: relatively loud, high-pitched, rapid, and copious. He initiates conversational turns and asks many questions; the questions culminate in a request for goods. (Recall that acts of petitioning are also connected with the "griot" speaking register, via the image of griots' and other low-ranking persons' dependence on the higher ranks for material support.) On other occasions, however, MF spoke quite differently. In outdoor, group settings he said very little, as in the conversation represented in Example 1.5 above, when he happened to be present.

These kinds of contrasts, between a griot-like register and a high noble register, were consistent patterns of conduct in MF's speech. For example, one afternoon he stopped by where Irvine was talking with two other people, MK (a noble of a junior lineage, about MF's age) and SG (a noble woman). MF greeted us, but in such a low mumble that he could hardly be heard. He asked only one question (*na ngga def?* 'How are you?'), although the greeting routine normally calls for many; it was MK who asked more. And in another conversation in which MK was again present, MF spoke very softly and seemed reluctant to repeat himself when Irvine asked for clarification. After MK left the room, MF began to speak much more clearly, loud enough for Irvine to hear, and offering explanations without hesitation. The topic – a recent conversation between Irvine and a local elder – did not change; what changed was the departure of MK.

Evidently, MF's behavioral contrasts depended on his interlocutors and, relatedly, the purpose of the conversation. Apparently he considered himself higher ranking than MK, who might be considered genealogically his junior, though not junior chronologically. Later, MK commented – apparently without sarcasm, but it's hard to be sure – that you could tell MF was a *grand patron* (a big shot) by his manner of speaking. (As for MK himself, though he spoke relatively loud and copiously with MF, his voice dropped sharply in volume, pitch, and quantity when he accompanied Irvine to an interview with a *jaam* 'slave').

Let us now turn to a *gewel* (griot) for a case study illustrating another aspect of this ideological complex. The individual concerned (MM3), also in his early thirties in 1975, was starting to build a reputation as a skilled performer of praise oratory and as a trustworthy confidant – someone who could be asked to carry important messages, to accompany a high-caste patron at political meetings, and to make confidential inquiries on a noble's behalf. In this last capacity, he offered his services to Irvine. In one of our conversations, he produced the narrative below (Example 1.8) – partly, one may surmise, in evidence of his good character and skill in his profession. These qualities are not simply to be taken for granted. So one of the interesting things about the narrative, which recounts his experience at a noble patron family's celebration of their sons' initiation into manhood, is its presentation of the ethics of griot conduct. In effect, the narrative gives a griot perspective on the relations between the castes: some ways in which griots share in nobles' understandings of the relationship, and of the stigma attaching to their caste; and some ways in which they do not. In addition, the text is itself an example of the griot register, with its extended and dramatized narrative, and its detailed descriptive vocabulary.

(1.9)   MM3, N9:59 French insertions in Wolof are in italics, in both the Wolof text and the English version

Ni nu baaxo ci sunu-b cer di Ngewel:	This is how we ought to behave [what makes us good] in our section, which is Gewel:
Mooi am yarr ak xamé lan moi géer.	It's this, to be polite and to recognize what a noble is.
Bi ma ko xamee, looli la:	If I understand it, it's this:
Nofflay amatul.	There must be no laziness.
Neexadëkkal né ma, moo né,	A neighbor says to me, he says,

"Yów de, xewxew am na ci sa nyoñ yiu K.B.S. te ngga ko némékoji."

"Hey you, there's an event at your nobles' [family you are attached to] place in K.B.S. [name of town]. So you should go look for it."

Ma né ko, "Kon nak di naa fa dem wërlujiko."

I say to him, "So I'll go there and see if it's true."

Ba ma jógé ba yegg fa

When I set out, so that I arrive there,

Jub kër ga dégg sarxolé ya ak nyalaw-nyalaw ja ca lawbé ya,

entering the house, [I] hear the Sarakholés [=Soninke] and the wailing of the Lawbés.

Ma fekk leen nyu róogóo am caxxi sumaari,

I find them – they are wearing a necklace of sumaari nuts;

Dall di rôonu, siisu, nyu watu,

They have made a cross mark in cinders on the forehead; parted the hair; and shaved;

lëkkayu da di dógg seen-ub kurél.

wrapped a cloth from behind the neck to form their turban.

Ma dall ni bajoróo:

I start to declaim:

"Sarr-O jiin la, Talata Jojo Sarr Ndei Jambar Malik,"

"O Sarr [clan name], [praise-epithet plus name of their ancestor]"

Ba ma ko waxee, nyëpp né tekk di ma déglu.

When I say it, everyone falls silent and listens to me.

Ibra Sarr, moi lamdu ja, dal né "Waaw góor Parr ! May naa la sexug baay ga mu ma joxoon."

Ibra Sarr – he's the first boy to be circumcised – says "Yes indeed, Griot! I'm giving you the rooster that my father gave me."

Gora Sarr, moi tokko la, né ma "Maai góoru Jaynaba, mooi bëñleget. Du ma daw muuq.

Gora Sarr – he's the last-circumcised – says to me, "I'm the brother of Jaynaba, she's the bëñleget [nurse of circumcised boys who cares for their wounds and represents their sisters]. I never run away.

ndax jirim laa, te li mai nekk-nekk jirim kàt garmi laa.

I am an orphan, but what made me be an orphan does not take away my noble rank.

Ndax bu *guerre* takkoon, da ma sóobu ci biir, di añee *balle*, di reeré ay *kano*.

Because if a *war* broke out, I would immerse myself in it, lunching on *bullets*, dining on *cannons*.

Kon war ngéen-a xam né
garmi laa."
Walbatiku, né ma "Eh, nyenyo,
may naa la alfuun."

Biraan Sarr ma waroona nekk
bootal ba, jóg, né ma, "Maa
donn Biraan Demba Jigéen
ma dai górél jaam nya. Dal
maané may naa la siqetub
Ngulux-ngulux."

Dellu ca tekk, né ma, "Nyëpp
la yeené ndax sumburóo, ta
niileuloo sa nyoñ ngir xarxarle
seeti nyu léen ëppële.

Waay, géer nyëpp waraan na
nyu donn baay nde kon ngga
feetewoo askan wi."

So you all ought to know I'm a
prince."
Turning around, he says to me, "Hey,
nyenyo, I'm giving you a thousand
[dirhams; = 5,000 francs cfa]."
Biraan Sarr who must have been
the bootal [man in charge of
circumcised boys], got up and
said to me, "It's I who have taken
the place of Biraan Demba Jigéen
who freed the slaves. That means
I'm giving you the ram [named]
'Stuffy-Nose.'"
Returning to add, he says to me,
"Everyone respects you as a
serious person who doesn't come
perpetually around begging, and
you don't hide your own nobles
[ignore them, fail to praise them],
in searching for people who are
richer than they.
All nobles ought to have been
like fathers to you; but then you
would not have been attached to
this lineage." [He wants the griot
MM3 to serve only the Sarr family,
although the griot deserves all
nobles' patronage.]

In the narrative, MM3 reports that he was called to the household of a noble
family (in the Sarr patriclan) to which his own lineage segment is traditionally attached; that is, the griot family has a permanent clientage relationship
with these nobles, and a special responsibility for knowing and maintaining
an account of their genealogy and family history. On arrival, he finds that they
are celebrating the completion of male initiation (circumcision and traditional
instruction) of their sons. MM3 performs praise oratory for the family; the narrative represents the oratory only in abbreviated form, by recounting its open-
ing line. The nobles, MM3 reports, fall silent and listen attentively. Afterward,
they offer him substantial gifts, and tell him he is an excellent griot whom
all noble families would want to patronize; fortunately for the Sarrs, he is
specially attached to them.

Notice first that MM3's good character and skills are stated in negative terms: not being lazy; not coming around perpetually begging; not ignoring your noble patrons; not abandoning your traditional patrons for people who might have more money. Important aspects of the stigmatized image of the griot as greedy, annoying, and undeserving of reward are here represented as what this particular griot is *not*. (And by implication, other griots are – a view MM3 offered in many other conversations.) There are a few positive characterizations (being serious, polite, and "recognizing what a noble is" – i.e., acknowledging the relationship and being aware of one's responsibilities as a griot to praise the noble publicly), but stigmatized characterizations are presented as well. Notice too that any praise, in this case commendation of the griot himself, must be put in someone else's mouth. Even a griot cannot praise himself. Here, MM3 is complimented by the initiated boys and their mentor. Only the narrative frame permits MM3 to utter these compliments.

Moreover, in showing why these nobles' opinion is important, and why their compliments matter, the narrative has the nobles themselves speak to their own importance and background – "I never run away," "I'm a prince," "I'm giving you a thousand," and so on – utterances they were unlikely to make in real life. In the actual event, it would be the griot who would say these things about the nobles, while the nobles' gifts to the griot, silently yet ostentatiously displayed, gave evidence of their veracity. Thus the narrative implies that MM3 is worthy of being praised even by nobles, although it recounts a scene in which his narrated self acts within the conventional griot role (as he also did in recounting a dramatic narrative to Irvine).

While the narrative's representations of the role and image of the griot, and of the griot-noble relationship, are consistent in many ways with nobles' representations of them, there are differences too. Nobles valued taciturnity ("If you really knew what you were talking about you wouldn't be talking about it," as one noble succinctly put it), and plain speaking; griots valued aesthetic elaboration, dramatic performance skills, and verbal fluency. The narrative displays these values, including knowledge of relatively esoteric or unusual vocabulary, although MM3 does not claim them explicitly. But if a griot's professional prestige and command of rewards derived from this activity and fluency, it was the nobles' value on taciturnity and immobility that trumped them in the local context – that recursively supplied the model of higher ranking conduct, even within griot family events.

Incidentally, the fluency and esoteric Wolof vocabulary of this text contribute to making the narrative a good example of *wolof bu xóot,* 'deep Wolof' (or *wolof piir, wolof bu set* 'pure Wolof,' 'clean Wolof'). In Chapter 8, we explore how the rural speech registers, collectively called 'deep Wolof' and exemplified in narratives like this one, contrast with urban varieties of Wolof. In a contemporary urban context, the fractal recursions we have discussed are still to be found, but as we will point out, the values attaching to them are not quite the same.

Wolof Language Ideologies in Historical Perspective

The contrast in discursive practices between nobles and griots goes back many centuries. It is found widely in the Sahel region, and is attested in early written sources (e.g., Fernandes 1940 [1509]). Oral traditions also place the relationship between nobles and griots far back in time. Epic historical narratives recounting the foundations of Sahelian states and societies in the thirteenth and fourteenth centuries cite caste affiliations in a way that presumes categories such as nobles and griots already existed. Thus the story of Sunjata, the great epic of the Mande empire, relates interactions between Sunjata's father and his principal griot, as well as Sunjata himself and his griot (the famed Bala Faasigi Kuyaté), and shows the importance of these relationships in moving the historical events forward.

Mythological stories about the very beginnings of social life also speak to the interdependence of noble and griot. In many stories there is an original pair of brothers, the elder of whom does something praiseworthy that places the younger one forever in a position of dependence. For example, there is a Just-So story in which the elder brother defends the family against enemies, while the younger brother stays out of the fighting; on the elder's return from battle, the younger brother praises him. Forever after, the descendants of the elder are warriors and the descendants of the younger are praise singers. These stories about brothers not only represent the noble/griot relationship as fundamental to Wolof (and other Sahelian) society but also represent, in abbreviated form, the recursive hierarchical relationship that likens the higher/lower caste relationship to the senior/junior kin relationship.

While the evidence of oral history and early travelers indicates that the general outlines of a caste system with differentiated communicative practices is historically deep, and is seen as fundamental to Sahelian social traditions, this does not mean that the ideological picture we have drawn has been unaffected by more recent events. One such event, which looms all the larger because evidence of earlier times is fragmentary, is the French conquest of Senegal in the second half of the nineteenth century. The final and utter defeat of the Wolof kingdoms and the dismantling of their state apparatus considerably undermined the credibility of the traditional princely families. Anticolonial sentiment in the early twentieth century tended, instead, to look to Muslim religious leaders, who professed ascetic values and modeled a more contemplative kind of conduct than the Wolof kings had done. In fact, that difference between the clerical leaders and the princes had begun well before the French completed their conquest of the region. Some of the Muslim clerics, though certainly of *géer* ("noble") rank, had even earlier established themselves in political opposition to the traditional kings and their armies of crown slaves. Moreover, the community in which Irvine's ethnographic work was carried out had been a center of the religious opposition party as early as the eighteenth century. Despite these historical and local particulars, however, the picture of relatively silent nobles relying on griot praise singers and spokespersons in public and intercaste settings pervades Wolof history and ethnography, as well as other parts of the Sahel.

Among the many other consequences of the conquest – although one that came only decades after the beginning of French rule – was the colonial abolition of slavery as a legal status. Although some persons in the *jaam* category stayed with their "masters," others took advantage of new opportunities: the new lands being opened up for peanut cultivation in the Ferlo region under the leadership of a new religious movement, the Mourides. The exodus of a large number of people from the *jaam* category might have increased the tendency to binarism in the ideology of language, and its tendency to ignore the slave category. But the *jaam* were never professional speakers. Their social category largely connotes menial manual labor, performed by persons (and their descendants) who were demoted from other ranks. Linguistic expertise does not apply to them, nor does especially flamboyant conduct.

In recent decades, increasing rates of emigration from rural areas to urban centers – and emigration outside Senegal altogether, to Europe and North America – have created situations in which Wolof linguistic variation and repertoires are reconfigured. The salient units of comparison shift along with speakers' change of social positioning. We explore these matters, and the issues of scale, global relations, urban/rural distinctions, and ideological recalibration that they involve, in Chapter 8.

2   German-Hungarians in Hungary

Like many settlements in southwestern Hungary, the town of Bóly (G: Bohl) is known as German-speaking. About half the five thousand or so residents are descended from families that migrated in the eighteenth century from various German territories to Hungary. People who grew up in such families before the Second World War speak German; so do most of those born in the 1950s and 1960s. Even many younger people understand German and easily partic- ipate in familial interactions that include German, but are often reluctant to speak it. Everyone speaks Hungarian. Yet, when elders talked about the two languages spoken in Bóly it was not at all this German-Hungarian bilingualism they emphasized. Much more interesting for them was another form of speech variation:

(2.1) *Das wissen Sie jo, das in Bohl*   You know of course that there were
       zweierlei Sproch' worden.   two kinds of language in Bóly. The,
       Die, die Handwerker haben a   the artisans wanted to be a little
       bissl so feiner wollen sein, die   more refined, they talked differently
       haben anders geredet wie die   than the farmers.
       Bauersleute.

                    (M90:3A8:45)

Ignoring the presence of Hungarian, this woman in her sixties focused on two kinds of German "language." Each had a conventional, metapragmatic label, each was linked to one of the two major categories of people types in prewar Bóly, a time when everyone in town was German-speaking. *Handwerkerisch* (H: **iparos nyelv**) was the way artisans talked; *Bäuerisch* (H: **paraszt nyelv**) the language of farmers.[1] The rich artisans and farmers of the prewar era are remembered as pillars of the town's life. Linguistically, artisans and farmers understood each other perfectly well, yet the speech differences attributed to them were enormously significant. Another woman offered this response when asked about her late husband's language use:

(2.2) *... er hat schöner Deutsch*   ... he spoke a more beautiful
      gesprochen wie ich weil ich   German than I did because I speak a
      kann so echt Schwäwisch.   kind of real/genuine Swabian.
                   (87:23A2:48)

This made sense, she reasoned, since her husband had been an artisan and she was from a farming family. Following local convention, she used the term *Schwäwisch* (H: **sváb**) Swabian – after a region of Germany – interchangeably with *Bäuerisch* (from *Bauer* farmer) to designate farmers' speech. (We will follow suit.) Like everyone else, she contrasted the more beautiful with the more genuine. For everyone, explanations of the differences between the two ways of speaking relied on the presumed characteristics of the social types "farmer" and "artisan." Such explanations are part of the language ideology that shaped these practices and rendered them interpretable.

Although named for occupational categories, these forms of speech were not lexicons of technical, work-related terms. They were social registers. The differences extended to every part of the linguistic system: Lexical and phonological contrasts abounded, not as firm boundaries but as different frequencies of variable features. Intonational differences were striking; in morphology there were a number of shibboleths, as also in systems of address, use of titles, and everyday greetings. Some of these differences – for instance, the idiom for "going home": z'Haus versus d'Ham – (artisan versus farmer) were immediately offered as examples by speakers; others were not remarked at all. These registers were not simply correlates of speaker identities. Rather, they indexed the social types – the figures or personae – of artisan and farmer that organized social life along an axis of differentiation. Any speaker could, on occasion, take up and enact either type; speakers were evaluated against these two contrasting and complementary images.

In what follows, we ask what counts as "beautiful" versus "authentic" speech for speakers and what other qualities make up this axis of differentiation. How do the values of local language ideology unify diverse linguistic features, enregistering and contrasting them as Handwerkerisch versus Bäuerisch? How is this contrast connected to stereotypical qualities of artisans and farmers? What is necessarily erased to achieve this result? What do these local forms of German have to do with the contrast between Hungarian and German that seems today more significant? The answers take us to the semiotic processes of differentiation that structured not only linguistic practices but all of social life. To show how this worked, we examine the social organization, expressive culture, and value systems of Bóly in the interwar period, when these differences mattered most. Finally, to see the relationship between what seem like very different linguistic distinctions – Hungarian/German and Handwerkerisch/Bäuerisch – we locate Bóly in historical and geographical scales that go beyond the town itself.

Forms of Evidence

Despite the salience of the farmer/artisan contrast in the 1980s and 1990s – when Gal did fieldwork in Bóly – independent farmers and artisans had disappeared by the late 1940s. These centuries-old ways of life were ended by state socialist collectivization and nationalization of private enterprise after the Second World War. In another drastic change, almost half the German-speakers were expelled in 1946–1947 and Hungarian-speakers settled in their stead as part of postwar population transfers.[2] Nevertheless, local stories of an orderly life before the war were kept alive during the communist period (1949–1989). A proud town "spirit" was held responsible for Bóly's past and continuing economic success relative to neighboring settlements. After communism, Bóly has become even more prosperous and civic-minded. Amid small towns in the region that are often in disarray due to poverty and neglect, Bóly's streets are strikingly clean, its garbage collected; carefully tended gardens flower around well-built homes. Public institutions thrive, including a small shopping mall, a swimming pool and sauna, a bilingual (German-Hungarian) kindergarten, and a German track in schools.

In Bóly, as in all of the former eastern bloc in Europe, stories of the past increased in salience in the 1980s, as people responded to the end of the Cold War by celebrating what they believed to be precommunist social arrangements and values. Even those born in the 1960s and 1970s kept track of whether their families counted as artisans or farmers. Many younger people recognized the contrasting sounds of Handwerkerisch or Bäuerisch/Schwäwisch. They could argue about who speaks or spoke which forms. When Gal was documenting these linguistic differences in 1997 with two grandmothers, one from each category, one of the elderly women grew tired. Her daughter – aged about forty-five – offered to help: *Ezt velünk folytatod. Majd az uram játtsza a Marika nénit, én meg az anyámat, jó?* (97A1:41) (You'll continue this with us. My husband will play Marika and I'll play my mother, okay?).

The younger people could well "play" the parts – a telling description to which we will return – even though they did not experience directly the social world that created them. The memory of these distinctions remained alive. However, the material presented here is based on recordings of elders, conversations *among* them and *with* them about the past. These are speakers who were about sixty-five to eighty-five years of age at the time of Gal's fieldwork. They had actively participated in the distinctions discussed and continued to maintain them.[3]

Ideological Visions before and between the Wars

From the 1870s to the 1940s, the social categories of "artisan" and "farmer" organized virtually every aspect of communal life in Bóly, although there were always residents – Catholic priest and nuns, school teacher, local landed aristocratic family and their servants – who did not fit into either. Through formal organizations, the categories of artisan and farmer were turned into self-conscious social groups that disciplined the town's practices.

While neighboring villages had only a few artisans during these years, Bóly was a market town and census records show that its population was evenly divided. Artisans were of many kinds, producing and selling goods and services to local and regional customers. There were house builders, carpenters, turners, coopers, furniture makers, knitters, wool spinners, millers, bakers, butchers, and tailors. Farmers were also diversified as independent producers of milk, grain, cattle, and other livestock, and the fruit of vineyards. Both categories were, ideally, family-based capitalists. Farmers considered themselves the economically dominant force. Yet census records and outside observers suggest complementarity and a transactional relation: families in each category relied on the other's products and patronage.

In smaller settlements, where artisans were few, they were relatively poor and denigrated (Wild 2003:45). In Bóly, however, economic stratification occurred *within* each category, as Kovács's (1990) social history of the town has shown. Even in the economically difficult 1930s, some artisans were rich, were highly skilled, and owned their own shops, employing apprentices. Others, however, had fewer or negligible skills and sold their labor. Similarly, some farmers had large acreage, vineyards, and as many as fifteen dairy cattle with the newest Swiss milking equipment. Others had only gardens, had no fields, and did day labor for wages. Rich farmers practiced primogeniture and maintained their core holdings (the *Sessionfeld*) by marrying mostly among themselves. Marriages between artisans and farmers occurred only if the prospective partners' economic means were roughly equal. A poor bricklayer's son could marry the daughter of a landless farm laborer. A farmer with large holdings could allow his daughter to marry a wealthy furniture maker's son. In this way the daughter would be spared heavy farm work, and the artisanal family would be in line to inherit vineyards (Németh 1900).

Economic distinctions were matched by political arrangements. The wealthy of each category ran the town. An informal agreement guaranteed an alternation in the mayor's position: already in the nineteenth century, the election of a farmer was followed by the election of an artisan. The rich families also supported the formal societies of artisans (G: *Gesellenverein*, H: *Legényegylet*) and farmers (G: *Jünglingsverein*, H: *Ifjúságiegylet*) that were established in Bóly in the 1880s, on the model of such associations in German lands.

These societies turned the social categories we are describing into groups and fixed them in everyone's consciousness. Each group had a house of its own, officers, and weekly meetings. For the young men of each, the societies functioned as clubs with adult education classes where new ideas and techniques were introduced. There were also moral lessons from the Catholic priest. The societies provided libraries, newspapers, periodic balls, and annual theatrical productions. Everyone in town was invited to the plays, but the dances were separately held by each society, for members only.

The ideological binary embodied in these societies implied the equivalence of the members of each and their parallel with the other society. Yet, most of the town's residents lacked land and apprenticeships; they were relatively poor and did not participate in governance. No special linguistic forms distinguished the poor, nor those like the priest, the noble family, and their servants who did not fit this binary scheme. The ideological vision and the *Vereine* had the effect of denying (erasing) the town's consequential hierarchical differences based on wealth and status.

Schooling brought children together in a different way. In the interwar period boys were taught by a schoolmaster and girls by nuns. The language of education was Hungarian, with literary German taught in weekly lessons. In the schoolyard children were directed to avoid Bäuerisch or Handwerkerisch. Friendships across categories were common, since networks connected those who were neighbors, whether at home or at the wine cellars. Neither space was segregated by occupation. Higher education was available in Hungarian in nearby cities or (rarely) in German when students went outside of the country. It was accessed mostly by artisan families, though younger sons of farming families sometimes became teachers. The language of the state, too, was Hungarian from the mid-nineteenth century. But town government was another matter. Mayors made announcements from the balcony of the town hall after Sunday's high mass and it was a matter of pride that officials were smart and articulate, reading or speaking in what was considered literary German. Handwerkerisch and Bäuerisch were said to be inappropriate. For town events, literary German was superposed on the two local registers, in implicit contrast to them and to the official Hungarian of the state.[4] Thus, before World War II, Hungarian was learned, but was not in local use; it did not fit with the town's artisan/farmer distinction.

Ideologically Shaped Practices

Just as the associations of artisans and farmers were supposed to parallel each other, so the speech forms associated with artisans and farmers were imagined as parallel. Neither was considered primary or more fundamental.

As one farmer said, *ők is másképp beszélnek, mi is* (they speak differently and so do we). Even though many people mentioned that there were elements of urban speech and even literary German (*irás után/nach Schrift*) in the speech of artisans, they added that both Handwerkerisch and Bäuerisch committed "errors." That is, neither was seen as "correct" according to school usage.

Individuals and families were normatively classified as artisans or farmers, yet given the right circumstances, anyone could potentially "play the parts," as the young woman remarked, because everyone was familiar with the characteristics and speech forms associated with each social type. The metapragmatic labels themselves created an image of separate "languages," erasing the variability and situational fluidity of linguistic practice.

What qualities were conventionally attributed to artisans and farmers? One farmer generalized about farmers, *egyszerű emberek vagyunk* (we are simple people), and summarized the stereotypical differences this way:

(2.3) *Die Bauern, die haben die*   The farmers, they have tradition,
      Tradition, gel, die haben die   you know, they have the old
      alten Gebräuche, die alten   customs, they carry on with the old
      Sitten mitgenommen weiter.   ways. The artisans, they orient to
      Die Handwerker, die haben   higher culture. They wanted always
      sich schon der höheren Kultur   to be something more. The artisan
      angepasst. Sie wollten immer   felt himself always to be something
      etwas mehr sein, ja? Der   higher than a farmer, something
      Handwerker fühlte sich immer   better.
      etwas Höher oder etwas
      Besseres wie ein Bauer.
                          (M90:8)

But his grin revealed irony: artisans saw themselves as "better," but farmers were not impressed. Indeed, farmers and artisans were seen to operate with stereotypically contrasting, complementary values and aesthetics. They were seen as different human types, forged by contrasting ways of life.

Knowledge and skill, brought from apprenticeships in the wider world, were supposed to be characteristic of artisans. The artisan vision treasured expertise in crafts and in the interpersonal aspects of marketing to diverse customers. For the stereotypical farmer, on the other hand, accumulation of land, not knowledge, was the goal. New agricultural techniques were appreciated, but more important was hard labor in the fields and frugality in every sphere: as much in speech and display as in finances. Artisans saw themselves as more refined; farmers knew themselves to be richer. Even rich artisans lacked large tracts of land, so in terms of the farmer-standards of value artisans were relatively poor and dependent. One farmer typified the past this way: *A parasztok gazdagok voltak. Itt úgy volt, ha a paraszt jól állt akkor jobban állt az iparos is, mert ha a parasztnak nem ment, akkor az iparosnak pláne nem ment. Az iparos a parasztból élt* (The farmers were rich. The way it was here, if it went well for the farmer, it went better for the artisan too; if it went badly for the farmer it was worse for the artisan. The artisan lived off the farmer. 97:6A35:56).

This totalizing ideological vision was enacted through the signs of daily life. People were judged in terms of complementary qualities, organized in an axis of differentiation: farmers' restraint and artisans' elaboration. Rich farmers built houses that conserved the floor plan, decoration, and materials of past generations, but vied with each other over the exact height of the roofline, which signaled relative wealth. Farm women retained till the 1930s the kinds of dark kerchiefs, aprons, and multiple skirts worn by their grandmothers. Even for festive clothes, which were often made of expensive materials, farm women favored long-established designs and somber colors, as did the men. Rich farmers ate amply but with little variety. For their celebrations, they hired brass bands to play polkas. Rich artisans, by contrast, competed with each other in the style and variety of their houses, clothing, food, and entertainment. Artisan women followed urban fashion; in the 1990s they spoke avidly about the seasonally refreshed wardrobes, hats, and purses they had worn fifty to sixty years earlier. They varied and elaborated meals by consulting cookbooks and inventing new dishes. Artisan men changed suits according to the season. For dances, artisans hired Gypsy musicians and jazz bands and danced in a variety of styles (Kovács 1990).

Language itself was a form of expertise for the artisan view, but not for stereotyped farmers. The artisan vision defined work more broadly than bodily labor; it was an exercise of skill, and language was a skill worth cultivating. Handwerkerisch required effort: one had to exert oneself (*bemühen sich*) to speak it. The daughter in a family of turners remembered her father's reprimand about her slovenly pronunciation; he urged her to leave that to her farmer friends. Even in the 1990s, the wife of an artisan reproached her husband for sounding *bäuerisch* when he returned from an evening of camaraderie with farmer friends at the wine cellar. In taped interviews, some artisans criticized their own speech, saying it had deteriorated; other artisans said they welcomed the opportunity to "practice" Handwerkerisch. By contrast, farmers recalled their elders denigrating speech: *ne dumálj, dolgozz!* (don't chatter, work!)

Rhematization and Explanation

Handwerkerisch and Bäuerisch did more than index these social stereotypes. For participants, the registers enacted them; they sounded like the complementary qualities of the conventional categories. How did people attribute the same qualities to speech as to people types? How did they explain and reason about speech differences?

Recall the elderly woman quoted at the start of this chapter, who contrasted her husband's German speech as *schöner* (more beautiful) with her own more *echt* (genuine) speech. There were also other and related characterizations, clusters of contrasting, relational and complementary qualities that made the two categories of speech iconic of the two speaker types in a process of rhematization. Thus, the abstract schema of restraint versus elaboration was enacted through speech forms as much as through the contrasts in housing, food, and entertainment we have described. The artisan register itself was described as comparatively *feiner, zivilisierter, edeler,* more *geschult* and *gebildet* than farmers' speech – in Hungarian: ***előkelőbb, tanultabb, finomabb*** (more refined, fancier, more schooled, more cultivated, more elegant). It was heard as relatively more various and newer. Farmers' speech was considered relatively simpler and older/more genuine.

What was it about these registers that could be picked out, by the ideological visions of speakers, as embodying these complementary, co-constitutive qualities? To figure this out, Gal elicited lists of register differences from speakers and noted the occurrences of differences in everyday talk. That formed the basis of Tables 2.1, 2.2, and 2.3, summarizing some conventional distinctions in phonology, morphology, and lexicon between the two registers. In addition, Gal asked two women who were childhood friends, one from a farm family, the other from an artisan family, to tell the same story. This was a staged performance; each woman had agreed to the task, so there was interactional pressure to display the differences for the recording. At various points in these sessions, each woman said *mir sog so* (we say this) and *die sog so* (they say this), dividing the world into "us" and "them." The same exercise was repeated with two more speakers, a man and a woman, also longtime friends.

The patterns of variation revealed by the recorded stories, when analyzed with reference to the conventional distinctions, help to specify how speakers interpreted features of the registers. For an outside observer, the differences were relative, certainly not matters of the stark opposition that the ideological vision created. Table 2.4 shows the percentages of two morphological variables and two phonological variables in the storytelling.[5] One morphological variable (variable 3 in Table 2.2: modal *können* + past participle) shows an absolute distinction between the two categories of speakers. This was a shibboleth of farmers' speech, a verbal complex particular to Bóly. For the other three variables, all four speakers produced some tokens that counted as Bäuerisch. In contrast to the farmers, however, the artisans also used, and with considerable frequency, forms that counted as Handwerkerisch. The artisans in these tapes also used a more diverse vocabulary and strikingly more verb tenses.

Table 2.1 *Phonological differences between Bäuerisch /Schwäwisch and Handwerkerisch*

---

1. Interconsonantal B/Sch [e] = Handw [i] in substantives, verbs

		Examples	
Bäuerisch/Schw	Handwerkerisch	Written form	English
khenn	khint	Kind	child
drenga	trink	trinken	drink (v.)
melich	milich	Milch	milk
wenda	winda	Winter	winter

2. Interconsonantal B/Sch [e] = Handw [i] when standard has u-Umlaut or o-Umlaut

		Examples	
steck	stick	Stück	piece
teschlesa	ti^{a}schlisl	Türschlüssel	door key
mest	mist	müsste	p.p. must
mecht	micht	möchte	(I) would like

3. B/Sch [a:] = Handw [au] in all positions

		Examples	
kra:t	kraut	Kraut	cabbage
scha:	schaun	schauen	look (v)
a:ch	auchn	Augen	eyes
a:	au	auch	also

4. Interconsonantal B/Sch [o^a] = Handw [u]

		Examples	
kro^{a}mbien	krumbien	Kartoffeln	potatoes
sto^{a}nd	stund	Stunde	hour
wo^a	wu	wo	where
so^{a}nto:g	suntog	Sonnentag	Sunday

5. Some preconsonantal sibilants: B/Sch [ʃ] = Handw [s]

		Examples	
do^{a}naʃto:g	dunastog	Donnerstag	Thursday
pa:ʃleit	bausleit	Bauersleute	farmer folks
eʃt	e^{a}st	erst	first

The registers also share many features. This a not a full list of differences between artisan and farmer forms. Only the feature in focus is specified here in some phonetic detail. See Wild (2003) for the fullest linguistic discussion of farmers/artisans in this region, but outside of Bóly. For artisan/farmer linguistic differences in other regions, see Manherz (1977).

Table 2.2 *Morphological and pragmatic differences between Bäuerisch/Schwäwisch and Handwerkerisch*

1. Endings of infinitives and of past participles of irregular verbs, Bäuerisch/Schwäwisch: –e, ø; Handwerkerisch: –n, –m. Examples:

Bäuerisch/Schw	Handwerkerisch	Written form	English
gewa	gem	gegeben	p.p. of give
kessa /kess	kessn	gegessen	p.p. of eat
kanga	kangn	gegangen	p.p. of go
soga	som	sagen	inf. of say

2. Diminutives in Bäuerisch/Schwäwisch built on –chen; Handwerkerisch diminutives built on –l. Examples:

medxje	maal	Mädchen, Mädel	girl
stechje	stickl	Stückchen	little piece
bisje	pisl	bisschen, bissel	a bit, a morsel

3. Modal verb können followed by past participle in Bäuerisch/Schwäwisch but not in Handwerkerisch. Examples:

mir kenn net anerʃ kred	mir könn nit anders redn	we can't talk differently
dass [ich] gut kann g'riech	dass ich gut riechen kann	so I can smell [you] better
ich koᵃn net gess	ich koᵃn nit essn	I cannot eat

4. Address terms and titles. Examples:

mutta, vota	mama, papa	to parents
grossmutta, grossvota	oma, opa	to grandparents
onkli, tanti	bácsi, néni/onkli, tanti	to uncles/aunts
bácsi, néni	bácsi, néni	to unrelated elders
[FN] wos, [FN]veta	her/masta, frau/nedig frau	servants to employers

5. Pronouns of address for second-person singular. Examples:

du – to age-peers	du – to age-peers, parents	informal
ihr/er – 2nd pers. pl. verb	sie – 3rd person plural verb	respectful

6. Conventional request forms. Examples:

ich v'lang wos zu essa	ich micht wos zu essn	I would like something to eat
ich v'lang sche wos zu essa	ich micht schön wos zu...	"
	ich micht schön bittn...	"
	sei so gut un geb mir....	"

Greater diversity in artisan speech, evident in the recordings, was generally noted by speakers and contributed to the "refined, cultivated" effect of Handwerkerisch. In lexical contrasts as well, farmers used only those items identified as Bäuerisch, artisans used Handwerkerisch forms and occasionally

Table 2.3 *Examples of Lexical Differences Between Bäuerisch/Schwäwisch and Handwerkerisch*

Bäuerisch/Schwäwisch	Handwerkerisch	Gloss
d'ham	z'haus	home, [to] home
gaul	ferd	horse
haint	hait	today
hart	sehr	very
henne	hindle	hen/chicken
keh	rindvie	cow
kiristo:g	weihnachtn	Christmas
kirsche	kerschen	cherry
krepl	krapfn	doughnut
kwant	kleid	garment, clothing
kwetscha	zwetschgn	plum
mannesbild	mann	man (male human)
mehreri	mehr	more
ness	nuss	nuts
ohrwaschl	ohr	ear
scho:f	lam	sheep
sei	schwein	pig
siewen uᵃ te o:wat	sieweni auf t'nocht	seven o'clock at night
stru:l	stritzen	strudel
stuwe	zimmer	room
teka	tuchat	bedcovering
weib	frau	woman
wesche	wosch	the wash

Table 2.4 *Percentage of Bäuerisch/Schwäwisch and Handwerkerisch features in storytelling by four speakers*

	pp. irreg. Vb		Kann g'Vb		e/i		a:/au	
	B/Sch.	Handw.	B/Sch.	Handw.	B/Sch.	Handw.	B/Sch.	Handw.
Farmer 1	93	7	100	0	85	15	75	25
	N = 29		N = 2		N = 15		N = 16	
Farmer 2	90	10	100	0	86	14	85	15
	N = 29		N = 5		N = 8		N = 13	
Artisan 1	42	58	0	100	30	70	50	50
	N = 12		N = 4		N = 13		N = 14	
Artisan 2	38	62	0	100	38	62	43	57
	N = 26		N = 8		N = 8		N = 14	

Bäuerisch ones as well. In titles of address and in conventional request forms too, the artisan register showed additional variants (see variables 4 and 6 in Table 2.2). These were cited by speakers as evidence that artisans had, as one farmer put it, "more politeness."

Metaphors that speakers constructed in narratives also show how they interpreted the two registers. While *finomabb/feiner/now'l* (more refined, elegant) characterized the artisan register, what might have been the contrasting terms for the farmer register – "less fine" or "coarse" – were not heard in the 1990s. Yet, the distinction was signaled when a woman from a farming family was setting the scene for a story about her experience in the aftermath of war. By implicitly analogizing food and speech, she alluded to the quality they shared in displaying the ideological contrast of artisan and farmer:

(2.4) Kati M. (97:5A35:30)

soha nem felejtem el, pont	*I'll never forget, I was just making*
palacsintát sütöttem, nemol	*palacsinta, never palacsinta,*
palacsinta, ksocht Pfannkucha,	*we said pfannkucha, because we*
wal palacsinta hom mir nemol	*could never make palacsinta,*
khaan kmocht, tes wor jo zu	*that was way too fine/refined.*
noowl. Pfannkucha! Ez csak	*Pfannkucha! It was just poured in,*
így belett öntve, sűrűbb mint	*denser than palacsinta, and then*
a palacsinta és akkor meglett	*it got cooked, like palacsinta only*
sütve, mint a palacsinta, csak	*thicker. And then we spread jam on*
vastagabb volt. És akkor	*it or walnuts, and I was just making*
kentünk rá lekvárt vagy diót,	*this, when …*
és pont ezt sütöttem …	

Palacsinta is a delicacy, a thin, light crepe made of water, eggs, and flour. *Pfannkuche* is usually translated as pancake. They are identical in ingredients and mode of preparation, nicely representing the unity of the town. They differ in the one quality – best glossed as refinement or its absence – by which each matches the parallelism enacted here: *palacsinta* = artisan; *pfannkuche* = farmer. The speaker started narrating in Hungarian, then switched to Bäuerisch while telling of the distinction: [e] rather than [i] in *nemol*, [a] rather than [ei] in *wal*, the distinctive Bäuerisch verbal complex *khaan kmocht*, and the vocalic rather than nasal ending of *pfannkuche*. She seems to interrupt herself, saying *nemol palacsinta* (*never palacsinta*) with enhanced volume, enacting the authoritative voice of the farmers' world intruding into her story, forbidding her from making the fancier, finer food. She created and enacted a culinary-linguistic metaphor for the artisan/farmer contrast.

Could some aspects of Bäuerisch be heard as "thick" and "dense," matching the qualities of the pancake that farmers stereotypically prepared? The phonological variables in Table 2.1 show that the farmers' vowels – in comparison to the artisans' – are generally lower or backed; the artisans' forms more fronted and higher. This, plus the backing of many preconsonantal sibilants (s vs. ʃ), and a general hoarseness, could give an impression of "thickness." Intonation patterns, which differed markedly, could have the same effect, as also the tendency of farmer women to be full-throated and lower pitched than artisans. The stereotype could well have been projected onto sound patterns, which – in a circular logic – would then be heard to support the image.

The terms "thick" and "dense" (in Hungarian) imply not stupidity (as they might in English) but rather ampleness or abundance. From the ideological perspective of farmers, moreover, refined and thin were not positive qualities. Asked to name someone who knew Handwerkerisch, one farmer mentioned a current drinking partner, adding,

(2.5) *a Gábor az tud, az még beszél,*   Gábor can, he still speaks [like that],
      ha egy pár szó megüti az   if a few words hit one's [my] ear, a
      ember fülét akkor sokszor   lot of times I say to him, hey, your
      mondom neki, hát, megint   artisanship is showing again.
      kilátszik az iparosság, ugye.
            (97:1B31:36)

The joking yet accusatory tone suggests that artisan speech, though recognized as a form of skill, was also, from a farmer perspective, a kind of swagger (*felvágás*). It was called *rongyrázás* ("shaking the rag" = putting on airs), being conceited (*eingebildet*). The stereotype for the farmers' register as *echt* (genuine), as maintenance of the old and "traditional," constructed a contrast with the artisan form devoted to variety, novelty, and the foreign.

Conventional narratives explained the reason for the two registers and their qualities. Farmers' speech, these stories asserted, was rooted in the past because it was what migrants "brought with them" from a specific region in western Germany in the eighteenth century.[6] It gave proof of origins. Yet, the work of historians shows that German-speakers who entered southern Hungary in the course of the eighteenth century came from many German principalities. The migrants' difficult travels down the Danube forced the mixing of people; families were often separated. After arrival, individual families moved repeatedly within Hungary, searching for better conditions (Fata 1997).[7] Linguistic analyses of Hungary's German dialects support this view. They show a mixture of features attested in the past in many disparate regions of today's Germany and Austria.[8] These external observers' views differ from the town's understanding, in which the term *Schwäwisch/sváb* for farmers' speech suggests an origin in

Swabia. But this name was given by Hungarian observers; historical accounts show that Swabia contributed very few migrants. Nevertheless, the term came to mean anyone in rural Hungary whose family spoke any form of German.

Artisan speech, by contrast, was understood to be formed not by origins but by artisan men's travel as apprentices to Austrian cities. According to one farmer, **Hazahozták az intelligenciát** (they [artisans] brought home intelligence). Novelty and the foreign belonged, by ideological framing, to artisans. The interwar innovations of farmers – new agricultural practices, high-tech Swiss milking equipment – were erased in the conventional narratives. The traveling life, it was said, changed artisans' nature, their very form of humanity. As one artisan put it, *die waren viel in der Welt ... in Wien* (they were [the kind of people who were] much in the world ... [even] in Vienna). Yet the traveling artisan was more an idealized figure than a description of practice. Many did not travel at all, nor did the female family members who were often credited with the "best" Handwerkerisch. Nor would travel to Austrian cities account for the fact that artisans were credited with learning Hungarian more eagerly and earlier.[9] With language, as with food and clothing, the artisans were stereotyped as the ones who brought the new to Bóly.

There were indeed linguistic details of the artisan register that resembled forms attributable to Vienna, or to literary German.[10] And the category distinction of farmer/artisan with its linguistic aspects is certainly a very old one in German-speaking lands; there are word lists documenting the contrast in the eighteenth century. The *distinction* itself might well have been imported by migrants. But Bóly's specific version of the contrast between Handwerkerisch/Bäuerisch is a *local* phenomenon. When Bäuerisch forms happened to be close to an Austrian or literary pronunciation, speakers of Handwerkerisch innovated *away* from them. One observant man from a farming family who had an interest in language remarked, *wenn der Bauer das richtig gesagt hat, da hat der Handwerker bestimmt das Wort anders ausgesprochen* (When the farmer said something correctly [i.e., matching the literary form], the artisan would be sure to say the word in some other way). For example, *Kirsche* was the Bäuerisch form for "cherry" and also the literary form. Handwerkerisch lowered the front vowel to <u>Kersche</u>, a shift that otherwise would have sounded typically Bäuerisch. The maintenance of distinction took priority.

Voicings and Fractal Recursivity

Despite the importance of the register contrasts, either could be taken up – in quotation or other voicing effects – by any speaker, regardless of how that speaker was normatively classified. Artisans imitated Bäuerisch, and vice versa, as in this conversation around a kitchen table, largely in Hungarian. The women – Klára from a farming family, Marika a tailor's daughter – recalled their friendship as girls in the 1930s.[11]

(2.6) Klára and Marika (97:3A6:12)

KLÁRA: *az iparosok elvettek parasztlányt de egy paraszt egy iparos lányt nem vett el* [overlap]

MARIKA: *Du wast doch, **hogy hol volt nekünk a Mariperink,** ott fönn? és egyszer jött a Kluch bácsi, der aldi, a Kluch Jóskának az apja. Asz mondja – hát én úgy tettem-vettem ott a Tuka, vagy Mariperiben ottan – megáll, leteszi a vödröt, mondom ez mit akar most, azt mondja, hát, hot'e ksokt, i' hom gemant di Masta Schnedera tie oawada nix. Owr jetz se ichs. **Ő azt hitte az iparosok nem dolgoznak, de most látom hogy igenis dolgoznak.***

KLÁRA: **Marika, mert úgy volt hogy az iparos lányok azok ki nem mentek dolgozni.** [she lists the work artisan girls did not do in the fields since they had no fields] *de a **Marikának örökké kellett dolgozni** tess vegess ich net, tes ... hogyha mentünk litániába, szerettünk is menni, addig se kell csinálni semmit ... Hát az iparosok is dolgoztak, de otthon, hát az különbség volt, ugye? Hát akkor én is noch kschwind fuot minél előbb eltudjak menni. Na megyek Marikához. Marika jössz a litániába? Hát jövök, ich khumm, ich khumm. Hát akkor jött az anyja, ti Marika khummt, ti Marika muss erst abwoschn. Hát ich homme halt stehn, no muss wart pis ti Marika hot aa oupkwosche. Ti Marika hot imme mes oawet. **Örökké kellett neki dolgozni.***

KLÁRA (FARMER'S DAUGHTER): *artisans married farmer-girls but no farmer would marry an artisan's daughter –*

MARIKA (TAILOR'S DAUGHTER): *But you know, **where we had that** [vineyard] **on Mariaberg, up there?** And once along came Kluch bácsi, the old one, Jóska's father. He says – I was just bustling about up there on Tuka, on Mariaberg – he stops, puts down his pail, I thought what does this guy want, he says, well, he said, I thought the master tailors, they don't work. But now I see it. **He thought artisans don't work, but now I see that yes they do work.***

KLÁRA: **Because Marika, the way it was then the artisan girls did not go out to work** [i.e., in the fields; she lists many kinds of work in the fields]. **But Marika always had to work** this I'll never forget, this ... if we went to litany, we liked to go, didn't have to work while we went ... well, the artisans also worked but at home, well that was a difference, wasn't it? Well, then I was quick get out fast **go out as fast as possible. Well I go to Marika's. Marika are you coming to litany? Well I'm coming** I'm coming, I'm coming. **Well then her mother came** Marika is coming, Marika has to wash up [the floors] first. Well, I had to stay there a lot, must wait till Marika finished washing up. Marika always had to work. **She had to work all the time.***

Behind Klára's bald statement about marriage practices, one could hear the typical farmers' accusation that artisans do not really work. It is potentially offensive to her artisan friend since working hard was a value claimed by everyone. Marika's anecdote is a veiled response. In the story, Marika enacts/voices old farmer Kluch, showing that he acknowledged her "real" work, that is, farm work. Farmer Kluch, ventriloquated by artisan-Marika, comes to life with the lowered front vowel in *g'mant* (thought), raised vowels in *Schnedera* (tailors), the vocalic ending on the infinitive *oawada* (work), and the characteristic intonation: all Bäuerisch forms. Klára the farmer then addresses Marika directly and ventriloquates Marika's girlhood self and her mother. The raised vowels of Marika and her mother in *khumm*, repeated several times, are shibboleths of artisan speech, as is the initial vowel in *abwoschn* (wash up). As the voice of Marika's mother, the vowel is short, when repeated as Klára's (farmer) inner speech it is diphthongized. These voicings accomplish a delicate job of interactional diplomacy around the initial bald statement, and hence around the artisan/farmer distinction.

Artisans adopted the farmer register – and vice versa – in particular interactions and were understood to do so in the longer term as well: farmers' daughters who married artisans were supposed to adjust their speech to their new families. A theory of inheritance was sometimes invoked. People with mixed parentage were said to speak sometimes this way, sometimes that. Or, the two categories were said to be reproduced in single individuals who were then subdivided, being a little of each.

These examples are instances of fractal recursivity: the ideological vision of a contrast between artisan and farmer is reenacted at a narrower scale, subdividing each category into artisan/farmer. This organizes, by analogy, other contrasts, such as voices and positionings in interaction, or as supposed divisions within an individual speaker. Fractal recursions can also be encompassments, unifying the contrasts and opposing the combined category with one that it opposes at a wider scale. Yet recall that Handwerkerisch included some farmers' forms, so the creation of the contrast itself relies on erasing the overlap in the forms that occurs in everyday speech. Fractal recursions rely on further erasures too, for in order to grasp the reiteration of the analogy, one has to ignore the ways in which the reproduction is never exact.

Examples of subdividing occur when, among speakers all classified as belonging to one category, the contrasting register is used for some interactional effect. One elder farming couple invited another for a birthday celebration. Gal did not go, but asked them to record parts of the celebrations, in which no Hungarian occurred. On arrival, one guest recited a customary German verse to mark the birthday, and soon thereafter the hostess started to question the guests. Many topics were discussed – children's schooling, a recent pig killing, the price of meat. Each topic started with questions by the hostess, asking about matters well known to everyone such as "So, did you just return from your trip to Germany?" The scene sounds like a staged interview, and the hostess used Handwerkerisch forms. Grammatical features such as *kann g'Vb* that strongly signal Bäuerisch – and which were otherwise common in her speech – did not occur at all. The hostess enacted the voice of the relatively more cultivated, worldly artisan, one appropriate to an interviewer. This might have counted as swagger under some circumstances. But here, in this small ceremonial and while taping for the foreign researcher, features of Handwerkerisch among farmers evoked no (recorded) negative comment from the other farmers.

An instance of fractal recursivity among artisans, by contrast, hinged exactly on such judgmental attention to speech, as befits the artisan stereotype. Three women gathered with Gal, and talk turned to the 1930s. All were born into artisan families: two were sisters-in-law married to brothers who were carpenters. Let us call them Emma and Róza. The third woman, Detti, was a neighbor; at fifty-five she was a decade younger than the other two. She was from an artisan family now living in Bóly but originally from a neighboring village, Pócsa (G: Posch). Here, as usual, the subject of difference between artisans and farmers came up, in this case leading to a kind of needling or teasing:

(2.7) Róza and Emma (87:29A2:21)

RÓZA: *Waa untaschied.*
Untaschied waa' in da Kladung.
Die Handweaka hom so kuaza
Klaada getroga, wie jetzt, und die
Baua hon langa Klaada getroga.

RÓZA: There was difference, difference there was in the clothing. The artisans wore a shorter Kleid [smock, dress] like the kind worn today, and the farmers wore a longer Kleid.

→ EMMA: *Kittl, Kittl*

EMMA: Kittl, Kittl [smock]

RÓZA: *Hát, langa Kittl, ugye,*
Baua so langa Kittl und Blusn,
und noch, ugyis, und noch woan
viela Bauaschmäda, di hom sich
scho umgezoga, di sen Sunntogs
in Klaada ganga und –

RÓZA: Well, longer Kittl, farmers had longer Kittl and blouse and also, many farmer girls had switched their dress [from traditional farmer clothing] and went on Sunntag in Kleid, and –

→ EMMA: *Sonntogs, sog doch nua*
Sonntags

EMMA: Sonntag, just say Sonntag

DETTI: *Mia hon, in Posch*
Sunntog hamma ksogt

DETTI: We, in Pócsa we said Sunntag [Sunday]

RÓZA: *In jedem Duof is an*
andere Mundort, oda wie man
scho sogt.

RÓZA: In every village there is a different dialect, or however you say it.

Róza described the farmers' dress, playing the authority for the inquiring visitor. She avoided the Bäuerisch term *Kittl* – even though she was describing farmer clothing – and instead used the artisan term, *Kleid*. Emma corrected her (at first →); Róza accepted the correction. Next, Róza's vowels became the center of attention. She had used a high [u] for Sunday. This was an artisan form. Like the farmer who razzed his artisan friends to stop showing off, Emma laughed as she made a second correction (at second →), directing Róza to just say it, that is, just say it the farmers' way. This could be an accusation that Róza was getting above herself, rather than being accurate. Although she is herself an artisan, Emma offered the farmer's word and the farmer's pronunciation. Detti tried to defuse this minor conflict by citing her own village's usage, and Róza defended herself by trying, once again, to play the expert, this time about inter-village differences. The artisan-farmer contrast is here used for diverse interactional effects among artisans.

Scalar Projections: Encompassments

The two people-categories typical of Bóly were not limited to the town itself. They were projected fractally to construct a wider system of relations, an entire cultural geography. Speakers used the local contrast to encompass and characterize social differences they imagined and encountered as they moved across geographical space; they also mobilized it to analogically interpret changes that occurred after the Second World War.

Given the definition of the artisan figure as bringing valuable knowledge back to Bóly, it is not surprising that, when asked to name the best speakers of Handwerkerisch, people pointed to rich artisans who had left Bóly to live in neighboring cities. The most stylish clothes of the 1920s and 1930s so lovingly discussed by artisan women often turned out to be presents from aunts who lived in cities. Their provenance gave these objects greater value; they evoked and typified artisan life.

By contrast, it is all the more surprising, given the stereotype of farmers' connection to land, that the farmer ideal was also located outside Bóly. The best examples of farmer tradition and *szorgalom, tisztaság, gazdagság* (industriousness, cleanliness, and wealth) were in villages. It turned out that Bóly's farmers were not so traditional after all, not so *sváb/schwäwisch*. The *echt Schwow* (real Swabian) in these discussions was always from a village that was said to "still" know the dances, songs, and ceremonies; to still tell ghost stories and wear kerchiefs and wooden shoes. Bóly's farmers were too cultivated for that. Farmer's speech in Bóly was described as *jobban svábos* (more Swabian) when the comparison set was (implicitly) the local artisans; it was described as *nem olyan svábos* (not so Swabian) when compared with neighboring villages (which were acknowledged to differ among themselves).

Bóly itself, as a place, was imagined through these comparisons. Those who considered themselves *hiesig Bohler* or **tüke bólyi** (original German-speaking inhabitants) spoke with pride about the diversity of people in town, even in the 1930s: the teaching nuns, the aristocratic landowner, and the full range of artisans and farmers – all of which, in their eyes, made Bóly socially special. The town itself was often called *stolz* (proud) by outsiders and described as **előkelőbb** and *zivilisierter* (fancier, more civilized) than the surrounding settlements. In a typical anecdote, it was said that when girls from Bóly – farmers as well as artisans – went to the city, city folk thought them to be educated college students, not hicks. Those who had moved to Bóly from other places complained that the native families were **pökhendi** (arrogant) and *eingebildet* (conceited). One artisan woman from elsewhere was blunter: *Ich wea ka Bolyana mea. Ich wea ni ka Boola. Di Boola waa so stolz, sie hon di Fremde net fua glaichan Menschn genumma* (I will never be a Bólyer. I will never be a Bohler. The Bohlers were so proud, they did not take outsiders to be humans equal to themselves).

In this accusation one hears an echo of the claim that artisans think they are better than farmers. Indeed, all the qualities used to characterize the artisans were employed to describe the town itself. The comparison was an encompassing one between Bóly and neighboring settlements. The artisan/farmer opposition within Bóly was unified and re-created at a wider scale: all of Bóly was seen as the artisan, the other settlements as the farmer.

Wider Encompassments, New Comparisons

The conventional comparison of Bóly to the surrounding vicinity changed after the Second World War in response to a vastly changed political situation. An ally of Nazi Germany during the war, Hungary became part of the Soviet bloc after the war. The beloved societies for young men were abolished, as were the schools that supported the teaching nuns. As a result of forced population transfers, almost half of Bóly's population was expelled and replaced by monolingual Hungarian-speaking farmers from Slovakia. By the 1950s, businesses and farms were nationalized and collectivized by the newly communist government. The use of German was heavily stigmatized, seen as the enemy's language, and school instruction in German was suspended for a few years. For several decades, in the Cold War, Hungary's borders were in effect closed. Despite the trauma and hardship caused by these catastrophic events, they were interpreted – even normalized – through the ideological differentiation we are discussing, especially in enregistering Hungarian by sweeping it into the familiar local vision.

A narration of the new order through a local sociolinguistic perspective appeared in a conversation between Gal and two elderly sisters from a farming family. The elder sister, Rosina, recounted two incidents that, though told some ten minutes apart, and supposedly occurring some forty years apart, were poetically and politically mirror images of each other. They extend recursivity of the artisan/farmer axis to Hungarian and Hungarian-speakers.

(2.8a) Rosina (87:15B:7)

Mikor jöttek, mikor újak voltak [the Hungarian settlers from Slovakia, 1947]. *Ők is katolikusok voltak és a templomban, a templomból egyszer mentünk haza, mikor azt kérdezte – nem jut eszembe a neve – hogy nem-e haragszom ha most megkérdezi hogy honnan jöttem, ajaj gondoltam, most jöttek, mondom sehonan, én itt születtem. Hát ez nem lehet hogy maga ilyen tisztán beszél magyarul.*

When they came [the Hungarian settlers from Slovakia, 1947], when they were new. They were Catholic too and in church, we were going home from church once, when she asked – I can't remember her name – that I shouldn't be mad if she asked me where I came from, oh no I thought, they just recently came, I said I didn't come from anywhere I was born here. Well, that's just impossible [she said] that you speak Hungarian so well.

(2.8b) Rosina (87:15B:18)

Most [i.e., the time of telling, 1987] *ez a Jóska, ez a szomszéd hozott egy levelet egy ekkorát, nem volt olyan jaj de olvasható de eltudtam olvasni. Hát aszondja Rosina néni milyen jól tud németül. Mondom hát öcsém, hát itt születtem, hát maga magyarúl is tud. Hát persze.*

Now [i.e., the time of telling, 1987], this Jóska, this neighbor he brought me a letter [from Germany], a big one, it was not so very readable but I could read it. Well, he says, Rosina néni, how well you know German. I said, my boy, I was born here. Well, but you know Hungarian too. Well, of course.

In each of these anecdotes, a monolingual speaker of Hungarian is depicted as impressed by Rosina's remarkable linguistic abilities, first in Hungarian, then in both German and Hungarian. Rosina's explanation within the story, directed also at the fieldworker – and told in Hungarian – made distinctions within Bóly irrelevant. The wonder was not only Rosina herself but also Bóly, the extraordinary place where such linguistic prowess just (naturally) happens. The recursivity encompasses the newly arrived Hungarian monolinguals and their speech. Rosina is from a farmer family, but as the personification of Bóly, she is the artisan among farmers: notably skilled at linguistic diversity.[12]

This, however, was not the broadest comparative set invoked by speakers. There was an even wider parameter of contrast invoked in the 1990s, one that had emerged earlier, between the two world wars. To understand it, we must briefly glance back to the eighteenth and early nineteenth centuries when the ancestors of Bóly's German-speakers migrated to Hungary. They settled not as German nationals but as former subjects of many different German-speaking principalities. By the end of the nineteenth century, however, in Germany (unified in 1871) and in the multinational, multilingual Austro-Hungarian Monarchy, German nationalists were working to mobilize German-speakers to their supposedly primordial ethnolinguistic identities (Judson 2006). In parallel, and motivated by the same Romantic language ideology, the Hungarian government, though never financed sufficiently to achieve this, was trying to magyarize the country: persuade or force linguistic minorities to learn and speak Hungarian (i.e., Magyar).

In the Hungarian half of the monarchy, German-speakers were deeply divided in political predilection (Pukánszky 2000 [1940]). There were several regionally separate German-speaking groups. One was in the northern region of Szepes/Zips, where most German-speakers actively supported Hungarian independence in 1848, learning Hungarian and retaining German as well. The great ethnographer-linguist we will discuss in Chapter 9 – Pál Hunfalvy – came from that region and became a lawyer and member of the Hungarian Academy of Sciences.

Another category of German-speakers was city-dwellers. Indeed, many urban centers of Hungary were mostly German-speaking until the second half of the nineteenth century. And urban German-speakers adopted Hungarian language more quickly than villagers. In cities, many were sympathetic to the Hungarian nationalist movement against Austrian rule (1848–1849), sometimes vociferously magyarizing their own and other minorities. Another urban contingent, however, was loyal to the emperor and German high culture, quietly siding with the Habsburg suppression of the Hungarian revolution. A further category, perhaps the largest rural population of German-speakers, included Bóly's region of southern Hungary. They were neglected by politicians, thus unorganized, though often subjected to Hungarian teaching efforts, aided by the Catholic Church, as in Bóly's schools.[13]

To this fragmented scene in the 1930s came recruiters from Germany. They were first pan-German mobilizers and later National Socialists eager to invoke ethnonationalist ideology as a way to claim German-speaking minorities in Hungary and other eastern parts of Europe for the Third Reich.[14] Their activities in rural Hungary politicized and polarized the population (Spannenberger 2005). A suggestive record of this is provided by the census of 1941 that asked about nationality and mother tongue. Some German-speakers in Bóly signed on to an identity as "Germans"; others checked "Magyar" (Hungarian) as their nationality, but German as their mother tongue. Still others claimed Magyar as their mother tongue despite their everyday German practices.[15] The many different shades of political awareness, group consciousness, and political loyalty can be partially suggested by listing the many labels that were used then and since, by and for this bilingual population, each term heavily loaded with historical and political baggage: *magyarországi németek* (Germans of Hungary), *Ungarndeutsche* (Germans of Hungary), *Volksdeutsche* (Ethnic Germans), *német ajku magyarok* (Hungarians of German tongue), *Donauschwaben* (Danube Swabians) or *svábok*/*Schwaben*.

The first two terms have long been the official forms in Hungary; the third was preferred by Nazi recruiters, among others; the last term is today the colloquial one. Like many such labels, *sváb* is potentially insulting, if used without permission by those who have no claim to the category. Today, it can also be a mildly politicized claim to minority identity, a reminder of the discrimination that German-speakers suffered in Hungary after 1946. After communism, there was a noticeable increase in young people taking pride in it. For elders there are more complicated attitudes, as the layered result of magyarization efforts in the early twentieth century, recruitment by Nazi Germany, and the expulsions of the 1940s. Speakers in Bóly – variously interpellated through these labels – became aware of their potential ties to other populations of German-speakers in Hungary and in Germany and those living as minorities in other parts of Europe and globally. To speak Schwäwisch could thus refer to speaking one or more of the many village forms of German in Hungary but also in other parts of the world.

The suppression (erasure) of the farmer/artisan distinction in Bóly, while evoking the contrast between Hungarian-speakers in Hungary and German-speakers in Hungary, occurred frequently. In an interview about language, an artisan woman corrected herself: She had been inspired to compare Handwerkerisch with *Schwäwisch – net Schwäwisch, wir sind ja auch Schwowen* (– not Schwäwisch, really we're of course also Schwaben). Thus, the speaker moved from a Bóly-based contrast, where artisan and farmer speech differ, to one unifying those two as German, and reiterating the contrast as German/Hungarian instead. Others discussed the painful fact that even though their families have been in Hungary for centuries, Hungarian monolinguals sometimes noted their intonation and asked what foreign country they were from. In discussing one such incident, an artisan woman dismissed (erased) the difference between Handwerkerisch and Schwäwisch – with some bitterness – and asserted an overriding unity:

(2.9) *Magyarul mindannyian svábok*   In [speaking] Hungarian, we are
      vagyunk   all sváb/Swabians.
              (M90:7)

This declaration had multiple ambiguities: It could mean merely that Hungarian has no subcategories for *sváb*. Or that when speaking Hungarian everyone with a *sváb* background has the same accent; or that from a Hungarian point of view, "we" *sváb* people are all alike, contrasted to Hungarians, and stigmatized.

Thus, among the elders in Bóly, an encompassing recursion of the artisan/farmer distinction erased the differences within Bóly and the contrast in qualities was (partially) reproduced at a wider scale, this time opposing German-speakers to Hungarians in Hungary. But in this newer comparison, there was an important change. When Rosina, in her narrative at the start of this section, made herself the emblem of Bóly, she took up the linguistically knowledgeable artisan's position. But when Hungarian-speakers are stereotypically contrasted with German-speakers in Hungary generally, the German-speakers are cast as the farmer figure. They are said to have many of the features that supposedly marked the farmers of Bóly vis-à-vis the artisans: hardworking, rich, clean, and restrained in expression. A woman from a farmer family, who became school inspector for German-language instruction across the whole region after the war, characterized this well. She was speaking in an interview and thus ex cathedra, as a representative of German-speakers in Hungary: *Minket úgy neveltek, ha ezt kell csinálni, nem kell dumálni hanem meg kell csinálni* (That is how we were raised: if there is something to be done, don't chatter, just do it).

If these are qualities of *Schwaben/svábok*, what is the stereotyped image of Hungarians? Explicit discussion of Hungarians, as a category, was very rare in Bóly. After a difficult early period, peaceful coexistence with transferred Hungarian families was seen to require utmost tact. "Mixed" marriages have been accepted since the 1960s. Nevertheless, one can detect subtle contrasts: In telling of the first encounters between Bólyi and in-migrating Hungarians, the Bólyi were invariably characterized as *csendes, békés, nem káromkodós* (quiet, peaceable, not given to cursing). A contrast is clearly implied. Hungarian figures in anecdotes from earlier years were sometimes described as *nagyszájú* (big-mouthed). The first Hungarians who came to Bóly after the war were described as *nincstelen magyarok, gumi csizma meg rongy, nem is tudtak nem is akartak dolgozni* (penniless Hungarians, rubber boots and rags, they didn't know how and didn't want to work). Much more frequently, however, characterizations of Hungarians as poor, overly expressive, and indolent were firmly dismissed as inaccurate. They were pointedly denied in the case of the current Hungarian monolinguals of Bóly. Yet, historical and ethnographic works about this multiethnic region have been preoccupied by just these mutual stereotypes.[16] It was not unusual to hear both locals and visiting Hungarian monolinguals quietly attributing the outstanding cleanliness, orderliness, and prosperity of the town to its supposedly ethnic (*sváb*) characteristics.

In sum, Bóly's speakers extended the scope of their categories. By recursively and more encompassingly applying local distinctions, speakers categorized distant people and places in terms of local contrasts, which themselves were changed in the process. They established equivalence between contrasts of different scope by using the same term – *sváb/schwäwisch* – to refer to different entities, people in Bóly or in all of Hungary; by using the same adjectival descriptors for different categories (*előkelőbb* for artisans and for Bóly as a whole); by enregistering languages; by personal deictics, us/them, that are always shifters; and by inviting inferences of equivalence through narrative juxtapositions. One might say that the local language ideology encountered ethnonationalism and swallowed it, though not without becoming, to some extent, what it ate.

Perspectives and Blockage

Since the 1970s, the people of Bóly have journeyed widely even outside Hungary for work, schooling, and tourism. Before the end of communism and increasingly since, people have commuted to work in Germany. They have visited relatives there who were expelled in the 1940s, and are visited in turn. In fractal fashion, German-speakers from Bóly are known as "the Hungarians" to their kin in Germany; and they call their visiting cousins "the Germans." Some from Bóly have acquired German citizenship through their German family background; via marriage in Germany some have created fresh kinship links. Speakers from Bóly have had the opportunity to compare themselves to diverse others, and to learn how they were perceived by observers in varied social locations.

These experiences have led to new conundrums of scale and positioning. We have seen how speakers can *pivot* from one to the other category of differentiation by taking the position of "farmer" vis-à-vis one interlocutor, but voicing an "artisan" position in comparison to others, even within a single event. The logic of co-constitutive ideological schemas makes this possible. Yet, such fractal comparisons and pivoting are undermined by any stricture that *permanently* allocates people types to one or the other "side" of what participants construct as an axis of differentiation. (An imaginary example would be a regulation that those who ate potatoes every day must always identify as farmers, and can never adopt an artisan voice.) If enforced, such a stricture creates what we call a *blockage* of recursivity. The dilemma of an artisan woman, let us call her Terus, provides an example. She was in her sixties, from Bóly.

In 1990, Gal asked a young German-Hungarian bilingual from northern Hungary (Mari) to record an interview with Terus. Giving examples of "artisan language" and "farmer language" in the interview, Terus enacted an artisan persona by displaying elaborate expertise in communication. Then she unexpectedly launched into a story of a time when she moved away from Bóly and lived in a Hungarian-speaking village. There, she said, she spoke German with the few farmers who, like her, were German-Hungarian bilinguals. Erasing the farmer/artisan distinction, she voiced a farmer persona in that scene. The story then segues to an international scene, a group trip to Germany, where a German performer (not from Hungary) recited a Hungarian poem for Terus's excursion group. To this, Terus reports a strong emotional reaction: "I said then, I don't know what, what this is in me, I am still, after all, Hungarian, the Hungarian anthem, it so moves me and even so I like German. I don't understand this in myself, what this is." The speaking stops; one can hear Terus quietly sobbing. The interview unfolds in this way:

(2.10) Terus and Mari (M90:3A9:50)

Mari: *... andere Beispiele, die Unterschied?*
Terus: *Muss einfalln. Fällt mi nix ein*
Mari: *Bei uns sagt man geh Ham.*

Terus: *Wenn ich zusammen komme mit gewissen deutschen Leute, tue ich gern, ich war auf solchen Dorf gelebt nur Ungarn warn nur eins-zwei schwäbische Frau warn dort. Wenn wir uns getroffen haben wir haben immer nur Deutsch weil ich habe gern das deutsch Wort. Jetzt hab ich die Fernseh die Parabola und ich schaue meistens nur Deutsch. Näher ... ich weiss nicht, wir waren vor zwei Jahren in Deutschland d'raus ... dort haben wir die, eine, die war aber eine Reichsdeutsche, die kann so schön Ungarisch sprechen. Sie kann "Este van este van ki ki nyugalomba" gyönyörűen elszavalja. Des is ein ungarische –*

Mari: *... other examples, [of] the difference?*
Terus: *It has to occur to me. Nothing [more] occurs to me.*
Mari: *By us, they say "geh Ham."*

Terus: *When I get together with certain German people, I do [this] gladly. I lived in a village where there were only Hungarians, there were just one or two Swabian women there. When we met in the street we always spoke German because I like the German word. Now I have a TV and a satellite dish and I mostly watch German. Closer ... I don't know, we were out in Germany two years ago ... there we, she a, she was an Imperial German, she could speak such beautiful Hungarian. She knew "Night has come, night has come, to each in repose" she recites it so beautifully. That's a Hungarian –*

Mari: *Dichter*
Terus: *Dichter, den haben wir
lieb, der hat schöne Dichtung,
sie hat das ganz so, wir waren
so überrascht, dass sie so schön
Ungarisch gelernt hat und so ein
schweres, doch ... und dort haben
sie, sie haben alle gern den unseren*
Himnusz *und* **a Szozat**. *Und das
haben wir dort gesungen. Und sie
hat, kann auch alles mitgesungen
und ich, hab ich damals gesagt ich
weiss nicht was das ist in mir, ich,
doch ein Ungar, der* **Himnusz** *und*
Szozat *so drückt. ... Und doch habe
ich das Deutsche [gern]. Das kann
ich in mir nicht so verstehen was
das ist.*

Mari: *poet*
Terus: *poet, whom we love
very much, he has beautiful
poetry, she did this so, we were
so surprised, that she learned
such beautiful Hungarian and
such a difficult [language]
still. ... And there they, they all
liked our* **National Anthem**
and **the Pledge**. *And we sang
it there. And they sang all of it
along with us and I, I said then
I don't know what, what this
is in me, I am still, after all,
Hungarian, the* **Anthem** *and*
Pledge, *presses [my heart]. ...
And even so, I like German.
I don't understand this in
myself, what this is.*

In the space of a few moments, Terus presented herself as differently situated in a series of linked comparisons, each an encompassment at an increasing social scale, each one iterating the farmer/artisan distinction by invoking its conventional axis of qualities. The contrast remains restraint/elaboration, but *the linguistic forms that invoke the contrast of qualities shift from one comparison to another.* In the narrating event, she is the artisan, implicitly contrasted with the farmer type. In the narrated Hungarian village, she joins with the few German-bilingual farmers, speaking German, enacting the "plain, farmer" in contrast to Hungarians. The third scene is international. Marveling at the German performer's recitation in Hungarian, Terus calls Hungarian "difficult," thereby evaluating it as elaborate vis-à-vis German. In this scene, Terus inhabits neither the artisan role (vs. farmer), as in Bóly, nor the simple German-speaker (vs. Hungarians), as in the village. Instead she is, ironically, the (elaborate) Hungarian vis-à-vis Germans, calling the Hungarian poem and anthem "ours," switching to Hungarian to praise the performer. Terus changed her position by fractal *pivoting* repeatedly, on the artisan/farmer axis. By juxtaposing the three comparisons in this one narrative, she equates the fractal recursions in the three scenes, erasing their differences. And she places herself differently in each one. This evidently made sense to her. In a fractal world, such pivoting among contrasting perspectives is to be expected.

Why, then, the sobbing? The source of trouble is the exclusionary logic fundamental to European ethnonationalism: When language is made a sign of national loyalty, it must be unitary. Any system that forces participants to take up fixed, exclusionary categories creates blockage of recursivity. European linguistic nationalism was famous for doing so. Terus was evidently troubled by her emotional bond to two languages and her ability to pivot between them. She knew that ethnonationalism's demand for monolingualism undermined her claim, as a bilingual, to both German and Hungarian ethnonational identity. She could count on Mari, her interviewer, to understand since the interviewer was in a similar social position.

The fractal pivoting was not a problem in Bóly, with the farmer/artisan contrast, but Terus's experiences had taken her well beyond the scale of Bóly and ethnolinguistic ideology had itself come to Bóly with a vengeance in the 1930s. The exclusionary logic had further results moving into the twenty-first century, problems noted by students and teachers of German in Hungary, by young German-Hungarians, and even by Terus's elderly generation. Terus equated *Schwäwisch* and *Deutsch* in her narrative. Many in Bóly insisted on the latter term for the local varieties. Yet there are enough differences between *Deutsch* (or rather *Standarddeutsch*) as heard on German and Austrian TV and Bóly's local forms that although people mostly understand the various standards, they routinely spoke of "translating" them into local forms. Speakers in Bóly were also aware that they have incorporated large amounts of Hungarian material in their everyday speech. Some of this borrowing is centuries old and unnoticed, but some is judged by the speakers themselves: *Misch ..., ich misch viel ... tu ich jetzt so zamischn. Nemme so, tas man nur teutsch oder ungarisch tät* (Mix ... I mix a lot ... I do these days a mixing together. It doesn't happen anymore that one speaks only German or only Hungarian).

How then, should children's fragmentary knowledge of homegrown German varieties in Hungary be handled? What standard version of German should be taught in schools? Following Hungary's EU accession in 2004, how should German-speakers in Hungary construct a contemporary German-Hungarian ethnic identity, indexed by bilingualism? This is now officially recognized as possible, as it was not for Terus's generation.[17] For decades children were taught in school to devalue their parents' local German speech; now, educators lament its disappearance, even as more young people are interested – for economic reasons and as a badge of identity – in learning standard German. These concerns are being formulated through continent-wide ideological frameworks, constructed by teachers, by intellectuals, and with their feet by young workers of German background who find lucrative work in Germany or find the German language an economic resource in contemporary Hungary and a prestigious practice across the European Union. We return to such questions of scale and international relationships in Chapters 8 and 9.

Part II

Semiotics

The ethnographic chapters presented close-up and "inside" views of how people make relative judgments and switch vantage points in everyday life when they take *perspectives* and make shifting *comparisons*. These are ways of organizing knowledge and action through signs. To explore how sign relations constitute the work of ideology, the chapters of Part II disassemble and explain the semiotic process of differentiation, proceeding from simplest to complex ingredients.

Chapter 3 shows that signs are not separate from the hurly-burly of social life. Human beings make signs by conjecturing – guessing, hypothesizing – about the meanings of everyday phenomena. Just as the ingredients of a dish are not separately evident in the culinary result yet are crucial to the taste, so the creation of signs is not always obvious, yet is indispensable for the constitution of the ideologies with which we act and interpret social practices. Conjecturing about signs is ongoing, revisable, and open-ended. Thought experiments in Chapter 3 illustrate the basic principles, drawing on works in linguistic anthropology. While explicating our reading of Peircean sign-relations – icon, index, symbol – we also build on other philosophical traditions. The focus is on people's metasemiotic communicative practices: typifying, construing similarity (iconicity) and contiguity (indexicality), transforming sign-relations, and making simple erasures. We discuss the special place of linguistic practices as signs.

But that is not yet the semiotics of differentiation. Chapter 4 turns to more complex sign relations. It shows how ideological work draws on – and organizes – specific frameworks of knowledge through the process of differentiation. We look more closely than in previous chapters at how this process is composed of *axes of differentiation*, qualities and *qualia*, *rhematization*, *anchors*, and essentializing narratives as well as *fractal recursivity* and *erasure*. Together these produce novel categories in social life that are sometimes only momentary, but can be stabilized in institutional practices. Sociohistorical circumstances may motivate *multiple axes* and their relationship. Hegemony is exerted in the related process of *blockage*, as exemplified in standardization. The chapter illustrates differentiation step-by-step, by tracking the conjectures of an early nineteenth-century traveler, as she makes sense of people, landscapes, and social practices in the new United States.

Axes of differentiation often seem fixed and stable, yet they change. Chapter 5 shifts analytical strategies to explore how axes are transformed under historical pressure. Axes shift whenever they are deployed in situated action for diverse – often opposed – political projects. To illustrate such changes, we draw on expressive practices in the United States between the 1770s and 1850s. Memoirs, travelogues, and literary materials provide the evidence. This was an era of great regional upheavals, following the Revolution and before the Civil War. The political stakes were high and are ever-present in our discussion, as we focus on how participants both intervened in historical transformations and made sense of them. The historical developments are illuminated by our analysis. But the larger point is to exemplify the semiotic process itself: axes are changed in successive uptakes, by *splicing*, shifting *salience*, and *pivoting*. Some twenty-first-century examples show how change in axes organizes social projects of purification and conflict as well as forms of solidarity.

3   Ingredients: Signs, Conjectures, Perspectives

What are the ingredients of language ideological work? What are the semiotic processes that compose it? How is the logic of those processes assembled from simpler sign relations? Ideological analysis made sense of our ethnographic materials. So, why do we need to know more about signs? Indeed, what is the connection at all between ethnographic description and this chapter's more abstract discussion of semiosis? Metaphors suggest an answer. Sign-relations are like armatures in sculpture: they are not separately visible, yet they are part of it, giving shape to the clay – to the sociocultural materials. In another image: cell processes rely for their activity on the nutrition provided by the rest of the organism even as they are necessary for the workings of that organism. Similarly, sign processes are indispensable as the organizing logic out of which ideological presumptions and change are made. Like the colors of thread in a tartan cloth, sign relations constitute the patterns of social life. Armatures, cells, and colors are not separate from what they constitute. So too, sign-relations do not stand apart from the social world, simply representing it. On the contrary, sign relations and the ideologies constructed with them are part of the social world. They are produced by it, are subject to its historical contingencies, and enable meaningful action in it.

"Sign relation" is an apt phrase for explicating the ingredients of ideologies. First, it highlights signs in general – not language alone. Sign relations invariably organize many expressive modalities, including those that do not involve language at all. Second, the phrase implicates differentiation by focusing on relations. A sign is the *result* of relationships; it does not preexist them. Any phenomenon may be a sign if it is posited to stand for something, in some uptake, from some vantage point. And there are always many vantage points. This multiplicity of vantage points in part reflects the fact that every social aggregate, even the smallest, provides multiple social positions. Some social theories go on to suppose that vantage points can be read off from participants' social positions. Yet, as students of interaction have noted, participants do not mechanically "give off" signs of social position. Instead they have differential access to knowledge about how positions are conventionally signaled, which allows them to enact various points of view. With that knowledge, an individual may take up and inhabit (perhaps only momentarily) various perspectives – even in a single scene.

How should one conceptualize *perspective*, in semiotic terms? C. S. Peirce's notion of "interpretant" is a good entry point for doing so. We read Peirce as suggesting that interpretants are fragments of cognitive activities in which human beings engage: they construe as signs various aspects of a complex socio-material world. We call such actions conjecturing, which is an alternative term for Peirce's sometimes confusing label "interpretant." Participants conjecture – we could equally say they guess or hypothesize – by turning attention to potential signs. Existing knowledge suggests what could conceivably be a sign, as contrasted against its surround. Attention and contrast are presupposed in conjecturing something as a sign. And as social actors rely on frameworks of preexisting knowledge to make conjectures, they also create more knowledge by reasoning with signs. Reading Peirce for our own purposes, we take him to mean that conjectures (intepretants) accomplish three sets of "tasks": typifying signs; creating iconic; indexical; and symbolic sign-relations; and transforming these relations on the basis of further knowledge.

Peirce did not explore the specific scenes and histories in which conjectures are made. Our goal, by contrast, is to draw out the implications of that social locatedness. In other ways too, our theoretical purposes are different from his, so we also rely on other lines of thought. Although conjectures are surely open-ended, provisional, and reinterpretable, just as Peirce taught, we do not assume they lead to the converging, objective portraits of the world for which he hoped. On the contrary, in this chapter we take up each of the tasks of conjecturing in turn, and argue that when clusters of these tasks are accomplished together, in specific sociohistorical circumstances, the result is the construction of perspectives that are partial, conventional, and positioned. They are potentially diverse vantage points of social life.

To discuss abstract semiotic relationships as lucidly as possible, this chapter illustrates each step with thought experiments. But, because empirical materials are more persuasive, the chapter ends with an example of a single writer, as she switches among multiple perspectives in a first-person narrative. Anne Newport Royall (1769–1854) was an author and journalist in the early United States. A scene from one of her travelogues vividly renders her situated experience of conjecturing with signs in a way that would be difficult to glean from ethnographic observations or interviews.

Although expository writing requires us to present our discussion of perspective in some sequence – and some aspects of the process presuppose or entail others – our order of exposition does not mirror a temporal or onto-genetic order. Rather, the goal is to illustrate how conjectures are the semiotic armature of perspectives.

Conjectures Constitute Signs and Objects

Knowledge that social actors already have makes it possible to notice and pick out phenomena in the buzz and bustle of a constantly changing, socio-material surround. It allows guesses about what might be signs and a search for what a sign might signal, what it might stand for. Nothing is a sign in itself, but any phenomenon recognizable by participants can (potentially) be taken as a sign, guessed about, and perhaps acted on. Not only words or gestures, also acts of all kinds, events, pictures, qualities, feelings, abstract configurations, even thoughts. By the same token, anything can potentially be what a sign stands for, its "object." The quotation marks are important because the term does not mean a physical object, but any kind of phenomenon at all. And we will use the term "object" in this sense, sometimes specifying "semiotic object." Selective attention picks out qualities, things, acts, events, practices, people, and situations that exist in the world and that, by conjecture (a guess), might be linked to each other as sign-and-object. But, noticing a possible connection is not enough. Only if the co-incidence of two phenomena is interpreted so that one is taken as a sign of the other can we talk of sign relations. This last moment is the crucial reflexive – metasemiotic – step of construing (taking up, conjecturing) and thereby constructing sign-relations.

Since conjectures rely on and are embedded in frameworks of knowledge, they presuppose and are guided by knowledge practices that have been socio-historically created, often over long periods of time. They are part of those frameworks, elaborated through explanations and practices, sometimes fixed in social institutions. In Chapters 4 and 5 we examine how sign making draws on and organizes frameworks of knowledge. Here, for the sake of explication, we zoom in on the several ways that conjectures construe sign-relations – how conjectures make perspectives – paying less attention to the preexisting knowledge in which they are inevitably embedded.

Yet it remains crucial that knowledge and communicative action are moments of a single process. The link between thinking and signaling is fundamental. Unlike the usual Cartesian view, in which thought is rooted in radical doubt and introspection, our view is that thinking requires some sort of expressive form – signs – to convey the objects of thought. For Cartesians, communication is secondary, other people's minds remain a mystery, and minds are separate from the materiality of bodies. For us, thinking starts *not* with doubt but with previous knowledge, with matters that at any historical moment are familiar to some knowers, to some extent. Signs are the products and tools of such knowers in social relations. Instead of a Cartesian split between mind and bodily matter, between individual thinkers and social groups, we are interested in how such realms – once separated in one major philosophical tradition – are connected, and how signs mediate the connection.[1]

To this basically Peircean view we add other dimensions: As scholars interested in cultural difference, we maintain that any epistemological realms recognized by participants may be the source of phenomena taken up as signs and semiotic objects. Furthermore, signs are always hypothesized within social scenes of some kind, which are themselves part of sociohistorical process. Social scenes are the crucibles in which ideas (knowledge, conjectures, guesses) are formulated as communication and communicative forms are taken as tokens of knowledge. Social encounters – face-to-face or in some other medium, even with oneself, and in all their linguistic and nonlinguistic aspects – are the means by which we as participants and as observers obtain access to communicative forms and to the wider organizations of knowledge in which such forms exist. Thus, the ideologized visions and practices of knowledge with which conjectures take up signs are themselves the results of an existing world of social arrangements – made by earlier visions and actions – and which participants enter in midstream.

When, in the course of everyday life, on the basis of their knowledge, interests and projects, people make conjectures about what might be signs and what objects they might represent, those conjectures sometimes turn out to be accurate inferences. When the leaves at the top of a tree are moving, it is a safe bet that there is wind. This is in part because, just as signs (movement) *represent* objects (wind) for a conjecture, so objects (wind) *determine* the signs (movement) that represent them, for some act of noticing (conjecture) that links the two. Further, in a triangular and metacommunicative relationship, signs-and-objects (movement + wind) together specify (*determine*) the conjecture (guess) that notices them. The conjecture connects a phenomenon posited as a sign to some other phenomenon conjectured to be its object. The result is that signs (movement) mediate between objects (wind) and conjectures (the guess that wind has caused the movement). That is, signs allow people to guess about objects. But, of course, not all movement at the tops of trees is related to wind. It might be birds bickering. Nevertheless, such a conjecture is a guess that can lead to others.

This way of describing the process may sound tediously roundabout. It is nevertheless crucial: while the mediation of a sign enables an object to have an effect on the conjecture (hypothesis), it is actually the conjecture itself that has allowed this, by linking the sign and object. One might say the conjecture *erases* its own action of creating the sign and takes the sign as having a separate existence of its own. It is a kind of bootstrapping operation: an active construction of sign-object relationships and the elision of this action are built into the Peircean understanding of sign relations. Furthermore, acts of conjecture lead to other conjectures in chains of guessing. Let us see how this works with a simple example:

Suppose that on an early morning walk through our urban neighborhood during a lengthy dry spell we notice a large, apparently wet patch of pavement.

To notice it at all, there must be some contrast between this bit of pavement and other bits, a little surprise in seeing it. So the presupposed start of any interpretation is attention and contrast within a frame of expected sameness: the pavement. The noticed bit can be taken up as a sign of many potential semiotic objects: Perhaps it is evidence of welcome rain; was there a downpour last night? Or perhaps it is only the runoff from the neighbors' lawn sprinkler; or maybe a passerby has spilled a bottle of soda. But wait, perhaps the bit of pavement is not wet at all, only in shadow, or is newly painted a dark color. An observer's previous knowledge about pavements, shadows, paint, and liquids will be mobilized and adapted to understand the scene. Checking for trees that might cast shade, and finding none, we as observers settle on a diagnosis of "wetness." If the lawn next to the patch of pavement also looks "wet," and if its wetness is construable as similar to the wetness of the pavement, then linking the two could solidify the inference – a conjecture – that the wet lawn and wet pavement, by dint of being taken as similar, constitute signs of each other for the conjecture that construes them in that way.

The similarity goes along with the construal of connection or co-occurrence between the lawn and the pavement. If they had not been contiguous, their similarity would not have prompted the same attention. Seeing them as similar and together invites another semiotic step. It allows the inference that the two wet objects could signal a single act, the neighbor watering. More abstractly put: the neighbor's (hypothesized) act is taken as a semiotic object that can be seen to have *determined* or created the sign that *represents* it (the wetness of grass and pavement), for the conjecture that our observer adopts. "There are, thus, two opposed yet interlocking vectors involved in semiosis, the vector of determination from object to sign and the vector of representation from sign to object" (Parmentier 1994:4). A conjecture brings the two vectors into relation, in a metasemiotic move. In our example, the conjecture connects two phenomena: wetness (of lawn and pavement) and an act of watering ("it must have been the neighbor sprinkling the pavement and lawn"). The wetness (sign) is determined by its presumed object (lawn watering) and in turn determines the observer's conjecture that the wetness and lawn sprinkling are causally connected. At the same time, the sign (wetness) also represents the semiotic object (neighbor's act) for the conjecture that reflexively presumes the link between wet lawn/pavement and sprinkling to be a sign relation.

Peirce's philosophical project was to clarify the correct ways for a scientific community to reason in order to reach universally convergent conclusions based in part on empirical evidence.[2] We, however, are just as interested in the ways our observer of pavements might have used impeccable semiotic logic and empirical clues yet reached a conclusion seen by others as mistaken, or later revealed as wrong. Perhaps the observer failed to notice the children playing with water balloons nearby; or it was the city's street cleaners who sprayed the sidewalk and lawn with water. And what about the possibility of painted sidewalk that was not pursued? Many other contingencies come to mind. The goal of our investigation, in contrast to Peirce, is the multiplicity of knowledges as formulated by various possible inferences, rather than any single, correct inference. We are just as interested in *differentiation* in the way observers take up signs, as in convergence. Taking Peircean insights in novel directions, we reread some of his analytical distinctions to serve our own purposes.

We also draw on the arguments of others. Nelson Goodman's philosophical commentary on language and art helps us take the theme of signs, representation, and reasoning in more "constructivist" directions. Peirce was looking for the "Real ... whose characters are independent of what anybody may think them to be." By contrast, Goodman emphasized the various "ways of world-making" that are enacted by diverse modes of sign interpretation. Each mode is in keeping with *differing* objectives, interests, and conventions (Goodman 1978).[3] For us, the logic of Peircean semiotics undergirds the way sign relations invoke and rely on objectives, values, interests, and conventions, but these may be quite diverse. Conjectures may rely on and invoke different knowledges, in different "worlds."

It is an important complication that conjectures themselves can be taken up as objects and also as signs. How can they be objects? When people make a conjecture in order to understand the relation between a posited object and its presumed sign, that conjecture itself can be construed as an object, if signaled by some other sign, for yet another conjecture. Chains of (metasemiotic) conjecture are formed in this way. Let us see how the conjecture that linked the observed wetness to the actions of a neighbor could be taken as the *object* of another sign. The uptake of wetness-created-by-neighbor (earlier a conjecture, now an object) could be signaled by, for instance, the observer's back and forth shake of the head, which is a sign. In turn, noticing-wetness-created-by-neighbor (object) + head shake (sign) might be connected in an uptake by a new conjecture (perhaps another observer's) that construes them together, perhaps as a conventional gesture of "disapproval" ("In the midst of this drought the neighbor is watering the pavement!").

How does it work when a conjecture is taken up not as a semiotic object, but as a sign? As this brief scenario unfolds, the conjecture that first noticed the wetness, taking it as a sign of the neighbor's act, could itself be a *sign* of another object for another conjecture. The very gesture of noticing wetness and taking it to be a sign of a neighbor's act could be construed, by another guess in this series (the observer's or someone else's), as a sign of yet another object, for instance: already existing tensions among those who live on this street. The successive conjectures lead to a question: are people watching and policing each other?

Conjecturing about sign-object relations and successively (metasemiotically) taking conjectures themselves as signs and objects – all these are acts of inference-by-hypothesis. Peirce called these abductions. Chains of abduction imply communication, even if merely with oneself. But one need not assume a single observer conjecturing. It could be an encounter, with two or more people responding to wet pavements and one another's conjectures. They could be making different hypotheses. For instance, let us say one observer takes the other's conclusion as a sign: head shaking (a conjecture) at the sight of wet pavement, observed by another participant, is taken to signal something, but not about the neighbor or the street but about the person whose head is shaking. A guess might take the head shaker to be a judgmental character; another guess, perhaps by another participant, might hypothesize that the head shake stands for a worry about saving water. These are differential hypotheses about aspects of other participants in the same scene.

It is noteworthy how quickly a rather trivial observation of a wet spot under one's feet invites inferences about possibly consequential difficulties in social relations among neighbors ("Are they policing each other?") or can produce hypotheses about other people's character ("judgmental"). Indeed, if the scenario takes place in drought-prone California, the trouble between neighbors over lawn watering could itself be taken to signal larger political disputes: an observer might interpret the lawn-and-pavement watering as a sign about the neighbor's rejection of environmental regulation concerning water use, and signs of "disapproval" could be taken as an environmentalist commitment. On the other hand, further inquiry could lead to construals that notice aspects of the scene neglected before, inviting conjectures that revise or undermine earlier ones. The pavement turns out to be painted and not to be wet at all; or the neighbors, it happens, are away on vacation. They could not be directly responsible for using a sprinkler.

Through an active, constructive, and reflexive enterprise of successive conjectures (metasemiotic abductions), some guesses are rejected and others come to seem more persuasive and detailed. Existing knowledge is invoked to produce new conjectures, and novel observations become the basis of further conjectures, adding to the frameworks of knowledge. Conjectures never occur in isolation, they are connected and embedded in differences of preexisting knowledge, interests, and values, and in real-time scenes. Conjectures are ideological work. They might mobilize action, be justified by narratives, and may be communicated to a wider network of people. In this thought experiment, we zoomed in to examine the logic by which chains of conjectures create ever more knowledge in an open-ended process that links hypothesized signs and posited objects. What else do they accomplish?

"Tasks" of Conjecturing: Typifying

Our walking observer on the urban street experienced a historically unique moment. It was a singular combination of, say, a dry spell, the quality of light, the time of day, the look of grass, the hardness of the pavement, perhaps a feeling of strain in the shoulders and worry about the morning's news report. All of this specificity will never occur again in just the same way. In a deep philosophical sense signs, objects, and conjectures in a social scene are always singular. But in conjecturing about the street, the observer apprehended the unique patch on that unrepeatable day as a non-unique sign, "a case of" an abstract quality – wetness – present on a surface understood as an instance of a specific cultural category: a pavement. Both these leaps are typifications, accomplished by conjectures. Typifications are crucial to semiosis because real-time phenomena that are taken to be signs, objects, and conjectures can always fit more than one socially recognized category. Even our very small example of a morning walk showed that dark patches could be many things, requiring detailed worldly knowledge.

Philosophers and social theorists of many kinds have noted the importance of typification. Peirce's approach distinguishes among all phenomena in the world according to their ontology, their mode of being. He called this their "degree of reality." Abstract qualities are potentialities or "Firsts"; they are immaterial, like the possibility of redness or the idea of wetness, or worry. "Seconds" are singular, existing scenes, events, and objects in the sensuous world. They are emplaced uniquely in space-time: a particular case of a wet lawn; the precise worry one has today. "Thirds" are generalizations, systematic regularities that are socially recognized by some population. Thirds are phenomena that are "a general type which, it has been agreed [by some set of people], shall be significant" (Peirce 1955a:102). For us, they are not simply "agreed." They are the result of arrangements that are embedded in systems of value, for particular populations. Thirds are *types* and therefore cultural categories. They are generalizations and conventional expectations. Instantiations of types, in real-time encounters, are the *tokens* of types.[4] Tokens are always Seconds: they occur as part of singular, real-time events.

It is only in the realm of Seconds – the humanly experienced, real-time world – that signs and objects can be noticed, taken up, and connected by people's conjectures. But in every such uptake, signs and their objects are linked, by conjecture, to abstract potentials (Firsts), and shaped by generalized, conventional categories (Thirds). Another way to say this is that generalizations and regularities (Thirds) are *instantiated* in real-time actions, scenes, objects, and bodies (Seconds) that are then understood as their *tokens,* by those making conjectures. Similarly, abstract qualities (Firsts) must be *embodied* in material

objects and experiences as well as instantiated as examples of cultural categories (Thirds). Potentials of quality (like wetness), when embodied and experienced as cultural categories, are *qualia* (Seconds). In the everyday world, it is
qualia and tokens that conjectures take up and connect.[5]

It follows that conjectures, as metasemiotic moves that typify signs and
objects (and can be taken as signs or objects), are themselves also tokens of
types. The (re)actions we identified as conjectures in the thought experiment –
head shaking, tensions among neighbors, personal character, or political commitment of observers and neighbors – these are all themselves instantiations
(tokens) of recognizable cultural categories (types). Any uptake (another word
for conjecture) is located in a real-time scene and consists of an act of some
kind (a token) that connects an experienced sign (a token of a cultural category) and an experienced object (another token of a type). The uptake can
be an experience of affect, a thought, a gesture such as a head shake, or a
verbal comment or other act. All conjectures are (re)actions in real time and
therefore Seconds; they are themselves tokens and qualia, hence the results of
typification.

As scholars have long observed, labeling is a powerful form of typification –
making experiences into instances of types; invoking types to identify
instances – channeling and shaping experience. Was the spot "wetness" or
"shadow"? Was reaction to wetness an embodiment of "irritation," "rage," or
"admiration"? Is the person who waters the lawn a "neighbor," an "enemy,"
or a "stranger"? Does the reaction to watering count as "blame," "warning,"
or merely "complaint"? Even if only a thought, the conjecture must be made
recognizable according to some convention, some cultural category. The same
holds for actions. Is a head shake "disapproval" or "agreement"? What if our
observer, on seeing the wet pavement, disables the sprinkler? Was this act an
instantiation of "aid" or rather an "intrusion"? Each of these possibilities is,
of course, a dense category with a genealogy, a locus of regular practice, with
many further implications. For instance, labeling a sign as intended (watering),
accidental (spill), dangerous (storm), or benign (rain) has effects on the kinds of
further conjectures that can be made about its objects.[6]

But linguistic labeling is only one means of tying instances to types. Types
are established by many kinds of practices. They can be made by discourses
about the characteristics of categories of people, events, qualities, and
actions; they may be "secured" to tokens by standardization, made hegemonic and presupposed in frameworks of understandings that are spread in
innumerable ways, or fixed by institutionalized practices. To be sure, they
also may be more fleeting and are certainly subject to transformations. Yet,
whether fleeting or durable, types (stereotypes) are accessible only to populations that have familiarity and knowledge of such practices and frameworks, not to others.

Conjecturing Similarity and Contiguity: Perspectives

There are several ways that signs can be linked by conjectures to semiotic objects. This is another task for conjectures. Peirce distinguished three kinds of linkage, calling these three different "grounds": iconic, indexical, and symbolic. We discuss iconic and indexical links first and return later, in a separate section, to symbolic ones. It is customary to say that iconic relations pick out some similarity between sign and object; that iconic signs *depict* their object. It is customary to say that indexical relations display a contiguity or co-occurrence between a sign and its posited semiotic object, perhaps some aspect of what created the sign. Yet it is important to note that similarity and contiguity are presupposed possibilities attributed by conjecture and not self-evident features of signs.

Indexical signs, by virtue of contiguity, seem to point to their objects. As Seconds (real-time phenomena), they can be directly affected by the object they represent. The object can be understood to cause the sign, and this is often an accurate inference. But causation itself is only attributed to the indexical sign relation and is not necessarily involved. (We return later to discuss some of the problems with attributions of causation.) Recall that conjectures erase their own "work" of creating sign-relations by seeming merely to notice signs presumed to already exist. In the same way, conjectures posit iconic relations of similarity and indexical relations of coexistence or co-occurrence between typified signs and objects, yet erase their own work. They make it seem as though relations of similarity and contiguity (or causation) were inherent in the world, rather than the result of conjecture working on the phenomena of the world.

It is important that while iconic and indexical relations are different, they nevertheless work together, even in the simplest cases. Something noticed and taken up as a sign may be conjectured to partake of both iconic and indexical relations. Peirce presented this link as the "incorporation" of icons in indexes. The classic example is a weather vane. It is taken as an iconic sign by noticing that its direction is *similar* to the direction of the wind. But it must also be indexical, coexistent, and contiguous with the particular wind being observed, otherwise it is useless as a wind vane. In our thought experiment, too, a conjecture took up the "look" of wetness, located in grass and pavement. The conjecture took them to be similar, in iconic relation (same qualia). Yet they were also noticed as being in contiguity, located together in a particular place, hence indexical of each other. Further uptake of the wet spots as a sign includes the iconic link (wetness) and some aspect of the conditions that created the contiguity (indexicality). By the incorporation of an iconic relation in the indexical link, the observer's conjecture led to the question: What made the wet spots?

These examples are thought experiments that posit real-time signs. They are tokens, Seconds. Typification is involved because any real-time assessments of iconicity and indexicality are tokens of abstract, socially available concepts, that is, *types* of resemblance and contiguity (co-occurrence, pointing). Social conventions define what "counts as" similarity and contiguity between signs and objects, in specific sociohistorical scenes. In what follows, we show with examples that the "tasks" of conjecturing – construing sign-relations, typifying, recognizing "grounds" – when taken together, enact conventional ways of construing in the here-and-now sociohistorical world. It is by recognizing and enacting typification, similarity, and contiguity in stereotyped ways that participants take up particular *perspectives*.

First, we discuss the characteristics of each kind of ground, with a focus on ways in which they operate together, returning later to situations in which one kind of sign-relation (ground) is turned into another.

Iconicity Shaped by Indexicality

Defined by Peirce as the simplest sign relation, iconicity is one in which, as we have noted, a sign is taken to represent an object through some similarity between them. They are similar if they share real-time features, that is, qualia. (Sign and object may also be similar by a more complex "formal resemblance," to which we turn in Chapters 4 and 5.)[7] Qualitative similarities may include, for instance, redness, darkness, wetness, slowness, directionality, excitement, smoothness. For a long time, similarity was believed by philosophers to be such a self-evident aspect of observables that it could form the explanation for more complex relationships. It was thought that ascertaining "likeness" between observed phenomena was simply a matter of careful examination and inventory of their qualities.

Typification throws a monkey wrench into this approach. As we saw, an experience can be apprehended as the embodiment of many possible abstract categories ("wetness" or "shade"), and conversely, abstract categories may be embodied in various ways (e.g., even the wetness of lawns is somewhat different observationally than the wetness of pavements). Tokens may instantiate many different types.[8] Such tokens and types may be differentially recognized by various populations of social actors, or by the same groups on different occasions. Thus, recognition of qualities is not simply forced on us by objects and signs themselves. Conjectures mediate between phenomena-as-experience and the conventional categories that they "count as."

There is a second and equally grave problem with the traditional philosophical view of similarity as based on observation alone. Even after embodied qualia are construed as instantiations of particular abstract qualities and conventional categories, another semiotic step is required in order to ascertain similarity: a conjecture must pick out which qualia, of the many that are potentially detectable in both sign and object, in the specific situation, are to be matched with each other, in order for the sign and object to be construed as "similar," hence in iconic relation, in that scene. As Nelson Goodman argued: "anything is in some way like anything else" (1972:440). Similarity is insufficiently constrained by observation alone, even when observation is constrained by typifying inferences. The problem is that "every two things have some property in common [if only existence] ... [but] of course no two things have all their properties in common" (1972:438). As Goodman suggested, there must be some way that resemblances are picked out from among the vast possibilities that the world provides. Judgments of similarity depend on what Goodman called "circumstances." He provided a thought experiment:

[S]uppose we have three glasses, the first two filled with colorless liquid, the third with a bright red liquid. I might be likely to say the first two are more like each other than either is like the third. But it happens that the first glass is filled with water and the third with water colored by a drop of vegetable dye, while the second is filled with hydrochloric acid – and I am thirsty. Circumstances alter similarities. (1972:445)

Thus, the conjecture of similarity is dependent on aspects of the scene in which the judgment is made. The act of positing a similarity between two liquids is *part* of the scene. That act is not itself a similarity, not in iconic relation to the phenomena judged to be similar. Rather, for an observer's conjecture, the act is contiguous and co-occurrent with those phenomena. We can restate this by noting that the conjecture of similarity is an indexical sign pointing to various aspects of the "circumstances" in which the similarity judgment was created.

Most importantly, Goodman highlights the momentary bodily state of thirst of the person making the similarity judgment. This particular act of judgment picks out qualia that were not obvious: the red liquid as similar to one of the colorless ones in being potable. Making this iconic link is an act – as construed by the author or another observer – indexical of the author's condition of thirst. But it also entails some background knowledge of chemistry, the very possibility that hydrochloric acid may look like water. And this implicates esoteric expertise within a history of knowledge as well as what frameworks of knowledge are familiar to the individual participant. In this sense judgment of resemblance is multiply "relative and variable," as Goodman puts it (1972:444), reliant on ways of construing similarity that index differences among participants in bodily state and in access to frameworks of knowledge.

In another thought experiment, Goodman explores other aspects of a situation:

Consider baggage at an airport check-in station. The spectator may notice shape, size, color, material, and even make of luggage; the pilot is more concerned with weight, and the passenger with destination and ownership. Which pieces of baggage are more alike than others depends not only upon what properties they share, but upon who makes the comparison, and when. (1972:445)

In contrast to the previous thought experiment, this one concerns types of people and the types of judgments they are stereotypically likely to make, not biographical individuals (not the "I" who is thirsty). We think it is worth distinguishing among several senses of Goodman's "who" and "when." These help us to parse the indexical (co-occurring) aspects of the situation that point to the different judgments of similarity that Goodman distinguishes. "Pilot," "spectator," and "passenger" are social roles; a pilot on one day may be a passenger the next. A particular biographical individual, even if not working as a pilot and not even trained as one, can nevertheless enact much of the stereotyped role of a pilot, perhaps in the theater, or as a joke. Conversely, an individual trained as a pilot, traveling as a passenger, might adopt a spectator role and the conjecture that displays that role, by grouping luggage according to shape, size, and color.

Many social roles are specific to typified speech events (e.g., defendant and witness are specific to trials). Longer-term stereotypes of personhood – *personae* – are sustained across events: lawyer, pilot, pirate, revolutionary, or yuppy. Both roles and personae are connected by social conventions to likely actions, interests, and access to knowledge. Goodman's scene depicts a stereotyped setting in which pilots care about safety and know that safety depends on the load an airplane carries, so they attend to the weight of luggage. Biographical persons can take up (inhabit) roles and personae by virtue of the fact that both roles and categories of personae are understood to imply typical forms of conjecture – conventionalized and often even institutionalized ways of attending to types of things, people, qualities, activities, and events. Such clusters of conventional conjectures, indexical of personae, constitute what we call *perspectives*.

There are limits to the perspectives that biographical persons can take up. They are constrained by social positions and experiences that provide differential access to the stereotypes and frameworks of knowledge associated with (indexical of) typified social roles and personae. This shapes but does not determine what kind of conjectures they can propose. An extension of Goodman's scenario illustrates one aspect of the partial indeterminacy between social roles and perspectives. If we presume the airport scene is a real-time situation (rather than simply a typified one), we can be sure that people attend not only to roles and personae but also to the moment-by-moment creation of social relationships through gestures, utterances, and other signs. Conjectures that pick out some dimension(s) of evaluation on which to judge similarity (weight vs. destination vs. style of luggage) may be construed by participants not as a change in role or personae but as more fleeting. The pilot, momentarily adopting a spectator perspective, smiles together with the passenger/fashionista, as they look at designer luggage, displaying their similar appreciation of it. Within the indexicalities of role and personae, this is a similarity (iconicity) of judgment, creating interactional alignment (similarity between interactors) as construed by participants themselves.[9]

Further Conjectures about Indexicality

There are always more construals to make and more links among signs. To follow how indexical and iconic signs intertwine, we propose some further thought experiments. Just as everything is in some ways similar to everything else, as Goodman said, so every existent thing in the world is in contiguity with every other existent thing, so potentially every existent thing could be an index of every other. As with iconicity, ideological work relies on frameworks of knowledge and real-time conditions to orient what participants notice, and to limit what ideologized connections, contiguities, possibly causations they are prepared to conjecture about. Indexical relations are by no means self-evident. One way to explore the implications of this is to further extend Goodman's thought experiments. He started with idealized scenes in which different similarities were created. What if we reverse the procedure? What are some of the semiotic objects that the construal of a single similarity (iconicity) between two phenomena may index?

Consider Goodman's three liquids. The surprise of his example comes from the default assumption that the scene is in an ordinary kitchen, which would be indexed by the similarity of the two colorless liquids. The thirsty philosopher's dilemma, however, is more likely to occur in a chemistry lab. What other scenes might a judgment of similarity between the colorless liquids index? It might point to a children's party scene. The children identify the two colorless liquids as similar and reject them (taking both to be water), selecting instead the red one (as soda). This choice among liquids might index many other phenomena too. Conjectures could focus on one child's judgment of similarity, and on aspects of that act, perhaps taking it to index the child's straitened home life ("mom never buys soda") or the child's character ("Robin always does what the others do"). A guess focusing on a single child's choice might itself point, by stereotype, to the conjecturer as a school psychologist or a parent. Teachers might focus instead on how orderly the judgments are for the whole group, making conjectures about characteristics of the class ("they are too tired to behave"). The judgment of similarity between glasses of colorless liquid might index yet another kind of scene: a basic eye test for color perception, so that conjectures and inferences would pertain to the competence of experts (eye doctors) and the physical abilities of participants. Local frameworks of knowledge about personhood, intent, and ethics would be immediately relevant.

The very terms we used to describe these scenarios – lab, party, exam, teacher, parent, psychologist, doctor – were conventional categories, types of event and of person. So was "choice," both as a philosophically complex act and as the various gestures by which it might be signaled (a nod, pointing, or reaching). It is typifications such as these that, when instantiated in real-time scenes, enable participants to take up diverse perspectives. Our description of conjectures – like those of Goodman – relied on our own culturally inflected notions of typicality in order to invent plausible scenarios.

In sum, wherever one starts, a chain of abductions unfolds through acts of conjecture, metasemiotically building on previous conjectures, typifications, and sign relations of both iconicity and indexicality. As these thought experiments suggest, conjectures necessarily rely on – and simultaneously organize and extend – frameworks of knowledge. Perspectives are variously taken up and enacted. Frameworks of knowledge and communicative action are entwined. Moment-by-moment chains of conjecture (of abduction) allow for momentary perspectives: these are reinterpretations of previous inferences about ongoing events, actions, and circumstances, and revised alignments among participants. This lesson about potential revision, in somewhat different terms, is equally emphasized in the interactionist work of Goffman (1981) in his studies of replies and responses, as well as by Bakhtin's (1984) notion of unfinalizability in art and social life.

Symbols: Linguistic Forms as Signs

We have not said much so far about symbols. It has been customary in linguistic and anthropological theory to define symbols as different from other sign relations by virtue of being "conventional." But, as we have been at pains to demonstrate, perspectives typify indexical and iconic signs, and typification depends on social conventions. Earlier, we quoted a phrase from Peirce that bears repeating: all typified signs are ones that have been "agreed [by some set of people], shall be significant" (1955a:102).

The distinctiveness of symbols, therefore, does not lie in their reliance on social understandings. Rather, unlike wet pavements, glasses of liquid, and luggage, symbols in the Peircean sense are *necessarily* signs and depend for decipherment on a specific delimited system. Words and grammatical patterns are excellent examples of symbols, but so are all signs that rely on a code. The color coding of traffic lights is a nonlinguistic example. Like other typified signs, linguistic forms – when pronounced or displayed on particular occasions – are real-time phenomena (Seconds) that are instantiations of abstract regularities (Thirds). Speech regularities are tokens, quite particularly, of linguistic systems. For example, no two pronunciations of the sound-concatenation "stick" are entirely alike, yet if the sounds are taken to be tokens of a linguistic category they are all construed to be examples of the *word* stick, an abstract linguistic form in a specific language system. The object called a stick can also be a sign, with many conventional (typified) but nonlinguistic construals in a social world: as cane, as weapon, as a measuring standard; or in a game, as doll or dance partner. Unlike the stick as object, or the earlier examples of glasses of liquid and pavement, the uptake of utterances *as* linguistic expressions requires, minimally, specific kinds of conjecture, informally characterized as "knowledge of some language." Those uptakes recognize the abstract phono-lexico-grammatical categories, sense distinctions, and combinatorics of which the spoken forms are construed to be instantiations. Otherwise, the linguistic tokens cannot be taken up as linguistic signs at all. They could be heard as sounds and even as a language of some kind, but further access is largely occluded.

Yet, the specific linguistic knowledge that construes linguistic tokens as symbols in this narrow sense is never sufficient for understanding real-time linguistic utterances and practices. To be sure, linguistic forms are taken up as specific linguistic knowledge. But other conventional conjectures are also required for their interpretation. They must also and *simultaneously* be interpreted by additional conjectures – what we have called perspectives – that construe them as indexically related to the specifics of speech event and personae they instantiate. So, in some ways, linguistic practices are much like the nonlinguistic yet conventional sign relations we have been discussing. Now, let us examine iconicity and indexicality in the realm of linguistic signs.

Similarity in Linguistic Materials

Iconicity is evident *within* linguistic systems. As Jakobson noted, any linguistic sign involves two modes of arrangement, *selection* and *combination*. The first of these he called "similarity." Since the selection between alternatives implies the possibility of substituting one for the other, selection requires the two to be similar in some respects (1990 [1956]:119). Similarity, as a mode of arrangement, operates at all levels of linguistic systems, contributing to distinctive features, phonemes, morphemes, and syntactic and semantic units. Knowing the relevant linguistic system enables one to pick out resemblances between two or more linguistic units in some system-defined way: similarities of phonological shape may signal similarity in grammatical distinctions, as when similar endings of nouns signal co-membership in noun classes. More broadly, any two forms are similar when/if they can be substituted for each other. The principle of selection (paradigms) implies degrees of similarity/iconism and thus substitutability connects terms in absentia.

In contrast to this system-internal view, there are iconic relations that link instances of the code and the world. Western scholarship focuses on how words and expressions represent the real-world objects for which they stand. But linguists have rightly rejected the idea that denotation depends on direct imitation (similarity) by linguistic forms of the objects they denote. Iconicity between word-as-sign and its denotatum as object – onomatopoeia – is rare and marginal in linguistic systems. When onomatopoeia does occur, the object's "sound" (animal, machine) is apprehended in terms of the specific phonological system in question. That system also shapes what is recognized as the sound's imitation by the human voice.

In contrast to onomatopoeia, another form of iconicity in the linguistic realm is best called pragmatic iconism and is of great interest for us. Forms identified *as* linguistic, and taken up by specifically linguistic knowledge, are further construed as similar to (sharing qualia with) nonlinguistic phenomena, although the linguistic forms do not denote those phenomena. Different sensory modes are often connected in this way. Vowel quality may be understood as "light" or "dark," for instance, even if those descriptors are more usually applied to sight phenomena, not sound. Across social groups, speech features and linguistic practices have been likened to many nonlinguistic phenomena, although *not* denoting them. The ethnographic record provides examples of speech types characterized by speakers (or outsiders) as conventionally "oily," "sweet," "upside down," "hard," "soft," or "harsh" (Gal 2013). A major goal of Chapter 4 is to conceptualize how ideological work creates these kinds of iconicities in speech.

Contiguity in Linguistic Materials

How is *indexicality* evident in the realm of linguistic signs? For almost a century, this question has inspired much important research. As Jakobson noted, the second "mode of arrangement" of linguistic signs is *combination* – which he also called contiguity. Contiguity is as ubiquitous in linguistic organization as similarity/iconicity. Combination connects linguistic units with other linguistic units and thereby creates a context for both:

[A]ny linguistic unit at one and the same time serves as a context for simpler units and/ or finds its own context in a more complex linguistic unit ... : combination and contexture are two faces of the same operation. (Jakobson 1990 [1956]:119)

With larger and larger linguistic units, context comes to include the situation or event in which speech occurs. For this reason, Jakobson argued that there are always (at least) two kinds of knowledge (conjectures) necessary to interpret linguistic signs, one that refers to the code and the other to a situational context (1990 [1956]:120). Whatever an utterance signals, *qua* token of linguistic form, it is at the same time a token in indexical relation (contiguity) with the other linguistic forms that co-occur as its "co-text." And, for conjectures taking it up, it is simultaneously also indexing (as a pointing sign) aspects of the nonlinguistic circumstances of its occurrence as a sociohistorically located signal, much like any other indexical sign we have discussed. This would be its more broadly construed "context."

But "context" does not preexist semiosis. On the contrary, indexicality constructs context. Silverstein has theorized it this way:

Any indexical signal form, in occurring (a contingent, real-time, historical happening with possible causal consequentiality), hovers between two contractible relationships to its "contextual" surround: the signal form as occurring either PRESUPPOSES (hence indexes) something about its context-of-occurrence, or ENTAILS ["CREATES"] (and hence indexes) something about its context-of-occurrence, these [are] *co-present* dimensions of indexicality. (1993:36, emphases original; see also Silverstein 1976)

The presupposing moment of indexicality is one conjecture ("What, in its surround, does this phenomenon stand for, if taken as a sign?"); and the entailing moment is another ("This phenomenon is hereby taken to stand for X in its surround"). But, as we have emphasized, the world of potential contiguities is vast; a focus of attention is necessary in order to pick out something as a sign and to conjecture what it likely stands for. Silverstein proposes a typifying level that "regiments" how the surround is to be chunked into types of events, activities, and the genres and person types that go along with them. Since the relation of signs to their surround is known in linguistics as "pragmatics," he dubs the typifying level *meta*pragmatics, the realm of metapragmatic categories that are embedded in what he earlier dubbed linguistic ideologies (Silverstein 1979). Metapragmatic regimentation typifies linguistic "indexicals into interpretable event(s) of such-and-such type that the use of language in interaction constitutes (consists of)" (Silverstein 1993:37). Many examples of naming we earlier discussed are metapragmatic terms typifying events – for example, lecture, chat, rant, prayer. But event types are also signaled through (genred) poetics (metrics, conventional parallelisms).

Silverstein's abstract proposal suggests that specific cultural knowledge (motivated by ideological presumptions) fills in the relevant categories ("such-and-such"), providing the types (of event, persona, interactional move) instantiated and recognized by a social group. In our terms, these also provide the ingredients for perspectives that social actors adopt and enact. So, linguistic utterances in interactions are at once "symbolic" in the narrow Peircean sense (tokens of code). In this aspect they are what Silverstein calls "denotational text," conveying propositions about the world. Simultaneously, utterances are also always tokens of interactional moves that speakers adopt, and thus are "interactional text." When examined as interactional text, utterances operate like the other conventional indexical signs we have discussed. They instantiate perspectives and events. Interactional indexicality, organized by metapragmatic typification, is not independent of linguistic structure but reverberates throughout it. There is no line between "linguistic" and "extra-linguistic" phenomena; no *fixed* separation between linguistic form and "context."

As in earlier examples, linguistic utterances participate in chains of abduction. Consider again the thought experiment about liquids. We extended Goodman's scene by imagining other scenes of choice among liquids: ordinary kitchen, party, eye exam. A name for the event, plus (propositional) discussion of the event, its participants and procedures, would all be metapragmatic discourse, characterizing various phenomena as signs, organizing them into the culturally recognizable personae, timing, and expressive forms so named. Further, like any instance of propositional talk (denotational text), metapragmatic discourse about an event occurs within particular social interactions. It therefore has its own uptakes, its own interactional text, including the conjectures with which it is interpreted. Registers of linguistic materials index typified events and participants, relying often on shibboleths. If the label used to characterize the party were "ceremonial," for instance, or for the eye exam "opthalmological," this would indexically project the speaker as one kind of persona (educated, adult, teacher) rather than another (small child). Discussion of the ongoing event by its organizers could be taken as self-congratulation and contested by those who disapprove of it. As in our simplest examples – the morning walk – construals of linguistic signs interpret denotational text as moves or stances in social exchange (interactional text), and conventionalized conjectures about them – perspectives – become further signs and objects of interactional text, swept up in social encounters and in threads of cultural knowledge.

Conjectures Change the "Ground" of Signs: Indexes into Icons

Knowledge is also involved in the construal of the difference between iconic and indexical signs, whether these are linguistic signs or signs of any other kind. We have already mentioned that in Peircean semiotics indexes *incorporate* icons, and we have given several examples of this even for very simple cases: weather vanes involve both. It is also clear from our several illustrations of abduction chains – the sequences of conjectures in the early morning walk, as well as in extensions of Goodman's scenarios – that conjectures about indexical sign relations build on iconic ones and further indexical and iconic relations also follow on each other, so that there is always an intertwining of the two kinds of sign relations.

In addition, sometimes a conjecture can *change* the relation (the "ground") that is hypothesized to exist between a sign and the semiotic object it stands for. Increases of knowledge about signs and objects and differences in frameworks of knowledge with which signs are identified can change conjectures about the grounds of sign-object relationships. Some background knowledge is always required for noticing and conjecturing. With changes in ideological work, a sign relation can be rethought, from iconic to indexical, or from indexical to iconic. This has the important implication that people with different kinds of presumptions will make different conjectures about the way signs represent objects.

Peirce's example of this is a yardstick. Yardsticks are signs that are instantiations of the type category of a yard, which is a standard of measurement. Everyday yardsticks seem to work by their similarity to that standard. But for those who know the history of yardsticks, that is not their secret. On the contrary:

[T]he very purpose of the yardstick is to show a yard nearer than it can be estimated by its appearance [i.e., by resemblance]. This it does in consequence of an accurate mechanical comparison made with the bar in London called the Yard, either the yardstick used or some one from which it was copied having been transported from the Westminster Palace. Thus it is a real [indexical] connection which gives the yardstick its value as a representamen [sign]. And thus it is an *index*, not a mere *icon*. (Peirce 1998 [1895]:14)

Those who know the history of yardsticks can recognize them as indexically linked – by actual physical chains of contiguity – to the standard-setting yardstick. Those who do not know this presume that similarity is the key. In our thought experiments too, additional knowledge could have changed conjectures. If an observer had seen Goodman's two colorless liquids poured from a single pitcher, contiguous with each other just moments before, then the judgment of similarity would have been changed, making them intimately and indexically related as well (whether acid or water). Sign relations thought to be iconic may be rethought as (also) indexical, when the conjecturer gains more knowledge. When the direction of change is from index to icon, Parmentier (1994:18) called it downshifting. The change can also go in the other direction. Peirce used the term "rheme" to refer to signs that could be conjectured as iconic by some guesses, yet taken by other guesses to be indexical, depending on the presumptions and knowledge of those who make the guesses. We will return in Chapter 4 to the term "rheme" in order to present a more complex form of reasoning with signs – what we call rhematization – that involves a shift in not only the "ground" of the sign-relation but comparison as well.

The difference between taking a yardstick to be an icon or taking it to be an index seems trivial. It does not have big implications for the yardstick's place in social life. But the contrast between similarity/depiction on the one hand and contiguity/co-occurrence on the other is deeply consequential in social relations. The difference allows quite different attributions of causality and different lines of explanation for why people, places, times, and things are the way they are, how they could be different and how they are or might be transformed. The changing of sign-relations from indexical to iconic, explicated in later chapters, is one of the most important aspects of ideological work.

Erasure in Sign Relations

In each semiotic step we have examined so far, the process of erasure has been evident. It has appeared in several forms, even in the most basic act of constituting a sign. In noticing a phenomenon as a potential sign, erasure allows selective attention, ignoring the surround, thereby separating figure and background. In picking out the qualia that might be relevant to a judgment of similarity or the co-occurrence posited in construing an indexical relation, whole worlds had to be elided and ignored. Vast possibilities of similarities and contiguities are eliminated in the making of any sign relation. They are eliminated by ideological work, in which erasure is a key element. Significantly, typification too requires erasure of all the possible alternative tokens and qualia that may instantiate a type in favor of what ideologizing highlights and what is key for the particular moment.

Perhaps most consequential is the systematic forgetting – erasure – of the metasemiotic step by which conjecture itself creates the link between sign and object. And similarly, the erasure of the conjecture's role in constructing and construing iconic as opposed to indexical links between sign and semiotic object. Repeatedly in our examples, once something was identified as a sign, its semiotic object posited, and the sign-object relationship created, that relationship came to seem like a feature of the world, not a consequence of conjecture – unless and until it was challenged and revised by another hypothesis that revealed the constructed nature of the sign-object relation. In chapters to come, we track how erasure becomes more complicated, more socially embedded, institutionalized, and socially consequential as an element of the semiotic process.

On the Road: An Illustration

Thought experiments are useful for explicating semiosis, but empirical materials are more convincing. The following brief text illustrates the interdependence of the tasks of conjecture that we pulled apart for analysis in this chapter. The scene is from the first travelogue by Anne Newport Royall, the nineteenth-century American writer. We will follow her work more closely in the next chapter. Here, we track various perspectives her narrative takes up in the moment-by-moment process of describing interaction in a scene. The scene also gives a sense of the sociohistorical embeddedness of semiosis, and its quality of always being in medias res.

Published in 1826, the book gave American readers what they craved: description and detail about their relatively new country. She was one of hundreds of people writing travel books in which the poetics of adventure was of key importance. This required a realist mode and a distinctive, individual narrative voice to comment on encounters and surroundings. Born into modest circumstances in Baltimore in 1769, Royall was raised in western Pennsylvania where her mother taught her to read. She married a wealthy planter when her family moved to western Virginia and she joined him in his large house whose library provided opportunities for self-education. When inheritance battles following her husband's death left her penniless, she reinvented herself as an author, selling her books on subscription as she traveled. This was one of the few respectable occupations at the time for educated women in financial straits. At first she traveled with her own carriage, visiting acquaintances; later and with less money, she took stagecoaches and stayed in taverns. Eventually settling in Washington, DC, she became controversial as a sharp-tongued commentator on national politics. Opinionated and colorful, she was curious, observant, and interested in language. Her books contain chatty vignettes of social life, geography, history, and local gossip, written in the first person and meant to sell.

As in any first-person narrative, the references to "I" and "me" are always multiple: "I" is the real-time writer as well as the represented narrator; "I" is also the traveling woman, the "figure" in the story, who is occasionally distinct from the narrator telling about the traveler's experience. The text's past tense places the action as shortly before the act of telling, almost contemporaneous with the events described. But we know that it took many years between the trip Royall took – itself many months long – and the publication of her book. The writing could have happened in many places; it surely involved corrections and revisions. The publishing process was problematic because Royall did not yet have a writer's reputation. Further time elapsed between the initial publication and distribution of the book (as text artifact) and its acquisition, perhaps in the 1890s by the Chicago library that holds our copy, and finally our reading of it more than a century later. These multiple Bakhtinian chronotopes are laminated yet analytically distinct.

In the context of the book's genre, the trivial little scene that is our focus probably worked as evidence of the author's vicissitudes and hence the reality of her adventure, much as, in one ideology of realism, insignificant "found objects" from a faraway place prove that one has been there. The brief text shows how the narrator reasons about and apprehends unfamiliar surroundings. Each conjecture is embedded in preexisting knowledge and in the various perspectives – drawn from her life experience – that the writer mobilizes to focus on objects of attention.

In this scene, the narrator notes that she (as traveler) is in the midst of a long stagecoach journey and has promised to write and post a letter to an acquaintance. Conveniently, the little town where the coach stops for the night has a post office and inn:

One tavern only in the place, and every room engaged ... all but one, which no one would have, as it was immediately over the bar room, and which necessity compelled me to accept. (1826:33)

The narrator/traveler knows that the room over the bar has a flaw, and presumes the reader would know this as well. (Perhaps in the 1820s everyone did know this.) But it is not named till the next few sentences, in which the narrator reports on the traveler's further experience in the guest room:

> Several men were assembled in the room beneath me. They were talking, singing, laughing, drinking and swearing, all at the same instant of time. Being compelled to write, I ... sat with the pen in my hand ... waiting for some fortunate intermission in the noise below, or that they would finally close and disperse to their respective homes – all in vain. (1826:33)

Here, the room's fault is named as "noise" – a shared quale that links barroom and upstairs room iconically. Another conjecture reconfigures this experience: the sign is not simply "noise" and the objects are not rooms. The sign is sounds of human activity: "talking, singing, laughing, drinking." The reconstrued semiotic object is the activities of "several men," and the sounds are an indexical sign pointing to the men (contiguous and posited to be caused by them). The men surely differ from each other in many ways (in height, background, hometown) that would make them similar to men *not* in the bar. But this is ignored, as the narrator/traveler's developing perception of "several men" links them iconically to each other, by virtue of the sounds made by "all at the same instant of time," all from "below," so that she can refer to them together as a unit, as "they."

The labels "noise" and "men" and the various activities "talking, singing, laughing" are tokens of linguistic labels, instantiating the names of cultural categories. The particular noises they name are themselves tokens of typified indexical signs within the narrated scene. The naming erases aspects of the sounds that may not have fit. Let us pause to note that the narrator/traveler's conjectures could be wrong about the signs and the objects posited, as also about the way they are typified. Perhaps the sounds are singular and not produced by men at all, or are coming from a stagecoach on the street. Such fanciful alternatives are useful to highlight the traveler's active construal and how it relies on conjecture, inference, and attribution.

In the next few sentences the traveler is depicted as picking out, on the basis of further conventionalized experience, increasingly specified, typified indexical signs:

> As I could hear most of what was said and sung, it came into my head, (since I could do no better,) to take down the conversation as it struck my ear, in short hand, and see what budget of nonsense it would display on paper. The reader has, no doubt, seen the conversation of a club, written by Goldsmith. This was not half so entertaining, but it was equally absurd. (1826:33–34)

Here, the indexical relation picked out by the narrator/traveler's construal is not between sounds representing men but "what was said and sung" as signs whose object is "conversation." Note the conventionality invoked: this conjecture ignores (erases) the possibility that the men are singing to themselves, or separately producing vocal displays.

Following the segment quoted here, the book's text presents a set of sentence fragments, in quotation marks, representing snippets of conversation, as the narrator/traveler posits social identities for the supposed speakers. They are "shoemakers, the drunkards, spellers [arguing about orthography]," their identities inferred on the basis of the style and content of their talk. Culturally recognizable speech types index types of speakers: this is a small case of the traveler/narrator's sociolinguistic theorizing.

The conjectures evident in these thirteen lines of text index various typical perspectives, all in a single setting. Alone in her room as an unratified and irritated overhearer of the barroom, the traveler's perspective is presented through the sign ("noise") she notices. Subsequent conjectures enact a writer-persona recognizing "material" for (possibly) witty narration. The physical fact of having "pen in hand," and the biographical fact of knowing "short hand," suggest this perspective. So do the sociolinguistic observations about overheard speakers. The literary parallel – "the conversation ... written by Goldsmith" – alludes to his play, *She Stoops to Conquer*, still popular in the 1820s. Mention of this prestigious literary work indexes the perspective of a cultivated person. Directly addressing the reader and assuming the reader's familiarity with the play, the writer-narrator – not the traveler – aligns (iconically) with the reader, flattering those who hold the book by projecting for them a similarly cultivated persona.

Conclusion

Sign relations are worth studying because they undergird ideologies, showing how the ideologies are thereby organized. This chapter demonstrated how perspectives – a key ingredient of ideologies – are built up out of simple sign relations. However solid and separate from human action the sociohistorical world seems, it is constructed out of semiotic processes that we ourselves create. There are no originary units in semiosis: signs are the results of relationships, of cognitive acts and chains of conjecturing. Conjectures are meta-semiotic (reflexive) moves that constitute sign-object relations. They are the key to the *processual* and – in principle – always reinterpretable and unfinalizable characteristics of semiosis. As the terms "conjecture" and "hypothesis" suggest, knowledge and communication are two sides of a single process. Put differently, interaction and encounter are the crucibles in which knowledge of the world – simultaneously with the relations of social life – are made, unmade, and remade.

At the same time, while the constructed perspectives on social life are contingent and transformable, they are also necessarily typified and conventionalized. They are made into recognizable and often long-lasting conceptualizations of events, persons, times, and places (chronotopes), and linked to social positions. Typification draws on discourses about stereotypes, once again a moment of knowledge. Yet communication is also implied in typification, for conventional knowledge (stereotypes) is instantiated in the tokens and qualia displayed in real-time interaction. Conventional, stereotyped conjectures, linked to roles and personae, constitute perspectives for social actors. Biographically specific people take up and inhabit perspectives, based on their access to knowledge, itself reliant on their experiences and social positions. Yet even in a single encounter, people enact multiple perspectives as they momentarily take up the perspectives of others in utterances, switching roles and creating alignments. Indeed, it is through the type/token relation that the iconicities of alignment are made possible.

The thought experiments in this chapter were deliberately chosen as abstract, stripped-down illustrations, with only enough information to make the logic of semiosis clear. The metaphors were chosen with a similar aim: Just as cell processes are nourished by the organisms they constitute, so sign-relations undergird but also rely on discursive forms. Just as armatures and tartan patterns are made by people, as they constitute sculpture and cloth, so sign relations are human-made and embedded in cultural presuppositions. Just as the weave of a cloth is without necessary boundaries, so semiosis is also open-ended. We argued that the ideologized knowledge that constitutes conjectures may also alter how sign and object are understood to be linked to each other. Iconic and indexical sign relations – similarities and contiguities – are intertwined in several ways: as incorporations in each other, as sequential uptakes in chains of conjecture, and in transformations of index to icon and back.

Sign relations and semiotic processes will continue as a theme throughout the book. In Chapters 6 and 7 they help us define sites of ideological work. But first, in Chapters 4 and 5, we develop further how relations among signs and perspectives create *comparison* and constitute the full-blown phenomena of sociocultural and sociolinguistic differentiation.

4   Comparison: The Semiotics of Differentiation

†

Traveling in nineteenth-century America, Anne Royall was heading toward the Atlantic coast, crossing the Blue Ridge Mountains of the Appalachian range, when she saw the "East" as different:

... different in all respects from what [it] is west of the Blue Ridge [Mts.]. ... No rich land, no bold rivers, no lusty timber, every thing *dwindles to nothing*. The people are *small*, the cattle are *small*. ... The most prominent traits of distinction in the personal appearance of the people of [the] East are their *diminutive size, ignorance, assurance ... effrontery*. Persons of the same class ... in the western country, form a direct contrast to these [in the East] in all respects. They [in the West] are **stout, able-bodied** men, **modest** and **unassuming** in their behavior. (1826:94, emphasis added)

Is this an accurate description? No matter. We are interested in what Royall's descriptions reveal about her ways of seeing the world. How is this particular view organized? What role do her highlighted word choices play? What logics are evident in the description? The brief text goes beyond the simplest ingredients of ideological work. It relies on *comparison*, which is a more complex way of reasoning with signs. Comparison is a step in ideologies of differentiation. This chapter characterizes comparison in abstract terms, specifying how it works as semiotic process.

Some comparison is already involved in guessing that a phenomenon is a sign, since it must be compared to what is *not* a sign. Picking out a semiotic "object" is also a comparison against what the sign does *not* represent. As we argued in the last chapter, rather than observing a link between a sign and object, a conjecture posits both and *makes* the connection that it seems merely to notice. This performative logic never operates in a vacuum. What are the existing understandings – of and in the world – on which a particular case of conjecturing depends? *How* does semiosis constitute the ideologies on which it draws? Frameworks of preexisting knowledge orient attention, defining what can constitute possible *signs* that deserve or demand comparison and the field(s) of semiotic *objects* worth distinguishing. They also provide ontological, cosmological and political warrants for taking some phenomena as signs. These frameworks may become matters of dispute, precipitating cascades of comparison, provoked by or inciting social transformations.

We argue that while all forms of differentiation operate by the same semiotic principles, they are embedded in different frameworks and in different political economies. In this chapter we explicate the process of comparison – a moment in differentiation – with examples that speakers experienced and explained as *spatial* or geographical contrasts. Whole chronotopes – matters of personhood, time, and events – were also implicated. But in Anne Royall's travel writings, the emphasis is on spatial imaginings. In her era, travel narratives were a specially appealing genre in the United States. The mobile and literate population was eager to know more about its new and quickly expanding country. Writers drew on visions of geography and society that were specific to their time. We explore their semiotic logic.

Spatial ideologies of social and linguistic variation are familiar around the world. In the past, linguistics and anthropology used concepts like "dialect," "region," and "boundary" to explain the spatial distributions of speech and cultural features, and we return to the views of scholars in Chapter 9. Here we aim to rethink these approaches. By analyzing historical materials, we also deal with ideologies of written representation. However, this is not a full-dress historical ethnography. Rather, the examples are meant to illustrate our abstract descriptions of semiotic process.

Ideological Frameworks: Signs and Geographies

Since any perceivable phenomenon is potentially a sign, communication requires some constraint on what *sorts* of phenomena participants should notice as signs and how to guess what to make of them. What are they signs of? Well-established presuppositions (forms of knowledge) direct attention to particular aspects of the world and justify that attention by connecting signs to theories and values. For analysts of differentiation, therefore, presuppositions and their frameworks are good places to start.

What did Anne Royall attend to, in her travels? To find out, we read closely her published letters and earliest travelogue – 1818/1830, 1826 – treating her books as one would an interlocutor in ethnographic research. At the time of these writings she was a widow in her early fifties, recounting many months of journey from her home in western Virginia to Alabama and from there to Boston. En route, she took the following *kinds of* things to be signs: features of landscape, climate, settlement pattern, agriculture, and human features: body size, weight, skin coloring, dress, voice, pronunciation, lexicon, and comportment. What she made of these signs depended on what she called commonsense knowledge. Her social position also gave her access to certain philosophical and political theories, which themselves formulated regimes of value in her time and place.

According to one of those theories, expressive forms reveal what kinds of people the speakers "really" are. Taking this seriously, Royall was participating in the "elocutionary revolution" of the late eighteenth century. Following British models, Americans embarked on a "new, affective understanding of the operations of language, one that reconceives all expression as self-expression" (Fliegelman 1993:2). Earlier, there were rules for speaking in accord with the speaker's social position and the event type. According to the newer ideas, the way one spoke reflected an inner self. Persuasive speech should work not by argument but by giving sincere signs of internal emotions. Royall extended this to other kinds of signs:

I have always fancied that the bonnet or hat took the tone of the wearer, and gave some indication of the predominant disposition or quality of the mind: I have thought I could perceive cunning, pride, prodigality, wisdom, folly, taste and refinement by the turn of the bonnet or the hat, and have been displeased with my friends when they put on a new one which made them appear not themselves. (1826:103)

The connection between overt sign and self was a question of "manner." Royall used this metapragmatic term for what we would call comportment. Similarly, an American elocutionist wrote in 1764 that meaning depends not upon the words spoken but on "'the *manner*' ... of speaking them" (cited in Fliegelman 1993:30, emphasis original). Manner was a performance, a "spectacle of sincerity" (Fliegelman 1993:2). There is a note of distrust in Royall's comment about hats. And no wonder: the theory's logic suggests the possibility of speakers' duplicity or pretense. It suggests a lack of reliability in sign-object relations that haunted the heirs of the elocutionary revolution (Gustafson 2012).

When these ideas became current, Royall was stepping into a social position that was new to her. The child of Scots-Irish immigrants, she married a rich and prominent planter in western Virginia whose library, well stocked with European and American works, she eagerly consumed. As in her allusion to Goldsmith in the passage we analyzed in the previous chapter, her writings often signal her range of reading. For instance, when explicating an interest in facial gestures, she notes, "That inimitable writer, Voltaire, observes, 'that to convey a just idea of the characteristics of men, you must strictly observe the expressions which accompany their actions'" (1969 [1830]:197). Other Europeans – Walter Scott, Lady Morgan, Alexander Pope, Lycurgus – were her heroes of high culture. Their names were signs of the well-mannered world in which she located herself for the reader.

Royall was also interested in frameworks that focused on linguistic differences and education. She adopted the views of language reformers of her day like Noah Webster who argued for a distinctively American English that would separate the new country from Britain, while retaining a connection to it through the heritage of English literature. The reformers – though never in agreement – partook of wider European political debates, arguing that any self-respecting nation-state must have a single, uniform language. In the late eighteenth century and into the nineteenth they campaigned for geographic homogeneity of speech and writing in the United States. They wanted to inculcate a standard of "correctness" in pronunciation and writing through school spellers, grammars, and dictionaries.[1]

Allegiance to the reformers' framework is evident in Royall's writing practices. To convey the impression of sound in quoted speech, she relied on the reader's expectation that printed matter would follow schoolbook conventions. Unusual spellings signal what sounded to her like unusual pronunciations. She labeled these "dialect." Such spelling, then called "cacophony" (Looby 1996:256–265), is now called "eye dialect." If school spelling was the "correct, right" form, so was the pronunciation it was presumed to represent, in contrast to what was unusual and therefore, in this framework, taken to be mistaken. Differences in orthography (as iconic stand-in for pronunciation) and differences in manner suggested differences in the inner selves of speakers – their "dispositions" and "quality of mind," as Royall put it. What distinctions were assumed to exist among different kinds of inner selves? What theories of inner selves oriented a search for the semiotic objects of interest to Royall, namely differences in manner, dialect, and accent?

One salient answer, for Royall and her contemporaries, was geopolitics: social locations defined by geopolitical institutions and formulated as conventional personae. Only those deemed to be Americans were said to speak "dialects" and display differences of "manner." Foreigners had "accents." The difference between Americans and foreigners seems a political one, but colonial settlers saw it in geographical, spatialized terms. For spatial imaginaries the Revolution was a watershed. Those siding with independence and therefore deemed "American" rejected colonial peripherality in relation to Britain. Instead, they advocated stronger connections among the former colonies. Yet the colonies were suspicious of each other. An ideal they could agree on, however, was equality between *places*. Many political struggles within the newly established country were attempts to prevent the formation of any seat of power as a spatial center replicating London (Onuf 1996:14–15).

England and France remained important, however, as eastern sources of cultural value. Books, consumer luxuries and fashions, as well as notions of personal refinement came from Europe. Manners and ideals of civilization – like the elocutionary revolution – were understood to radiate from the elite of England and France to America's coastal cities and from there to the western countryside. The rural and western, in this view, were rude and rough, lacking in refinements and amenities, temporally lagging: not *yet* civilized. Thomas

Jefferson, though a planter himself, nevertheless invoked this progress narrative when he placed "man's most improved state in our seaports and towns" (cited in Smith 1960:219). It was widely assumed that the agricultural settlements in the near-west were less developed than the coast; and that the backwoods of the frontier west, on the fringes of white settlement, were even less so. The colonial mode of emulating practices that came from further east, from Europe, was in tension with the insistence in the United States on the value of political and cultural independence.

Royall was passionately American, and certainly felt these tensions: She admired European high culture, yet honored her husband's activities as a Revolutionary War officer. Later, she requested that "The Union Forever" be inscribed on her tombstone. Born in 1769, in an era of Enlightenment secularism and women's active participation in politics, she refused to retreat to the private sphere and to women's moral campaigns when the ideology of "separate spheres" became dominant in the nineteenth century. Her public engagement with men's domain of electoral politics made her a controversial figure. For many of her eighty-five years she was an outspoken critic of national politics, editing and publishing a Washington, DC, newspaper in which she took politicians to task for corruption and criticized the increasing influence of evangelical religion.[2] The people she met on her early travels, who were religiously diverse and came from many parts of Europe and South America, constituted foreigners for her, although they might well have been immigrants planning to stay. She often admired their fluency in English, but did not compare them to Americans.

Although post-Revolutionary national consciousness located the United States in contrast to European countries, after independence Americans focused on spatial differences *within* the country, juxtaposing US regions to each other as parts of an envisioned whole. Europe versus the colonies was imagined geographically as East versus West. This contrast was projected onto the eastern and western United States. Compass points – East, West – were seen not as directions of travel but as *territorial units* with *culturally* significant characteristics. A united government – and its institutional forums – provided the venues in which American culture, economy, and landscape could be formulated as contrasting with foreign countries on the one hand, and on the other hand as features of regions envisioned as different from each other in intra-American political struggles (Ayers and Onuf 1996:8; Onuf 1996:11–27).

It is ironic that, while Americans wanted to distance themselves from Europe, their leading frameworks for understanding social differences – geography and correctness – were dominant European theories in which landscape, climate, and spatial settlement supposedly explained human differences. But there were many ways to slice up the spaces of the United States.

People were classified as "New Englanders," "Southrons," "Philadelphians," "natives of the Great Western Valley," or as "Tuckahoes," "Cohees," "Yorkers," "Yankees"; as "Kentuckians" or "Virginians"; but also as "well-bred" and "low-bred." The borders of all these units were continuously disputed and revised but also policed. Settlement itself changed ecologies and landscapes. Social mobility was as ubiquitous as geographical mobility. In the early decades of the nineteenth century, there were vast migrations and frequent travel. Hardly anyone, not even slaves, stayed in place for long. Yet, Americans adopted a British theory of stable dialect regions. Indeed, in the face of all this movement, the reigning commonsense view that variation in speech and communicative styles was *caused by* location seems to us a striking achievement of American language ideologies.

Stepping back from specifics, we see *several* frameworks that organized selective attention to communicative signs and the fields of semiotic "objects" that they signaled. Some we would now call psychological theories (true inner selves, personal refinement), others were epistemological (gauging dispositions), or moral and status hierarchies ("right" and "wrong" ways to talk, relative progress), and political economic projects (colonial relations, nationhood). How were such frameworks organized by semiotic principles?

Axes of Differentiation: Qualia and Schemas

The segment of Anne Royall's travelogue about "East" and "West" that we quoted is a good example of how frameworks were put to work. It draws on geopolitical theory and – as we shall see – also implicates theories of selves and dispositions. It is a detailed comparison, creating both difference and similarity. Any comparison recognizes some qualities shared by the phenomena being compared (in this case land, rivers, timber, people) and some qualities that differentiate them (big/small, rich/thin). The semiotic analysis of this process of differentiation (amid posited similarity) consists of two steps.

First, the attention to shared qualities creates similarity, which is an iconic relation. In the simplest iconic signs, a conjecture posits the same qualities in two phenomena, rendering them similar. Our thought experiment about wet pavement and wet grass – where two instances of wetness were taken to be signs of each other – was an example. To understand the semiotics of contrast in Royall's description, however, we must turn to a more complicated iconic sign relation, the *diagrammatic icon.* In Peirce's terms, diagrammatic icons "represent the relations, mainly dyadic, or regarded as such, of the parts of one thing by analogous relations in their own parts" (1955a:105). Like all icons, diagrammatic icons signal similarity. Unlike simple icons, however, they do not match their objects via shared sensual qualities. Rather, a conjecture seeks to construe a formal similarity between sign and object. Diagrammatic icons display, in their own configuration, some aspect of a relationship that can be projected onto the objects they are conjectured to represent.

In abstract terms, diagrammatic icons are analogies (a:b :: x:y), inviting the hypothesis that whatever relationship is conjectured to exist between a and b (as posited signs) should be sought, imagined, or projected between x and y (as the signs' semiotic objects). This is a very fertile semiotic device, able to represent many kinds of relationships and to inspire novel understandings.[3] The specific formal relationship of interest for our purposes is qualitative contrast. Two qualities, ideologically construed as standing in co-constitutive contrast, provide an example of a simple diagrammatical icon. This semiotic configuration undergirds what we call an *axis of differentiation*. Contrasting, complementary qualities – formulated as defining each other in some socio-historical imaginary – constitute an axis. Axes usually consist of large clusters of paired, contrasting qualities that make two contrasting multidimensional *images*. Since the qualities of these contrasting pairs are complementary, one "side" of the contrast is ideologically defined as what the other is not. The images constructed out of such clusters are stereotypes: forms of knowledge within an ideological framework. Any axis of differentiation is a totalizing *schema*. When invoked it divides a whole world of phenomena into qualitatively contrasting *images* or "sides."

The second step in the semiotics of comparison hinges on typification. An axis of differentiation is not itself a specific occurrence. It is a pre-supposed template – a type-level phenomenon in terms of which people construe actions and other phenomena. The qualities distinguished and contrasted in axes are abstract ones. They become experienceable when enacted or projected in real time. It takes interpretive work, situated in interaction, to invoke (index) a schema/axis and to interpret real-time phenomena as instantiations or embodiments of the qualities that are part of that axis. We use the term "quality" to name the abstract categories of the schema. By contrast, their embodiments as signs are "qualia" (qualisigns). The terminological distinction calls attention to the fact that qualia are not self-evident. The phenomena of experience are not inherently of some quality. Rather, as Chumley and Harkness (2013) emphasize, *attributed qualities* projected or presumed to be "found" in phenomena can act as signs. Participants learn what "counts" as an instantiation of a quality and its co-constitutive contrast via experience. They must learn what aspects of linguistic form and nonlinguistic features are likely to show the relevant qualia; they also learn how a particular quality – softness, loudness, sharpness – is recognizable in various media and modalities, in linguistic and nonlinguistic sounds, or in clothing or food.[4]

Recall that perspectives are clusters of conjectures (uptakes) that connect sign and object. A further conjecture – a reflexive, metasemiotic step in a chain of abduction – compares and contrasts perspectives as well, by locating them on one or the other side of an axis of differentiation. Axes are extendable and productive in two senses: First, novel phenomena never experienced before may be taken up and interpreted through an axis. Second, new qualitative contrasts may be added to an axis, transforming it. Schemas (axes) shape experience, but some experiences may challenge schemas; other experiences may reinforce or change them.

East/West as an Axis

Like her contemporaries – as against today's travelers – Royall saw the direction of her journey from Alabama to Boston as a trip from *west* to *east*. In that era, this conceptualization was the major way of making and grasping regional differences. Since much that she saw was new to her, her descriptions illustrate how axes shape the interpretation of experience. Looking from atop an Appalachian peak toward the Atlantic coast, she wrote more than the few lines quoted earlier. Here is the fuller record of her first reaction to what she called the "East":

… different in all respects from what is west of the Blue Ridge. … The face of the country, the productions, the manner of cultivating, the appearance of the people, and the livestock, are no longer the same. No **rich** land, no **bold** rivers, no **lusty** timber, every thing dwindles to *nothing*. The people are *small*, the cattle are *small*, stock of all sorts are *hardly worthy the name*. … [N]o more hills and dales, no more **luxuriant** meadows … the sameness is now and then relieved by the seat of some demi-lord. The land is *thin*. … The most prominent traits of distinction in the personal appearance of the people of [the] East are their *diminutive size, ignorance, assurance … effrontery*. Persons of the same class … in the western country, form a direct contrast to these [in the East] in all respects. They [in the West] are **stout, able-bodied** men, **modest** and **unassuming** in their behavior. The distinguishing trait of countenance in one [East] is *impudence*; that of the other [West] **modesty**. The same disparity is visible in their minds. … [T]he western people speak very **slow**, these [eastern people] speak *quick*; the first **say little**, the latter a *great deal* … even **waggoners** of the western country are readily distinguishable from those others … by **giving us** the road, while the eastern waggoner shows no preference but *for himself*. (1826:94, emphasis added)

We have put in **bold** the terms the narrative uses for "western country" and *bold italics* for those of "eastern country." More than a rendering of what she sees, this is a snapshot of *how* she sees. It reveals what philosophers call the "description under which" she perceives her surroundings.

In the geographical framework Royall takes up, the complementary, co-constitutive qualities form an axis of differentiation, creating two images, one "western," the other "eastern." These include evaluative, ethical, and activity dimensions as well. The (potentially) noticeable qualities of landscape and people that do not fit this model are ignored – erased – to make a unified vision. Everything in the world can be swept into this schema, by characterizing its qualities as belonging to one or the other image of this axis.

Royall surely knew many aspects of this schema before her encounter with the territory east of the Blue Ridge. As a framework or discourse, it was widely available, in newspapers, philosophy books, novels, and everyday presumptions. With it, more and more instances could be included, and deemed the "same" contrast. This ordered and regularized the scene so that it invoked the schema. The terms that are taken to summarize the entire schema, to be the best characterization of it, are East/West. These also identify the framework, in this case geography, from which the contrasts are seen to arise. Such terms – which in other cases may be people types or other abstract categories – are those taken by participants to be the best exemplars or most "real" aspects of the schema. We call these *anchors*.

Big/small is the *master trope* that summarizes many of the more specific qualitative contrasts evident in Table 4.1. It is comparative, as are all the contrasting qualities. There can be no "big" without a "small." In ethnography, one would check out what – in the ethnographer's terms – the description casts as big versus small. Here we rely on the details of lexical choice to grasp the possible instantiations Royall imagined in various media: *luxuriant* meadows, *rich* land, *bold* rivers, *lusty* timber. Even people's body types (*stout vs. diminutive*) are drawn into the contrast, as is comportment ("manner"). Note the irony of pairing "demi" (small) with "lord" (big) to convey the pretensions of an eastern social type – the aristocrat – that only pretends to be great.

Other examples from Royall's work add more contrasts to this East/West axis: quickness versus slowness in speech; hardness versus softness of disposition, as

Table 4.1 An East/West axis in the nineteenth-century United States

Western	Eastern
big	small
rich, bold, lusty, luxuriant	thin, not worth the name, nothing
stout, able-bodied	small, diminutive size
unassuming, modesty	impudence, effrontery, assurance, ignorance
speak slow, say little	speak quick, talk a lot
gives to others	concerned only with self (takes)

in the remark: "Atlantic people [are the opposite of] western generosity, they ...
are as hard-hearted as the flinty rock" (1969 [1830]:271). Thus easterners as
people match the proverbial hard rockiness of eastern soil. States are divided into
"old" versus "new," according to the order of white settlement: the East is "old."
The text presumes a habit of hierarchy in the East, with its "lords" and under-
lings, its "impudence" and "effrontery." By contrast, her anecdotes note "a native
bold independence in the people" in the western country (1969[1830]:117).
Literary surveys of this historical period show that many authors drew on these
stereotyped images, depicting the agricultural land just west of the Blue Ridge as
"vast," "bounteous," and "teeming," the people "hardy, sturdy plowmen" (Smith
1960:124, 142), and "laconic yeomen" (Justus 2004:62).

Just as Royall's readers interpret her text as typifying and comparing eastern
and western vistas, so another and *simultaneous* uptake compares the text's
perspective to that of other texts. Royall's writing bristles with conjectures that
laud the West and qualities attributed to it, and disparage by comparison those
attributed to the East. The inference is that she aligns with the West and wrote
in the persona of a westerner. That is, perspectives too are distinguished as East
and West; axes of differentiation characterize the perspectives that define them.

Royall's characterization of big, stout, slow, and pleasantly sociable westerners confronted by small, quick-talking, selfish, impudent (i.e., contemptuous) easterners did not go uncontested. Other writers portrayed easterners and
westerners differently than she did, though one can see that the same behaviors
were being described yet differently evaluated. While she cast westerners as
"speak[ing] slow, say[ing] little," they were depicted by an eastern perspective as "tight-lipped, grudging in giving information to strangers" (Justus
2004:62), "like trees and rocks," that "don't ask too many questions" (Smith
1960:82, 84). In such texts, western yeomen were seen as independent, but
also as "over-hospitable," "undeferential"; "sociable" but also rude and rough,
in an uncivilized way. Some writers claimed that "western mothers encourage
their children to fight" (Smith 1960:216), making them *excessively* social, with
"belligerence and cranky independence" (Justus 2004:69).[5]

The strongest evidence for perspective in Royall's travelogue – and specifically for a western perspective – is the text's narrative organization. An
example is the depiction of her arrival in Baltimore, after the stagecoach ride
over the Blue Ridge. In her previous experiences, stagecoach travelers would
stay overnight at the same inn and dine together, as they waited to continue the
journey on subsequent days. But in this case:

From the time **we** got out of the stage to this day, **I** have never laid eyes on **my** fellow
travellers. What a difference! In the western country, **we** are not only more sociable
while travelling, but constitute one family during the route, at all times and places. From

the mutual dangers, the pleasantries, accidents, and privations, incident to travellers, an **attachment** takes place which is not dissolved, perhaps ever. But here in the east, they jump out of the stage, and each one sets out to his quarters with ***perfect indifference***, and even without taking leave. (1826:187, emphasis added)

While the earlier passage we quoted described a static scene, this one narrates a brief incident, and then uses habitual verb markers to typify actions that are contrasted.

East/West is invoked as anchor (see Table 4.2) by attributing the actions of "fellow travelers" to their location "in the east," and not – for example – to women versus men, or rich versus poor, which they also might have been. The first "we" indexes all the people in the narrated event, those riding the stagecoach along with the "I" figure. The second "we" indexes the stagecoach travelers who are coming from the West, or those "in the western country," if it is interpreted as internal to the story. But simultaneously, it may be taken as well to index the reader and writer in the storytelling event, inviting the reader's alignment with the narrator in judging the referenced object: "they." If the "I" as traveler and writer is located on the west side of the East/West axis, then "they" is the East and its people, whose behavior demands evaluation and explanation, relative to those of the implied reader, in the West.

Table 4.2 *The East/West axis in a nineteenth-century narrative*

In the western country	In the East
slow interaction (pleasantries)	fast interaction (no leave-taking)
stay together, constant	sets out to own quarter
one family, more sociable, attachment	perfect indifference

Thus, this segment of Royall's text displays a perspective: a set of typical conjectures. Simultaneously, it may be taken as a second order index of the persona enacted by that perspective (Silverstein 2003). Second-order process has been explored largely as indexicality. Yet indexicality alone does not reveal why the persona is interpretable as a western one. To do so, we turn to iconicity. We recognize another conjecture, one that places the persona on the axis of differentiation. Without such an axis, there would be no way to identify the qualitative *comparisons* that Royall's text proposed, and the side of the axis with which her narrator is aligned.

Rhematization

Considering all the comparisons of eastern and western phenomena that Royall's brief texts noted, it is striking that a single master trope could unify all their qualities. After all, landscape, animals, people's appearance, their dispositions, speech, and actions are ontologically distinct. Yet, for the narrator, all things assigned to one side of an axis resembled each other, while those on the other side were defined as opposite in quality and similar among themselves. What processes create these unlikely similarities?

These are not simple iconic relations but the results of enacting a schema, an axis of differentiation. Enactment or instantiation of such a schema occurs when real-time signs are understood to point to (index) the participants, objects, and practices of the scene or interaction in which they occur, while they are simultaneously taken to be icons of (resembling) the abstract relationships presumed in the schema. Let us see how the axis (schema) of differentiation (qualitative contrast) operates in a specific situation.

Royall's narrator, observing the "land" on the other side of the Blue Ridge, took it as a sign. As a simple indexical relation, the land could point to anything seen to be in contiguity with it: the whole countryside is one likely object. But the semiotic task Royall's narrator takes up is to identify how the observable world can be taken as similar to the schema: What observables can be compared to each other in such a way that they form qualitative contrasts? The first conjecture noticed land as indexical of the countryside; a second one seeks to compare two signs as similar (both instances of land) and also posits qualia that distinguish them. The specific contrast at stake is defined by the ethnographically relevant axis of differentiation and its master trope. The real-life lands are taken to contrast, while each is also taken as indexical of the countryside around it. In accordance with the schema, whatever one land qualitatively is, the other is not: thin land versus rich land. This is true of the signs (the lands) and by analogy (following the schema's diagrammatic iconicity) equally true of their objects (the countrysides). Thus, the contrast between sides simultaneously creates a similarity in qualia on any one side of the axis (the qualia of sign + object). On the western side of the axis the land is "rich" and by implication so is the country; on the other side the land is "thin," the countryside "dwindles to nothing." With more and more contrasts, the process makes entire contrasting images of each side.

A relation of indexicality (between two cases of land and countryside) has been transformed into a resemblance (iconism) between the sign (land) and its object (countryside) by being construed together as part of an axis, a schema of contrast. Sign-object relations seen in one conjecture as contiguity are seen via a further (meta-)conjecture as (also) resemblance. This is the process we call *rhematization*: the grounds of sign relations seem to be shifted, by a conjecture, from merely index to (also) icon. Signs that have been called indexical icons (or iconic indexes) are created in the process. Recall Peirce's yardstick: it was an icon for some guesses, but for conjectures that knew its history, it was an index. In our current example, a conjecture makes an indexical relation into an iconic one. In both cases, once a conjecture posits a sign-object relation, a further conjecture can transform its ground. In both cases, more information enables the shift. Peirce called a sign a "rheme" if it had been changed by a further conjecture from an index to an icon, hence our term: rhematization.

More is happening in rhematization, however, than a change in ground. This is not only a "downshifting" from index to the simpler iconic relation (Parmentier 1994:18). In rhematization, sign relations are apprehended not singly, but as part of a schema of contrast that is invoked (indexed) to characterize a scene. The second conjecture, moreover, changes signs and objects, not only their grounds. After rhematization, it is *not* (only) the land that is a sign of the East, but rather the *comparative* thinness of the eastern lands is construed as a qualisign distinguishing some lands from others. Similarly, it is not a river that is the sign but rather a river's *relative* boldness; and the meadow's relative luxuriance in contrast to some other meadow. Thus, rhematization is a creative moment. Royall's narrator, projecting an East/West axis, is actually also positing "East" and "West" as imagined entities in relation: The large and bountiful West is an ideological unit (creating a unity, erasing patches of infertility). It becomes perceivable as such only in comparison to what is projected, in contrast, as an agriculturally small, impoverished East.

People types and their characteristic manners are also ideological units, similarly defined in qualitative relation. Royall's narrator selected the axis and its qualities as a schema to characterize the landscape, but also to posit person types (eastern and western personae). Big, slow, sociable westerners were apprehended in *contrast with* small, fast, hurrying easterners. Only through comparative and selective attention are qualia of big/small stature, slow/fast speech, lingering/hurrying activity – characteristics of bodies, speech and actions – observable *as regional* characteristics. Only in this sense did Royall's conjectures "find" the instantiations of her schema. Erasures abound in efforts to achieve rhematization. Perceived qualities that do not fit the schema are ignored, denied, or eliminated.

The contrasting characterizations of manner mentioned in Royall's texts include what sociolinguists call registers. They include specific speech forms and typical expressive gestures. Enregisterment, building here on Silverstein's (2003) definition, is the metasemiotic step of assembling such register distinctions along some axis of differentiation and identifying them as indexing speaker types, for some population of language users. Enregisterment has been discussed mostly as an indexical process.[6] Yet, qualitative contrast is always necessary for the perception of speech and other expressive forms as registers. Rhematization enables speech forms to seem qualitatively similar to the stereotype of the speakers who use them. "Slowness in speech" is defined with reference to some idea of "fast," in scenes described or observed. Through rhematization the images of person types arrayed on one side of an axis are apprehended as sharing qualia with the expressive forms that index them, in contrast to the other side. In short, to be able to pick out a speech variety (register) at all, one needs knowledge of the relevant axis and its qualia-contrasts: axes are prerequisites of enregisterment. Contrasting qualia of speech may be projected onto person types, or the qualia of speakers may be seen as primary and projected onto speech. However, when registers seem to stand alone it is invariably because one side of the axis defining them – and the registers instantiating the oppositions – has been suppressed or denied by participants, or by scholarly observers.

Narratives of Rhematization

Once differences in appearance, manner, and speech are noted by an observer's conjecture, people invariably proceed to explain, motivate, and justify perceived differences by reasoning with the qualia they have themselves posited through rhematization. What is the logic of these explanations?[7]

In the first of Royall's narratives, qualia of speech and manner are generalized to actions, in building an axis of East/West. If "western people speak very slow" and easterners "speak quick" then this is made parallel to western waggoners "give[ing] us the road," while the eastern waggoner "shows no preference but for himself." Linking each pair on an East/West axis enables positing pervasive and contrasting "traits of countenance." These are attributed to constructed and opposed person categories. Easterners have "assurance, effrontery and impudence," westerners show "unassuming modesty." Where do these traits come from? To answer this question, the narrator posits internal causal entities with matching qualities: "The same disparity is visible in their minds." But how does slow speech match "big" as a master trope for the West? A story explains: Slow, limited talk is evidence of a big heart, a form of largesse that lets others speak. Fast, profuse talk restricts attention to self, signaling an ungenerous hence small heart. Qualia of unseen, posited organs match qualia that are seen: *big* hearted/minded people contrast with *small*-minded/hearted ones. A scene is made comprehensible in terms of geopolitics and a theory of (metaphoric) inner organs.

These brief narratives give unseen causes for difference. A second kind of narrative depicts some behavior as perplexing or problematic, inciting people to reason about it and to weigh alternative explanations. Narratives of this second kind draw on presumed frameworks to make inferences about alternative causes of the behavior or incident. Royall's reflections on arriving in Baltimore provide an example:

... [in the western country] an **attachment** takes place [among travelers] which is not dissolved, perhaps ever. But here in the east, they jump out of the stage, and each one sets out to his quarters with *perfect indifference*, and even without taking leave. This difference is no doubt owing to their superior numbers, to their journeys being shorter, and the numerous imposters, who are constantly on the wing seeking for prey and flying from one seaport to another. Admitting these causes, however, in their widest sense, I cannot reconcile [to] that ***unsociable deportment*** which wears such obvious marks of ***groundless suspicion***. (1826:187, emphasis added)

To explain the behavior of those classified as "easterners," the narrator posits an internal trait indexed by their behavior: social indifference. Through rhematization, the qualia of urban conditions match qualia of urban behavior: fast, indifferent. Searching for the cause of this indifference, the narrator alludes to urban population density. In the East more people are packed into a smaller space; they are forced into stranger sociality and thus exposed to the danger of imposters. Easterners and westerners differ because they are reacting to different conditions of life. This theory was widespread. A Cincinnati newspaper editor of the time opined that if you take people from the eastern states and settle them in the West, any one of them would soon become "a different man: his national character will burst the chains of local habit" (Hall 1828:245). In this view, environments determine character traits.

But Royall's narrator is not satisfied with this explanation. An alternative step in reasoning connects the trait, now called "unsociable deportment," not to environment but to an unseen force – "groundless suspicion" – posited to exist inside easterners. This too echoes the comparative qualia of the regional social types. No longer mainly geopolitics, this hypothesis draws on theories of the elocutionary revolution, in which outward signs display but also hide inner selves. Notice that qualia of speech and demeanor may be projected onto person types and, vice versa, qualia of person types may be projected onto speech. In both cases perceptions are shaped accordingly. Here, "forces" like suspicion are posited as ultimate causes. In other cultural contexts, equipped with other theories, the ultimate causes may be hypothesized as interior "essences" or substances that match outward signs in their qualities, and are therefore seen to cause those outward signs. The temperaments, analogous to Galenic humors, discussed in the Wolof case (Chapter 1) are an example. In still other cases, internal causal substances are posited that do not match the externally evident qualities, for instance hormones or DNA.

As defined by Ochs (2004) the first kind of narrative displays patterns for further consideration; the second opens up a puzzling event for reasoned speculation that will resolve it. Both unfold in a circular logic: Signs are construed as qualitatively different on the basis of theories about regions. The signs are taken to index inner entities like minds or dispositions. The differences between observable signs become evidence for qualitative differences in minds and dispositions. The empirically accessible expressive signs and their qualia are taken as confirming evidence of the theory of differences that inspired the rhematizing construal of qualitative differences in the first place. Once such a circular structure of differences is conventionalized, individual social actors are under constraint: if their own practices match the theory, they seem to produce independent evidence for it. Confounding evidence in the behavior of participants, on the other hand, is often ignored (erased) or considered exceptional, or is stigmatized. There is social power in rhematization: its stories are often the basis on which policy and action are proposed and justified.[8]

Rhematization need not be a last step in semiotic inferencing. Further conjectures in chains of abduction can re-ideologize axes. Differences can be recast as contiguities (indexicalities). In Peirce's terminology, conjectures (interpretants) that take icons to be indexes are *dicents*, hence such a step is "dicentization" (Ball 2014). As we will see in Chapter 5, another kind of change is also common. Another discourse can invoke an uptake to reinterpret some of the same qualia (slow/fast speech; big/small stature) as belonging to different axes or as differently arranged and explainable, denying resemblances that had seemed self-evident, changing the salience of qualia, adding new knowledge, or denying what was previously accepted.

Fractal Recursivity

But even without such drastic changes, axes of differentiation produce cascades of differentiation when they are fractally reiterated. In Royall's time, arrogance, hierarchy, and pretensions to aristocracy were features that many Americans expected to find in Europe. After the Revolution, they contrasted these traits to the ideal egalitarian values of a republican America. At the same time – as Royall's narratives suggest – it was conventional to project some European qualities onto eastern regions of the United States, and those qualities deemed American were projected onto the western regions. Thus, an axis of differentiation, once established, has the potential to create ever more differentiation. Whatever items have been classified as belonging on one side of an axis – including perspectives – can be subdivided using the same contrasting qualities. Or the contrast can make more encompassing categories, as detailed below. This is the process we call *fractal recursivity*. Before explaining the term, let us look at the semiotic logic of some more examples.

Royall's eastern, impudent "demi-lord" is a caricature of Europeans, when contrasted with the "modest, unassuming" and independent westerner, which was one ideal type of the American. The allusion to Europe is palpable in the use of the term "lord," which was ironic, since the new country vehemently refused noble titles. But Royall did not stop there. Recounting travels west of the Blue Ridge, the narrator describes the keepers of an inn. Instead of comparing them to easterners, the narrator compares them to their own neighbors, to other westerners. The qualities that "constituted the character" of the hostess – she was short of stature, "presumptuous ... arrogant, ignorant, self-important ... all bluster, bustle," issuing peremptory commands, contemptuous of everyone around her (1969 [1830]:95) – are traits established in earlier passages as "eastern." This is a subdivision of the West into yet another East/West. "Eastern country" was subdivided too. Recounting a boat trip from Philadelphia to New York City, on which men and women, strangers to each other, converse familiarly, the narrator admires:

... the republican simplicity of their manners. The ladies unembarrassed, modest. ... In this respect they differ greatly from their ... neighbors [i.e., Philadelphians]. ... Here was no silly affectation among the females, no impertinent forwardness amongst the men ... these I thought must be New-Yorkers, which proved to be the case. (1826:236)

Instead of Philadelphia's "affectation" and "impertinent forwardness," in a New York hotel there is such "independence of manners as would be admired even in the land of Jackson [i.e., Tennessee]. ... I never found myself more at home in my life" (1826:241–242). New Yorkers, when compared to other urbanites along the east coast, are the westerners of the East: familiarly independent, egalitarian, modest, and sociable. Royall, as the west Virginian narrator, approves and thus aligns with New York.

Even when traveling on the eastern coast, Royall's writings consistently value and thus align with whatever she views as western. That enacts a western perspective and establishes her western persona. In subdivisions too, she aligns with whatever is comparatively western. Can Royall ever claim an eastern persona? Only very rarely does she approve of the eastern in a subdivision, thereby *pivoting* her perspective. Only once in her travelogue does she enact the kind of westerner who delights in eastern qualities. In Baltimore:

[a] host of wonders burst upon me at once, the vast number, height and density of the houses ... the number of well-dressed people in the streets overwhelmed me with astonishment. ... [T]his remark may excite a smile particularly in those who were never out of a populous town ... but till now I was never in one. (1826:188)

The "splendid houses" of Baltimore please the narrator in this rare passage, and she momentarily admires and thus aligns with the East.

The key to all such re-invocations of an established axis of differentiation is *comparison*. In particular: the narrower subdivisions versus broader encompassment that comparisons enact. All the phenomena judged as showing western qualia (e.g., big/slow/modest) in one comparison, can be considered again, with respect to each other, and subdivided, using the same criteria. This again creates two images or "sides," both sides "western" from the first comparative perspective, yet differentiated as "East" versus "West" for a perspective that compares them only to one another.

The relation between broader, encompassing comparisons on the one hand, and narrower, subdividing ones on the other, is clarified by the example of

Tuckahoes and Cohees. These terms were conventional, mutually derisive labels in nineteenth-century Virginia and the Carolinas. Royall sometimes used them. The generally known stereotypes were co-constitutive: Cohees were western, mountain folks, hardworking, independent, sociable farmers. Tuckahoes were "impertinent" slave owners of the relatively flatter landscape called Tidewater (East), with a "sense of imaginary superiority ... inclined to hold everybody else ... inferior" (Paulding 1817:91–93, 105–106; Royall 1969 [1830]:95). When Royall's narrator starts with divisions of the whole country into imagined East/West regions, her discussion of the Tuckahoe/Cohee distinction can be seen as a subdividing recursion, projecting the whole country's supposed East/West divide onto one section of the United States. But Royall grew up in western Virginia and in her early works she praised independent Cohees and was dismissive of Tidewater Tuckahoes. That more local, narrower distinction might have been her anchor – the most "real" for her, the best exemplar and starting point, projecting the East-Tuckahoe/West-Cohee contrast in an encompassing way. The whole country, then, would be divided by the East/West qualia of Virginia, making the United States into Virginia writ large.

Moving from a narrower comparison to a more encompassing one (and back) is a matter of *reparameterization*: shifting the bounds of a category (East/West and/or any of its qualities) to accommodate a revised vantage point. Thus, although the referents of "East" and "West" shift considerably in moving between more and less encompassing recursions, many of the same stereotyped qualities are evoked nonetheless. "East" can be the entire Atlantic seacoast, or Kentucky, or Philadelphia, or the Tidewater of Virginia. And some of the salient qualia shift as well. In Royall's comparison New York counts as the West – republican, modest, not at all impertinent – but it is hard to imagine that its denizens, even then, were comparatively "slow" and "said little." Indeed, elsewhere Royall emphasizes the hustle and bustle of New York, a characterization she erases here.

How any item of the moment – including the speaker's persona – is classified on an axis depends on what it is contrasted to, hence on the perspective taken by the comparison. The same practices, things, and people can count as instantiating one side of the axis when judged from one perspective, but may embody the other side when a more (or less) encompassing comparison is proposed. As a final step in this process, the comparisons involving different encompassments are ideologically equated, seen to be versions of the "same difference," erasing the inevitable disparities between them.

We call such differentiations *recursivity* because the distinctions are repeated, in linked and positioned comparisons. The recursions are relative judgments, creating categories of objects that are self-similar. The comparisons produce analogies: diagrammatic icons within diagrammatic icons, indexically invoked in specific situations. As in all analogies, the terms and distinctions are never perfectly replicated. What remains the same is the *principle of contrast* that is established, and the similarities that result, through qualities arrayed on one axis of differentiation. We label these repetitions *fractal* because each contrast repeats a pattern within itself, in a way that resembles fractal patterns constructed in geometry. Although fractal repetition has also been found in biological processes, we are concerned with the semiotic construction of fractal patterns through social practices, not their existence in the natural world.

Because fractal recursivity in social life creates categories, it is important to emphasize how these differ from other types of categorization. Taxonomies are nested, one set of categories included in another. But fractals do *not* form taxonomies. In fractals, the relation between or among the more encompassing terms is recapitulated among the more specific ones. The same difference is reproduced at each level. In taxonomies, the distinctions at any one level do *not* reiterate those at other levels as they do in fractals; the classificatory principle in taxonomies may be different at each level. Nor do fractals simply make a linear scale. They may do so, as an elaborate way of using dichotomies to represent a continuum. But the distinctions we are interested in are not gradations: East does not turn into West by degrees. On the contrary, they are complementary, relative to each other; they stand in contrast by definition (like griot/noble, farmer/artisan). The qualities arrayed in the axis – its schema – are *defined* as opposed and co-constitutive.[9]

Although our inspiration is recent geometry, the idea of a small version embedded within a large version of itself is an ancient conception. The notion of microcosm is one example; another is the human homunculus in reproduction, thought to have a homunculus of its own. Both of these are analogies. Our own examples are dichotomies that produce more dichotomies by analogy. The replication of dichotomies is familiar in fractal geometry. The figure called "Cantor dust" is made from a line that is bifurcated, the resulting segments also bifurcated, until the segments of the line become mere points (dust). But dichotomies are not the only configurations that can be made with fractal recursivity, in geometry or in social life. We will return to nonbinary social examples later, in considering standardization. (Recall, also, the three-way Sahelian person-categories discussed in Chapter 1.) A three-way figure in geometry suggests some of the possibilities. The Koch snowflake starts with a triangle, then by dividing each side into three equal parts and dividing the resulting sides in the same way, repeatedly, the figure comes to resemble a snowflake. As in our own examples, repetitions of the same principle of distinction make figures that look somewhat different in each iteration, yet also retain some of the properties of earlier instances (Gleick 1987:98–99).

How does fractal recursivity work in interaction? In analyzing Royall's vignettes, we saw that the narrator's conjectures divided the landscape into East/West. Simultaneously, her alignment with the West in those vignettes enabled readers to construe her as a western persona, locatable – as a second (order) conjecture – on the same axis of differentiation as the distinction she made, and implicitly contrasting her with easterners. Second order (iconic) indexes are the results of the process of fractal recursivity. An 1817 letter written by Royall to amuse a lawyer-friend in western Virginia provides another example of fractal recursivity in a narrated interaction. We focus first on the reported event, the story told in the letter. Royall as narrator recounts an evening she spent at an Alabama inn. Though presented as her personal experience, the scene was probably a familiar set piece. Mrs. Wells, the innkeeper, was tired and so was not going to cook specially for the late-arriving guests, a "gentleman" and "a perfect dandy, or fop." The fop is not satisfied with what Mrs. Wells has prepared. He observes, "without addressing anyone in particular":[10]

FOP: I believe you have no tea, no coffee in this country.

MRS. WELLS: (with great composure) Sometimes.

FOP: You doesn't have any flower hea' neither

MRS. WELLS: (sings out) Sometimes.

FOP: I b'lieve you' all savages in this country.

MRS. WELLS: (with good humor) Savage enough.

GENTLEMAN: (with great spirit) What country may you call yours, sir?

FOP: I ar' from Norfolk, Virginny, su'!

GENTLEMAN: And how do they live there?

FOP: Why, su' they live, su' like gentlemen, su'; I hasn't seen a bit of victuals fit to eat since I left Norfolk, except in Nashville.

GENTLEMAN: That is a great pity, sir. But we, of this country, do not rate ourselves by eating: we rate ourselves by fighting. Would you like to take a shot? (The little man dropped his feathers quite low.) (1969 [1830]:112–113)

The "fop" was a stock character, a boastful, vain, and condescending male figure conventionally defined as a "Europeanized American" (i.e., a fractal) with pretensions to refinement (Stein 1965:464). As denotational text, the exchange shows the fop faulting the meal and the "country" (i.e., region) for what it lacks. But more is accomplished interactionally. By mentioning "country" the fop invokes regional differences. With "savage" he displays the conventional view about the West from the supposedly "civilized" East, as he does when denigrating the rural "here" in comparison with coastal Norfolk and other cities, the presumed seats of civilization. Mrs. Wells's responses, as typified by the narrator, are conciliatory: "composure" and "good humor" in the face of insult. But her reactions and the fop's complaints are not only individual, nor only second order indexes. For those who can take it up, this is an interactional invocation of an East/West axis. Through the invoked axis, Mrs. Wells can be seen as the (rhematized) embodiment of *western* affability and the fop as a specifically *eastern* example of arrogance, issuing *eastern* insults. The gentleman (western, "of this country") denotationally redefines the issue as a matter of comportment, not food. The invitation to shoot enacts a polite ("sir") yet pugnacious – thus western – sociability.

Within the story told, the humor hinges on turning the tables: in response to arrogant eastern charges of deficiency in refinement, the gentleman names an East/West distinction – willingness to fight – in which it is the easterner who is deficient. Considering now the storytelling event – the letter in which Royall recounts this story – the East/West axis is also invoked there, but with a different fractal parameter. It categorizes narrator and reader in an encompassing contrast on the same axis, projecting for readers, then and now, a persona aligned with the West as the narrator's persona clearly is. The incident is amusing only for an uptake that is familiar with the axis and adopts a western perspective. Yet, a puzzle remains: Why is the speech of the eastern character spelled so unusually? To answer this, we must consider another axis.

Multiple Axes

Alternate axes arise in the wake of great social transformations, like the American Revolution. The East/West axis that had organized the colonial vision was projected by fractal recursivity to signal East/West contrasts within the country, but language reformers initiated more radical differentiation. They argued that American patriotism required rejecting British patterns of speaking. A prescriptive ideology that aimed to standardize linguistic practices for everyone was in full swing in eighteenth-century Britain (Mugglestone 1997:4). Ironically, to achieve full separation, a similar American campaign was in the making. There were many justifications. Separate spelling rules and dictionaries would free Americans of reliance on British books; American books would stop Americans from aping British style and would enliven the American printing industry. As late as 1817, the novelist James Kirke Paulding wrote, "We cannot be truly independent ... till we make our own books and coin our own words – two things as necessary to national sovereignty as making laws and coining money" (cited in Simpson 1986:128). The coastal cities in the East were the centers of American publishing and literary activity, the centers of intellectual authority. Regardless of their origins, all writers adopted an urban, refined persona (Smith 1960). Yet, American reformers claimed that the new standards relied not on East/West geographical distinctions but on "correctness," although the regime of value that would judge this quality was a matter of some dispute (Baron 1982; Mathews 1931).

The anchor categories of this new axis were linguistic and literary practices: standard and dialect. Its master trope was "high/low," lexicalizing the presumption that linguistic practices were indexical of hierarchy via "breeding" (education, social class). This ideological vision posited diverse dialects, distributed geographically in all directions, while correct forms were imagined to float above them in a deterritorialized space. The standardizing axis contrasting anonymity with authenticity as emplacement is familiar from European standardization, as Woolard (2016) and others have shown. It was apparent in the early United States as well.[11] Noah Webster, the early American standardizer, wrote, "[W]ell bred people resemble each other in all countries [regions]," but "local practices" are "disagreeable" and "incorrect"; less good than the written norm to which they failed to conform. Despite disclaimers, however, there was a *hidden* geography, as many have remarked. It was in "towns" that "people lost most of their [linguistic] singularities." And towns were in the East. Besides, "in eastern states there are public schools to instruct every man's children" (Webster 1967 [1789]:107–108, 288–289).

Like any axis, the high/low axis was totalizing: it focused on language but categorized every sort of semiotic object. Yet, it was also significantly different from other axes: it claimed a single perspective, defined by an institutionalized center of authority – schools, dictionaries, books, and mass mediated fashion – that would fix the criteria (linguistic and other) of correctness for an entire population. Unlike the distinctions we have examined so far, taking up this axis implied erasing perspectival possibilities; this axis claimed to represent a "view from nowhere." The high/low axis did not ignore East/West differences, but rather *subsumed* them. Anything western had a place on the high/low axis – as in the colonial vision – as rude, rural, incorrect, and therefore socially "low." Through the institutionalizing and obfuscating efforts of the standardizers, "West" was subordinated not to Europe but, it was claimed, to the national standard of the "well-bred."

Royall rejected a subsumption of the western. Though a westerner, she claimed a standardizing persona. She wrote from a western perspective, yet also admired the reformers; she was well educated and in favor of education for all. Her writings reveal a configuration rare in her era and not evident in most works about early American language ideologies. A closer look at the scene in Mrs. Wells's inn provides an example. The unusual spellings representing the fop's speech suggest "incorrect" pronunciation and grammar, thus the narrator displays the fop as not only eastern but also socially "low." His speech and rude manner belie his typically eastern claims to civilization, showing them to be mere pretense. That makes him even truer to western stereotype of the East: he is false as well as condescending, and thus ridiculing him is even more amusing from a western view. It is those with western traits who are socially "high" in this story. They (and the narrator) are represented with standard spelling. This narrative effect was the direct *opposite* of literary conventions in Royall's time, when writers assumed the "social inferiority" of westerners (Smith 1960:216), casting them as rude dialect speakers.

For Royall, the fop character was only one of many forms of "low." For all standardizers there were eastern and western forms of "low." What distinguished her perspective was that she also presumed some westerners would be "high." For her, the two axes coexisted as maps of the social world.[12] Royall, and the lawyer-friend to whom she wrote her letter, and probably many others claimed the persona of educated (high) westerner that was unimaginable for the hegemonic, standardizing (eastern) perspective. We call this *blockage*, when – through an exercise of power and institutional authority – a category is socially disallowed, unrecognized.

A High/Low Axis: Standardization and Blockage

Let us look at some of the semiotic processes of standardization. Here is Royall's view of dialect, which was in perfect accord with Webster:

If you wish to ascertain the dialect of a country, you must seek for it amongst the common, or in other words, the lower order of the people, as all well bred people speak alike. But the children of both classes are good specimens of dialect, as the better sort, in this [part of the] country particularly, consign their children to the care of negroes and illiterate white nurses ... then [parents] are at much pains and cost to unlearn them what they need never have learned. (1969 [1830]:201–202)

This axis, like any other, consists of co-constitutive contrasts: dialects are socially, linguistically and geographically diverse as opposed to the homogeneity of elite, educated speech. Other contrasting qualities were correct/incorrect, intact/mutilated. For instance, Royall condemned the unschooled speakers in the mountains of Virginia: "Their dialect sets orthography at defiance ... the whole English language is so mangled and mutilated ... that it is hardly known to be such" (1826:58). Elsewhere she judges dialects in aesthetic terms as "ugly" in contrast to "beautiful speech." The two sign types (dialects vs. the English language) each index people types as their semiotic object. The view that "negroes and illiterate whites" were the source of dialect was widespread, erasing the fact that schooling was sparsely distributed and denied to "negroes"; literacy itself was forbidden to slaves.

Royall's many examples of dialect are visually striking against the standard orthography of the surrounding commentary. She presented them (1969 [1830]:202–203) to show that no region is immune to dialect, which she elsewhere called "ignorance":

TENNESSEEANS AND NORTH CAROLINIANS: "Oh there was a proper sight of people – you never seed the like! ... and there was some monstrous purty gals there, and some dinged ugly ones, too. ... I tell you what ... they was going to fight. ... Then these fellows that lives on Flint, had liked to abin whipped steppin about."

BEDFORD (WEST) VIRGINIANS: "You know da is heap of baw (bear) on da Kenhawa ... Kenhawa mighty far – so we walk – we walk – last we come to da Kenhawa, b-i-g river, for true – Tell you what, it skears me. ..."

PENNSYLVANIAN: "Jim, where are you and Sam; why but 'ye's' pit (put) you cow in the pester (pasture) 'am sure a towled ye's the morning. –Ye's cruel bad children –and there a fine job ye's done to leave you gears out by."

YANKEES (NORTHEAST): "Flora you want (ought) to wash them clothes right away. You hadn't ought to left 'em so." "What say?"

TUCKAHOE (EASTERN VA. AND CAROLINAS): "Luke an't you done totin them taters yet? – I 'spose you at the fire again ... make up a good fire, you hea ... I 'spose you'll lend him ten dollars again ... you will fool away all your 'state. ..." (1969 [1830]:96–97)

The correctness of the surrounding text is taken for granted. The dialects seem to contrast only with each other as divergent subdivisions of the "language itself." The more basic contrast of each with a (written) standard is erased. These are rural cases, East and West. Royall also named some city dwellers as dialect speakers in Boston and Philadelphia. Royall's descriptions are not technically accurate in present-day terms. We should read them as rhematized stereotypes and shibboleths.

By omitting letters, the unusual orthography makes the dialects look "deficient": in/ing, 'spose/suppose, baw/bear. Transposing letters and syntax makes them look "mangled" or "mutilated": purty/pretty, da/there, towled/told. In a rhematizing move, these qualia are projected onto imagined speech. The socially low activities are loci of rhematization. The Tennesseans party and fight; western Virginians tell tall tales; and so on. These were stereotypes in the journalism of the period.[13] In further rhematization, the qualities perceived to differentiate the contrasting signs ("dialect" vs. "English") are projected onto speakers' (posited) *minds*, which are also supposedly lacking, mangled, and distorted. In Philadelphia, the "higher classes pronounce the English language with purity and even elegance." Yet, "[t]he dialect of its citizens, particularly of the children ... is very defective ... extremely disgusting ... [they are] *ignorant* of grammar, geography and history" (1826:229, emphasis ours). In Boston, Royall was amazed: Not only the "higher classes" but also the "lower class" were educated. Nevertheless, the dialect of the lower is "wretchedly defective," showing "ignorance." She added: "All the learning in the world will never break them of these vulgar habits" (1826:325). Thus, among the "better sort," dialect was reproduced when illiterate caretakers contaminated children. But, for the "lower classes," rhematization reversed the causal arrow. The bad qualities of speech were understood to be products of the same qualities in minds; they could not be eliminated.

Though similar to other axes in some ways, the standardizing axis is also significantly different. It has an asymmetrical "shape." It is not a simple dichotomous figure, but rather like an outspread fan. A single pole of correctness contrasts with many differently incorrect forms that are seen as geographically distributed. The East/West axis relied on a regime of value; so does the standardizing axis. The values of the standardizing axis are more obviously supported by institutional levers of power and authority: the details of its history show how it was imposed and policed, its shibboleths guarded by a literary elite.

Royall's trip to the east coast gives us an example of blockage in interaction. She made calls – as was customary among the well-bred – on the dignitaries of the day, known to her through reading and reputation. In Washington she visited John Quincy Adams, then attorney general, who received her cordially. In New Haven, she called on the "celebrated" Noah Webster, whose writings she admired. She "knocked at the door with more than common enthusiasm" because, she notes, "though we back-woods folks are not learned ourselves, we have a warm liking for learned people." Mention of learning evokes the standardizing axis; "backwoods" denoted the forested western frontier, as defined in Webster's 1841 dictionary. Its use here is ironic self-deprecation: Royall was a well-to-do widow from the agricultural near-west, not from the frontier. The two mentions of "we" are Bakhtinian double voicings. "We" westerners who are (generally) uneducated implicitly contrasts here with a subcategory of "we" – Royall herself – who admire the educated because "we" are also educated. This acknowledges her westernness, but also claims a persona as "high." But when Webster finally appears, Royall is mortified by his contempt: "He eyed me with ineffable scorn and scarcely deigned to speak at all." She was angry and "sorry for his sake I ever saw the man" (1826:388). The passage suggests Royall sensed Webster was not just being his famously cranky self, but was insulting her. He was unable to discern an educated, well-bred westerner, one worthy of conversation. The persona of which Royall was so proud was blocked, unrecognizable to the archetypal standardizer.

Standardization itself is fractally recursive: When one politico-linguistic center of authority challenges another, a new standard is created. By adopting Britain's ideology of standard, American reformers elevated "colonial English" into an American norm that recursively reduced other American forms to derogated, provincial dialects – another fan-like topography – with the same asymmetrical contrasts, but now judged, compared, and disciplined from a different – and only purportedly nongeographical – center of institutionalized authority.

Conclusion

The semiotic logic of comparison is ubiquitous in everyday activity. Differentiation depends on comparison, and all comparison is ideologically shaped. Axes point us toward the ideologies constituted through comparison and in which axes are, in turn, embedded. The process is robust enough to be evident in the writings of a single author and some of her contemporaries. We looked over the shoulder of Anne Royall, and read her narratives ethnographically, taking her points of view. Other frameworks, other ideologies, and other political economic circumstances display different qualities. But they too are organized into axes of differentiation and into contrasting *images* or depictions, authorized by regimes of value, and invoked as qualia in specific interactions. Perspectives, registers, and personae are parts of such schemas, whenever they are created. Experience that does not fit is erased. Rhematization and its narratives justify the differences and similarities that axes organize. Narratives formulate causes and motivations for difference; they authorize knowledge of differentiation by linking it to already existing values and frameworks. In this chapter, the narrative organization of text segments suggested ways in which knowledge of differentiation is evoked, enacted, and sometimes erased in interaction. Fractal recursivity proliferates difference through changes in perspective. But it can also be blocked.

Axes often seem stable and fixed. Yet, axes invariably change. Because the creation and construal of difference serves interactional and political goals, it enables sociopolitical alignments and conflicts that lead to social transformations. We ask in the next chapter: What is the role of axes and the entire differentiation process in historical change?

5   Dynamics of Change in Differentiation

What happens when existing ideological distinctions are put to work for novel social and political projects? How do existing axes shape new situations? Doing semiotic work invariably results in altered comparisons – rearrangement of contrasts, omission of some, addition and emphasis on others – so that axes are themselves altered. The differentiation process – like the chains of abduction that constitute it – is open-ended and creative. There is always a next uptake. And it may be transformative. By proposing new comparisons in historically novel circumstances, participants change the categories and instantiations of axes, which in turn changes their abstract conceptualizations and their later enactments. Such ideological permutations reframe social relations and reconstruct the social organizations in which they happen.

Here is a quick example. In 1834, shortly after Anne Royall's first travelogue was published, a Virginia physician wrote a novel that drew on American regionalism to display differences among the characters. His story revealed dilemmas Royall did not see. The hero, a South Carolinian, writes a letter to his friend in Virginia:

> You say you "hate Yankees" my dear fellow, you forget that you and I would be considered Yankees in London or Paris. ... 'Tis galling to our southern pride, I grant you, that we should be a mere appendage, in the eyes of a foreigner, to a people totally dissimilar to us. (Caruthers 1834:71)

The letter-writing character is discussing the East/West contrast by which all Americans were called "Yankees" in Europe. In Royall's terms, as discussed in the previous chapter, these characters count as denizens of the east coast. But, unlike her stereotypical easterner, the letter writer, while recognizing the East/West contrast, does not fractally reiterate it. He does not place himself and his friend on that axis as more "civilized" and "genteel" when compared to Americans further to the west. Rather, he *refuses* the characterization that Yankee-equals-American and as we will see, he reorganizes or *splices* the qualitative differences, creating a North/South axis on which the two friends are both "southerners," who are therefore in contrast to Yankees (as northerners), not equated with them. How is the East/West axis both coexistent with, yet also semiotically transformed, to make North/South? And how should we conceptualize the ability of participants to dispute how others see them?

To explore these questions, we change our analytical strategy. In the last chapter, we followed a single author whose writings, in a limited time-frame (ca. 1820–1830), illustrated the basic logic of differentiation. Here, instead, we track successive uptakes of a single axis over many decades by participants who are diversely located in space and across institutions. Reacting to previous invocations of the axis, they change it by creating new comparisons and categories. We observe throughout how semiotic change has institutional provocations and consequences. Uptakes imply action, shaping how people form schisms and alliances in social organizations. These groupings may create conflict, but also produce new kinds of solidarity. Even as the components of the semiotic process remain the same – axes, rhematization and its narratives, fractal recursivity, erasure – successive uptakes, motivated by different projects and values, produce ideological, linguistic, and organizational change. Time is central to this process in several ways. The successive (re)assemblages of an axis and its enactments as qualia – in speech as in other social action – build on and are often framed to echo past configurations. They may also invoke temporally distant causal events and origins. Explanatory narratives also change, calling on novel theories and values. In this chapter, we continue to draw examples from early US history. "Yankee" as label and stereotype serves as the main illustration of semiotic change, supplemented by some twenty-first-century examples.

Successive Uptakes

What does "Yankee" mean? For Charles William Janson, an English visitor to the United States in 1807, "Yankee" personified America, like "John Bull" for England. What did Janson see as distinctively American? Arriving in Boston, he was "amazed" by evidence of "American equality" when the ship's cook boy joined the passengers at dinner, reached across the table with his dirty hand, took a tumbler of rum and declared, "Good folks, here's to ye." Appalled, the passengers sent him away. The boy muttered about the "haughtiness" of "the proud English." Later, Janson was "astonished" by the "pertness [insolence] of republican principles" when he knocked on the door of an American acquaintance. He asked of the young woman who opened the door: "Is your master at home?" to which she replied, "I have no master." "Don't you live here?" "I stay here." "And who are you then?" "Why, I'm Mr. X's *help* I'd have you know, *man*, that I am no *sarvant*" (1807:9, 88, emphasis original). As Janson later found out, black slaves were known as "servants" and white employees, though often indentured for many years, rejected the label.

Visitors from Europe invariably remarked on the lack of deference and refinement in American manners and speech (Appleby 2000:137). Most of them – Gall from Germany in 1819–1820, Tocqueville from France, Martineau and Trollope from England in the 1830s – saw this as the effect of politics: how a republic differed from an aristocracy.

Americans agreed. Well before Janson's visit, one of the first plays written in the United States was titled *The Contrast* (Tyler 1970 [1887]). First performed in 1787, it satirized a Europeanized gentleman with fancy clothing who had pretensions to refinement. The character is a cold, insincere fop, who worships "rank" (hierarchy, aristocracy). The American characters, on the other hand, show rustic independence and insist on equality and on frank sentiment. One of them sings *Yankee Doodle*. The two sets of qualities are set up as opposites and melded into contrasting figures of masculinity. The American hero is named "Mr. Manly." Indeed, "luxury, effeminacy and corruption" was a triad as well-known in the Revolutionary period as its opposite, "life, liberty and the pursuit of happiness" (Kerber 1992). The play presents an American view that condemned duplicity and linked it to hierarchy. Those who dominated but did not deserve their authority were exercising a kind of deceit. Evidence for the contrast was projected and "found" in all aspects of life.

But Yankee as label and stereotype has a longer history that reveals semiotic change. Like "East" and "West" in Royall's writings, "Yankee" is a shifter (but one that Royall rarely used). Its referent changes, as do some of the qualities it implies, depending on who is using it, for what comparison, in what era. In the mid-eighteenth century, Yankee was a slur hurled by the British military at American colonial militias. It was probably first used in writing in 1758 by James Wolfe, a British commander in the French and Indian Wars. He alternated between "Yankee" and "American" in expressing contempt for the colonial soldiers under his command. He wrote to a fellow officer, "I can afford you two companies of Yankees, and the more as they are better for ranging and scouting than either work or vigilance." In another letter the "Americans" were "the dirtiest most contemptible dogs ... there is no depending on them in action ... [they] desert by battalions, officers and all" (cited in Wright 1864:376, 392). For him, Yankees were unruly and unreliable. They did not take orders well. At about the same time, Yankee was derisive slang used by New York and Pennsylvania colonists to name tough New Englanders in conflicts over land claims (Fox 1940).

In the Revolutionary War, however, the Yankee label was adopted by those fighting for independence. As often happens when a pejorative term becomes the focus of mobilization by those it names, Yankee was taken up with pride. It was recuperated by colonists as one step in the lengthy process of transforming themselves from British subjects to American citizens. Thomas Anburey, a British army officer stationed in New England in 1777, wrote, "The name

[Yankee] has been more prevalent since the commencement of hostilities. The soldiers [British regulars] at Boston used it as a term of reproach, but after the affair at Bunker's Hill [colonists' victory] the Americans gloried in it. *Yankee Doodle* is now their favorite paean, a favorite of favorites" (1789:50–51). Actually, both the British regulars and what Anburey calls the "Americans" sang the song. The British sang contemptuously, with nasality, which they took to be typical of American speech, and with lyrics about a "tattr'd crew" whose leaders were not gentlemen but "dealt in horses" (Nickels 1993:34–35). The derision spotlighted rank (hierarchy) and polish (refinement): qualities the British claimed to have, but denied to American fighters.

The American/British contrast evoked by "Yankee" was taken up again by colonists, fractally dividing all those the British called "Yankee." New England Tories (loyal to Britain) taunted as "Yankies" those of their neighbors who wanted independence (Sonneck 1909:81–82). This stereotype invoked the qualities that Major-General Wolfe decried – lack of deference and lack of fidelity to the Crown. And it added a new contrast: wanting/not wanting political independence. Other considerations, like residence in metropole or colony, were elided. In a fractal analogy, Tories took up the British perspective and projected onto those they called Yankees *some* of the distinctions the British evoked in comparing themselves to Americans. So, pejorative use of the term "Yankee," by a colonist, identified the speaker as sympathetic to the Crown.

With independence and republic gained, and Tories (mostly) gone, a "Yankee" stereotype was taken up in other projects. Among those New Englanders who had all supported the fight for an independent republic, urban groups rejected the Yankee label for themselves. In fact, what identified them was the use of "Yankee" for those unrefined "common folks" – farmers and peddlers – who refused to defer to the New England elite. One example was farmers in western Massachusetts who rose up in 1786 in a tax revolt against the eastern ruling class. Boston leaders took on much of the role that the British had played against "Yankees" in the revolution; the farmers staged a replay of the American role. Echoing General Wolfe, the elites cast the farmers as disloyal, unreliable types. But the qualities were reconceptualized: not military discipline, but political and economic; disloyalty not to Britain, but to Boston. Comparing themselves to Britain, the New England elites saw themselves as an egalitarian establishment (Conforti 2001:154–155). Yet, comparing themselves to the westerners on the frontier, they saw themselves as aristocrats of a sort. In 1802, Connecticut minister and geographer Jedidiah Morse approvingly (and fractally) noted, "The clergy ... have preserved a kind of aristocratical balance in the very democratical government of the state" (Grasso 1999:379).

A narrower contrast, the opposition between the earliest political parties, was also cast in terms of this axis. John Adams's Federalist Party approved of hierarchy in various forms against the radical egalitarian rhetoric of Jefferson's Republicans in the 1800 presidential election. Federalist writers lampooned New England Republicans as disloyal louts and rustic "Yankees," representing them in print as ignorant bumpkins, speaking in nasal-voiced dialect (Nickels 1993:44–56). The axis had long been political; now it formulated even party animosities. Here, as in earlier examples, use of Yankee identified a referent, but also identified users of the term – for those in the know.

These illustrations show how the contrasts in qualities that evoked a Yankee/Britain difference for colonists were remapped and revised multiple times. The locus of the anchor – Yankee as a metapragmatic label of a typified figure – slipped from geopolitics (colony/metropole), to national politics (independence/fidelity), to social status (commoner/elite), to party loyalty. Later, the regional component of the axis continued to be reconceptualized: In the eighteenth century, East/West had been important. By the end of the nineteenth century, most Americans saw Yankeeland as located only in the northern parts of New England, where rural residents claiming English ancestry adopted the Yankee label for themselves, as distinct from European and Canadian immigrants (Conforti 2001).

The instantiation of master tropes also changed. What General Wolfe considered unreliable was not what the Boston elite worried about; Morse's definition of aristocracy was not King George's. Some qualities were omitted, others added. A gender distinction, based on stereotypes of the era, contrasted the Europeanized and feminized fop to the "Manly" American, and gender appeared again when farmers in the West attributed "foolish women's" desires for feathers and ribbons to their urban Federalist opponents (Formisano 2008:39–40). The Yankee label was derisive for some but worn proudly by others. Either way, the use of the label identified speaker type as well as the referent. The label's continuity erased the multiple redefinitions. The term's power lay in the echoes of earlier comparisons projected onto new referents and new users, as construed by those in the know.

"Yankee," as label, is readily locatable in documents. Yet for any axis there are also non-lexical contrasts, the kind accessible ethnographically: distinctions in nonreferential indexicals, expressive genres, discourse patterns, and visual matters of dress and custom. Such signs – embodiments of the axis – are enregistered. In interaction, speaker types are identifiable by the way they formulate the referents of talk. This formulating can create interdiscursive relations among events and achieve fractal reparameterizations: comparing ever broader categories, or analogizing to narrower ones. It is a crucial point that contrasts of opinion – e.g., about independence or taxation – can be enregistered to align with expressive forms understood to signal an axis. Here we have stayed with a single historical example, but the enregisterment and recursivity of political opinion and political aesthetics are evident also in quite other cases

(Gal 2018). The display of opinion, implicating value, ethics, and aesthetics, then conveys speaker personae and other features of the axis, just as nonreferential shibboleths do. When opinions are enregistered in this way, they too are rhematized and justified by explanatory narratives.[1]

Encompassments and Splicing

The distinctions illustrated so far have been *subdivisions* of the colonial axis. But there were also unifications – encompassments – in comparisons of the United States to Europe. Mapping the new country, Jedidiah Morse's influential *American Geography*, published in 1789, argued that New England was uniquely representative of America because homogeneous in manners. Ignoring slavery in New England, Morse took New England's homogeneity as a sign of equality and republicanism, in contrast to Europe and to American regions that were more intensively slaveholding, "imperious" and therefore supposedly more like Europe (Conforti 2001). For Morse, America was – or ideally should become – New England writ large.

But during the Revolutionary War, people from other regions had different projects of comparison. James Thacher, in his Military Journal, remarked that among the troops "we too frequently hear the burlesque epithet of Yankee from one party, and that of Buckskin, by way of retort, from the other" (1823:61). One soldier, James Fallon, fighting in Fishkill, New York, wrote home to South Carolina in 1779:

> The inhabitants here abouts are all Yankees ... their manners are, to me, abhorrent. I long to leave and get clear of their oddities. They are for the most part a *damned* generation. (quoted in Alden 1961:22, emphasis original)

"Here abouts" was evidently not New England but a generalized north. Fallon was comparing Yankees not to the British, but to South Carolinians. He did not specify the "oddities."

A few years later, Thomas Jefferson did specify them, in a 1785 letter to the Marquis de Chastellux in Paris. Jefferson knew the colloquial word "Yankee," but avoided it in his formal and famous tabular description of differences in his country.

The evocation of the axis of differentiation in Table 5.1 shows Jefferson's view of what he called the "characters of the several states." His contrasts might well have included Fallon's complaints. For Jefferson, however, neither side is abhorrent, suggesting that unlike Fallon's southern perspective, the speaker here is not aligned with those "in the south" as one might expect from a prominent Virginian. Instead, Jefferson employs a different kind of encompassment by splicing (interweaving) the familiar distinctions to establish a new – specifically American – perspective. How is it done?

Table 5.1 Thomas Jefferson's "Characters of the Several States"

In the north they are:	In the south they are:
cool	fiery
sober	voluptuary
laborious	indolent
persevering	unsteady
*independent	*independent
zealous of their own liberties and just to those of others	jealous of their own liberties but trampling on those of others
interested	generous
chicaning	candid
superstitious and hypocritical ...	without attachment or pretentions in their religion

Boyd (1950:468).

As in any axis, the qualities here are co-constitutive contrasts. But there is a striking exception. For Jefferson, those in the north and those in the south are *identical* in being "independent" (note asterisks added). Jefferson was constructing northern and southern stereotypes via these contrasts. But by asserting that the stereotypes shared one crucial feature he also unified the two, without making the country an image of either one, writ large. This logic becomes clear when we see the letter's addressivity, its part in an interaction. Jefferson was presenting both regions to a specific recipient, a European aristocrat. By framing both regions as "independent" with all this implied in the rhetoric of American values, Jefferson constructed his own perspective and persona as distinctively American, in contrast to his aristocratic French addressee, who was exemplary of hierarchy and therefore of "dependence" as a system.

Jefferson's set of contrasts is newly arranged, but familiar. It is a *splicing* or interweaving, a rearrangement, of the contrasts of the colonial axis: a reassembling of the same qualities. Unlike New England–based comparisons, neither side alone resembles the British stereotype, nor the American. The qualities are redistributed – spliced – and the anchor becomes a north/south geography. Thus, "cool/fiery" contrasts the stereotyped cold, formal sociality of the British (but also those in the north) with the intensity and frank fieriness of American (and southern) relationships. "Indolent-voluptuary" versus "sober-laborious" point to conventional effects attributed to hierarchy, the first set characteristic of those accepting aristocracy or slavery (British and southern), and the second typical of those rejecting it (American, northern). "Interested," "chicaning," and "hypocritical" are those who seek profit by deceit, in contrast to "candid," "unpretentious" relationships. The British were seen by Americans as profiteering, but so were those in the commercial north, in contrast to those in the agricultural south. "Zealous/jealous" was Jefferson's veiled allusion to slavery. With the words "liberty of others," Jefferson excluded (erased) enslaved populations from this map of the United States.

The images created were explained by the rhematizing narrative of environmental determinism, characteristic of that Enlightenment age: heat makes tempers fiery, yet saps strength into indolence, and so on. Accordingly, Jefferson conceptualized a gradient, with Pennsylvania as the happy medium. He wrote that travelers could detect the latitude by checking people's virtues and vices. In Virginia "the warmth of ... climate ... unnerves and unmans both body and mind." This gradient and its explanation were widely recognized. James Winthrop of Massachusetts could not have known of Jefferson's letter, yet he wrote in 1788, "A people inhabiting various climates will unavoidably have ... different modes of life. ... The idle and dissolute inhabitants of the south require a different regimen from the sober and active people of the north" (cited in Storing 2008:93). He too presumed to speak for "a [single] people." Neither writer included African-Americans or Native peoples. This was not an oversight. When applied to individuals, independence (also called "liberty" and "freedom") presumed property ownership. Being property or having none, blacks, women, and Native peoples were deemed incapable of personal independence, as the constitutional debates testify. Independence was the defining quality of elite masculinity (Smith-Rosenberg 1992).

Jefferson's mode of encompassment is importantly different from one that made Yankee stand for the entire country. But it is equally fractal. This second kind of encompassment distinguishes sides/images at one level of comparison, while uniting them at a more inclusive level on the basis of a quality that they share. Yet, that quality identifies a contrast with a category at the more encompassing level. By splicing (reclustering), colonial contrasts were eventually crystallized as a North/South axis, no longer merely compass points but reified sections. This encompassment envisioned regions as subsumable only in an image of the country as a whole, compared to a stereotyped France, Britain, or Europe.

Encompassments and Markedness

The two kinds of encompassment recall the markedness relations of binary oppositions as identified by Roman Jakobson. Markedness, often illustrated by distinctive features in phonology, is not limited to sound systems. Writing to Trubetzkoy in 1930, Jakobson emphasized its relevance to conceptual domains:

Your thought ... [about] a mutual connection between a marked and unmarked type ... has a significance not only for linguistics but also for ethnology and the history of culture, and that such historico-cultural correlations as life-death, liberty-nonliberty, sin-virtue, holidays-working days, and so on are always confined to relations a/non-a, and that it is important to find out for any epoch, group, nation, etc. what the marked element is. (Jakobson and Pomorska 1990 [1980]:136)

Somewhat later, Jakobson added a further insight. The poet Majakovskij had just committed suicide and had written that death was easy, to make a life was markedly more difficult. "We realized," wrote Jakobson, "that according to his upside-down view of the world, not death but life 'required motivation'" (Jakobson and Pomorska 1990 [1980]:136). The unmarked (life as usual) versus death (marked) implies the possibility of its reversal to death as usual, against which it is life that needs justification. For our analysis, the difference between marked/unmarked depends on the perspective from which the opposition is taken up. For Royall, the West was the unmarked background against which the East needed explaining. In the early Republic, "Yankee" was the marked term for those who used it, until it was recuperated by those it named.

Jakobson also specified a hierarchical aspect of markedness: the unmarked term includes both the marked and the unmarked in some contexts, thereby eliding the binary contrast (Waugh 1982:302–303). Lexical polarities are illustrations of this and occur in all languages. So, day/night is a pair in which we understand "day" as the unmarked, and it also names the period of twenty-four hours that includes both light and dark. Like Majakovskij, we can also imagine a reversal of this, as in *One Thousand and One Nights*. Classic structuralist analyses in anthropology understood cultural oppositions as complementary, yet they often neglected markedness. Louis Dumont, however, emphasized the hierarchical aspect of cultural oppositions, calling hierarchy a "relation that can succinctly be called 'the encompassing of the contrary'" (1980 [1979]:239).[2] He also noted that a reversal is possible; the encompassed can become the encompasser.

We also find a further permutation. In early American examples, Morse's encompassment was the "hierarchical" kind that Jakobson and Dumont identified. The double meaning of "Yankee" (as either North or the whole United States) shows this hierarchy. The Jeffersonian mode, however, is something else: an *unmarked encompassment*. Southern and northern perspectives face each other; what is marked for one is unmarked for the other. But when comparing to foreigners, a novel position with its persona is created, markedness is denied, thus unifying those "in the north" with those "in the south," with neither included in the other. This parallels feminist theory's replacement of "man" with "human," rejecting the universal/particular gender distinction that allowed "man" to encompass the man/woman contrast (de Beauvoir 1968).[3]

The concept of markedness helps clarify the differentiation process. But our analyses also differ importantly from Jakobson's and Dumont's. We reject the structuralist claim that the relation of marked to unmarked depends on the "structure of the whole ... system" (Jakobson 1990 [1980]:133), or that "differentiation does not change the global setting, given once and for all" (Dumont 1980 [1979]:243). On the contrary, we show that people innovate, making unifying categories as well as distinctions, creating further levels of subdivision and encompassment, sometimes attempting to undo markedness relations. The categories are not already existing structural determinants. Fractal recursivity is productive, analogically proliferating categories, both new distinctions and potential new unities. Axes and their presumed qualities change as they are mobilized for new projects. Ideological differentiation is productive and open-ended. Yet, it differs from several other visions of productivity.

The productivity we describe is not one of added taxonomic categories or levels, where the principles of classification at one level are unrelated to those at another level of inclusion. It is also unlike Hegelian dialectics, where thesis-antithesis is "transcended" through a "lifting up" (*Aufhebung*) that produces a new synthesis. As Dumont noted about Hegel's dialectic, "By the negation of the negation, a totality without precedent can be produced synthetically" (1980 [1979]:243). The differentiation process we describe produces no final synthesis or totality without precedent. A unity of contrasts is built from elements that make it up, which form a partial precedent, yet will be changed somewhat by new comparisons (not a synthesis) that are brought into being.[4] Neither a structuralist nor a Hegelian system, nor a characterization of holistic social forms, the process we outline is Peircean in inspiration: it presumes a (re)making of concepts (categories, types) when their tokens are put to work in the ideological projects of participants, drawing comparisons in the world of events and interaction.

Interacting Perspectives in Social Relations

Interaction implies response. An axis of differentiation is often co-created in social relationships by participants who, in reacting to each other, take up opposed perspectives. We saw one way this worked in colonial Massachusetts when soldiers responded with pride to being called Yankees by the British, though Yankee was then a derogatory term. More generally, Gregory Bateson coined "schismogenesis" to name a reciprocal process "of differentiation in the norms of ... behavior resulting from cumulative interaction" in a system of relationships (1935:175; 1958 [1936]). For example, more insult as a reaction to insult (symmetrical) intensifies animosities overall, as in Revolution-era Massachusetts. More submission, say, in response to assertiveness (complementary) creates more extreme difference. We join Bateson in emphasizing – as Simmel had in discussing conflict as integration (1971 [1908]:74–95) – the ethical and psychological effects on groups and individuals of interaction as differentiation.

Unlike these theorists, however, we distinguish conceptually between *semiotic* distinctions and *social* relationships. The two are never simply isomorphic. Contrast (a semiotic relation) may organize conflict or its opposite, cooperation (both social). Encompassment (a semiotic relation) may be taken as a sign of social and emotional oppression and be refused (recall: it was "galling to our southern pride," to be "a mere appendage" to Yankees), or it may be welcomed as alliance against a jointly recognized foe. We are interested in the way cumulative interaction *changes* relationships – beyond intensification – and how the resulting differentiation is understood and justified. Much sociolinguistic change can be analyzed in this way (Gal 2016a).

The American press in the early nineteenth century illustrates such interacting perspectives. Novel technologies of mass publishing enabled distant readers to engage in virtual conversation. Newspapers responded directly to each other. For instance, official celebratory toasts in cities on the Fourth of July were published in other towns with derogatory or approving commentary, to which further replies were printed (Waldstreicher 1997). Publishing incited and also reacted to a wave of Romanticism, a moral self-examination across the country, about what was then called "national character." The issue was pressing because the country was experiencing rapid capitalist growth, huge waves of immigration from abroad, vast population movement to western territories, and fervent Christian revivals – all of which raised ethical doubts about new market relations and about slavery. Early in the nineteenth century, slavery had lost economic significance in the northern states, but was still legal in every region, yet was also globally condemned (Appleby 2000; O'Brien 2010).

Despite these shared dilemmas and despite networks of kinship, professional ties, educational connections, and business relations across regions, by the middle of the nineteenth century most Americans considered their country divided into homogeneous and contrasting "sections." Instead of a single people arrayed on Jefferson's gradient "in the north" and "in the south," most saw a "North" and a "South" – capitalized to signal their reification – that were two separate regions supposedly inhabited by distinct person types: the Yankee and the Southern Gentleman (aka Cavalier), whose complementary characteristics are yet another turn on the axis of differentiation we are examining:

The Yankee in his thrift, his industriousness and his asceticism was a praiseworthy figure, yet [also] ... mercenary, hypocritical and Philistine. Similarly, the gay, pleasure-loving and generous-hearted Southerner won admiration for his indifference to pecuniary drives and his ... genteel ways; yet [was] ... weak, vacillating and self-indulgent ... [or] wild. (Taylor 1961:21)

"Yankee" – with its southern counterpart – became "the major figure in an American debate over the lineaments of the national character" (Conforti 2001:158). The striving, competitive Yankee, an ambitious, self-made man, was juxtaposed to the gracious, elegant southern aristocrat, caricatured in the northern press as effete or even effeminate.

One could point to political economic differences between regions to justify this contrast. The Northeast had larger cities, commerce, and industry. More importantly, the Louisiana Purchase (1803) resulted in the revival of profit in slavery when the vast acreage of the Mississippi valley was turned to large-scale production amid rising world prices for cotton. White planters, with capitalist investors from North and South, took advantage of global markets by intensively and brutally exploiting black slave labor (Du Bois 1896; Johnson 2013). Supporters of the war with Mexico (1846–1848) envisioned the United States as a colonial slave empire expanding to the west and south. Labor was key. Whether the slave economy would be extended to the new western states and how to deal with forms of capitalist wage work in a newly market-oriented world were the urgent questions that drove politics.

Yet, stereotyped images of a North and a South were not simply reflexes of political economy. Boundaries of sections were ever shifting and highly contested. The conventional images actually erased the vast differences of economy and opinion *within* each envisioned region as well as the indispensable social, political, and especially financial connections between them. We agree with historians who warn against reading these early decades of the nineteenth century anachronistically as foreshadowing a preordained Civil War. On the contrary, the images of North and South and the person types that were eventually seen as their natural inhabitants were a *product* of debates in which participants challenged each other to justify divergent visions for the future.

Differentiation through interaction was ubiquitous in these debates. They highlight how expressive practices are invoked and transformed in *reciprocal* rhematizations, as speech and other expressive signs were taken up to signal social types and modes of social relationship. Speakers disputed and refused each other's stereotypes and those of foreigners.[5] The colonial distinctions were selectively retooled – independence versus hierarchy, honesty versus deceit – and the locus of anchors moved from geography to what was called "race." Explanatory narratives shifted from environmentalism to origins and genealogy. Features that did not fit were erased.

Competition was one social relation evoked via perceived differences. New Englander Ralph Waldo Emerson visited Charleston in the 1820s and formulated his experiences as comparative deficiencies of ("us") Yankees:

Southern people are almost all speakers and have every advantage over the New England people, whose climate is so **cold** that 'tis said we do not like to open our mouths very wide. ... The Southerner always beats us in politics [because] ... [he] has personality, has temperament, has manners. ... The **cold** Yankee ... has not **fire** or firmness ... and is shamed and scared and manipulated. ... The southerner owes to climate and slavery his suave and picturesque manners. (quoted in Floan 1958:52–53, emphasis added)

Cold/heat was the master trope linking the northern landscape of proverbial "granite and ice" to the inhabitants' demeanor, as opposed to the stereotype of a warm, fertile, and abundant South. Other northern writers were critical of southern abundance, the "stream of words, words, words that could talk a Yankee dumb" (*New England Magazine* 1834, quoted in Floan 1958:94). New Englanders were proud of their "frugality," in words as in money. The Boston poet James Russell Lowell celebrated rural Yankee reticence by extending the stereotype to phonology, writing fondly that the "genuine Yankee" omits certain consonants (r, g, d in final position) as a "piece of self denial" (1977 [1848]:42); non-Yankees seemed immoral, self-indulgent.

A southerner rhematized the North, in reports of his travels to New York and New England, concluding that "in affability to inferiors they [Yankees] are definitely behind us" (Minor 1834–1835:218):

[S]everal times I have experienced discourtesy [from servants]. ... The simplest and most harmless question ... has occasionally been answered with a gruffness ... an abrupt, surly, unmodulated tone uttered without even turning [the] head. (Minor 1834–1835:217)

Climate and slavery explained the difference, because they give the South "greater leisure to cultivate *manner* ..." that is, "politeness and respectful address." Writers in New York and New England criticized this politeness, calling it a "fondness for titles and ranks," explaining it as "a spirit of domination, engrafted on the southern character" (Floan 1958; Kerber 1970). Verbal skill was a related matter of contention. The journal *Southern Literary Messenger* (1835) praised a southern novelist's "warm, fluent, figurative language ... characteristic of southern orators and writers," while the same author was dismissed by the *New England Magazine* for "verbosity and incorrectness" of style (1837 in Floan 1958:92). The southern counterattack charged that "[t]here is no such thing as eloquence in New England. Cause: the cold, phlegmatic, matter-of-fact character of the people" (*Southern Literary Messenger* 1842:8:1:68).

Southerners called the Yankee disposition "unchivalrous," "frigid," and "selfish," all signs of unsociability. The Yankee defense called it "cautious and reserved":

a manner ... of self respect and love of consistency ... [among us], each being able to depend on himself, there is no motive for servility, and arrogance is awed by the certainty of a prompt and effective rebuke. (*North American Review* 1837)

That is, southern sociability for New Englanders was a sign of aristocracy ("chivalry") and hence hierarchy. Speaking the same way to everyone was a sign of egalitarianism. Noah Webster had written that New Englanders say "you had better" instead of "you must," to avoid the hierarchy implied in giving commands (1967 [1789]:107).

But rhematized images were not always competitive. Fractal recursivity was sometimes a means of self-criticism. Lucian Minor (1802–1858), a Virginian traveling in the North in the 1830s, found the stereotyped northern virtues of orderliness and education and wished to establish them in the South. But he also noted virtues in the North that he identified as southern: "of Yankee *hospitality* there is a great deal" (emphasis original). By finding some piece of the South in the North and praising the North, Minor took up a northern perspective for and among his southern readers. James Kirke Paulding, a novelist from New York, signed himself "a northern gentleman," when he published his *Letters from the South*. Finding in the South the northern virtue of a lively city, he added self-criticism: Unlike "our cities" in the North, Richmond is not "exclusively monopolized by money-making pursuits" (1817:48). Despite his persona as northerner, he voiced a southern perspective to his northern readers. Just as most visions of the West were written by self-identified easterners, so too many plantation novels that popularized the image of the slaveholding gentleman-Cavalier were written by admiring northerners, including Paulding (Taylor 1961).

Mutual provocation was more common, however, formulated as accusations of deceit. "Cunning fraud," "dishonest transactions," fake products, and insincere piety were legendary traits of Yankees in southern eyes (*Southern Literary Messenger* 1837). New Englanders argued rhematically that the problem was not fraud but the gullibility of southerners. Yankees were *quick*-witted, their southern customers were *slow*-minded. Deceit, they wrote, was more characteristic of fine southern "manner," which hid ruthless racial domination. Jacksonian Democrats eliminated property requirements for voting by white men and claimed to be "the democracy." Many northerners saw this as "prevarication and hypocrisy": a party led by slaveholders claiming to support egalitarian values (Kerber 1970).

These accusations recall the elocutionary revolution of the early Republic (Gustafson 2012), but now worries about the unreliability of signs were taken up in novel ways. For instance, William Grimes (1784–1865), an African-American slave writing of his escape, created an encompassing recursion for the North/South axis. In 1815, Grimes fled from Georgia to Connecticut, where he was still legally a slave. In 1826, he wrote and self-published a memoir.[6] Grimes wrote as a southerner, explaining southern colloquialisms to a presumed northern readership. He judged southern people as violent, hence *fiery*, and the northern climate and its people as *cold* and *hard*hearted. Yet, rather than only contrasting North/South, he picked out their sameness: in New Haven as in Virginia and Georgia he was cheated, deceived, and betrayed by everyone. He advised against slaves leaving good masters, stressing the parallels between enslavement in the South and forced poverty, discrimination, and prejudice in the North. People like him,

he wrote, cannot trust anyone, anywhere. Real escape would require something different than North or South:

I would in my will leave my skin as a legacy to the government, desiring that it might be
taken off and made into parchment, and then bind the constitution of glorious *happy* and
free America. Let the skin of an American slave bind the charter of American liberty.
(1826:103, emphasis original)

In this poetic leap, Grimes created an unmarked encompassment, opposing a
dishonest America (North and South) not to any physical place but to the image
of a freer country temporally displaced into the future, and inheritor of a free
legacy.

By midcentury, temporal displacement was also typical of the broader debate.
The environmentalist's causal arrow was reversed. Writers drew "a contrast
between ... the character of the people of the Northern and the Southern parts
of the Union and the *consequently* opposite conditions of the countries that they
inhabit" (*North American Review* 1837, emphasis ours). Or environment was
replaced entirely in explanatory narratives. The ideals of the southern Cavalier
were found in rural England – the "Southrons" of Walter Scott. A southern writer
identified a "Southern Yankee" social type with all the "unscrupulous" characteristics of all Yankees, but living in the South (Hundley 1860:136); northerner
Harriet Beecher Stowe did the same in *Uncle Tom's Cabin* in 1852. Region
was backgrounded in favor of temperamental differences traced to genealogy.
Rhematizing narratives became tales of origin through kinship claims, as in
the Romantic imagination of nations in nineteenth-century Europe. The North/
South axis was extended temporally, lining up deep historical events along the
axis, in parallel with then current differences. So the characters of the stereotyped Yankee and Southern Gentleman were claimed to be bodily inheritances
from the first settlers of the North and South, who were supposedly on different
sides in the English Civil War of the 1640s. The Yankee was cast as the descend-
ant of the Puritan Roundhead, the Southern Gentleman as scion of the English
Cavalier. Differences between the two images were called matters of "race" or
"blood" (Taylor 1961:15).

Serious historians rejected this fanciful narrative (O'Brien 2010). But it was
a staple of popular magazines, as in one lead article: "A contest for the suprem-
acy of the race, as between the Saxon Puritan of the North and the Norman of
the South" (*Southern Literary Messenger* 1861, 1860). Theories of language
presumed the same story. The Vermont philologist George Perkins Marsh
argued, in 1859, that the Saxon heritage kept English vital, the Latinate (as in
Cavalier speech) was pompous, to be avoided. To James Russell Lowell, the
Boston poet, "the Yankee dialect was ... a sign of a thriving organic connection
with Saxon traditions" (Cmiel 1990:111). Geographical distinctions did not
disappear, but people types were ideologized as focus of attention.

Axes of differentiation build on entire chronotopes. The highlighting of one element (space, time, or persona) does not eliminate the others, but shifts their relative *salience*. Recall Jakobson's (1960) observation that the functions of speaking are simultaneous, but may shift in salience. Shifts in salience build on the social organizations through which the axis is normalized, institutionalized, and explained.[7]

Institutionalizations: Pivoting, Blockage, Branching

Social actors' institutional location does not determine the perspectives that they can take up; but location and perspective are not independent either. There is a space of indeterminacy between a social location and the speaker's inhabitance of a perspective/persona in interaction. In this space, fractal processes operate: *pivoting*, *blockage*, and *branching*.

Sixty years after Jefferson's environmentalist gradient, the genealogical view that North and South were separate and distinct races was normalized, indeed firmly institutionalized. By this we mean, first, that access to signs necessary to indicate one's social location with respect to this axis depended ever more on law, government, schooling, churches, and occupations. These institutions policed expressive forms and uptakes of stereotypes. The institutions were often reshaped around the values and practices associated with changing axes. Second, the stereotypes were discursively elaborated in ever more domains: as much in historical narratives as in linguistic theory, as much in print as in live entertainment. In calling Lucian Minor a "southerner" (above) we followed the practice of his contemporaries, who knew him as a professor at William and Mary College, born and educated in Virginia, a state allied with interests constituted in Congress and elsewhere as "southern." He was a valued contributor to Richmond's *Southern Literary Messenger*, a journal of specifically southern values. And he aligned narratively with "us southerners" in his writings, using shibboleths that others identified as indexing southerners. Parallel observations could be made for "northerners." The stereotypes and their conventionalized perspectives became recognized social facts, materialized and disciplined by multiple institutions.

For individual social actors, knowledge of the typical conjectures discursively linked to their institutional location is an indispensable part of claiming (or rejecting) that location and the stereotypes of self and others it establishes. So is validation of one's claim by others. The location enables experiences that provide knowledge about other corners of the social world, or limit such access. Social systems differ widely and over time in the extent to which they stabilize axes, which ones are matters of greatest attention, and how much movement they permit by participants across the resulting social categories.

Recall that Anne Royall, claiming a western persona, divided and subdivided the world into eastern and western qualities. By consistently aligning with whatever she found to be (comparatively) western, she enacted herself as a westerner. She only rarely adopted an eastern perspective. But consistency like Royall's is rare. Southerner Lucian Minor's strategy is more usual: in some writings he subdivided the South into a North/South distinction and on that subdivided distinction, he aligned with the North. Minor's move is a *fractal pivot*. It does not change the axis, nor the institutionally defined social location of the participant. But it has effects: Lucian Minor's reports, when discussed in an influential southern journal, helped define a southern person type that was sympathetic to northern values.

Fractal pivoting is an interactional move that changes the social actor's perspective, switching (usually temporarily) to the other side of the invoked axis: easterners acting like westerners; northerners like southerners; Americans like British. It works by evoking (voicing) one stereotyped persona in a scene that, for the speaker, conventionally calls for another persona. Quotation, citation, double voicings, ventriloquism, theatrical portrayal, and everyday mimicry are all forms of citation in which authors and speakers, relying on conventional linkages, take up a persona framed as "me, for now." These are ways of achieving fractal recursivity. The interactional effects may be impersonation, ridicule, and parody. But effects may be framed as serious and earnest – and longer term – as in Minor's reports.

A more elaborate example of earnest pivoting comes from the Revolutionary era letters of John Adams (1743–1826), later the second president. Adams's institutional location was never doubted by his contemporaries: he was a Massachusetts man, fought for independence, and represented the new United States in diplomatic relations with European countries. The axis that distinguished republic from aristocracy – with all the related contrasting qualities in that period – was one he invoked often. Letters to his wife Abigail provide glimpses of how he placed himself with respect to refinements that he considered the dangers of aristocracy: "Whenever ... love of Pomp and Dress ... great Company, expensive Diversions and elegant Entertainments get the better of Principles ... there is no knowing into what Evils, natural, moral or political, they will lead us." Yet, when he arrived in France for the first time in 1778, aristocratic qualities enthralled him. He wrote to Abigail, "The Delights of France are innumerable ... Stern and hauty Republican as I am, I cannot help loving these People ... The Politeness, the Elegance ... the Richness, the Magnificence, the Splendour, is beyond Description." Subdividing among republicans and their qualities, he placed himself on the aristocratic side. Yet among those republicans aristocratically inclined in France, he was once again a republican, expressing his preference for Braintree, Massachusetts, over Paris (quoted in Bushman 1992:199–200).

Adams never stopped being a republican vis-à-vis Europeans. Yet, the love of "splendour" was part of the demeanor he cultivated in comparison to other Americans. It was not simply a matter of propositional statements ("hauty Republican as I am ... delights of France") but also of gestures, speech forms and consumables. He insisted his children show elegance of bearing and dress, and famously recommended that the US president be addressed as "your Highness." It is tempting to see Adams as peculiarly ambivalent or even self-contradictory. But that ignores the ubiquitous potential of fractal differentiation. All subjectivities are potentially "divisible," and capable of what Du Bois (1903) called "double consciousness," with multiple perspectival views of the self.[8] It is more revealing to ask what pivoting produced. Among US politicians, Adams often inhabited a discursive position that valued (relative) hierarchy. He embodied in America some of the values that American rhetoric denied. Many disagreed with him – he lost the 1800 election; Washington rejected the address form Adams suggested. But no one forbade these pivots. Pivoting gave Adams his distinctive political voice at this time in his life.

But fractal pivoting of perspective is not always possible, or not for all axes and all participant types. We discussed *blockage* as the imposition of limits by some powerful authority (law, education, church, state), on the personae a speaker may legitimately take up. As Royall's experience suggested, standardization produces blockage. People types, objects, and practices defined as educated and well-bred by some institutionalized authority were deemed "correct" and standard. They were supposedly everywhere alike. Royall demanded respect as a well-bred, educated person and assumed her practices would qualify her for that persona. She was a western standardizer. But the eastern literary establishment, claiming uniformity of standards, in practice counted anything "western" as incorrect. They blocked recognition of the persona she claimed. Here we explore blockage in more depth, linking it to fractal pivoting, to show its several forms.[9]

Race theory and its categories also illustrate how blockage restricts fractal pivoting. In nineteenth-century America, this was more institutionalized in law and custom than standardization. Practices that distinguished "free citizen/black slave" added matters of "color" to the independent/dependent contrast. They erased free blacks entirely and restricted those in the marked, stigmatized category from some recursive moves and the categories they would create. William Grimes, the escaped slave, wrote, "My father was one of the most wealthy planters in Virginia," yet "I was in law a bastard and a slave," because Grimes's mother was a slave. Once, in Savannah harbor, with his "best suit and rattan [walking stick] in hand," and followed meekly by a free black sailor from the North who did him this favor, Grimes embodied the persona of a well-to-do white planter: elegant in dress, with swagger and a black slave. The white militia guarding the harbor took him to be white, a fact that enabled his escape.

However, on his arrival in Connecticut "they called me ... *negro*," yet in a New Haven boarding house, they "took me to be a white man" (1826: 29, 85, emphasis original). Grimes considered himself "three-quarters white" by birth, and lamented the fact that there was no legal place for this category in his world. If found circumventing the race binary or its enforcement, Grimes would have been held in contempt as "passing" and punished. By contrast, race theory permitted those who were unmarked citizens (white, free) to represent black personae for politics and profit. Thus, Boston newspapers printed cruel cartoons and eye-dialect representations of the dress and speech of New England free blacks when they mobilized for abolition in the 1830s (Waldstreicher 1997:328–348; Melish 1998:163–209).

A more complex example was blackface minstrelsy, which became popular in the 1820s in northern cities and remained so for a century. The performers and audiences were men, recent immigrants, mostly from Ireland. On stage, with painted faces, they pivoted to the black side of the racial binary, caricaturing the songs and dances of slave figures. Blackface minstrelsy was decried as stolen "skin" by Frederick Douglass, the black abolitionist (1950–1975 [1849]), but admired by some white critics as America's truest folk culture (Kennard 1845).[10] Key to minstrelsy's communicative effect was the position of Irish immigrants as wage labor, which involved no ownership of property, hence was seen as *dependent* and demeaning in American terms, in contrast to independent farming and artisanship. It emasculated immigrants as mere "hirelings," locked into humiliating capitalist work discipline, which was likened to slavery – "wage slavery." Immigrants and free blacks shared impoverished neighborhoods and competed brutally for jobs. Although "white persons" could be naturalized as citizens by law, it was not clear that Irish immigrants were "white" in this social sense (Ignatiev 1995:41). Poverty and dependence marked them as inferior in the eyes of Yankees, a label adopted in the mid-nineteenth century by northern nativists, as distinguishing them from immigrants. Yankees – factory workers as well as business elites – claimed the virtues of "discipline, sobriety and reliability" that they denied to immigrants (Foner 1995 [1970]:230–232). Minstrelsy's sexually charged, derisive imitation of the very figures that were the usual foils for American manhood – black men, women, and "Indians" – constructed a kind of masculinity, while underscoring that the performers – and their audiences – were merely playing with the racial (and sexual) binary and therefore implying they must surely be "white."

This alternative masculinity, a contemptuous mimicry of African Americans based on fractal pivoting via ventriloquation, was a form of privilege. It was transformative, helping to create a new category – the specifically *white* waged worker. Yet it was also a product of blockage. A more recent example clarifies this, exploring the fact that all axes have two *branches* – sides – and showing that these can be separately subdivided.

In the mid-twentieth century, a theory of "ethnicity" emerged in reaction to the civil rights movement and created novel stereotypes that Grimes and Douglass would have recognized. It subdivided the marked branch of the existing racial binary, yet blocked elaboration of the unmarked branch. The stereotyped qualities of the white/black distinction were reiterated, but *only* as subdivisions of the (black) stigmatized branch. The ideal American remained white. The fractal repetition of the race binary on the stigmatized branch produced two kinds of distinction. As Urciuoli (1996) has shown, neat, safe, and limited difference was called "cultural," while a difference framed as dangerous and disorderly was called "racial." Upward mobility and a foreign pedigree were requisites of *cultural* difference, which created many new stereotypes colloquially called hyphenated Americanness: Irish-American, Italian-American, and so forth. Reminiscent in semiotic "shape" of dialect differences in systems of standardization, each is "low" in its own way. Descendants of European immigrants, who were treated as racially different on arrival, claimed this category ("white ethnics"), and so did upwardly mobile African-Americans (note the label's frequent hyphenation). But this fractal subdivision reproduced the old stereotype of poor and nonmobile speakers of dialects and non-English languages who continued to be stigmatized as *racially* different.

Yet another kind of blockage is one that obstructs encompassment. To illustrate, we stay in mid-twentieth century but leave the United States, turning to Frantz Fanon's classic discussion of the French colonial world. In *Black Skin, White Masks* (1967 [1952]), he reveals a colonial axis of differentiation that casts civilization, whiteness, intelligence, respectability, Europe, and the French language on one side, representing the colonizer as the unmarked "human." In co-constitutive contrast was the stereotype of the colonized: savagery, blackness, vulgarity, and Creole – denigrated as corrupted French. Fanon's project was to persuade the colonized to reject these distinctions. He described what we call recursivity of the colonized branch. While both the Senegalese and Antilleans were colonized, Europeans allowed Antilleans to enact a "European identification" vis-à-vis the Senegalese, to be the Europeans among the colonized. Further recursions in the Antilles made Martinique the stereotyped European vis-à-vis Guadaloupe. And in Martinique, a man who had been to Paris seemed whiter, more civilized to his colleagues than those who had never left (1967 [1952]:19).

Linguistic practices invoked these distinctions, since the colonized accepted French Republican language ideology. It posited that "to speak a language is to take on a world, a culture" (1967 [1952]:38) and so "mastery of the French language" would be the sign by which people from the colonies would be judged in Paris. For the colonized, writes Fanon, it seemed that "to speak French ... is the key that can open doors which were still barred [to the colonized] fifty years ago." French language ideology offered a promise: "The Antilles Negro who wants to be white will be whiter as he gains mastery of the cultural tool that language is" (1967 [1952]:38). Yet, Antilleans in France were not treated as "white," no matter how well they spoke French. The French addressed Antilleans in a "pidgin French" that was "an automatic manner of classifying ... primitivizing ... decivilizing" them. The reason: "The European has a fixed concept of the Negro ... an archetype ... [an] eternal ... essence ... an *appearance* for which he is not responsible" (1967 [1952]:35, emphasis original). The promises were lies for "dupes and [by] those who dupe them." The French in France recognized only the black/white distinction.

Despite the recursions institutionalized on the colonized branch, an Antillean in Paris, speaking fine French, who had expected to be treated as a Parisian, would be blocked. Fanon suggests that French Republican language ideology promised an *encompassing* recursion that would eliminate markedness and by which all French-speakers – in metropole and colony – would be united by the French language they shared, as against, say, German- or Russian-speakers. This encompassment was obstructed by European race theory – the "eternal ... essence ... the archetype" – enacted through the rhematizing linguistic practice Fanon describes. Despite recursivity on one branch of the axis, race theory legitimated the institution of the color line, blocking encompassment across it.

Standardization, race essentialisms, and European monolingual nationalisms are among the ideologies that create blockage. Ironically, one *response* to blockage is a fractal reiteration of standardization, creating a new center of authority. Fanon feared that Antilleans would fail to standardize Creole, but imagined that the Senegalese would exit the colonial bind exactly by making a standard Wolof. With just this logic, an American norm for English in the early Republic was justified as opposition to British denigration of colonial speech. American English was to purify American speech by eliminating the supposed corruptions wrought by the London stage and Court (Baron 1982). Similarly, on seceding from the Union in 1861, the Confederacy envisioned instituting an English of its own that would have its own dialects and be purified of "Yankeeisms" (Faust 1988).

Purification, Polarization, and Solidarity

Purification is an organizational process as much as a linguistic one. Any contrasting stereotypes that speakers impute to each other have implications for constituting groups. Social categories and groups are not the same, of course, but group mobilization builds on categorial difference, enabling participants to form coalitions and split into factions.[11] To start with a classic example, Evans-Pritchard's description of Nuer segmentary politics shows categories mobilized into groups:

[E]ach [tribal] segment is itself segmented and there is opposition between its parts ... the members of any segment unite for war against adjacent segments of the same order and unite with these adjacent segments against larger sections ... the larger tribal sections were almost autonomous groups and acted as such in their enmities and alliances. At one point they would be fighting among themselves and at another would be combining against a third party. (1969 [1940]:142, 144)

Tribal segments are territorial and genealogical (lineage) categories that subdivide fighters: social obligation to mobilize as a group to fight in concert with a particular segment is expressed in a kinship idiom (1969 [1940]:143). Evans-Pritchard, like Simmel and Bateson before him, emphasized that outside threat produces unity among otherwise distinct segments. The segmentary dynamic is an important and familiar one, by no means limited to Nuer. Its logic follows a semiotics of differentiation.

But Nuer segments, in Evans-Pritchard's account, were never called on to choose which of two mobilized groups to join. Fractal pivoting, however, does create positions that are often perceived as "in-between" the distinctions of an axis (the change or difference in level of encompassment is unnoticed, erased) and thus social actors may be called on to join mutually exclusive alliances. Lucian Minor and James Kirke Paulding, had they lived long enough, would have had to decide which side to fight in the Civil War. Purification, polarization, and solidarity are aspects of grouping – of factions and alliances – that are undergirded by fractal recursivity, and more specifically by fractal pivoting or accusations of it. To illustrate, we track unfolding events in two ethnographic accounts of group formation and schism in the twenty-first century.

The first is an episode of purification in American negotiations around gun use. The National Rifle Association (NRA) started as a shooting club in 1871. Since the 1970s, through a change in leadership, it has become one of the country's largest civil society organizations (Cole 2016). Member recruitment emphasizes "freedom," as a masculine ideal of self-made independence. Thus, it relies on the changing axis of differentiation we have been examining. While wage work was a signal of dependence at the start of the nineteenth century, by century's end wages were generally seen as the instantiation of *independence* – redefined as control of one's own labor – and cause for masculine pride (Foner 1998). Gender distinctions had shifted for women too. From the mid-nineteenth century, waves of women's movements for equal rights undermined "separate spheres" ideology and framed paid work as freedom for women from political and economic dependence (Fraser and Gordon 1994). Today, the NRA is a tireless defender of self-sufficient masculinity, as emblematized by gun ownership and ensured by Second Amendment rights. It charges that these values are endangered by feminists, women in public life, effeminacy in men, homosexuality, and more broadly an intrusive, feminized, regulatory "nanny state" that is seen to produce dependence (Melzer 2009). These factors are framed not only as contrasts to masculinity, but as constant threats that effectively mobilize the category, making the NRA an activist group. It wages a no-compromise "war" with these opponents. The group's tasks are to link gun manufacturers to consumers and join with other civil society groups to lobby Congress for pro-gun legislation, opposing all gun regulation within a self-styled "gun-rights" coalition.

The NRA's immediate enemies are groups attempting to limit gun ownership and regulate gun safety through legislation, litigation, and negotiation. Their values and methods oppose those of the NRA, a contrast that emerges in the encounter we analyze. In 1998, the mayors of Chicago, New Orleans, Boston, and Detroit set out to sue gun manufacturers for product liability in order to get their cooperation in increasing gun safety and reducing handgun trafficking linked to rising rates of criminal activity at the time, especially murder. Courts refused to hear the suits, arguing that only legislatures can impose restrictions on a legal industry. The Secretary of Housing and Urban Development in the Clinton administration joined the mayors, asking cities to pledge they would buy police weapons only from companies that negotiated toward gun safety regulations (Osnos 2016). The mayors, the administration, and numerous civil society groups formed a "gun-control" coalition.

Some gun manufacturers were willing to negotiate, fearing the already draining costs of litigation as a danger to their companies and the whole industry. In March 2000, the CEO of Smith & Wesson, then the largest gun maker in the United States, signed an agreement promising child safety devices on handguns, internal locking devices with keys, smaller capacity magazines, and arrangements with dealers to reduce illegal resales. Smith & Wesson's CEO argued that his company had already been planning to develop some of these devices, while other points were too vague to cause trouble. The production and distribution of guns – perhaps even increased sales – would continue unimpeded; the industry was simply being asked to police itself.

Smith & Wesson was part of the gun-rights coalition. Yet it negotiated. The NRA found the agreement a violation of the Second Amendment. But the CEO of Smith & Wesson, himself a member of the NRA, said, "[Y]ou don't have to sacrifice the Second Amendment to get this [the lawsuits] resolved." He added, "I believe it is an absolute right for me to have them [my guns] and if they [government forces] went so far, I would be willing to give up my life, [for my guns]." This was NRA talk. The formulations – sacrifice, absolute right, give my life – are recognizable chunks of a gun-rights register, evident in NRA publications. Yet, continued the CEO, "I'm also a pragmatist," and the manufacturers "have to save the business" of making guns. The NRA, he caustically noted, no longer has much to do with guns. "Their job is to prove 'we can get your candidate elected.' They're [nothing but] a political force, period" (quoted in Brown and Abel 2003:195). For the CEO, taking a narrow view from within the gun-rights forces, the NRA was playing politics, not protecting gun use.

The NRA, defining a broader contrast, cast the CEO's action as taking the other side, and a threat to gun rights.

When the agreement was publicly announced, the NRA sent to its then 3.2 million members a summary that characterized the agreement as a "betrayal." Shortly thereafter, the following message blanketed gun-friendly internet sites:

If we all stopped buying new S&W firearms, knives, hats and accessories for the rest of 2000 and 2001 there would be no S&W to keep the deal with the Clinton Administration. No one has to go without a gun, simply go without an S&W gun. (quoted in Brown and Abel 2003:214).

Within days the Smith & Wesson CEO was receiving death threats. Sales of the British-owned company plummeted, as did its stock price. The NRA president, in a TV interview, told the "redcoats" to go home. Smith & Wesson offices received shipments of tea bags, an allusion to the Revolutionary War's Boston Tea Party. The CEO stepped down in the autumn of 2000. The company, which had been bought in 1987 for $112 million, was sold in 2000 for $15 million (Osnos 2016:36–45). The boycott was dazzlingly successful. Yet, as the trade magazine *American Handgunner* commented, "if Smith & Wesson perishes in a consumer boycott the only winners are the anti-gunners" (quoted in Brown and Abel 2003:227). Ironically, the gun-rights coalition had almost destroyed a major gun maker.

That logic characterizes purification generally. In our semiotic analysis of the episode, the gun-rights/gun-control distinction was reproduced among gun-rights forces, and some of the gun companies pivoted. Difference in encompassment was erased. One participant invented criteria for belonging to its side and disciplined allies to obey. Waves of purification eliminate practices that pivot to the values of the other side. This process increasingly distinguishes and socially distances from each other those who represent the two sides of the axis and results in polarization, displaying the coercive power of those who discipline.[12]

But fractal pivoting can also be a different kind of power move, making evident a form of solidarity. To illustrate, we turn to the World Bank, where "human rights," not gun rights, are at issue. Like "Yankee," "rights" is a shifter that has been invoked in diverse comparisons in US history (Rodgers 1987). Human rights became a focus for advocacy and NGO activism only in the 1970s; it appeals to an international legal order, not to states, and protection is sought for individuals against governments (Moyn 2010).

The World Bank is an intergovernmental agency headquartered in Washington, DC, with a mandate to alleviate world poverty. Led by a board of member countries, it cultivates an apolitical, technical image that attracts clients: countries needing help but wary that help may encroach on their sovereignty.

The image also attracts donors: rich countries that pursue their often neo-imperialist policy goals through contributions to this seemingly neutral organization. The agenda has expanded to fund anticorruption campaigns and environmental and health projects. However, the World Bank resists supporting "human rights," despite pressure from NGOs and private financial institutions to do so. Many factors motivate this refusal. As Sarfaty (2012) has argued, a neglected one is the bank's internal discourse, which we reanalyze here, with an eye to differentiation.

The World Bank is run by economists, and economic frameworks have the most influence in decision-making about what development projects to fund, where, and at what levels. The bank also employs lawyers, sociologists, and anthropologists. For most employees, regardless of discipline, human rights are outside the bank's mission. As they see it, the World Bank's charter precludes them; remaining apolitical legitimates the bank. This hegemonic, *economistic* position bases the bank's work on international protocols and quantitative evidence, seen as objective. Yet, internal discussions among World Bank professionals have produced ideological fission. Many lawyers, social scientists, and some economists have come to consider the protection of human rights an ethical responsibility. This *reformist* position opposes the *economistic* one. The reformist position is itself divided, recapitulating the initial distinction: one side frames human rights *instrumentally*. It is ethically important only insofar as it supports economic development and is based on well-defined, quantitative evidence. The opposed reformist position frames human rights *intrinsically*, as a universal, transcendent value, based on the international legal regime and on ethical principles and imperatives (Sarfaty 2012:115–130).

This fractal pattern is a matter of positions – not groups – signaled by register differences. Some professionals warn their colleagues to abjure ethical questions and instead discuss "trade-offs." That is the economistic register. The term "human rights" in a report marks a reformist position. Phrases like "universal principles, dignity and quality of life" signal the intrinsic-reformist position. By contrast, "inclusion, accountability, good governance, empowerment," while they seem to cover similar concerns, are nevertheless understood to be "more easily defined, more receptive to measurement." They signal the instrumental-reformist view.

It is evident that the reformist positions (instrumental or intrinsic) could be mobilized to pivot to differing factional positions in decision-making situations. Instrumentalists can sometimes form alliances with those taking an economistic view, at other times with those who take up intrinsic views. Intrinsic positionings can mobilize in alliance with instrumentalists, or even with outside groups. In the early 1990s, an internal conflict arose over the funding of power plants in one of the richest botanical reserves in Southeast Asia, which is also the ancestral home of six indigenous groups (Sarfaty 2012:93). Rights-minded professionals at the World Bank, positioning themselves as intrinsic-reformers, constructed an alliance against the project with community groups and NGOs. This was a rare case in which a project's funding was withdrawn. The incident illustrates the potential power of fractal fissioning.

At the World Bank, economists tended to be economistic, lawyers and anthropologists were often reformers. Thus, when professionals and staff took up positions in decision-making, action might be based on a Durkheimian organic division of labor, in which disciplines work in complementary combinations. Or there could be mechanical solidarity, uniting experts into groups in a single discipline. But the various positions on human rights cut across disciplines and across the bank's administrative and regional specializations. Registers signaling positions on human rights provide ways of recognizing allies or opponents even among people one does not know. This makes possible a fractal solidarity: perceived similarity in the positioned contrasts one enacts (Abbott 2000). Distinct, contrasting registers and the situated (ideological) positions they signal in particular events provide an alternative way of forming coalitions for action, no matter where the social actors are located organizationally or disciplinarily.

Conclusion

We moved from Yankees in eighteenth-century colonial militias to human rights in a twenty-first-century intergovernmental agency. This chapter illuminates the substance of these changes, but is centrally about the process. The apparently large leap across time and scale supports the generality of our argument. The goal was not to explain these many circumstances, but the reverse: to exemplify the logic by which the process of differentiation changes axes, which in turn changes the circumstances that they organize.

The three chapters of Part II have shown the semiotic armature that sustains differentiation. Yet the same process enables permutations of what counts as difference itself. Thus, ironies abound: change in axes seems conservative, since it relies on already constituted distinctions. It is also creative, contingent, open-ended: qualities are reordered and reinterpreted as they are taken up to formulate and organize new projects, values, and interests. This is how people both intervene in historical process and learn to interpret it. Cascades of differentiation also make new and unexpected similarities. Distinctions separate, but they also connect, in two senses: different kinds of scenes are linked to each other by changed axes; and abstract values and qualities are connected to their instantiations in organizations and in diverse sites – times and places of social interaction – as we discuss in Part III.

Finally, differentiation constitutes and also transforms the social world, creating novel forms of difference and social organization. We return to these processes in Chapter 8, on scaling. Sometimes transformation is due to power lodged in centralized authorities. Thus, blockage is a familiar power effect, constraining and controlling participants. The same may be said of purifications and erasures. But differentiation more generally is better characterized as productive power, recalling Foucault's sense. It creates classifications and spreads their differentiating effect extensively in time and space. The semiotic process described here provides the routes and channels by which power reaches into the tributaries of social life. Differentiation and comparison create novel categories, assembling the distinguishing signs of those categories, constructing the armature of organizations that support them and the rhematizing narratives that render them taken-for-granted, presupposed.

Part III

Sites

What does our approach imply for the observer's analytical strategies in identifying and interpreting ideological work? Where should you start looking for ideologizing about language and communication? And how do you move forward from there? While the methodological concerns of investigators dominate our discussion in Part III, such concerns are not qualitatively different from those of other social actors. Everyone is an observer. Everyone needs to grasp what is important to pay attention to, what it signifies and what it leads to, in relation to their own roles and projects. Outsider investigators have their own backgrounds and points of view, but these vary among all participants in social life.

Part III builds from simple to complex. Chapter 6 lays out a minimalist, sign-based definition of *site of ideological work*. It is an *object of joint attention* – "object" in the philosopher's sense of something the mind takes cognizance of, whether concrete or abstract. It is a site *for making interpretations*, construals. Joint attention to this object implies a plurality of actor gazes, viewpoints that are relative to their backgrounds and their lines of sight upon the object. Like a camera that can focus on more or less of the social world, this attention-based definition of sites posits them as inherently unbounded. Many questions are implied. Who picks out an object for scrutiny? What and who are excluded? What practices are involved in the construal, and what semiotic properties are accorded to the object? The investigator's gaze adds a meta-move, tracking participants' gazes as well as the object of their attention itself. We start by choosing a simple site – doors and their implications – to illustrate how even an apparently trivial (and wordless) example reveals multiple gazes, varied responses, and ideologized interpretations.

In Chapter 7, a whole array of ideological processes – typification, explanation, authorization – is illuminated by analyzing them as different kinds of connections between sites. Even the simplest site leads to many others. Again we start from a simple everyday site, this time a bench at a city bus stop. From that starting point our discussion builds outward to explore a wide range of uptakes to still other uptakes, all implicating social positionings and differences. What ideological work must be done to connect the sites and scenes of difference in these various ways?

Chapter 8 inquires into the complexities of scales and scale-making as practices linking sites in arrangements that are variously subject to differential evaluation or measurement. Scaling starts with a semiotic process of comparison among sites. Innumerable aspects of human activity can be compared and thereby scaled, but there is no single mode of calibration. Rather, making any scale is an ideological project that identifies what aspects are worth comparing, on what dimensions, in what context, and how justified and enacted. Examining some complex scale-making models shows that some models build social differences or shifts of perspective into the ways they link sites, while others deny that human perspectives are even involved. Finally, we consider approaches that reject scale-making because they deny commensurability. Some versions of incommensurability rest on contestations about what dimension of an activity is to be scaled. Other versions call attention to a dimension of (differential) power that renders commensurability on any other dimension impossible.

What Is a "Site" of Ideology?

Where should one look for ideologies of language, communicative practice, and social distinction? Where and when does evidence about the propositions, presuppositions, and construals that we call ideologies become apparent? Put another way, what are the "sites" of ideologies, where do they "live," and where can one find them in empirical investigations? These questions focus on investigation and its strategies, but they also entail some important problems regarding the nature of ideologies and their possible manifestations in the world of human social practice. They further entail some problems regarding investigation and analysis themselves, undertakings that are not the sole province of outsiders. All social actors are in some sense analysts of their situation.

These questions and problems need some rephrasing before they can be usefully addressed. Ideologies are not things, like rocks one might stumble over or buried treasure one might dig up. As the discussions in Part II emphasized, ideologies involve active processes of construal and uptake, applying theories about the world (linguistic and otherwise), and constructing sign-relations that may take complicated shapes. So a better way to pose our initial questions would focus on *sites of ideological work*: moments and practices in social life in which experiences and ideas are swept up – drawn into ideologized interpretations. Where can one see ideologies at work? And are there sites that require or invite more work, or different kinds of work, than others? Is there work that pertains specially to the researcher?

These are problems for research on all kinds of ideologies, not only ideologies of language. In particular, ideologies of communicative practice, and ideologies of differentiation – formulations of our topic that fall within our broad purview, as we have discussed in previous chapters – are equally subject to these research problems.

Meanwhile, the concept of "site" has itself become a topic of scholarly discussion. One strand in that discussion that we find interesting, though not yet sufficient, is inspired by Heidegger and his notion of a "clearing" (*Lichtung*) or "open" (*Offene*).[1] The "clearing" is a *space of intelligibility* in which any

existing thing, including humans, shows up (Schatzki 2005:469–470; see also
Schmidt and Volbers 2011). Supposedly, the "clearing" is ontologically prior
to all representation; Schatzki compares it to an empty stage in a theater before
the action begins. We find the emphasis on intelligibility useful, but the image
of the "clearing" or the "empty stage" becomes problematic inasmuch as it is
envisioned as bounded and, especially, as ontologically *prior* to semiosis. For
us there can be no preexisting theater space. Imagine, instead, a band of street
performers who establish – by and through their actions – a "stage" for their
play. *It is the semiotic activity that creates its site: the arena of acts, things,
people, or anything else that are made available for joint attention.*[2]

While that semiotic activity may include some initial framing ("Welcome to
our play," for example), the framing is not prior to interpretive attention. And
as soon as someone focuses attention on something, the attention effectively
leads to a sign. Even if we say that a site is a "space" of intelligibility and
therefore of the possibility of attention, the space can never be empty. It must
have an object of attention "in" it, semiotically grasped – made into a sign.
Ideological work must always involve semiotic materials. Moreover, a site cannot be definitively bounded. Regardless of framing, the semiosis of sites, we
will argue, always escapes any such boundaries.

We enclose the word "space" in quotation marks because it is to be taken
metaphorically rather than literally, even though there are sites that do in fact
have a spatial extension. However, our own favorite metaphor for sites of language ideology plays on the pun of "sites" with "sights," perceivable phenomena that can be viewed (or heard, or felt, etc.).[3] The pun offers a useful heuristic
because one can imagine a site of ideological work as like a camera's field of
view. Imagine, then, the positioning of an ethnographic or sociolinguistic lens
whose focus encompasses a particular range of observational detail that is analyzed with the question of ideological construal and activity in mind. Cameras
can be variously positioned, thus observing different things. And even if the
camera itself does not move, the focus of a gaze through the lens can shift,
by changing the width of the lens and the depth of the field. A camera's field
of view can be made wider or narrower, shallower or deeper, in the course
of observation, encompassing more or less of the field of observable objects,
activities, and events; and it can pick up more or less detail in what is observed.

Setting metaphors aside for the moment, how can we conceive of a site in
semiotic terms? A site is not a representamen; it does not stand for something
else.[4] One way to think of a site semiotically is as the *purview of indexicality*:
the "here" and "now" in which an indexical sign is taken to be meaningful,
particularly while the sign is under construction. If I hear and attend to a street
vendor's cry (as in Peirce's example of an index), the cry acquires an auditory
representation – a sign. On the basis of my experience with such cries, I take

this sign to be an index of some source from which it emanates, and I then look for this source (the indexical sign's object) in the environment. Notice that the scope of this environment is not independent of the theory – the presuppositions, the social knowledge, the interpretive schemata, the accustomed paths of construal – that I bring to the interpretive moment. I assume the source of the cry is spatially closer than Mars, for example, and temporally very close, and I inspect my visible surroundings for a person or animal I assume to be its source. So I have already identified the nature of the sign, to some extent. As a related – but separate – step, made on the basis of my experience or prejudgments, I hypothesize that the likely source is a street vendor. Peirce's discussion of *abduction* is relevant here: the hypothesis, or guess – especially the guess involved in forming a perceptual judgment – is itself an interpretive moment. "The abductive suggestion comes to us like a flash. It is an act of insight" (Peirce 1955b: 304; see also Chapters 3 and 8).

The site, then – to return to metaphors – is like the scene in which something construed as an indexical sign is in play. It is not prior to that snippet of "theory" that consists in identifying a representamen as an index, and construing a certain realm of available perceivables as the likely scope of contiguity within which to search for the indexical sign's object. It is the *arena of abduction*. So, any phenomenon becomes a site of ideology when it is a focus of interpretive attention.

Although the vendor's cry is a simple example, the signs in a site might be much more complex, built upon one another, in ways we have explored in Part II. Moreover, sites themselves can be linked. A given site can be a frame of reference – an interpretive anchor – for other sites, informing the interpretation of talk in them. The researcher's analytical efforts afford one such complexity: representations at a remove – at a meta level, if you will – from the representations created by participants (participants in the ideological work the researcher seeks to understand). The researcher's gaze is not the same as the participant's. Even in "participant observation" or in autoethnography, where researcher and participant are one and the same person, the gazes that accompany these roles are distinct. ("Researcher" is a stance, a role, not the permanent identity of a person.) The participant's ideologized construal – her or his taking something to be a sign – is the researcher's focus of attention.

Such a metacommunicative step is characteristic of semiotic processes and their analysis. This step is not automatic or passive. Instead, the researcher's analytical gaze selects what is to count for the purposes of study as a site of ideological work. Identifying sites for analysis is thus a matter of one's imagination, perspective, and/or theoretical agenda. Yet, even though the analyst in a sense creates or "determines" the site by selecting objects of attention, these objects – participants' talk and activities, reflecting their own foci of attention – already exist in the world, and the site's properties, from an analyst's perspective, can be examined.

In short, any social activity, and any existing object in the world that is socially interpreted, can offer an example of ideological work and thus engage a field of view for analytical attention – a site. The question of course remains as to whether the particular site is an interesting one, how if at all it is linked to other sites, and how the analyst might assess its ingredients.

Lest this concern with attention appear to be a Euro-American analytical monopoly, consider the Mande concept of *kolosi*, "paying attention," discussed by Henrike Florusbosch (2011). For villagers in rural Mali, *kolosi* is the analytical center of social life. It is not just that one ought to pay attention to important things; what matters most is the question of *what* things and events are signs requiring attention and construal. Then follows the question of where to look for the signs' (Peircean) objects. A broken stick lying in the road may be merely the effect of a gust of wind, or it may be a sign left by a previous traveler, to convey some message to those walking along the road later. How recently might that traveler have passed by and left the broken stick? Frequently admonished to "pay attention," because she had apparently not taken something to be a sign – or had focused on the wrong thing – Florusbosch found that *kolosi* and the problem of sorting out important from insignificant phenomena, and exploring the scope of their significance, were themselves objects of attention and theorizing in village life. Attention and the scope of signification are to be negotiated.

Once participants pay attention to something, whether in their action or in their gaze, their attention – or, rather, the act that signals their negotiated attention – becomes, in turn, a sign for us the observers, allowing us to identify the participant's gaze and its object as a sited sign, and to ask: How exactly is the material in focus interpreted by participants? What aspect of the material they identify draws their attention? In what sort of framework, in what perspective, with what conjecture (interpretant), hence with the aid of what ideologizing do they respond to it? Do the participant gazes we can identify differ from one another? If a site is a field of view affording the possibility of joint attention, then there can be more than one viewer, more than one perspective on that field and on any semiotic object in it. The researcher's gaze is focused on the multiple gazes of others.

Why "site," a spatial term? Even in our metaphor of gaze and sighting, our image of the camera that "views" a field invokes a spatial imagery too, although emphasizing the camera and its manipulation rather than taking the spatial field as given. One reason for drawing on this kind of imagery is simply its familiarity and utility in the social sciences. In fact, the use of spatial imagery for attention and other cognitive processes, projected as located in space, is very old in the Western intellectual tradition. So too is the connection of these processes and projections with language – with its creative uses as well as with conceptions of common, conventional or authoritative knowledge. That connection, via spatial imagery, of the conventional and the creative was articulated by scholars and orators in Antiquity and in medieval times. Spatial imagery, such as envisioning the rooms in a large and complicated building, offered a series of *loci* or *topoi*, through which one could amass and remember "commonplaces" – the already existing ideas of others – and among these, distinguish among different arguments or perspectives on an issue, as well as the facts bearing upon them. The architectural structure would serve as model for the images' order and organization.[5]

Although the architectural image has been largely forgotten, the spatial metaphor persists, sometimes recognized as metaphor, sometimes taken more literally. In recent scholarly writing the term "site" can mean a number of rather different things: a geographical location, a position in a social system, a complex social institution (e.g., "the laboratory"; Foucault 1972:51), a nexus of social practices (Schatzki 2002), a text. Anthropology has had its own "site" discourse, especially regarding the "field site," an expression of long standing in the discipline. While anthropologists still maintain the spatial metaphor of "field site," work by George Marcus (1995) and others in the late twentieth century pushed the notion of ethnographic research site away from literally geographic conceptions, and especially away from the village studies that had dominated ethnographic research for many years. As Gupta and Ferguson (1997) conclude, all ethnography is a matter of a framing or form of attention, not necessarily of place. One can be "in the field" in one's own neighborhood, or "not in the field" in the New Guinea highlands, depending on one's frame, gaze, or attitude. Ethnographic attention "in the field" focuses on some range of observational detail, usually taken to be a slice of some larger process or system.

We agree with Gupta and Ferguson on this point. We also agree with those scholars who connect the notion of "site" with those intellectual traditions, exemplified by scholars such as de Certeau, Lefebvre, and Foucault, that question the possibility of discovering universal, eternal truths about human social life, preferring to consider all such knowledge as situated and all social facts as linked to historical contexts. Our notion of site is consistent with those arguments. We press further, however, rethinking the concept of "site" itself via our semiotic approach.

There is another advantage to a concept of "site" for our purposes. Considering "sites" in relation to ideological work conveniently affords paying analytical attention to activities and social relations, as opposed to seeing all ideology in terms of persons and minds. So "sites" may help circumvent some aspects of Euro-American ideologies of language, those that locate language firmly and only in the "mind-brain" and imagine language ideology as only someone's attitudes toward kinds of persons. "Sites" may allow us to bracket some difficult philosophical problems attending notions of belief and consciousness. Perhaps it also helps us recognize that ideologies, to be effective, must be produced and reproduced. They are positioned, but they cannot be utterly private.

If it is the analytical gaze that picks out a phenomenon for scrutiny, thereby taking it as an object of ideological work, then a site of such work can be anything or anywhere at all. Training attention on some "object" implies a series of questions about its siting: Whose eyes (besides the analyst's) pick out the object? Whose eyes are excluded or pay no attention? What are the perspectives through which attention is paid to this site? What is observably occurring within the field of view of our gaze and that of the (other) participants? Where does the gaze reach if its purview is widened (or narrowed)? Gazes may not hold still or stay within boundaries. What are the semiotic properties of the objects and events at the center of participants' attention? As an act in the world, or an object in the world, how is the site or activity produced and with what consequences? What institutional context is needed for its production, and what personal biography or group trajectory is accomplished or retarded by it? What other events is the site linked to, implied by, imagined with? What events are its precursors and consequences, or imagined to be so?

These questions will be taken up in detail in the next two chapters. They are pertinent for the present chapter too, but only insofar as they necessarily arise even for our minimal, semiotically focused conception of a site of ideological work: a conception in which a site is like the arena of abduction for a Peircean sign. We will explore this conception by way of a very humble example from everyday life in the United States – an example we initially thought would be very simple, but which turned out to be more complex upon analysis. The example shows how *a site of ideological work is the locus of semiotic uptake under a (potential) plurality of gazes.* It presents a communicative scene that is subject to ideologized interpretations, and the interpretations depend on the social positioning of the gazes on the site – that is, the positioned perspectives of the people for whom this site, and the scenes in which it might figure, is an object of attention. In this example, an apparently trivial or everyday object, involved in some ordinary communicative practice, is swept up in interpretations that draw upon larger-scale relations of social inequality and interestedness. Additionally, our minimalist example will allow us to draw some lessons about a few issues that have loomed large in scholarly discussion of sites and the empirical means by which one "finds" ideologies of language.

Site and Sighting: An Example

In producing such a minimalist conception of sites, we asked ourselves: What is the minimal set of considerations necessary to "sight" ideological construal at work? We deliberately chose to focus on something small and everyday, yet ideologically construed by participants. There is no text or talk directly involved in this site. Even the uptake and interpretation of its semiotic ingredients initially showed up only in nonverbal behavioral responses, and were given utterance only considerably later. Moreover, no single person, institution, or dominant force can be credited with actually "having" the ideology participants took to be revealed in this site. Yet, we observed that the ideology participants took to be revealed – created, to be sure, through their own (ideologized) assumptions and projections – was an interpretation powerful enough to change some participants' behavior.

At a certain American university there is an office building, renovated in about 2003. As part of the renovation, many interior doors, especially including the doors of faculty offices, were outfitted with a small vertical pane of glass, just above the door handle. On moving into their offices after the renovation, some faculty members covered the glass from the inside with a thick material; some covered the glass with a thin material, which showed whether there was a light on the other side of the door but afforded no visual detail; other faculty members left the glass uncovered. Among those people who did not tape anything onto the glass from the inside, some hung coats or sweaters inside the office in such a way as to obscure most of the view through the glass; some pasted posters or student sign-up sheets on most of the outside of the glass; others left the glass as is; and still others left the door entirely open whenever the office was occupied.

These responses to the glass doors were patterned, at least to some extent. A year or two after the faculty moved into the renovated building, some observers among the faculty noticed that the treatment of the glass roughly (but only roughly) coincided with faculty subgroupings according to academic discipline. A story began to circulate alleging that the pattern reflected disciplinary differences in faculty attitudes toward conversation with colleagues and students. People in discipline A, so the story went, were independent-minded, devoted to private contemplation, and averse to collaborative work. They covered the glass panes because they generally strove to restrict access to themselves as much as possible, believing that great ideas arise in privacy. People in discipline B, it was said, got along well with one another and had overlapping intellectual goals, so they did not mind if someone knocked at their door. They thought interaction fostered productivity, although (some versions of the story sourly commented) they spent too much time simply gossiping and socializing. These people were the ones who covered the glass only partially or not at all, so that it was obvious whether they were present in the office or not. Meanwhile, people in discipline C, the story claimed, favored team projects; they kept their office doors open – although in this department's case it was said that the faculty members disliked each other, so the teams consisted of students who worked with a single faculty member, not the faculty working with one another. (The doors were open for the students, who came and went, but the faculty member's desk was actually hidden from the view of anyone standing outside in the hall.) Some versions of the story speculated that the glass panes were placed in the doors by fiat of some administrator – unnamed, but presumed to be outside the particular departments housed in the building – who wanted to promote "transparency" in university life and thought faculty should be more accessible to students.

In short, the glass panes were interpreted in terms of ideologies about communicative practice in an academic setting: who ought or ought not to be available to interact with whom, which disciplines favored sociability and of what sort, and whether conversation fostered academic productivity. An ideological construct about faculty motivations, accessibility, and relationship with students was projected onto the intentions of some anonymous administrator(s), who allegedly had attempted to manipulate faculty communicative practice.

The responses to the glass panes roughly differentiated the faculty along lines that already existed, but that might not previously have had any obvious connection either to door design or to conversational practices. Yet, these differentiations and the accompanying story attributing them to disciplinary essentialisms appear to have been sufficiently powerful as to influence individual actions and the interpretation of anomalous cases. Professor X, loyal member of discipline B, might have preferred to cover her door's glass but did not; instead, she placed a coat rack near the door so that a heavy coat blocked the view of her desk from the hall. Eventually she stopped using that office at all except during published office hours. Professor Y, also a member of discipline B but who covered the glass with a paper screen, was said to have "leanings" toward discipline A. Professor W, also in discipline B, placed sign-up sheets all over the glass, partly obscuring the view of her desk – but a few years later, she increased the number of sign-up sheets and obscured the view entirely. Meanwhile Professor Z, who produced some of the most detailed versions of the essentialism story, left the glass uncovered. The story itself went unchallenged.

That narrative and the reactions to the glass came from faculty members. But there was also a narrative we heard from a staff member, who offered a different perspective. In a confident tone of voice she claimed that the glass panes were a matter of safety: being able to see who was inside the office before you entered it. So if there were an intruder, you would not have to confront or speak to the individual at all – you could just call security. Notice that she assumed the view of someone outside the door rather than inside; and she did not mention the possibility that the door might have been locked (lowering the probability of an invisible intruder within). This staff person, incidentally, had once or twice found it necessary to confront dubious-looking people in the hallway outside her department's main office. So her story sprang from her own experiences – which did not usually involve faculty offices directly – and from her perspective as staff rather than faculty. She said nothing about faculty-student interactions. Yet, her story, like the faculty members' stories, assumed that some powerful outside persons had designed the doors with a communicative rationale, just a different one. Visibility, in her story, meant *not* having to talk to someone one would prefer to avoid.

Actually it is not clear whether the glass-paned doors were the result of anyone's design for the behavior of faculty, students, or staff. In the process of renovating the building, we heard, the contractors may have made some mistakes – installing interior walls in the wrong place, for example – and there were also some unexpected costs and changes in availability of materials that led them to depart from the original plans. (Whether these changes or mistakes had anything to do with the office doors we do not know; the stories about the contractors did not mention doors.) So while the notion that glass-paned doors were to promote accessibility and interaction is certainly plausible, as is the idea of security (i.e., that visibility makes it possible to avoid talk, rather than promoting talk), it's quite possible that there were no such plans and, instead, a certain quantity of this type of door happened to be available at low cost. Alternatively, it might have been an architect, rather than a university administrator, who selected the door design – on aesthetic grounds rather than from notions of how faculty should behave.

(We must make it clear that the example is historical, not now contemporary. As of the time of writing, there have been changes in faculty, staff, office assignments, and door coverage, and the explanatory narratives seem to have disappeared.)

This example suggests that constraints on, or pressures toward, particular discursive practices can be literally built into an institution – becoming part of the built environment and its affordances – regardless of whether there is any individual who actually subscribes to them. Interpretations that rationalized these constraints and these forms of uptake were attributed to other people's supposed ideological commitments and projects. Faculty members articulated ideologies about intentionality and about the availability, frequency, and desirability of conversations with students, ideologies they themselves did not have – that perhaps nobody had.

At the same time, the ideological work of attributing motives was done on the basis of presuppositions about various categories of people who might be found in the building. Whether articulated by faculty or by staff, these ideologizing narratives focused on social inequalities within the institution and drew on some outside it. Regarding a doorway differentiating outsiders from insiders, faculty accounts emphasized the difference between faculty (located inside offices) and students (located in the hallway), while the staff account focused on people who belonged in a university building versus people who did not – people who were somehow threatening. (How threat was determined was not clear, but probably by some combination of clothing, age, facial expression, body size, and race.) Further differentiations within the faculty, the disciplinary patterns, emerged with respect to the actions people took, or didn't take, or delayed taking, to cover the glass.

In short, ideologies – here, concerning communicative practices – could be said to be present, on the premises, as it were. But where the ideologies were present was in the interpretive gazes that made this building's doors a site of ideological work. Ideological work was on the premises; intentionality had left the building.

Our own interpretation focuses on the meta level: on the building occupants' actions and narratives that reveal their various kinds of uptake on the semiosis afforded by the glass-paned doors. It is at that meta level that we identify participants' responses, their positioned ideologies concerning visibility and availability to interaction, and the differentiations – some evidenced in practice, others in allegation – of staff and faculty, and of faculty members in various disciplines, according to ideologized concerns about communicative interaction. Differentiation – in semiotic practices, gazes, and interpretations – is to be found even in so minimal and ostensibly nonlinguistic a site of ideological work as this one.

Lessons from the Example, with an Excursus on Explicitness

An office door leads between two spaces and affords communication between them – or not. As such it offers convenient metaphors for communicative practices: an "open-door policy," for example. Yet, although we can say that the door itself "communicates" between office and hallway, it does so merely through its location. It does not speak, it has no intentionality, and its particular material qualities need not be specified. The door participates in semiosis only when people attend to it and respond to it. As soon as they do, it becomes a site of ideological work and an object of multiple gazes and interpretations.

The first lesson to be drawn from this example, then, is that *joint attention engages multiple gazes, from which proceed multiple uptakes.* No two responses could be precisely identical, and the differences between them are themselves available for uptake in their turn. In the doors example the narratives about faculty members' responses also focused on differentiations – the contrasts among responses, and putative explanations of the contrasts.

Since the narratives went on to attribute motivations for the door design to some unknown university administrator, a second lesson to be drawn from the example concerns the *locus of ideology*: if those motivations are understood in ideological terms, whose ideology is it – if anyone's? Even if people postulate its existence, an ideology might "belong" to nobody. The motivations articulated by people who produced those narratives all concerned the ideologies of others, not themselves. Of course those statements can be examined as stemming from the narrators' own assumptions about their social world, as we saw. But these assumptions were not expressed explicitly in their statements (nor, obviously, in their nonverbal responses, such as covering the glass pane with a cloth).

So a third lesson concerns explicitness and the complicated matter of when, where, and why explicit ideological statements are made. *Ideological work need not be evidenced in explicit statements*. In the example, we see that as analysts of ideologies of communication, we cannot limit our analysis to actors' explicit assertions as if nothing else much mattered. In fact, we cannot even limit ourselves to linguistic utterances.

A fourth lesson is that a site of ideological work, because it engages multiple gazes, branches out in many directions toward other sites that are connected with it. The analyst's gaze is not the least of these. Therefore, *a site as we have defined it is not bounded*, except insofar as any boundary is constructed by the ideological work itself.

The last two of these lessons require us to elaborate. The issue of explicitness is sufficiently prominent in the literature, as well as important in its methodological relevance, to deserve some discussion in its own right. The question of a site's (lack of) boundedness will be taken up subsequently, in a section that will lead into the next chapter (7), on relations between sites.

Concerning explicitness as a possible feature of ideologies, and to pun again on site and sight: scholars have attended to the way ideologies of language are "sighted"; that is, whether they are revealed – or concealed – in discourse. Many scholars have studied language ideologies as (and only as) propositions about language found in denotational talk or in written texts. Ideology is taken to be metapragmatic discourse, consisting of propositions semantically referring to linguistic forms, practices, or beliefs. In such cases, the speakers or writers of the texts are usually taken to be holders, authors, or at least representatives of the ideologies they express. Other scholars have claimed that it is more important to examine practices that are based on unspoken, implicit, taken-for-granted ideological principles, those of which speakers themselves are not at all or not entirely aware. Whether people express ideologies explicitly or not has been attributed to the hegemonic power of socially dominant forces that constrain the expression of views unsupportive of the dominant class, possibly even blocking any awareness that nondominant perspectives might exist. In this view the speaker or author of some bit of metapragmatic discourse or text might merely be voicing someone else's ideas. As for such speakers' own ideas, their unspoken practice is deemed more revealing.

This question of the relationship between explicit and implicit manifestations of belief has been a persistent problem, much debated in the scholarly literature. Many matters that we would prefer to disentangle have been brought under its umbrella. Thus, some scholars have supposed that the explicitness (or not) of ideological propositions in discourse directly indexes the degree of speakers' conscious awareness of those propositions and of the social inequalities they entail. These issues have been linked, in turn, to the social occasions and genres of talk in which ideological propositions might be actively contested. Our argument here, however, is that dominance, conscious awareness, and contestation – though related in interesting ways in any particular case – do not follow automatically from the degree of explicitness of ideological articulation in talk.

Still, however many different aspects of communicative practice have been enfolded in them, questions about explicitness are part and parcel of questions about "sites" and "sightings" because they point toward where, in social life, ideologies – or particular aspects of those ideologies – are to be found. Moreover, where they are found has something important to do with what gaze(s) they implicate, and what their consequences may be. For some scholars, explicit metapragmatic discourse about languages and language use is the *first* place to look for evidence of language ideology, while for other scholars it is quite the opposite: explicit discourse is the *last* place to look for really powerful, hegemonic ideologies. Obviously, then, sightings are pertinent to the analyst's problem of research sites – the question of where to focus one's analytical attention – and evidence. Where should one look? Explicit statements may be easy to start with, but what if they cannot be found, and what implications can one draw from them anyway? We recall a conference in which a senior sociolinguist observed that in his view, studies of language ideology simply meant that the investigators were substituting informants' analyses for their own, and not doing their job, which was to look at behavior, not at claims about it. Meanwhile, many discussions evaluating evidence in terms of whether it is explicit or implicit seem to rely on a Western tradition of politico-linguistic ideology that posits an ideal of communicative transparency, honesty, and deliberative dispute in which the unspoken is a realm of deceit or subterfuge.

When the concept of "linguistic ideology" was first proposed by Silverstein in 1979, the definition focused on explicit assertions: "linguistic ideologies are any sets of beliefs about language articulated by the users as a rationalization or justification of perceived language structure and use" (1979:193). In contrast, some other scholars have identified ideology most crucially with the implicit and presupposed – those propositions about the world that are taken for granted. In that view, explicit statements are merely a sort of window dressing, while the really important things are the unquestioned certainties that are powerful precisely because they are never stated openly, hence never challenged or even available for challenge.[6] Curiously, while there are commentaries claiming that most studies focus on a task of revealing what is implicit – unmasking hidden agendas (Philips 1998) – there are also commentaries claiming that most studies focus on the linguistic ideologies revealed in informants' explicit metadiscourse (Tsitsipis 2003). In either case what is still needed, as Philips and Tsitsipis both point out (and see Silverstein's later statements, e.g., 1993, 1998), is close consideration of the varieties, relationships, degrees, and locations of ideological manifestations, in any particular case study.

The problems in question are more complex than they may seem. Although discussions of explicitness invoke questions about semiotic form, embedded in these discussions are several other issues: participants' conscious awareness of the meanings of their own statements and actions; the distribution of discursive practices (such as assertions about language) across genres and social settings; social asymmetries and inequalities; the possibility and form of contestation; and the role of outsider ethnographers. So, concerning conscious awareness, for example, Verschueren (1995:142) maintains that if powerful ideologies remain implicit, it may be because participants are not even aware of holding them: "the implicit meaning that we are dealing with represents supposedly common background knowledge at a level that may be insufficiently conscious to be voiced explicitly at all." Concerning the effects of power relations, Tsitsipis proposes that implicit ideologies of language partly correlate with "conditions in which hegemonic processes have been relatively successful" (2003:542); he alludes to Bourdieu (1991) on symbolic domination and inculcated dispositions, among other writings on power and agency. In other words, hegemonic processes have succeeded in making a dominant viewpoint on social life seem to be natural, and a dominant social segment's program for conduct seem normal (see also Verschueren 1995:143).[7] Notice that these arguments bear a close resemblance to Bourdieu's concept of *doxa* ("the world of tradition experienced as a 'natural world' and taken for granted"; 1977:164);[8] Habermas's "pre-understanding sedimented in a deep-seated stratum of things that are taken for granted, of certainties, and of unquestioned assumptions" (1998:236–237); and Brisard's "pre-predicative knowledge" (2002:xxv). These are closely related concepts, although the term "ideology" is not prominent in them.

Meanwhile, Philips (1998:223) suggests that scholars whose aim is to deconstruct implicit ideologies are appropriating the metapragmatic function to themselves, under the (implicit) assumption that the participants are ignorant or deluded – if not engaged in a process of deluding their fellows. Although (as Philips points out) the strategy of unmasking hidden meanings has long been part of ideological critique, anthropologists who are outsiders to the societies they study can be faulted too, if they presume that only the anthropologist can really know what the natives are doing.

Reflecting on these exchanges, we find that distinguishing among self-consciousness, active contestation or critique, social inequalities, and the distribution of genres and occasions in which disputation might occur is more useful than subsuming all these factors under the umbrella of a single variable, the explicit versus implicit articulation of ideologies. Only if we distinguish among the many variables that the literature has tended to summarize under "explicitness" can we attend to relationships among them. Regarding conscious awareness, for example, it is too easy to assume that if participants do not talk about something – itself too easily equated with not appearing in the ethnographer's notes and transcripts – they must not be aware of it. The ethnographer's problem is difficult. While it is obvious that people who explicitly discuss something are aware of it (sleep talking aside), it is not easy to demonstrate a negative – to make the case that people are unconscious of something. And when the case is not made, ethnographers can become prey to the temptation pointed out by Philips: that of appropriating all metapragmatic, interpretative authority to themselves.

Yet, the problem arises because there are several reasons to see awareness, self-consciousness, and attention as important factors linked to ideologies. Earlier chapters' discussions of erasure pointed out that ideological formations necessarily deflect attention from some things in the very fact of calling attention to others, as an important process in how ideologies are built and become effective. And Silverstein, in a well-known paper on "The Limits of Awareness" (2001 [1981]), showed that a speaker's (gradient) awareness of linguistic structures and their contributions to meaning was strongly influenced by those structures' semiotic form. We have witnessed, as well, the consciousness-raising effects of (for example) Jane Hill's work on "Mock Spanish," work that reveals the political implications of such expressions as *el cheap-o* and *no problemo* that occur in Anglo-American humor and light styles of talk (see Hill 2008). In politicizing them – reframing them – she brings them newly into attention. We have observed the unhappy surprise of liberal-minded Anglos in Hill's audiences who come to recognize their complicity as participants in a practice with racist overtones. We do not want to lose sight of these issues.

There is a difference, however, between being unaware of the ideological implications of what one says, and other reasons one might have for not expressing those implications in explicit assertions. One might not express something because it seems so obvious that saying it overtly would be unnecessary – perhaps even insulting to an addressee, because implying that the addressee was stupid or untrustworthy. Alternatively, one might be concealing – even, perhaps, from oneself – an assertion whose overt expression would invite criticism. Such masking is not only a tactic for the politically dominant. It can be seen also in the strategies of their less powerful opponents, as in the case of writers in Stalinist Russia who sought to evade the power of censors and the threat of arrest. Anna Akhmatova, for example, called her "Poem Without a Hero," a work begun in 1940, a "cryptogram" written in "mirror writing." The poem, comments Wendy Rosslyn (1995), "is a tour de force of periphrasis and quotation which locates the poem firmly as a late flowering of modernism and protected it from the onslaughts of censorship." Another poem ("Requiem"), less cryptic, could not be kept in written form at all. Instead, Akhmatova wrote it on bits of paper, gave these to a close friend to memorize, and then burned the paper over an ashtray. "Eleven people knew *Requiem* by heart, and not one of them betrayed me," she later remarked (Kelly 2005:64).

The circulations of Soviet-era oppositional writings through various genres and media, and through *samizdat* underground channels, indicate how wrong one can be to assume that what is not said explicitly has not been thought.[9] The example also points to the importance of attending to the social settings of talk (and writing) and the social positioning of texts' producers. Why, one should ask, is this person making this assertion, in this manner, and why now? If other people remain silent, can their silence be attributed to their social positioning (as friend of someone they don't want to betray? as someone who does not count as "expert"?) or is there some aspect of the social occasion that inhibits them although other kinds of occasions do not?

The making of explicit assertions about language is itself a discursive practice, subject to constraints on speakers, audiences, times, and places. Among rural Wolof, Irvine found it impossible to conduct garden-variety linguistic elicitation with certain kinds of speakers – women of the *jaam* ('slave') category, for example – because the local sociolinguistic regime offered no grounds for those speakers to feel authorized to pronounce on matters of linguistic form. *Jaam* women could, however, assert the (ideologized) principle that they were not language experts and "couldn't say" whether (e.g.) they had ever heard anyone utter such-and-such a linguistic construction. On this principle they quite agreed with the griot "experts" who appropriated expertise to themselves.

In short, explicitness, dominance, and contestation are not all-or-nothing matters. Ideologies (of language or anything else) cannot be taken as indissoluble wholes, even apart from questions of contestation. Two participants might contest a point, an idea about (say) what it means to speak in a particular way, while nevertheless concurring on the naturalness of other things. The Stalinist-era poets and the secret police shared the assumptions that poets are politically influential and that poetic form, in itself, does not protect a message from retribution. As Akhmatova's friend, the poet Osip Mandelstam, commented, "Poetry is respected only in this country – people are killed for it" (Kelly 2005:64).

Mandelstam was, in fact, arrested for a poem about Stalin describing "cockroach whiskers" and "fat fingers, like worms," even though the poem had not been written down. The oral channel did not protect him from a "friend's" betrayal. Of course, what he was arrested for was his explicit assertions about Stalin, not his assertions about poetry or language. Still, his case reminds us that ideologies of language are not ephemeral wisps or epiphenomenal structures having no bearing on other aspects of social life. They both shape and are shaped by the practices in which they are manifested, and the social relations they constitute. Ideological formations exist in history, and it is in history that they – or aspects of them – come into being, shift, acquire or lose "dominance," succeed or fail in drawing connections, and call attention to some things while erasing others.

The binary of explicit/implicit is too blunt an instrument for fruitful analysis of so many intersecting contrasts. These deserve to be separated, not conflated. The many degrees and ways of being (un)aware, the numerous ways of defining "explicit," the many modes, audiences, and reasons for issuing or bypassing explicit statements, the social positions from which these can emerge or can be seen to do so – all these vary across contexts, historical circumstances, and institutions, precluding easy correlations among the factors concerned. Notice too that if "explicitness" means assertions having truth value – thus deemed either true or false – many interesting bits of discourse using metapragmatic terms or metaphors but not conspicuously taking the form of assertions will be ignored, as will instances of lack of uptake.

As the office door example has shown, there is a similar complexity to the relationship between uttering a statement and "having" the ideology someone finds in it. Ideologies one abjures may be attributed to someone else, in the very move of abjuring them. What we saw in faculty members' claims about manipulative university administrators is a meta-move, an ideological projection, a process of *inferencing* – itself grounded in presuppositions about the someone else to whom one attributes power and objectionable principles.

Questions about Boundaries

Projecting ideologized commitments and projects onto other people is but one of several ways in which a site (of focused attention) branches out into other potential sites. Because a site, as we have defined it, is a semiotic construct – and in this sense differs from the usual social-science conception of a "field site" or "research site" – it potentially branches out to include whatever is encompassed in a particular gaze's field of view. And since there are multiple gazes, including the projections and meta-moves discussed above, no one gaze can definitively bound the site. Recall, in this regard, Peirce's discussion (1955a:100) proposing that the interpretant is itself a sign and therefore can give rise to an interpretant (conjecture) of its own. ("Interpretant," Peirce's term, for us always means "conjecture," and vice versa.) Put another way, the conjecture becomes the object of a meta-sign, potentially giving rise to a limitless series of signs upon signs. Signs are never alone; they exist in relation to other signs. Ideologized visions are never alone either. They always imply alternative views, seen from differently positioned perspectives. Just as a sign cannot be isolated from other signs and still remain significant, a site of ideological work, as we conceive of it, is not isolated either.

As a semiotic construct, our site implies differentiations, if only in the basic contrast between A and not-A, or figure and ground, that permits identifying something on which to focus attention. Contrasts will do more than that, of course; they organize relations, such that perceived entities are understood in terms of their differentiating features. The differentiation itself is what we focus upon. Such *differentiation is not – or not yet – a boundary.* "Boundary" implies confinement, limitation, duration. It is possible to make a boundary out of a contrast, but it is also possible to make a contrast disappear, by reaching for a more inclusive categorization – ignoring regional dialect differences, for example, in favor of "American English." Boundaries must be constructed, so that the differentiation they mark is accorded a sense of confinement and duration. Some boundaries may become so institutionalized, so deeply entrenched, that they are difficult to ignore. They tend to block the recursions that might regroup their contents into larger unities.

Some of the differentiations we have explored in this book involve major cultural features that have become entrenched in this way, such as the difference in linguistic structure between German and Hungarian, or between Wolof and French. These differences have been taken to be signs of exclusive national belonging. Recursions involving such differentiations have tended to be internal, that is, creating subdivisions rather than supercategories, and arraying more subtle features. An example of more subtle differentiae than the grammatical structures distinguishing Wolof from French would be the phonetic features that potentially distinguish grammatically standard French spoken with a Senegalese "accent" from similarly standard French spoken in Paris. Observe that ideological work is needed if someone is to notice and interpret, consciously or not, this "accented" way of speaking as French with Senegalese-influenced phonetics rather than just "French." The positioning of persons hearing this way of speaking would be relevant, with French residents in Europe more likely to pick up on the Senegalese phonetics than are many residents of Senegal itself. The positioning of an observer – of a gaze on a site – affects the salience of differentiae, even the identification of the site itself insofar as a particular differentiation is taken as central to it. These construals – of salience (of differentiae) and of what the site "is" – are important aspects of the positioned person's uptake of the site's semiosis.

In this regard, recall Fanon's discussion of Antilleans in France. Describing their struggles with the [r] of metropolitan French, Fanon (1967 [1952]) illustrates how "accented" French is made into a boundary within France, marking its speakers' exclusion from full belonging in a French national community. Whether (as he implies; see Chapter 5) the white French interlocutors themselves relied more on skin color than on "accent" is a separate issue; Fanon's Antilleans took the [r] to be crucial. A boundary is a sense of limitation and exclusion, and it must be constructed by ideological work that picks out a contrast as salient, definitive, and enduring.

To some extent, our argument here parallels some classic works in anthropology that rejected forms of analysis in which some social unit – such as ethnic group (Barth 1969) or caste (Marriott 1959) – is bounded off in order to examine what happens within it. In his discussion of ethnic groups and boundaries, Barth proposed that the ethnic groups between which some boundary had been defined should be thought of relationally. The boundaries, he argued, organized differentiae and relations between groups, rather than representing limits or edges of separate ethnic or cultural universes. Some people, perhaps including the members of such groups, might assume they inhabited utterly separate worlds, but the analyst should not. Since the cultural differentiae in the cases Barth discussed were relatively trivial, he argued that they could not in themselves be the source of an ethnic boundary; instead, they must be its consequence. Yet, we suggest, whether the differentiae are trivial or not is in an important sense irrelevant. Trivial in whose eyes? Although Barth asserts the perspective of group members for whom the "trivial" differences signal affiliation and relationship, it was more likely outsiders (such as colonial officials) – largely absent from his presentation[10] – who identified certain groupings as "ethnic" and placed them on maps and census lists. What Barth seems to propose, then, if we rephrase it in our terms, is that *for the participants* the ethnic difference is not a "boundary" in our sense at all. It is a differentiation across which relations are organized. The outsider perspective is likely the one that constructs a boundary out of this relationship.

In later years, other ethnographers followed up with their own critiques of analyses that remain internal to some bounded-off social unit. Focusing the critique especially on the old-style village study, where a village – taken to represent an ethnic group – was the field site for an analysis concerned with social life within it, these researchers recommended various ways of transcending the village boundary: multisited fieldwork, consideration of historical dynamics (avoiding arbitrary temporal boundaries), network analysis (avoiding spatial boundaries), and attention to circulations and flows. Perhaps some of this work merely trades one kind of unit-internal analysis for another, for example studying what happens within a social network. The move to problematize community studies, however, a move all these approaches share, is consistent with our own, although we conceive of the analyst's "site" differently.

Another option, less often pursued so far but especially relevant for our discussion, is to identify some "site" as centerpiece from which an analysis moves outward.[11] In effect, this is what our analyses do – whether starting from an American office building, a nineteenth-century term like "Yankee," or a small town in Hungary or Senegal: they explore how the differentiations "internal" to the centerpiece lead outward to track connections in space and time. Those connections engage our centerpiece site in a branching network of other sites and a series of ideological projections of differentiae onto those other sites. From the published literature another useful example of "site" treated as centerpiece rather than boundary is Cécile Vigouroux's (2009) study of a South African internet café. Focusing on language use and signage in the café, Vigouroux's analysis shows how her field site opens up in many directions. Many users, places, languages, interests, and visual styles intersect in this spot. Some users and languages come and go; some leave their mark upon it materially (in the form of signage and other marks of their presence); none are confined by its walls.

To summarize: as we have been arguing, the object of ideologizing, as an object of attention, is never bounded intrinsically, that is, absent any limits or confinement imposed by the ideological work itself. Meta-moves and other extensions are always possible. Since "ideology" (as we have pointed out from the beginning) implies multiple points of view – hence some form of social difference between the positions from which those views arise – the very fact of positioning entails differentiation, whether actors recognize it as such or not. The site – as semiotic construct and as ideological work – *always* entails differentiation among the perspectives upon it. Such differentiations can be constructed as boundaries, that is, edges and limitations, but such construction is an extra piece of ideological work.

Yet, boundaries are not limits to the construable universe, even if they are ideologized as such and have become institutionalized. Instead, and as a construct, a boundary affords comparisons and a view across the fence. That view has effects on what happens within the fence as well. In illustration, let us consider a favorite topic in interactional sociolinguistics: second-person pronouns. In our ethnographic field sites, these linguistic structures – "internal" to a particular language – turn out to be, on occasion, subject to usages and interpretations that reveal actors' awareness of languages "external" to the one being spoken. Some usage of structures understood as being of language X is influenced by, and socially interpreted in terms of, practices presumed to stem from language Y.

The ideological salience and social sensitivity of these pronouns have been noted in the considerable literature on them.[12] For the most part, studies have focused on the "familiar" and "formal" options for second-person singular, options known in linguists' shorthand as "T/V pronouns" (convenient for French *tu/vous*, but some languages have more than two forms, and in some languages the "formal" pronoun derives from a third-person form rather than from a second-person plural form).

Brown and Gilman's classic study (1960) showed that the social position and attitudes of a speaker govern what choices of pronoun are socially appropriate in addressing variously positioned interlocutors. Moreover, the social relationship between interlocutors is reflected in whether their usages are symmetrical (T/T or V/V) or asymmetrical (T/V or V/T). That study was so influential that subsequent generations of sociolinguists have found it crucial to examine the pronouns' distributions and positions, to discover how pronoun choices and usage are meaningful in discourse. It became obvious that forms of address such as second-person pronouns point to differentiated social roles and categories (including participant roles in discourse), as well as to social relationships and attitudes. In any situation that has such options in address forms, the linguistic forms entail social positioning, both in the role structure of acts of speaking and in the categories of persons who can inhabit those roles in those acts.

Notice now that because social referents and categories take part in regimes of differential value, the linguistic forms indexing those referents will be affected by those values, reflecting them in usage histories and likely showing up in commentary. Any site of usage of T/V pronouns extends, for its construal, into actors' experience of many other sites, of usage and of metacommentary.

We are hardly the first to point out the semiotic layering involved in social deixis, nor are we the first to note the flaws in traditional linguistic approaches that conflate these layers into a single "semantics" (see Silverstein 2003). What makes these sociolinguistic practices worth noting here, however, is the linguistic differentiation that informs their ideological significance. Differentiation and contrast are key: the fact that a speaker uses *this* form and not *that* one. Moreover, these address forms and their deployments are also analytically interesting because they point to ideological processes operating "on the fly," so to speak, when and as the forms are implemented creatively in interaction. When speakers creatively deploy T/V forms (or other social deictics) in interaction, their delicate self- and other-positioning shows that they are not just robotically reacting to some existing set of social fences and oppositions. Instead, they are engaged in constructing oppositions and crossing them. And this is a process in which – as in the recursive logic we have explored in other chapters – many kinds of difference, and boundaries too, can be invoked.

Our main ethnographic cases from Part I, European and African, will serve in illustration. In Bóly, the "respectful" (V) pronouns categorically differentiate Handwerkerisch from Bäuerisch, in that the pronoun *Sie* is only found in Handwerkerisch. Nevertheless, artisans are known to use the (farmer) form *ihr/er* as well. Therefore, the artisans have a larger pronoun repertoire, three forms total (*du, ihr/er, Sie*) while the farmers have only two (*du, ihr/er*). What is of interest about this situation is that the very fact of a larger repertoire is said (by people of both categories) to be a sign of the artisans' greater concern for elaboration and refinement.[13] At the same time, the *Sie* form (which derives from the third-person pronoun, used as respectful second-person singular) is also a feature of standard and is seen as more refined and educated than the *ihr/er* form. Thus the contrast between local German and school German may well have partially informed the Bóly-internal usage. Although the artisans' speech forms do not always coincide with school German (see Chapter 2), in this case the differentiation of pronoun forms resembles both the refined/authentic contrast and the temporality (new/traditional) stereotypically assigned to the artisans and farmers, respectively. In short, the distribution of the pronouns is construed ideologically (via rhematization), by Bóly residents, as an iconic index of the social category to which a speaker belongs – much as the two varieties, Handwerkerisch and Bäuerisch, are also construed as wholes; and a relationship with (extra-local) school German is brought to bear upon the local varieties' "meanings."

But there are other issues of perspective and evaluation that apply to these pronoun usages too. The logic everyone in Bóly applies is that more forms mean more politeness; and everyone says the artisans are/were more polite, or cared more about politeness. Caring more about politeness could be seen as a good thing, but it could also be seen as a sign of conceitedness, as we've mentioned above; or, artisans could be afraid that their usage might be seen that way. For instance, Gal was told that some artisans required their apprentices to use not just *Sie* itself but the more elaborate *g'nädige Frau* + *Sie* [+ plural conjugation] when addressing the artisans' wives. This report was controversial, however. Some artisans denied it in front of their farmer friends. Meanwhile the farmers said the artisans use *ihr* for politeness when they are not "showing off." And maybe they do. But regardless of the distributional facts, there are differing claims about what artisans do (or did) under various circumstances, and the claims themselves vary according to the contexts in which they are made – most crucially, whether persons from the opposite category are present. Both the usages themselves and the interpretive commentary upon them are sensitive to the delicate demands of particular social interactions.

Meanwhile, the Wolof situation is a bit different. In rural Wolof speech the uses of second-person pronouns do not follow a T/V pattern in which a plural pronoun becomes respectful singular. Other forms of address do offer many, and varied, ways to display respect; but not the pronouns. Instead, the plural *yéen/nggéen* is treated as simply plural, end of story.[14] Irvine did hear one person claim that the singular *yów/ngga* was actually more polite – the opposite of the French T/V pattern – since it would imply that the addressee was the head of a large following, whereas the plural would suggest he/she was merely one of many, such as a member of a family rather than head of household. Although this claim shows that the person making it was aware of French patterns and wanted to assert that Wolof expresses politeness too, Irvine could not confirm the claim in observations of actual usage.

However, the relationship between the French and Wolof patterns of pronoun usage becomes relevant to ideological issues in Senegal because of patterns of bilingualism and language "mixing," especially in urban settings. Consider the situation, encountered by Irvine many times, when a Senegalese taxi driver in Dakar addressed her in French with T forms (and she replied with V forms).[15] What does the taxi driver's usage mean? Was he simply importing a Wolof pattern into French, that is, using a simple singular with no additional pragmatic implications? Was he adopting a French pattern, and if so, which one? Was it the "formality" pattern in which the T form would not ordinarily be used for an adult stranger of opposite sex, except to be rude, or patronizing, or flirtatious? Or was it the pattern of French egalitarian ideology, which advocates widespread use of T (somewhat similarly to the Quakers and "levelers" of seventeenth-century England)? Or was it the adjusted version of this second pattern among French students and intellectuals, who use T forms to one another – whether previously acquainted or not – but may use V forms for elders and working-class people they fear would be offended by T forms? There is no way to know. Each of these possibilities represents a possible positioning of the interactants, so that the effect is indeterminate exactly because of the ambiguities created by larger patterns of usage. Each positioning also represents a possible gaze upon the event, a gaze that is in play whether any participant's construal actually corresponds to it or not.

As this example further suggests, where speakers are bilingual, social deixis in one of the languages – even in a conversation in which that language alone is spoken, with no switching – must be seen in light of the broader linguistic hierarchy and the practices that apply in the other language. The language not spoken casts an ideological shadow, as it were, on the situation at hand. Actually, just as French lurks in the background of urban Senegalese usage, so too does Hungarian lie in the shadows of usage in Bóly. Because the Hungarian system of pronominal address is much more elaborate than any of the German ones, including standard German, the artisans' apparent extra politeness may have been the effect of Hungarian usage, and makes them sound more like urban Hungarians, thus reinforcing their well-traveled image. For us as analysts taking a scene of pronoun usage in any of these cases as a site of ideological work, we see that the work points outside the site that was its starting point, invoking contrasts and looking across language boundaries.

In these examples, we have seen not only creative usages, engaging with the local social and linguistic differentiations. We have also seen how actors' usages and their interpretations of other people's usages are informed by the view across the fence: their sense of what happens elsewhere, and what options other languages, lurking in the background, could provide. In these cases and more broadly, a person's feeling of sociolinguistic appropriateness is partly anchored in some notion of a relevant "elsewhere."

Conclusion

What is a site of ideology – or, better put, of ideological work? We have explored ideological work semiotically, drawing on the Peircean concept of sign, in which a conjecture (interpretant) considers an object via some sign-relation. In effect, the site is the arena of abduction in which one can form a conjecture (interpretant) as to what the object, sign, and sign-relation are. Why call this a "site"? To ask about "sites" implies a researcher's perspective, as in the social-science discussions of "research sites" or, in anthropology especially, "field sites." The perspective of the researcher into ideologies of communication differs from a participant's perspective *only* insofar as it is necessarily a meta-move, an interpretation of an interpretation. In this chapter and in the next two, we explore such meta-moves and their semiotic objects of study: their sites.

A site as we have conceived it can be practically anything, thus possibly a sign with a very simple semiotic object. The office door, with its inset glass pane, was an illustration. But sites never stay simple. There were multiple gazes – ideologized interpretations – of the doors and the forms of communication they might afford, as well as the possible motives of persons who might have been responsible for the doors' installation. Among these gazes there is also the analyst's, a gaze distinct from a participant's even when these roles are only different hats worn by the same person. Even the most minimal site, then, offers differing perspectives on the same object. So sites inevitably open up into other sites, and a difference between perspectives on one object can always become the object of another site, with its own (differing) perspectives.

In the next chapter we explore some relationships among sites, especially those that involve the institutionalizing and regimenting of communicative forms.

7   Among and Between Sites

How are sites of ideological work connected with other such sites? The previous chapter suggested some connections in its discussion of the meta-moves of interpretive uptake that act upon interpretive responses to produce further interpretations. The narratives that "explained" why office doors were equipped with glass, and why faculty members responded to the glass in the ways they did, are meta-moves of this kind; so are the moves illustrated in our own analysis of the case. All such moves are afforded by the fact that sites are unbounded as potential objects of metadiscourse.

We have also seen that sites of ideological work, even for ideology of language (let alone a more encompassing notion of ideology), are not just to be identified directly with utterances, since such utterances are always embedded in some setting, starting from the space of abduction but also expanding to the various aspects of the communicative event as interpreted. Instead of focusing immediately on utterances for their own sake, it is useful first to envision how a site (of actors' attention) may be located in a scene of social and cultural activity. The semiotic forms in which ideologies are sighted – be they explicit or masked, overtly contested or apparently accepted – are relative to the interpretive frames provided by genres, social occasions, and shifts in participation. And while a scene of social activity may reveal presupposed principles that are acted out and made palpable, scenes also have connections with other scenes. Those connections involve ideological work in their own right, since they entail construals: construals of relevance; of what scenes offer models and precedents to be taken up, imitated, repeated, or somehow transformed; and of what can be imagined as sequelae and consequences of one's actions, for good or ill.

Our discussion of connections among sites owes an obvious debt to the literature in linguistic anthropology concerning interdiscursivity – links between stretches of discourse, including both spoken social interaction and written text.[1] With our emphasis on ideological work, its semiotics and its sites, we press this literature toward a focus on contrast and difference.

Sites afford uptake in complex ways, potentially branching out into many other sites. Such possibilities of uptake lead out into many and varied semiotic forms, revealing social issues and differentiations great and small, and potentially engaging large-scale and long-established institutions. We begin with an extended example, again starting from an apparently trivial object but showing how the varieties of uptake on a site draw connections in all these ways – including, in this case, how they lead into political institutions and major social tensions. The exercise will allow us to take a closer look at kinds of connections among sites, as well as to consider how the ideologized semiotic forms can undergo processes that authorize, regiment, and institutionalize them.

Benchmarks: Bus Stops in Baltimore

Sometime around 1990, benches at bus stops and parks in the city of Baltimore began to be painted with the following text:

READING ZONE

BALTIMORE, THE CITY THAT READS

Many images can be found on the internet showing one or more of the five hundred or so benches that were painted in this way. Some of these images show people sitting on them – reading, sleeping, or staring into space. Figures 7.1 and 7.2, drawings created from photographs on the internet, are examples. Treating any one of these benches, or the whole set of them, as a site for analysis with respect to ideological work, what sorts of inferences might this site allow, and what questions might be raised about its context?

First, consider the text and its location. Irvine observed such benches herself in Baltimore at the time. (To be more precise, she initially saw one such bench. The professional lettering style led her to infer that there were many such benches, established by some municipal authority. This inference was soon confirmed when she saw a few more, although she learned of the total number from other sources.) The placement of this bit of text on benches at bus stops struck her as an exhortation to read – i.e., to engage in a particular kind of linguistic practice – while sitting on the bench waiting for the bus. Perhaps the people seen in these various snapshots to be reading felt similarly exhorted. At any rate, the people in the two examples shown here are (dutifully? mockingly?) engaged in the very practice that has been urged. The second example (Figure 7.2) shows that reading material in the form of newspapers is available at the site, in case the careless traveler has neglected to bring any. A trash bin visible in that image permits – maybe even silently urges – the traveler to treat the newspapers as ephemera and throw them away

Figure 7.1. Baltimore, readers sitting on bench, 1990s
Drawing created by Jessica Krcmarik from photograph at http://cse.ssl.berkeley.edu/
bmendez/pics/gl/read.jpg.

Figure 7.2. Baltimore, reader sitting on bench, 1990s
Drawing created by Jessica Krcmarik from photograph at http://cse.ssl.berkeley.edu/
bmendez/pics/gl/morn.jpg.

after reading, or after the bus arrives. It is evident, however, from this and many other photographs of the benches, that any appeals convenient trash bins might silently make about clearing up abandoned ephemera have not been entirely successful.

The top line of the bench text, "Reading Zone," counts as the exhortation to read, since a bench might very well be described in quite other ways and not be used for reading at all. The regularity of the lettering on the benches suggests a professional sign-painter, presumably hired by the municipal authority responsible for the maintenance of public spaces. Moreover, there is a quality of coercion about the placement of this text on a bench: it commands attention (at least for the literate gaze, until one has seen it so many times as to become utterly inured, and no longer notice). So, whatever you do on the bench – either reading or not reading – becomes a response to a directive from an authority; it is framed as a reaction rather than simply an action. You are brought into an interaction with the municipal authority, and this becomes one of the frames for the bench sitter's behavior, in addition to any personal inclination to read or twiddle your thumbs. In fact, by virtue of reading the sign, the viewer is already participating, in a small way, in the commanded practice. But since some minimal degree of literacy is necessary to read the exhortation at all, the bench text can address only people who can already read (and read English). Despite its exhortation it differentiates between the literate and the utterly illiterate, excluding the latter.

Notice now that the second part of the text, "Baltimore, the City That Reads," is a slogan or formula whose form parallels other such slogans, whether for Baltimore itself (and Baltimore has had others) or for other cities ("New York, the city that never sleeps"; and even "Chicago, the city that reads" – but not at bus stops). The slogan takes its place within a system of intertextual relations, potentially called forth in the memory and imagination of the viewer.

This slogan did in fact stimulate a large body of commentary in the Baltimore press and elsewhere (such as personal weblogs), drawing on people's understandings of city slogans as a textual genre. Some commentators exercised their poetic talents in inventing counter-slogans: "Baltimore, the city that breeds"; "Baltimore, the city that bleeds"; "Baltimore, the city that reads ... at a third-grade level"; and many others, including our personal favorite, "Baltimore, the city with delusional park benches." Other commentators recalled alternative sobriquets from Baltimore's past: "Charm City" (creativity available here too: "Harm City"); and "Mobtown," a designation dating from the Civil War but striking some bloggers as having contemporary relevance. Still other comments compared the slogan with other cities' slogans. The bench text, therefore, is differentiated from other slogans, in ways that imply images of the city as well as differences between this city and others.

After the turn of the millennium, the now faded and splintering benches began to be repaired and repainted with a new text: "Baltimore – The Greatest

Figure 7.3. Baltimore, bus stop bench, 2012
Photo: J. T. Irvine.

City in America" (see Figure 7.3). Of course there were snarky comments on the change. "The City That Reads Now the Greatest City in America," ran the headline of a feature in the *Johns Hopkins News-Letter*, a university publication aimed at an internal and alumni/ae readership. The feature continued:

New York. Los Angeles. Key West. Baltimore. What do these places have in common? They all pop up if you do an AltaVista search for "the greatest city in America." But that's not all they have in common. All of them are prime destinations for both American and foreign vacationers (except Baltimore); all of them are legitimately recognized as places that people dream of one day moving to (except Baltimore); and all of them have residents who might actually endorse the notion that their city is, in fact, the greatest city in America (again, except Baltimore). This didn't stop Mayor Martin O'Malley from giving Baltimore that particular designation during his December 1999 inauguration speech, and the public benches haven't been the same since.

You may have noticed that, until recently, benches around the city were branded with the slogan "The City that Reads." ... Although the two slogans carry distinctly different messages, they are based on the same idea – if you believe it hard enough, it will eventually come true. Unfortunately, however, the whole "City that Reads" thing didn't actually get the city to read, just as it's somewhat doubtful that Mayor O'Malley's new slogan, now visible on benches throughout the city, will cause Baltimore to undergo some miraculous conversion. (Shapero 2001)

None of these comments question the notion that reading is a good thing and a suitable activity for public benches. Nor do they question whether cities can have slogans, or whether a slogan for Baltimore should be written in English. Instead, the comments use the bench slogans as a vehicle for disparagement of Baltimore and the city administration. For these commentators, the crucial question is whether the slogans can count as true and legitimate, given their reference to that city and their association with its government.

The mockery evident in these comments about the bench slogans, implying that putting that slogan on public benches was ridiculous and hopeless – that it signaled a municipal administration unable to cope realistically with urban problems, presumed to be worse in Baltimore than elsewhere – raises the question of who the commentators were. Whose gaze did these comments reflect? Not, obviously, that of the city officials, from whom the commentators clearly distance themselves. So what about the view from officialdom? About the project to repaint benches with the second slogan, Baltimore Transportation Department personnel wrote:

Each bench will be marked with the slogan "Baltimore: The Greatest City in America" and many will also adorn unique community names in order to highlight Baltimore's diversity of neighborhoods.

Approximately 60 benches have been restored since the start of this initiative. Once the program is complete, citizens will be able to rest comfortably on clean, refurbished benches throughout the city while waiting to ride a bus. The Department of Transportation is committed to making sure that "*the greatest city in America*" has some of the "greatest benches in America" for the citizens of Baltimore. (City of Baltimore 2004; emphasis original)

But were the Transportation Department employees responsible for deciding to put slogans on public benches, or merely for implementing a decision made higher up? We don't know. "City officials" is not a monolithic category or unique perspective either. In addition to the mayor's office and the various city departments, there are other bodies either tightly or loosely associated with municipal government, such as the Baltimore City Literacy Corporation and the Baltimore Area Convention and Visitors Association. There are also the advertising agencies hired by one or more of these groups to come up with a slogan – a "brand" that is supposed to improve a city's image. The city does not itself speak; there are many mediations.

Why a new slogan at all? The successive slogans effectively differentiated between two municipal administrations. The first slogan was part of a literacy program initiated by Mayor Kurt Schmoke, who took office in December 1987. Although the literacy program itself was not a target of scorn, Schmoke's administration came in for some harsh criticism during his last years in office (for not being more effective in dealing with Baltimore's problems; and, more relevantly for our slogans, for closing some branch libraries and removing some newspaper vending boxes). Martin O'Malley, who became mayor at the end of 1999, worked to distinguish his administration from the previous one. His many efforts included a new slogan and repainted benches – on which citizens were no longer urged to *read*, but instead (we gather from the Transportation Department) to *rest comfortably*. Subsequently, O'Malley developed an additional slogan, "BELIEVE," placed on banners, T-shirts, and trash cans. A mayoral trailer, the BelieveMobile, drove around city neighborhoods exhorting optimism, showcasing local entertainers – the trailer opened up into a performance stage – and advertising programs to combat drug use. The benches proclaiming Baltimore as the "Greatest City" were not replaced, although some soon deteriorated.[2]

Meanwhile, who were the mockers and cynics? To judge from what we found in a web search and some informal inquiries, this was a gaze identified, or self-identified, as outsider and cosmopolitan. Many people who wrote comments in weblogs were out-of-town visitors. Many who wrote letters to the *Baltimore Sun* or to the *Baltimore City Paper*, or wrote feature pieces in college publications such as the *Hopkins News-Letter*, were temporary residents who apparently expected to move elsewhere as soon as the opportunity arose. Even most of those whose writings suggest longer or even permanent residence in Baltimore refer conspicuously to other cities they have known well. "We are not from here," they seem to imply. Their gaze is oppositional and distanced, not only from the city government but also from the city itself.

By the 1990s, and in fact already well before that, the majority of long-term residents in Baltimore were African Americans. Does a distanced perspective on the slogan therefore represent a predominantly white point of view? The answer to that question isn't clear, but our site does have a connection to Baltimore's often tense race relations. Mayor Schmoke was the city's first elected African American mayor – O'Malley is white – and racial identity politics figured in mayoral campaigns in 1995 and 1999.[3] Although Baltimore's black citizenry were far from supporting every municipal institution or mayoral act in either administration, and their opinions have certainly never been all alike, our internet searches turned up relatively few negative comments about the bench slogans that were written by identifiably black writers or published in black-oriented media (such as the *Baltimore Afro-American*, a weekly newspaper, or radioblack.com). Of course this small proportion partly reflects a lower level of access to the internet. Still, African American criticism of Schmoke seemed to focus on other things. We saw comments denouncing some of his particular policies, and accusing him of "forgetting where he came from," but he was seldom mocked for excessive optimism in hoping to raise literacy levels. Some websites that were still accessible as of the time of writing showed Schmoke's "The City That Reads" slogan without irony: one, sponsored by a law school and devoted to African Americans in the law, included a poster from Schmoke's 1990 political campaign; another website that included the same campaign item featured a 2010 exhibit in the Loyola/Notre Dame University library, titled "The City That Reads: Novels in Baltimore." Meanwhile, during O'Malley's tenure as mayor, sources connected with his office and the "Believe" campaign complained that it was difficult to persuade white residents that they shared responsibility for taking action to solve the city's problems.[4] In short, a racial opposition seems to lurk among responses to the slogans.

What has become of the slogan "Baltimore, the City That Reads" more recently? By the second decade of the new millennium it had vanished from public benches. It has lived on in three places: in counter-nostalgic discourse (of some city residents and visitors, who still write about it); in occasional news articles promoting the Baltimore Book Fair; and, most tangibly, on a metal plaque on the outside wall of the Barnes & Noble store downtown. Installed in 1998, the plaque marked the slogan's appropriation into the private sector. "Baltimore: The City That Reads" turned into an ad for a bookstore.

The city continued its search for a "brand." In 2005, the Baltimore Area Convention and Visitors Association hired Linder & Associates, a company that had already "built brands" for places such as Madrid and Hong Kong, to come up with a new makeover for the city's image. While the "Believe" campaign was oriented primarily at the city's own residents, aiming to promote self-confidence and turn around a city "in love with its own victimhood," as a local policeman put it (Smith and Siegel 2001), the new campaign took a wider view, looking nationally as well as locally. To target these audiences requires countering a perception of Baltimore that comes from its portrayal on television programs (*Homicide: Life on the Streets*; *The Corner*; *The Wire*) as a decaying and depressing place pervaded by violent crime.[5] Especially important in the city's image campaign is an effort to differentiate Baltimore in a positive way from its neighbor, Washington, DC. In this optimistic view, Baltimore's waterfront setting, seafood cuisine, and low cost of living will attract new residents who will commute to work in Washington – and preferably attract high-tech companies to settle in Baltimore itself:

Baltimore is increasingly seen as a cheaper, more livable alternative to the high rents, horrible congestion, and antiseptic environment of tech-booming Northern Virginia. There's a rising demand for unique, cheap office space with nearby housing, things that Baltimore, with its surplus of abandoned industrial buildings and potentially charming waterfront neighborhoods, has in abundance. Local developers seemingly can't convert old factories into high-tech offices fast enough. ... Baltimore's cityscape, dotted with charming old neighborhoods, is an attractive location for the young "creatives" powering the ... software and content side of the digital revolution. (Smith and Siegel 2001)

As relatively affluent high-tech workers and educated office personnel, these sought-after new residents would contrast sharply with Baltimore's urban poor. Perhaps these "charming waterfront neighborhoods" revive some fragmentary image of Baltimore's "splendid houses" that so impressed Anne Royall in 1826.

How easily can perceptions of a city be improved? Not very. In January 2015, a new African American mayor, Stephanie Rawlings-Blake, signed an order for painting over the "Greatest City in America" bench slogan. The City Council had decided that a new slogan featuring Baltimore as the birthplace of the "Star Spangled Banner" would be less controversial and less easily mocked. But Baltimore's racial tensions could not just be painted over. In late April 2015 mass riots broke out in impoverished neighborhoods following the death of an African American youth in police custody. The city was literally on fire. Many Baltimoreans blamed increased police brutality on policies instituted by former mayor O'Malley, whose reputation for successful law enforcement had earlier helped his political career, including his election as governor of Maryland (2007–2015). O'Malley declared his candidacy for the US presidency in May 2015, but the city's recent troubles did not help his chances.

What is most directly and obviously a matter of ideologies of language in this case is the concept of city slogans and the notion – held at least by some people (outsiders? would-be outsiders?) – that such slogans ought to express things that are already true about the city, not things hoped for. Moreover, no matter which gaze we explore, some ideas are taken for granted: that reading is good; that Baltimore public signs should be in English; and that lettering of a certain form indexes an institutional, rather than a personal, statement. So some ideas about communicative practice are held in common, even while other important ones differ.

As with the office doors discussed in the previous chapter, we started with what might initially seem to be a very simple site: an ordinary object of everyday life in the city in which it is found. But sites of ideological work are never really simple, when they are interrogated as sites of language ideology. They always open up into fields of differentiation. In exploring this example we have considered various perspectives on our site, perspectives linked to major social divisions and racial inequality. We have discussed some of the semiotic properties that make the bench slogan count both as an instance of a particular linguistic genre and as a municipal government directive (and more than that, an interpellation) to engage in a particular discursive practice. We noted that the bench slogan, as an act in the world, served as a stimulus to uptake in the form of commentary on the municipality and its government – but not on the discursive practice as such, nor on the text's language. We also considered the bench slogan's placement within a particular local history, the possible connections with racial tensions, and some of the site's links with other practices and institutions (newspapers and weblogs, especially). The site opens up into many kinds of differentiations: in its immediate audiences, between the literate and the nonliterate; in its text, among various slogans, and among lettering designs; in its producers, between different city administrations, as well as among city departments and agencies; in its commentators' gazes, between locals and (hyperliterate) cosmopolitans, and between blacks and whites; and in its geographical setting, between two cities, Baltimore and Washington, in a regional economy that opposes affluent, well-educated high-tech workers and federal government employees to the urban poor. Differentiation – in semiotic forms, in gazes, in practices, in social types – lurks in any and every site of ideological work, including this one. Exploring these differentiations has taken us to many other sites, connected with our starting point.

Types of Sites, Kinds of Connection

If a site can open up into so many more sites, how might we usefully organize our thinking about the connections among them? In the case of the Baltimore benches, an obvious connection among sites is the *interpretive response, the meta-move* as we called it in Chapter 6. Those responses represent most of the connections we traced, and if we add the analyst's interpretations in with the actors', meta-moves can be considered as a great umbrella category. But there are more specific kinds of connections as well. There is the connection between a particular *text and its genre* (city slogans); there are moves that invoke *regional/economic contrast sets* (Baltimore and Washington); and there are moves that invoke *typifications*: of cities – e.g., the cities you would consider "great"; and of administrations – the actions that characterize a certain mayor. There are *temporal connections* between sites: the benches in 1990 and the same benches several years later. And there are *institutional connections* between the benches and media, government, and advertising, as well as – less formally – the *institutionalizing process* in which a painted bench becomes emblematic of a city, its aspirations, and its troubles. All these connections invoke scenes of social activity and the objects, people, written texts, and behavioral practices those scenes afford.

As we think about types of sites as scenes of culturally inflected activity, an important way such scenes are connected is through *modeling* – linking a model scene, as a normative prototype, with the scene that is understood as its replica, echo, or herald. (An echo replicates a prototype understood as existing prior to the echo; a herald, on the other hand, looks ahead to its model.)[6] As an example, recall Chapter 1's discussion of griot performances in rural Wolof social life. The griots' public performances, with their voluble, hyperbolic, and dramatic oratory addressed to an audience of higher caste patrons, serve as cultural prototypes for a register of "griot-[style] speech" in other settings. That is, voluble and dramatic talk addressed to someone of higher status may be likened to "griot speech" even if the speaker is not actually a griot. Similarly, acts of petitioning take on some of the linguistic characteristics of "griot speech" no matter who utters them, because they imply relations of rank and dependency. In Part I we discussed these ethnographic patterns as organized through recursivity. They also illustrate modeling, because the scene of griots' public oratory serves as model for other scenes where talk enacts and constructs relationships of rank and/or patronage. See also Part II, on images and recursivity.

Another useful illustration of modeling comes from Susan Philips's ethnographic work in the Kingdom of Tonga (Philips 1998, 2000).[7] As Philips shows, discourse in and about Tongan courtrooms demonstrates – as the just-mentioned Wolof case also does – that some culturally typified scene can serve as the reference point, the (ideologized) *locus classicus* of language use, without itself necessarily being an occasion on which commentary on language use takes place. The kind of usage at issue is "bad language": ways of speaking that violate the norms of proper talk between brother and sister. "Bad language" must be avoided in any social setting where people in a brother-sister relationship (including classificatory siblings such as cross-gendered cousins) might happen to be present. However, the proscription against "bad language" applies not only to those situations where the participants are known to include some brother and sister, but also to many situations open to a wider public. The courtroom is potentially such a setting, but a problematic one. Courtrooms are public – so persons in a brother-sister relationship might be present – yet "bad language" cannot simply be excluded from the discourse, since it might be part of the evidence in a court action, or actually be the offense brought before the court.

In short, scenes of brother-sister talk, evaluated as proper (normative, "good language") or improper ("bad language"), are the prototypes in terms of which other scenes of talk, such as the courtroom session, are assessed. There is a pragmatic calibration (Silverstein 1993) between the two scenes, the prototype and the here and now, involving evaluation and normativity. Although the calibration may remain implicit, on some occasions there is overt discussion of whether and how the courtroom discourse fits the norms of brother-sister talk. In that case, the commentators simultaneously enact and display their scene's connection with the model they both presuppose and discuss.

This example is useful for considering what kinds of scenes can be made into prototypes. That is, people assume an understanding of the prototype, so that whenever they are engaged in a scene they take to be its replica, they suppose they are instantiating the type. But the settings of prototype and instantiation can be quite different. The prototypical scenes illustrating proper (or improper) Tongan talk between brother and sister are not set in the courtroom, but instead are scenes of family life or scenes of intimate gatherings set in an idealized traditional village. These scenes provide the reference point for contemplating "bad language" elsewhere. This is quite different from the rural Wolof case, in which it is a public situation with wide attendance that serves as model for other settings, including relatively intimate ones.

That the Tongan case points to an idealized traditional village shows that the prototype scene does not have to be an event people have witnessed in real life. An idealized image of life in some Golden Age can serve as prototype just as well as a scene people have actually experienced. (Hence – in a different cultural milieu – the joke about a Bible-thumping fundamentalist arguing against bilingual education: "If English was good enough for Jesus Christ, it's good enough for the state of Texas.") Moreover, the prototype does not have to be something one approves of. There can also be counter-normative examples. The snarky comments on Baltimore bench slogans ("Baltimore, the city that bleeds") and on the "BELIEVE" banners ("BEHAVE!") echo an original they disparage.

Prominent among the kinds of sites that can anchor a cultural prototype are rituals that lay claim to some kind of value-setting effectiveness (Silverstein 1998). Ritual provides the grounds for indexical relations, such as participants' names and relationships, and the norms of talk and conduct, which – thus authorized and presupposed – will pertain in other settings. As Silverstein (2003, 2013b) has shown, "ritual centers" serve as "center point[s] of emanation," having wave-like connections with other social occasions that derive significance from pointing back toward that authorizing scene. Especially important for the emanation is the ritual moment that introduces, for the first time, some indexical relation that will reverberate in subsequent events. Such introductions can be considered "ritual centers of indexical baptism," or baptismal moments (Silverstein 2003:222). These moments, which we can call *baptismal sites*, are the particular occasions in social life that inaugurate some practice, or designation – such as bestowing a name on a child, or bestowing an attribution on a work of art – that is to be followed in all relevant future occasions. Those echoes refer back to the baptismal scene; the interdiscursive connection between sites involves presupposition and precedence. (In the case of a fraudulent attribution, the connection is false – not actually temporal – but is to be presupposed by the victim of the fraud.) Notice, however, that this kind of model scene is distinguishable from other model scenes in being normative only in a limited sense: as a site of inauguration of a very particular indexical relation. It is the consequence that matters – the dossiers that will be associated with the child, and the price the work of art will command. There is no general imperative requiring "Ferdinand" (say) to be the name of all children.

Since the baptismal site points ahead to future scenes in which the bestowed designation will be used, it differs in this directionality from most of the other intersite connections we have explored. That is, a baptismal site points ahead even if the social occasions it anticipates do not actually occur. (Suppose, sadly, that Ferdinand, his kin, and the baptizer all perish in an earthquake minutes after the baptismal event.) The sites that are instantiations, echoes, of a presupposed model point backward instead, even if the scene serving to anchor them is only idealized and never actually occurred. Note, too, that these echo sites include other aspects of an overall ritual scene, such as a baptismal font and template text, which point backward to presupposed moments that established their role and authorize the baptizing. As Silverstein (2005) has pointed out – and our example of fraudulent attribution also indicates – the relation between one utterance and the interdiscursive link to which it points is usually better understood as presupposition or entailment, rather than time itself.

This discussion has introduced the notion of *site as scene of cultural activity* (interpretively framing sites of attention encompassed within it), and *modeling* as a relationship between sites – so, between scenes or events. There will be more to be said on these matters. For now, we should just note that a relationship between model and echo, while superficially looking like a simple reproduction or reiteration of tradition or precedent, requires ideological work and creativity. Just as the cases discussed in Part II involved differentiation, rhematization, and erasure, the same processes apply in connecting sites. It takes ideological work to identify or imagine the cultural model that applies to and organizes a scene in the here and now, and to play down the differences between the model and its supposed real-world "echo." Moreover, differentiation is always involved – always an aspect of a site, whether that site is model or echo. Even if the site seems like a "thing," like a bench or like a physical place, there is still a differentiation between figure and ground.

Explanatory Sites and the Locus of Authority

When you observe ideological work in a site, what is taken to explain it? What is the locus of explanation, or of authority, over the site's interpretation? Or is the site itself a model that "explains" semiotic processes elsewhere?

In the Tongan case, reference to a normative domestic scene "explains" –
and in so doing, authorizes – behavioral norms that apply in the courtroom
scene that is anchored to it. In Ferdinand's case, the baptismal event "explains"
his naming – he is named Ferdinand because his parent declared the name at
his birth and the proper forms were filled out – though not why this particular
child was named with that name (after a famous bull?). Explanation, a variety
of which is reference to a model, is a mode of connecting sites by referring one
scene to another, taken to be its source.

Let us backtrack for a moment to consider the semiosis of explanation
itself. The semiotic processes we have outlined in previous parts of this book
rest upon a kind of "explanation." As we discussed in Chapter 4, rhematization
contributes to "explaining" an indexical relation by attributing some shared
quality to the indexical sign and its object. The ideological inference through
which Anne Royall – herself a westerner – imagined westerners as big-hearted
because their speech was "slow" and not copious follows this line of explanatory attribution, in which generosity was deemed the shared quality in both
their sociality and their speech (which left room for others to speak). The
same kind of rhematizing, exercised from a different social position, might
imagine a different quality and a different semiotic object, hence the northern
perspective that imagines southerners as slow-witted because their speech is
"slow." The rhematization projects the quality of slowness, found (supposedly) in speech, onto the mind of the speaker in a mutually entailing, and
possibly circular, explanation. (Why do they speak so slowly? Because they
are slow-witted. How do you know they are slow-witted? Because they speak
so slowly.)

Notice that this bit of reasoning, taken in itself, can only be an ideological
shortcut. Rhematization is actually the outcome of a more complicated process,
as we have shown in Chapter 4. The object you are explaining must be made,
via some relevant differentiation. So an "explanation" that rests on projecting
slowness as southern essence requires contrasting southern with northern – or
perhaps General American – speech/minds. If only the South is focused upon,
the whole non-southern side of the contrast is erased from view, although it
remains implicit as the ground for the southern figure. Our major ethnographic
cases all involve this kind of inference: in a differentiated sociolinguistic scene,
the distinctive qualities in the speech of some social category are deemed "similar" to the category's other indices (ideologically selected qualities of conduct,
dress, food, inhabited landscape and climate, or whatever) in which this social
category contrasts with another. Rhematizing narratives "explain" that these
indices are similar not only to each other, but also to an internal essence that
they manifest.

Usually, metapragmatic labels for linguistic varieties already "explain"
them to some extent. Those labels capture – and lexicalize – the interpretive

move that creates its own site of ideological work. The labels locate the varieties in cultural stereotypes of (categories of) persons or activities, and in so doing, they point to what explains the variation. Moreover, to the extent that the labels enter common parlance, they represent steps in institutionalizing the interpretations they label. Although there may also be elaborations on the explanations, such as the Just So stories explaining the origins of Wolof caste distinctions, these stories take the caste labels (and, therefore, the metaprag-matic terms derived from those labels) for granted. They "explain" them; they do not deconstruct them.

Explanations have, or seek to have, important social effects. They seek to authorize that which they explain, and to regiment it. When a site (of attention) is linked to a prototype scene through semiotic steps that "explain" it, then any anomalies or departures from the prototype can be ignored or explained away. Suppose you notice that a small creature having the general shape of a spider has only seven legs instead of the expected eight; you are unlikely to envision an entirely new genus of seven-legged arthropods. Instead, you imagine a narrative: the spider suffered an injury while still in the egg; or maybe it lost a leg in the Great Spider Wars. Your narrative explains the dif-ference between your prototype concept of a spider and the exemplar you actually observe, so that seven-leggedness need not be generalized beyond the individual case.

In other instances the regimenting effect may actually erase from view – impede the perception of – exemplars or usages that fail to conform to the authorized label or prototype. Our ethnographic materials in Part I illustrate this possibility. As we showed there, metapragmatic labels such as "griot talk," for example, often refer only to the stereotype – the griot's "typical" public performance – and may therefore, if taken literally, render a research-er's gaze blind to other usages. When Wolof townspeople were interviewed about the expression *waxu gewel* ("griot talk") by itself, they responded only in terms of members of the gewel caste in performance (doing "being a griot," in effect). Yet, people who were not griots sometimes spoke loudly and rap-idly – i.e., in "griot-like" ways – and, in context, were sometimes said to be speaking "like a griot," even using "griot talk." Such commentaries (about the speech of members of other castes) emerged only in conversation that was focused on an example of nonconforming usage, not in more general interviewing, in which interviewees were much less likely to move beyond stereotypes. The discourse practices into which an ethnographer taps have everything to do with what the ethnographer learns, as Briggs (1986) indi-cated years ago.

In short, metapragmatic labels are a form of regimentation. They skew what will be offered in illustration, and what will be remembered. Memory culture erases the subtleties of nonstereotypical usage; so do the practices of outside observers who rely only on interviews and have little chance of observing behavior that does not fit the stereotype. In such cases both the researcher and the participant who relies on relatively distant memory take metapragmatic labels such as "griot talk" too literally, and fail to discover the analogies and figurative usages mentioned in participants' explanatory commentaries. The analogies that had underlain the nonstereotypical performances in the first place likely go unnoticed. A similar problem applies to observers who rely only on transcripts and never explore metapragmatic commentary at all.

What makes a particular site explanatory? Which site do participants pick out, or invent, for an ideological elaboration explaining that site as the source for other sites? To our discussion of rhematization, we must add *anchoring* – a relation among fractal recursions, as discussed in Chapter 4. In anchoring, one iteration of a differentiation is taken as more "real," or "originary," than others, and therefore affording the explanatory locus – the "last analysis" – for the bundled contrast. Semiotic anchoring can be invoked, then, to describe those kinds of relations among sites in which one site serves as model and explanation for another. It is in this vein that we have been discussing Philips's work on Tongan sites, where an idealized picture of talk between brothers and sisters serves as a model scene that, for Tongans, "explains" norms for talk in other settings. Many origin stories and Just So stories work in exactly this way. So too do accounts that explain some deep antipathy between social groups as caused by a long-ago conflict, attributing the connection between the present moment and that earlier time – the anchoring model site – to "social memory." Meanwhile the (perhaps different) nature of relations in the intervening time is ignored, as are any problems in linking the "we" who experienced the conflict with the "we" of today. (Why are you fighting the X's? Because of what they did to us in the battle of ___ in the year 13--.)

Along similar lines, the explanatory locus of the Zulu/Xhosa custom called *hlonipha* lies in gender and family relations. In that account, the pattern of name-avoidance – actually name-sound avoidance – is attributed to women's speech, specifically a daughter-in-law's polite and modest behavior in reference to her father-in-law, the sounds of whose name she avoids uttering. But the pattern is much more widespread. Not only is there evidence that men do (or, not so long ago, did) *hlonipha* their mothers-in-law, but also followers avoid the name-sounds of important political leaders (Krige 1950:31; Dlamini 2005:88). There is an ideological process, then, such that the domestic scene in which a woman avoids the sounds of her father-in-law's name, substituting other sounds and other ways of referring to him, semiotically anchors – "explains" – the broader usage (Irvine and Gal 2000). Yet, this process, picking out a gendered domestic scene, has its own history, in colonial disbanding of the Zulu army (previously an important locus of male hlonipha usage) and in gender stereotyping in both colonial documents and Zulu national imaginaries (Irvine and Gunner 2018).

Many kinds of authoritative statement and practice, and the regimentations that follow from them, can be considered in terms of intersite connections via semiotic anchoring. Ethnographers often hear informants explain some practice simply as "because our ancestors did it that way" – thus invoking a model, remembered or imagined, that anchors semiotic practice in the present. But why should one do what the ancestors did? If we do something or other "because the gods decreed it," why those gods, and why follow their decree? If we are told to look something up in the dictionary to find out whether some expression is or is not English, or what a word means, what makes the dictionary authoritative? Why should courtroom talk, in Tonga or anywhere, follow the norms for brother-sister talk? What semiotic anchoring does not explain, exactly as Just So stories do not explain, is *why* the model is authoritative – why it anchors anything. The process through which the model gained authoritative power (and thus any role it may play in social domination) remains masked, erased from the picture. The public for whom the dictionary is authoritative does not generally know who its lexicographers were. Only when a new edition is produced – altering the text that had previously been taken as ultimate linguistic authority – is there public discussion of the lexicographer's procedures; then, the difference between the public's and the analysts' perspectives on "authority" comes to the fore. Otherwise, for the dictionary's users, erasure reigns.[8] Semiotic anchoring as an interdiscursive relation between sites is a relation based on diagrammatic iconicity. Its semiotic processes therefore include erasure, as an entailment of rhematization (see discussion in Part II).

Of course, a major fount of explanation and source of authority in sites of language ideology is provided by linguists and other language "experts." We will turn to them in Part IV.

Institutionalization, Regimentation, Sweeping Up in Complex Interdiscursive Webs

Regimentation and its attendant practices are a recurrent theme in recent literature in linguistic anthropology, including our own contributions. One strand of that literature and related sociolinguistic studies explores the connection with large-scale institutions: enduring systems of conventionalized practices having some sort of public character, and sometimes associated with special buildings in which their characteristic activities are housed.⁹ "Brick-and-mortar" institutions, as some are called (even though reinforced concrete is the more common building material nowadays), reach far beyond their physical buildings. Less like bricks than like giant squids, they have tentacles that reach deep into the sea of ongoing social life to regiment its practices. But can they reach everywhere? Is there any realm of activity that always remains outside their touch?

The case of the public benches in Baltimore offered an example of this question about sites of ideological work: the extent to which the semiosis in the site is swept up in interdiscursive webs that bring it into the regimenting effects of institutionalization. City government, media, commercial establishments, educational institutions, and long-standing race relations all were engaged. Like Chapter 6's office doors, this case suggests that there is no object, no bit of language or social conduct, that is utterly impervious to such effects. Ideology is already a form of regimentation; insofar as ideology of language permeates discursive practice, regimentation is already at work. Institutions small and large are also sources of formation of linguistic registers. Because institutions forge links across encounters, welding them to the institution's main purpose, they have a propensity to develop a characteristic "voice" or register of talk (see Agha 2005a, 2005b). Charles Ferguson's discussion of radio sports announcer talk is a well-known example (Ferguson 1983).

Thinking of regimentation and institutions may lead one – perhaps too quickly – to the state, with its bureaucratic and policing operations. Let us begin instead with some other kinds of institutionalizing processes, more local and perhaps more subtle. Not all institutions or institutionalizing processes involve a wide public. Consider, for example, ways in which a bit of talk can be made into an institutionalized object, a regularity or routine that gets hooked up to some aspect of social organization. In many American families, there are little sayings or routines that come to "belong" to the family, to identify them emblematically and invoke family sentiment, perhaps for decades. Some such sayings come from a child's "funny" usages prior to full linguistic competence; some come from what was said in an episode of family history; some routines are purposely invented (e.g., a distinctive tune to be whistled if children wander off in a department store or a crowd, to reunite the family). These bits of proprietary language and emblematic routines do not create the norms and roles of "the American family" as a sociological institution. They pertain only to the particular family, with its roles, routines, and sentiments. Still, the creation, form, and deployment of such family sayings does relate in some way to the particular shape of "the family" in America. Not for us the conventionalized routines that enact patriclans' "joking relationships" in

Senegal (and elsewhere in Africa) – not because we don't have conventionalized routines or joking, but because we do not have patriclans of the African type.

Processes that regiment social categories by concretizing them, thus turning categories into organized groups equipped with special places and norms, can be seen in our ethnographic cases too. In Bóly, there were two developments in the nineteenth century that institutionalized the categories of farmer and artisan in this way. First, in the middle of the century, an informal agreement was reached that guaranteed a strict alternation between the two categories in the election of town mayor: the election of a rich farmer as mayor was necessarily followed by the election of a rich artisan. It is not clear, however, whether the distinction between the two categories was quite absolute, at that time. Farming and artisanry were activities people engaged in, and perhaps some poor people who did a bit of both might not have been firmly and uniquely categorized in terms of one or the other activity. In the 1880s a second move reified the contrast more decisively, establishing formal organizations, the *Gesellenverein* (**Legényegylet** in Hungarian) for the artisans and the *Jünglingsverein* (**Ifjuságiegylet** in Hungarian) for the farmers. Set up on the model of interest-group *Vereinen* then burgeoning in Germany, these social clubs each had its house, its officers, regular meetings, libraries, and other activities, most restricted to its own membership. At that point, activity categories had turned into contrasting and exclusive social groups, with corporate property, membership rolls, norms, and routinized, predictable events. Contrasts in linguistic practice lined up with these institutionalized groupings.[10]

In rural Senegal, precise moments when social categories were institutionalized are much harder to pin down than in Bóly. Yet, institutionalizations there have been. For example, the town where Irvine did most of her ethnographic fieldwork was divided into named neighborhoods (*quartiers*), one of them called *ngewel* ("griotdom," one might say). The town was founded in 1809, though not in exactly its present location. It is not clear at what date a special griot quarter was established and named, as a quarter where only griots resided and which had its own representation on the town council, as was the case by 1970. But caste segregation (especially of griots) and representation, for many purposes – food provision, water, burial, seating at social events, and many other activities – has a long history and wide distribution in Senegal.

Let us turn now to a case where institutionalization is a much more ambiguous matter, not celebrated and valued the way the establishment of clubs was in 1880s Bóly. Take now as our site of ideological work a loosely defined group of midwestern Americans, described by Jeffrey Grabill and Stuart Blythe

(2010), engaged in grassroots environmental activism. For any group whose self-definition or self-image rests on a notion of "grassroots," institutionaliza- tion can only be an ambiguous value. Movements are called grassroots when they begin informally, outside the major established institutions normatively involved in the movement's purpose. Subsequently, a grassroots effort that develops successfully, becoming more organized and widespread, can itself become institutionalized and/or transform the established organizations. But then is it still "grassroots"? And – as the flip side of the same coin – if such a movement resists institutionalization, does it risk collapse? Between informal spontaneity and long-range effectiveness lies the process of institutionalization and the conundrum it sometimes presents for citizens' groups and community action networks.

What makes this particular community effort interesting for our purposes is the way the local environmental action group addressed the conundrum semi- otically, through their communication strategies. This group, the "CEC" – we are told only its acronym – was "a loose collection of individuals" (Grabill and Blythe 2010:189) in a midwestern town who met about once a month to focus on environmental issues and local politics. One of their projects was to gather information about a proposed storage facility for toxic waste, and to arouse local resistance to the facility's proposed location within the town limits. Grabill and Blythe's analysis centers on a flyer produced and distrib- uted by CEC members. The printed sheet had an arresting graphic on one side: a map of the town, with a bull's-eye superimposed on it and a skull- and-crossbones symbol at the center, the spot proposed for the toxic waste facility. On the other side was a text, in newspaper-like format, informing the reader about the proposed facility. The text offered ways to find out more, and it listed relevant community organizations. Producing and distributing the flyer required several meetings and various media, as group members worked through many presentational forms. They assembled published texts and graphics, engaged in conversations and oral reports, produced typed and printed statements, then more conversations, followed by revised versions. When they distributed flyers they were simultaneously talking to the recip- ients. There was a complex interdiscursive trajectory leading up to the flyer and its dissemination.

If we had taken the flyer itself as a site of language ideology – and it would be plausible to do so – we would have needed to follow these semiotic trans- formations, as Grabill and Blythe indeed do. The flyer is a semiotic artifact with a temporal trajectory, a history of transformations, and connections to various other sites and relevant sets of people: producers, audiences, people and organizations referred to in its text, and people whose interests it was created to oppose.

The site we are primarily attending to, however, is the CEC group, some portion of whose ideologies of language and textual artifacts the flyer represents. Considering this group during the period in which it was working on this project, one can observe the ways the group's members relied on ideologies of language, semiotic form, and communicative practice, in order to navigate between potentially conflicting pressures. On the one hand, they needed to organize themselves and their project systematically, effectively, and on a relatively large scale; on the other hand, they needed to maintain their identity and image (including self-image) as a local, informal, grassroots movement. They needed to win their neighbors' trust, by simultaneously representing themselves as "just your neighbor," outside any impersonal institutions with coercive powers, while representing themselves as having access to reliable scientific information about toxic waste and the disposal project. Interviewing K, a member of CEC, Grabill and Blythe report:

He [K] believes that information regarding environmental issues should be kept short and visuals should be used, hence the image-heavy design of the first page. He also said that people would not attend to data distributed by people they mistrust – a claim that was repeated often in this community, both by officials and residents. One aspect that can help gain trust, K said, was the look of a document. If it is typeset, like the bull's-eye flier, "It will look like it has truth to it." ... In producing the flier, he used the familiar, iconic images of the target and skull and crossbones in order to emphasize the threat posed by the project. He also used a map of the city to emphasize the location of the threat. His design works efficiently, telling his readers in one image (1) that a threat exists, (2) what type of threat it is – that is, poisonous – and (3) where it is located in their community. For those willing to read further, K also drew on the genre of the newspaper to complete the second page. In other words, he used a multi-column format, complete with headlines and datelines, in order to invoke in readers the sense of trust that might attend a reputable newspaper using similar visual conventions. (2010:199–200, 202)

Although K claimed (2010:198) "I'm not an activist," he took major responsibility for designing and producing the flier for which CEC members had gathered information. And at the same time as CEC members drew on the typefaces and multicolumn formats of "reputable newspapers," they relied on face-to-face interaction to accompany the flier. As J, another community member, explained:

J said that not everyone reads newspapers, but they can get people to pass around fliers. Plus, when they pass out fliers they can talk to people. J believes that face-to-face communication makes people more likely to participate. (2010:202)

This local community association is an example of ambivalent, perhaps incipient, institutionalization in a context of group political activity. People drew on ideologies of language, visual representation, genres, and communicative practice in mobilizing a group and constituting an ideologized representation of their group's composition and purpose. They played with issues of scale, keeping the local and face-to-face aspects of identification and discursive practice always in sight while also identifying with "reputable newspapers" through the flyer's iconic representation of newspaper typefaces and visual conventions. Newspapers offered models on which they relied, but so did the face-to-face conversation between neighbors. The double strategy linked the sites of their activities to two different kinds of model sites, associated with two different kinds of trustworthiness.

If we turn to more established institutions, we can observe similar processes at work in the formation and regimentation of institutional practice. Educational institutions, with their instruction in literacy practices, their college admissions essays, and their professorial job interviews, are obvious sites where language ideologies are part of institutionalization and regimentation processes. So are academic disciplines, with their technical terminologies, their texts, their preferred styles of talk and writing, their criteria of expertise, their regular national and international meetings (not for nothing are these often called "conventions"), and their grounding in university departments. So too, of course, are election campaigns, today increasingly swept up in media relations and practices where – as is well known – the projects of media personnel can intercede in and shape the political process and the presentation of candidates to a public. It requires no special conspiracy theory to see how American politics is entangled with the institutions of advertising, news media, and the blogosphere.[11]

In some cases of ideologically based institutional processes one can even observe effects on the social implications of linguistic forms themselves. We take an apt example from work by Thomas Bonfiglio (2002): in *Race and the Rise of Standard American*, Bonfiglio argues that the emergence by the 1940s of western or midwestern norms for a "General American" male voice for network broadcasting actually began in the early 1920s, when Harvard changed its admissions policies to focus on the western and central states and limit recruitment from the Northeast. Other Ivy League schools soon followed suit. As Bonfiglio explains, a key text – hence, for us, an important site of ideological work – was the report of Harvard's "Committee on Methods of Sifting Candidates for Admission," presented to Harvard president A. Lawrence Lowell and the faculty in April 1923 with an accompanying letter to Lowell from the committee's chair, professor Charles H. Grandgent.

What is important here is how this text was swept up in interdiscursive webs that ultimately, as Bonfiglio documents, institutionalized a "General American" accent and prosody, modeled on the network newsman's voice. The 1923 text itself makes little explicit reference to language, much less "accent," as a criterion for admission. What it discusses, instead, are race and geography. Preceding the formation of the committee was a set of statements by Lowell recommending limits on admission of Jews, statements that sparked considerable controversy among the faculty and in the press, even the national press. Countering Lowell's recommendations, Grandgent's committee rejected quotas based on race or religion. Instead, they proposed "the building up of a new group of men" from the rural central states and the West (cited in Bonfiglio 2002:184). As Bonfiglio comments (185), "Thus the committee denied the criterion of race and displaced the focus of recruitment onto geography. ... Instead of explicitly focusing on race, the committee focused on a metonym of race, i.e., on geographical location that was coded for proper racial content." To increase the proportion of rural midwestern boys in the student body was to increase the proportion of white Protestants.

Interestingly, Grandgent, the chairman of the faculty committee, was a philologist who only two years earlier had described urban northeastern [r]-deleting dialects as "decay" and Middle West [r]-production as "vigorous":

America has, in the main, followed about the same paths as the parent lands; but our enterprising Middle West, unwilling to abandon the r tradition, has developed and cherished an r-substitute, homely, to be sure, but vigorous and aggressive. What has the future in store? Will decay pursue its course; or will a reaction set in, restoring to the English-speaking world a real r of some kind, or a tolerable substitute? (Grandgent 1920:56; also cited in Bonfiglio 2002:185)

The same (rhematizing) ideological process that linked the "vigorous" midwestern [r] with its "enterprising" population promoted midwestern applicants as especially suited for Harvard admission. Thus the elite schools reconfigured their representation of the ideal American male and his ideal American speech – although the connection with speech was indirect.

According to Bonfiglio, this new standard was further institutionalized when network broadcasting adopted it in the 1940s. Important affirmation of that normative voice of American maleness came from the wartime reporting of broadcaster Edward R. Murrow (CBS) and the reporters trained by speech specialist James Bender at NBC. The long-range result of Harvard's changed admissions practices, then, and the adoption of voice training for news announcers on broadcast networks was to institutionalize – through many interdiscursive steps – a new "standard" for spoken American English. These standardizing processes worked to exclude or downgrade other linguistic varieties and the (ideologized) images associated with them from news broadcasting and other sites taken as authoritative.

Similar processes of exclusion can be seen in one of our own ethnographic cases. In Bóly, both the farmer and artisan registers were and are deemed "incorrect" from the perspective of German-medium schools, where a literary *Standarddeutsch* is the medium of instruction. Local German has no external support; recall that for Bóly's region, since the mid-nineteenth century the language of national affairs and most of education has been Hungarian. In education, only literary German has been offered, and only on the side, in weekly classes or in "mother tongue" primary school tracks, depending on the historical period.

These examples have directed our analytical attention toward national institutions and the state because they illustrate how a site, even if local and occupying only a brief historical moment, can have interdiscursive connections reaching to the state and beyond. We saw something similar – far-reaching interdiscursive connections – in the Baltimore example. What if our site of ideological work were the state itself?

While the state can have the power to decree language policy – and sometimes to impose it, which is not always the same thing – ideologies of language inhere not only in such policies but also in visions of the state's relation to its citizens or subjects and to other states. As Gal (2006) and others have argued, European ethnonationalism has rested on an exclusionary logic in which language, as sign and essence of ethnonational identification, must be unitary and singular: only one "mother tongue" per speaker. For people like the residents of Bóly, German-speakers in a Hungarian-dominated territory, this logic has subjected them to various and competing regimenting pressures, from German nationalists in the Habsburg and Nazi eras who tried to mobilize them for a German-speaking polity, to the Hungarian state pursuing magyarization projects. Again, one must not only observe the semiotic "stuff" internal to the site – here, the "mother tongues" and their entailments – but also consider the site's relationship to other sites from which it is differentiated. For German nationalists operating in the Bóly region, the relevant differentiation is between German-speaking states and Hungary. In an earlier era and in the regions unified as the German Reich in 1871, the relevant national differentiation was most often from France, and the linguistic opposition was between German and French. Today, according to some sources, the most relevant differentiation for German-speakers, at least in Germany, is from the United States and English (see Spitzmüller 2007).

As for French itself, recall that the language (in its metropolitan, literary form) was long considered the treasured possession of the French state, to be protected from the noxious influence of other languages. In the early modern period, when French was encroaching on political and literary domains previously reserved for Latin, French linguists claimed (in what has been called the "natural order debate") that French word order reflected the order of nature. Word order, as Claude Hagège has remarked, was "far from the purely scholastic pursuit of grammarians, [but instead] constituted the cornerstone of defense for the French language, and even for the prestige of the French state" (1990:118). In some quarters this view is still championed. But French has also been touted as a potential international language on the grounds of its claims to represent a universal rationality (clarity, logic) and universalist egalitarian ideals, the latter stemming from the discourse of the 1789 Revolution.

These French and German examples indicate how connections among sites branch out even beyond the state and into international arenas and global history. Such connections invoke questions about the scaling of interdiscursive relations – questions that deserve consideration in their own right.

Conclusion

The focus of this chapter has been on how sites of ideological work can branch out into other sites, potentially proliferating endlessly. Exploring, through the "Benchmark" case, such a burgeoning network of sites has led to considering how we may understand those connections between sites, how they work semiotically, and what effects they can have. All such connections can be considered "meta-moves": that is, they concern uptake – an interpretive response to a site's conjecture (interpretant). The response may be made by an actor who participates in the site's social milieu or it may be made by an analyst. Moreover, the responses and the sites to which they link – or sites they create – no matter how much they involve ideologized construals, are situated in history. As we have emphasized many times, real-world events, changes, instantiations, and comparisons affect semiotic processes, hence the ways sites of ideological work are linked.

It is useful to summarize the main forms of connectedness we have identified:

Chains of interpretive responses ("meta-moves"). Given a site as a focus of joint attention, uptake on the site links it to some response that at once interprets it and offers a new site, which affords new uptakes and new responses. For example, attention to the slogan on the bus stop benches in Baltimore involves reading the slogan and, in the photographs, to sitting on the bench reading some book or newspaper, which in turn provides a site that is responded to by photographing it. Different perspectives (points of view) on the site, as for example in the differing views of long-term city residents, city officials, and transient outsiders, lead to different response chains.

Typifications. Typifications situate a site as an instance in some putatively more inclusive set of sites or objects of attention. The bench slogan is linked to the genre of city slogans and "brands," in comparison to slogans attaching to other cities. Similarly, the environmental action group "CEC," in producing their flyer, situates its discourse as an instantiation of print media in the hope of enlisting the authoritativeness of newspapers and other institutionalized publications. Typifications necessarily invoke contrast sets – the kinds of things/actions the type contrasts with – another kind of connection among sites. When Charles Grandgent wrote about midwestern speech as homely yet vigorous forms of utterance, he not only offered a type, "midwestern speech," but also invoked a contrast set of American "accents" and their speakers. The bundled qualities he attributed to midwestern speech contrast, in his view, with the qualities of other regional forms, along an ideological axis of differentiation.

Temporal sequelae and historical connections. A series of slogans, on benches and elsewhere in Baltimore, each reacted to the previous one – but also, especially in the bench slogans, responded to the gradual physical deterioration of the benches themselves. *Baptismal sites* have forward-looking connections. They inaugurate a series of sites following their lead, as in naming a child or establishing an attribution for a work of art.

Modeling or "anchoring." A site is modeled by another site if it (the former) is construed as a diagrammatic icon of another (anchor) site, whether experienced or imagined. Examples have included Tongan courtroom discourse, understood as connected with brother-sister talk – its anchor; similarly, "griot-like" talk by Wolof people who are not themselves griots is understood with reference to (i.e., modeled after) griots' public performances. The connections between a baptismal moment and its consequent echoes are also of this nature, differing from examples like the Tongan brother-sister talk in that the baptismal site is a unique event that serves as anchor and inaugurates the series, rather than a general type.

Explanations. Exploring the effects of connections among sites led us to consider explanations as (attempts at) authorizing and regimenting – processes through which a site's semiotic materials are concretized and rendered iterable, but which also have the consequence that subtleties and possibilities for nonstereotypical behavior tend to escape notice and fall from memory.

Institutionalizations. Pursuing the matter of regimentation led us to consider processes through which activities become systematically organized and conventionalized, stabilizing them over time, and processes connecting sites with established institutions, including the state. These are institutionalizations.

Our strategy for discussing connections among sites was to start "small" and work toward "large." That is, many of the "larger" sites are broader-based in their personnel, temporal extension, and other features. But this strategy draws attention to questions of scale: How does ideological work move "up" or "down" in the scale of what its object encompasses? Are "up" and "down," as binaries on a metric of verticality, the best way to think about these matters? We turn to questions of scale in the next chapter.

8 Scales and Scale-Making: Connecting Sites

What does it mean to say that one site of joint attention and ideological work is "larger" or "at a higher level" than another? These are scalar claims. They entail comparisons and connections between sites, connections that, in many cases, are somehow measured. This chapter focuses on scales and scale-making as ideological projects, linking sites and their differentiations in the pursuit of increased value – whatever value may consist in.[1]

Some concept of "scale" is much relied upon in both the physical and the social sciences, usually under the assumption that a relevant kind of metric is "out there" in the world, external to the project at hand. Yet, scales are made, not found. Scale-making is a human activity that can work in various ways, whether it is done by researchers or, in the human sciences, by the people they investigate. As Bruno Latour has observed, analysts of social life should not assume the relevance of particular scales a priori. He comments (Latour 2005:183), "The problem is that social scientists use scale as one of the many variables they need to set up before doing the study, whereas scale is what actors achieve by scaling, spacing, and contextualizing each other." How, then, shall we conceive of scale, such that scaling can be seen as achieved by actors, not only by researchers?

What Is Scale? Scales and Sites

Scale-making and scale-invoking are forms of comparison among sites (foci of attention and ideological work). They require practice and activity, and they imply projects. Such projects are made; so too are the scales they depend upon. Even though the scales may seem to be objective principles, and even when the phenomena they measure are external to humans and their social lives, the scales themselves and the values of their measures are humanly constructed.

The concept of "scale" we draw upon is relatively abstract. It is based in a semiotics of comparison, which may operate on any feature of the world – physical or social – and examine that feature for commensurability with some other feature, a commensurability that may be found or denied.

Together with some other recent works in our field (e.g., Carr and Lempert 2016; Blommaert 2015), we reject the broad binary, assumed in many analyses of social life, that contrasts the "micro" with the "macro," as if time, space, and social activity all took place on a single dimension of bigness (or smallness). Our work also differs from analyses that assume a geopolitical scale, for example distinguishing local, national, and global "levels," as the necessary basis of scaling in any (other) aspect of social life.

More useful for our thinking are some recent approaches in human geography. They distinguish scale as a property of a geographical phenomenon from the analyst's view of it (Moore 2008). One might call the latter the degree of magnification, or the breadth or depth of field, with which a geographical phenomenon is to be examined. But, in our view, picking out some geographical phenomenon for study is itself a semiotic process, and is relative to ideological projects. To compare this geographical selection with the scope of an analyst's view is to compare one semiotic process with another, not to compare something material with something methodological. Furthermore, the kind of distinction Moore makes becomes more delicate, and the comparison more complicated, when the object of study is itself semiotic and ideological.

What, then, should one mean by "scale"? Matters of size, extent, generality, and degrees of interconnectedness have all been called "scale." The word itself is ambiguous. It can refer to some quality, dimension, or angle that might be measured, made into a ladder, as it were; or it can refer to a particular value, that is, a *magnitude* – a step on the ladder. If there were only one ladder that accounted for the "size" of all social phenomena, the term's ambiguity would not cause trouble. Perhaps the ambiguity conduces to one-scale-fits-all analyses, for that reason. But the sites and scenes of human life have innumerable qualities and dimensions that could be measured. What qualities are seen as scalable, and by whom? Are the scalar ladders seen as lining up together? Does a ladder change shape when viewed from a different angle? Is there a particular step on the ladder that stands out in importance? These are empirical questions about the ideological construction of scales in particular ethnographic cases. To assume, as is so often done in invoking a micro-macro binary, that scalable dimensions must coincide – or that there is only one kind of scale, or one way of scaling – is an ideological artifact, perhaps emerging from the institutions that regiment people's lives (including our own) and align scales according to some social project.

Scaling is a relational practice that relies on situated juxtapositions and comparisons among events, persons, things, and activities; that is, among sites of attention, as we have defined these in the preceding chapters. All human languages afford the possibility of identifying qualities – for instance in adjectives – and these can be made into dimensions of comparison by linguistic means: for example in morphology (e.g., *green* and *greener*, in English) or in other kinds of grammatical constructions (such as using a verb meaning something like "exceed," thus "this person exceeds that one in age," a mode of comparison found in many languages). Scaled comparison may be implied also through quantifiers and intensifiers, as for example in "That dress is so *you!*" (i.e., "that dress expresses the qualities of your personality better than some other dress might"). Here the qualities of your personality have been made into a dimension. Languages thus offer the possibility of juxtaposing entities for comparison and then making a scale out of some quality along which the entities are compared, even one like greenness, or you-ness, where no such scale was obvious until the utterance itself made one.

While these simple linguistic comparisons already imply qualities, and these can be scaled – along a dimension of greenness in the first example – scales can be made more complex. Indeed they are of several different kinds; and some scales may be understood as quantifiable. All these kinds of measures have an ideological aspect, which may remain largely implicit in the simplest comparisons but involves more ideological work as the comparisons among sites become more complex. Additional complexity and ideological work arise if multiple dimensions are measured and made commensurable. Moreover, like any other ideological project, scaling implies positioning, hence point of view: a perspective from which scales, as modes of comparison, are constructed. It is from such a perspective, a line of sight as it were, that aspects of the world are noticed, evaluated and compared.

It is worthwhile exploring this matter of perspective more closely, because it enters into our discussion in several ways. First of all, as we have said, all scale-making is located in projects, and therefore entails the perspective of the scale-maker. Perspective, in this sense, takes part in the broader notion of indexicality. All utterances have indexical dimensions relating to their conditions of production, no matter what the utterances themselves are like. Additionally, however, many utterances contain shifters, like the personal pronouns *I* and *you*, or tense markers – forms that depend for their reference on the (indexical) specifics of the situation in which they occur. In contrast to nomic utterances that purport to express eternal truths – even though those utterances too have their conditions of production – the indexicality in shifters cannot be ignored. In the same way, some kinds of scale-making, like utterances with shifters (which they may include), depend for their reference – that is, for the identification of what the measure is and how it works – on the specifics of a situation of use. Yet, other kinds of scale-making ignore, deny, or bracket this connection and posit that the scale is absolute, external to any act invoking it – a property of the world, not relative to the properties of the situation at hand.

To illustrate, suppose we say that a piece of cloth is seven yards long. The fact that we have picked out length as the relevant measure, and yards as the units in which to express it, reflects our projects of the moment: making curtains, perhaps, and making them in the United States, or somewhere else where imperial rather than metric scales are used. The utterance, like any other we might make, entails our project and our perspective. Yet, this utterance appeals to a measure of length – yards – that is external to the act of measurement and is even backed by formal institutions. Someone else, who knew nothing about our curtains, could assess the length of the cloth. Because of that appeal to an external measure, this kind of scaling contrasts with a kind that builds the situational particulars into the scale itself, not just into the reasons for scale-making at all. So, suppose we say that this piece of cloth is long enough (for our curtain) while that one is too short. The example still picks out length as the relevant measure, but there is no way to assess the degree of length without reference to our project of curtain-making.

We call the types of scale-making that rely on a property external to the act of scaling *aperspectival models* because they posit measures that are assumed to be independent of the point of view of the measurer and the situation of scaling. Even scales that are created ad hoc may have this form. (An example might include a ranked list of "our state's best Italian restaurants," scaling "bestness" from 1 to 10 and positing some authoritative measurement thereof.) In contrast, we call the shifter-like forms of scale-making *perspectival models* because the perspective of the scale-maker and situation of scale-making are built into how the scale works. Some perspectival scales may actually involve lexical shifters: "that music is so last year," where last-yearness is the scale. The same is true of the "that dress is so *you!*" example mentioned above. Other perspectival scales may be more complex, such as the scales that involve fractal recursivity, with shifts of point of view governing the very identification of contrasting units. We will return to these contrasting kinds of models in later pages.

In simple examples, perspective may appear not to be particularly relevant. In fact, there may be many everyday practices of comparison made in the interactional moment that are not ordinarily recognized as scaling at all. But as soon as examples (and sites) become more complex, they reveal perspective's importance. In one way or another, it is important in the ideological work of scale-making – even when commensurability, or joint participation in a site, or the possibility of different perspectives, is denied. Perhaps especially then.

Exploring Inclusion as Scale

One of the simplest forms of scaling involves inclusion. Two sites are compared; in relations of inclusion, one of the sites compared contains the other. The sites differ in scale exactly because of this inclusion, for example as a category contains its subcategories. It is important to see that not every case of scalar difference is inclusion. For instance, consider a geographical example: the United States is geographically larger than any one of its states, and includes each of them; this is inclusion. But the difference of size between Texas and Massachusetts is not a matter of inclusion. Massachusetts is not inside Texas – nor can one always think of Texas as a great big Massachusetts. Comparative scaling of beauty is also not a matter of inclusion. One might decide that flower A is more beautiful than flower B, but it does not follow that there is a relationship of inclusion, since the properties that make flower A beautiful – its color, for example – may be different from the ones that beautify flower B, such as the shape of its petals.

We must be careful not to confuse inclusion with quantification. If you quantify a scale, measuring (say) population figures, the greater quantity can be said to include the smaller one; but unless one population actually incorporates the other, the inclusion pertains to the quantification – a more abstract, external scaling device, applied to and aligned with the population – not actually to the population itself. To illustrate the abstraction involved in quantification, suppose you have eight oranges and ten apples. If you say you have more apples than oranges, you are comparing the *numbers* (of pieces of fruit, a more abstract and inclusive category). You are not comparing apples with oranges. Abstracting toward quantification is itself an important scaling device, especially characteristic of institutional regimes in modernity (Porter 1995). For many aspects of social life, quantification can become so thoroughly institutionalized that it is not perceived as a scale distinct from what it quantifies. But it is not the same as inclusion.

Having eliminated these "false friends," let us explore a more complex example of scale-making in which ideological work constructs an inclusion: the relationship between languages and dialects. The sites in this example show that there can be different kinds of inclusion. They also reveal the relevance of differences of point of view. People of different backgrounds or roles who attend to the site may disagree as to whether inclusion, or any other form of scale-making, is even at issue. There is a problem here for the linguist's object of study. Is the "language" described in reference grammars an empirical object? A generalization over variation? A literary standard? A polylectal summary? An imagined type? A normative model? Whichever kind of object the "language" is, do "dialects" or "varieties" inhabit the same ontological realm? And does the "language" contain them?

The answer depends on ideological work and perspective. For example, many scholars see a standard as just one linguistic variety – constructed and endowed with institutionalized authority – so, not including other varieties. But it is also commonplace to identify particular ways of speaking as a *dialect (or variety) of language X* (say, "English," or "Italian," or "French"). This is the logic that results in such expressions as "all the dialects of French." Some linguists, including Saussure (1967 [1916]:278–279), have explicitly described the relationship between "dialect" and "language" in inclusive scalar terms.

For French, does the comprehensive whole equate to metropolitan standard French? Saussure did not equate "literary language" or "official language" with the large-scale unity he contrasted with dialect. For many linguists, the whole that is "a language" represents not a standard, but a generalization over variation. However, in the ideology of standard language that has emerged gradually along with modern forms of the nation-state, the standard exemplifies the imagined whole, even though the standard as a norm of usage does not itself literally include the dialects (except perhaps lexically). Instead, the standard-of-use is to be considered the best and most elaborated exemplar of the (imagined) type, which does include the dialects. There is a tension, often swept under the rug, between conceptions of "standard": standard as common (so, exemplar of the whole type), and standard as best, most "correct" (Crowley 1997). Eliding the difference between common and best is itself a piece of ideological work. Moreover, to conceive of the standard as "best," or "correct," implies judgments of value, and judges who differentiate good from bad.

Clearly, there are differences among the dialects, even if we set "correctness" aside. But except when the language's boundaries are debated – is Haitian Creole a kind of French, or something else? What about Béarnais? Or Picard, officially recognized as a distinct language in Belgium but not in France? – the differences are often erased in discussions referring to French as type. The type, in that case, is imagined as some kind of whole – perhaps as an abstraction standing for a set embracing the tokens.

What sites "count" as an instantiation of the posited type, and what must be ignored in order to do so? Notice that what counts as "French" and who counts as its speakers is important for the politics of *la francophonie* as global connectivity.[2] And following similar reasoning, the posited linguistic "type" might include among its tokens a historical form of that language. When a language attested in ninth-century texts is called "Old English" – not "Late West Germanic," or even "Anglo-Saxon," but "Old English" – the label posits a national linguistic persistence over twelve hundred years and in spite of the incursions of Norman French (Segal n.d.). The choice among these labels is not politically innocent.

The examples illustrate, in the realm of "a language," its standard variety, and its related dialects, how type-token relationships can be constructed in ideological projects as relations of scale. The ideological work construes the linguistic relationships as inclusion, analogous to the idea that the nation-state includes its local provinces and class divisions. Moreover, when attention is called to type rather than to tokens, the differences between tokens become irrelevant. With coins – often the prime example of token/type relations – it is perfectly possible to notice a difference between one particular dime and another, as well as the systematic differences that result from changes in dime designs over time, like the change from the liberty head to Roosevelt's portrait. But when we use the dimes as money we ignore those things.

Type-token relationships are not simply the same as part-whole relationships, however, even though both might be construed as scalar. A type is a conceptual construct, sometimes lending itself to the possibility of illustration through "best" exemplars; tokens are real-world objects. Type and token do not occupy the same existential realm. Part-whole relationships do. The United States has various subdivisions, the states; both the parts and the whole have legal status and territorial extension, so they occupy the same existential realm, despite any other differences that make this whole more than just the sum of these parts. Yet, ideologically induced slippages between "whole" and "type" are not uncommon. Such slippages can arise when a site connects to two kinds of meta-sites (such as the conceptual abstraction and the set of comparable real-world sites), which are conflated.

Thus, norm, best version, type, and part/whole are all possible ways of thinking about inclusion. All occur in the ideological work that has surrounded named languages.

Finding the Indexical Sign's Object: Abduction as Hypothesized Scale-Making

A somewhat different example of ideologized scale-making comes from Peirce's writings illustrating an indexical sign-relation. The passage features a driver of a horse-drawn vehicle who calls out "Hi!" to attract the attention of a pedestrian and cause him to get out of the way. "[The cry, Hi!] is an index, because it is meant to put him in real connection with the object, which is his situation relative to the approaching horse" (Peirce 1955a:109). But where does the pedestrian look, in searching for the possible source of the cry – the object of the indexical sign? What is the scope of the sign's arena of abduction? How does that site, as hypothesized by the pedestrian, compare with the site that focuses attention on the pedestrian himself?

We recognize, of course, that scale-making is not Peirce's concern in this passage, nor is ideology. Moreover, the driver's construction of a scene of interaction, via a vocalization that the pedestrian may take as an indexical sign, may not at first glance seem ideologically saturated. Yet (we depart now from Peirce's own discussion), people who hear the cry – the pedestrian and others – impute motive to the driver, and perhaps evaluate this "Hi!" in comparison to other things the driver might have said (such as "Excuse me, sir!"). This interpretive move is an example of scale-making because it *places an act* – the cry – *within an embracing sphere* of relevant persons, their motives, their spatial positions, and potential responses. There is an implicit comparison between spheres, whether spatial or sociological, in which the source of the cry and its target (the pedestrian) might be appropriately located. And if we update the example, adding the honking of car horns in rush-hour traffic, with the hapless pedestrian trying to cross the road at an unauthorized spot, we enter the world of industrial work, the state, and their regimentations. Whatever sphere might contain the source of the cry is itself embraced by other spheres.

Notice that a hearer can refuse to participate in an interaction whose sphere of relevance is constructed in this way. If our pedestrian ignored the auditory warning of an impending collision, the consequences could be grave; but in other cases the situational dynamics may be different, revealing the importance of point of view. Consider a catcall – as in a scene in which a man addresses a wolf whistle to a passing woman, or calls out not Hi! but Hey Bitch! How does the addressee react? As a rapper from 2 Live Crew commented (Hill 2008:91), "When I say 'bitch,' you don't have to turn around."[3] Refusing uptake is not the same thing as not noticing the call (whether Hi! or Bitch!), or misjudging the distance of an indexical sign's source. Uptake is a separate social move. However, the caller (or an observer) might not be sure whether an unresponsive addressee is refusing to participate or is merely deaf – that is, whether, for the addressee, a sphere of potential interaction has emerged at all. In this case, assumptions about the addressee could come into play (e.g., in terms of gender, age, frailty, perhaps race, as potential explanations for not responding).

One could cite many other examples that reveal the ideological aspects of this form of scale-making. Is a certain kind of noise an indexical sign of a car backfiring or a gunshot? The two interpretations might suggest different distances for the source of the noise. More importantly, however, the choice between the interpretations depends on the hearer's assumptions about the environs. Is there a lot of traffic close by, is this a high-crime neighborhood, are we in a war zone? Or: you're in a theater; the actors are portraying an intimate scene, but even though you're in the back row you can hear everything they are saying. In real life they would speak softly, their voices not constructing an interactional sphere wide enough to include you; but you understand their louder volume as a convention of the theatrical frame. Everything onstage has to be done bigger, so that it can be picked up by the person in the back row. This convention of live theater overrides norms of appropriate "bigness" of speech and gesture, relative to the scale of the interactional sphere suggested by the content of the talk. (Yet, we all know people who are not actors onstage, but nevertheless "speak to the crowd" – in ringing tones – when we thought the conversation more intimate.)

Although the foregoing examples happen to involve physical distance, the scale-making they illustrate is not just a matter of geographical space. There are not two spaces of different size being compared as such, but instead, a sphere of relevance and action – a site – is constructed, via an indexical sign-relation, and compared with other potential spheres. Moreover, the boundaries of a sphere of relevance, like those of sites in general, are not fixed. Instead, the sphere is taken to include an indexical *origo*, whose identification depends on interpretive schemata applied by the person who construes something as an indexical sign. It is the *interpretive schemata that establish a scale of spheres of relevance*, not geographical space. The most relevant spheres might be social rather than geographical, anyway. Finally, relevance – and therefore its spheres – is in the eye of the beholder. It is a matter of perspective.

The example from Peirce that began this discussion is not detailed enough to permit comparison on these points, but the enormous literature on indexicality – including the variationist sociolinguistic literature that does not necessarily draw on the concept of indexicality explicitly – would surely offer many comparable examples.

Complex Scalings: Perspectival Models

We turn now to more complex scaling frameworks, and the models of comparison on which they rely. In these models, perspective is crucially and necessarily at issue. That is, these forms of scaling incorporate points of view and situational contexts in the very process of characterizing and comparing things. These are perspectival models. Later we will see that not all complex models of scalings rely on perspective in this way.

One perspectival model is the comparison involved in barter exchange. The issue here is the possible difference in perspective on goods and values. Items valued highly by one party may be much less valued by the other. And there are not always agreed upon commensurating practices like the use of a single form of money. For example, the story about the Dutch purchase of Manhattan Island for a few trinkets reveals sharp differences in perspective. Were the Dutch terribly clever to acquire such valuable property in exchange for trivial goods? Or did the Native Americans cleverly dupe them because the "sellers" didn't actually own what they sold? The point about perspective actually applies beyond simple barter. As Jane Guyer writes (2004:4), "[T]he very idea of comparative advantage [in trade] rests on the assumption of difference among trading partners: different goods, different values placed on them, and different mediating means of exchange."

Another example of a model that incorporates perspective is one we have discussed at length in this book – fractal recursivity. It is not often seen as a form of scaling, so we return to it here to draw out some of its scaling implications. Fractal recursivity incorporates the possibility of changing perspective within the process itself. The perspective or positioning of the comparer – and the ideological projects of that view – pick out the qualities and dimensions taken to be relevant for comparison of sites. An axis of differentiation organizes the sets of qualities on which sites are judged, and this process is invoked in situated action. How any item is judged on the relevant dimension(s) depends on the perspective that defines what it is contrasted/compared to and, accordingly, the scope of the contrast set the item (for the moment) belongs to.

Toward the end of the previous chapter, we considered processes of institutionalizing: the ways in which a site, and its connections with other sites, may become stabilized and regimented. We pointed to the state as an important means of "fixing" such connections. Many projects of scaling have such regimenting aspects, and we will return to them later in this chapter. But social actors, with models that incorporate perspective – like fractal recursivity – may draw their own connections, making their own scales according to different principles than those "fixed" or standardized or regimented by states or other authorities. As a result, the entities under comparison and the ways they are compared do not sit still.

In illustration, let us observe a conversation Gal recorded in Bóly in which the actors made comparisons. One afternoon, Gal was sitting with an elderly farming couple, call them Hu(sband) and Wi(fe), who were talking about a recent letter from a childhood friend, Feri. The friend, an artisan, had emigrated to Germany. In Example 8.1, the husband depicts Feri as fondly remembering, in his letter, the artisan/farmer relationship of equality and contrast in the 1930s, as enacted through food exchanges between artisans and farmers in German-speaking Bóly:

(8.1)   HU: *az apja pék volt. És akkor*   HU: his father was a baker. And
        mondja, mindig jött és cserélt a   he says he always came and
        paraszt gyerekekkel, a paraszt   traded with the farmer kids,
        kenyérért, ők meg a –   for the farmer's bread [i.e.,
                                                  homemade] and they –

        WI: *péki kenyeret*   WI: baker's bread.
        HU: *péki kenyeret. A parasztok*   HU: baker's bread [i.e., machine-
        szerették a péknek a kenyerét   made]. The farmers liked the
        ő meg a parasztok kenyerét   baker's bread, and he liked
        szerette. Azt mondta, emlékszel   the farmer's bread. He says,
        hogy cseréltünk mindig? a zsiros   remember how we always traded?
        kenyeret.   the bread, spread with chicken fat.

The husband's story within a story was followed by a second story (Example 8.2), contributed by the wife. The immediate juxtaposition of the second story, and the continuing topic of food create an analogy between two incidents, eliding or erasing that the second incident occurred forty years later; the subject was the couple's son Tibor; and the location was not Bóly but the nearby Hungarian-speaking city of Pécs:

(8.2)   Wi: *és mikor a Tibor* [the couple's son] *volt diák, az bejárt Pécsre, minden nap. Sonkás kenyeret kellett késziteni. Kis vajat rá vékonyan, és sonka darabokat. Mindennap elcserélte évekig azt a sonkás kenyeret, nem tudom én zsemléér, vagy kifliér. De ezt nem mondta meg csak késöbb.*

Wi: and when Tibor [the couple's son] was a student, he went to Pécs [nearby Hungarian-speaking city] every day and every day I had to prepare bread with ham. A little butter on it thinly spread and then pieces of ham. Every day he traded that ham and bread for years, for – what do I know – for rolls or pretzels. But he never told us till later.

Hu: *Soha nem ette meg, de mindig harapták. Jöttek a városiak, elkunyerálták tőle, és adtak mást, ugye ami neki nem volt. A Feri ilyen volt, mindig mondja hogy cseréltünk.*
(97:2B:29:50)

Hu: He never ate it, they always went for it. They came, the city folks and begged it away from him and gave him something else that he did not have. Feri was just the same, he always says, let's trade.

The contrasting objects of exchange were no longer homemade bread and machine-made bread, but Bóly-made food versus urban goods. The parallel was noted by the husband, with a good-natured guffaw; in both cases "they" (artisans in Bóly, Hungarians in the city) appreciated the product identified as "ours." But the stories elide the fact that the reference of "our" had shifted significantly, from farmers (contrasted with artisans) to all Bóly (contrasted with the Hungarian city of Pécs). The husband's perspective had also shifted between the two stories. He took up the perspective of farmer in the first narrative (in contrast to Feri, the artisan), but took up the perspective of Bóly (in contrast to Pécs) in the second (note: "they came," locating the city folks as distal).

In this conversation, as in similar examples in Chapter 2, the axis of differentiation remains the same, contrasting authentic, down-to-earth qualities as against the refined and overly fancy. But in the second story the social units are more encompassing than in the remembered earlier one. The earlier contrast was internal to Bóly; the second contrast puts those subdivisions together in a more encompassing unit, all Bóly as opposed to Pécs. Moreover, Bóly and Pécs are equated in the fractal analogy, which is accomplished through the juxtaposition of the two stories. Yet, we know nothing about the contrast between Pécs and Bóly in terms of more conventional scales external to this situated comparison, such as population size or territory. In fact, Pécs is a good size city and Bóly is a small town, but the analogy elides this difference. And although in conventional measures of time the two incidents are quite far apart – forty years – the analogy collapses that difference too. It is the narrators' switching of perspective that allows an analogical fractal scaling (an encompassment) that overrides (for the moment) the quite significant differences between Bóly and Pécs, interwar and postwar times. Fractal scaling can challenge conventional, standardized scales.

The axis of differentiation in this conversation remained the same, despite the changes in the narrator's perspective. Let us turn to our Senegalese case to explore sites whose connections involve changes of location that bring along much more drastic changes in vantage point, indeed changes that reconfigure an axis of differentiation.

Example 8.3 is a statement by a Senegalese woman, AT, who had emigrated from Dakar to the United States. Her statement comes from a small study Irvine conducted among Senegalese people in southeast Michigan in 2004–2005. After chatting about the study's investigation of languages and multilingualism, we asked AT who speaks the "best Wolof" – an evaluation that the rural Senegalese of Irvine's first fieldwork some years earlier generally attributed to griots. AT does not mention griots, however:

(8.3) AT interview, Ypsilanti, MI, 2005:

The people live in the farms, they the best people who speak Wolof. ... They can do Wolof the best ... the real Wolof. [When she first went to visit her auntie on the farm,] in the beginning, I used to say, what happened, what are they saying? I speak Wolof, but I don't know what they're talking about ... that is the real Wolof. ... Sometimes I have to say something and put French inside, it's not Wolof. ... The real Wolof is hard, yeah.

Let us first notice the various comparisons AT invokes. She contrasts "the farms" as site (i.e., rural areas) with Dakar, perhaps also the United States where she now resides. She also contrasts her aunt who lives in a rural area, with herself; and implicitly compares herself on a first visit to the farm with herself on later ones. There is a quality of authenticity: "real Wolof" is compared with her own (urban) Wolof, presumed less authentic, and this coincides, inversely, with the relative quantity of French "inside" a speaker's Wolof: the more French, the less "real." These two, authenticity and quantity of French, further coincide with the difficulty (of understanding), which in turn is lined up with ruralness. Time is not lined up with these other comparisons in AT's statement, except insofar as the biographical comparison suggests that she began to understand her aunt's Wolof better on later visits, although this comparison does not necessarily undermine some implication of rural Wolof's essentially greater difficulty; it only means AT became more competent in it (another comparison).

The various comparisons AT invokes were echoed in statements by other Senegalese people Irvine interviewed in the United States. In those statements, as in AT's, the "best Wolof" was almost always located among country people, "down home," and described as "true Wolof," "pure," "real," "not tainted," even "clean." It is "deep Wolof" (*wolof bu xóot*). And it is "old": the best Wolof is spoken by old people out in the country; it's "old-school Wolof," "village Wolof or ancient Wolof," "like how our grandfathers spoke." A chronotope lining up scales so that old-time rurality and purity contrasts with urban "tainted," French-infused modernity, has either replaced or engulfed the noble/griot register contrast.

Looking more closely at these reconfigurations and their history, we observe that the émigré's change in location is also a change in point of view. The gazes on the relevant sites are therefore not identical. The shift of location leads to a shift in salience among the units of comparison. When people move to diasporan locales, their changed vantage point is likely to reduce the salience of internal variation in the linguistic practices they have left behind – particularly if that variation is minor to begin with, and/or gradient rather than categorical, as is the case with Wolof. In diasporan spaces, whether urban or abroad, the most striking differences people notice are often with members of other ethnic groups or nationalities, or at any rate with people whose biographies differ from their own.[4] The new positioning of émigrés offers a new perspective on language, role, and identity, such that "internal" differentiation may fade from salience in favor of a different set of contrasts – for example between Wolof, French, and even English.

To what extent do these new positionings simply repeat a pattern of fractal recursions consistent with the rural ideologies from the 1970s? Or is there a shift, partial or complete, in the features seen as organizing the contrasts? The changes in salience, we find, have led to a reassemblage – a *splicing* – of the bundle of contrasting qualities (much like Jefferson's reanalysis of colonial American contrasts, described in Chapter 5, although we did not there point out the scalar implications).

Wolof and French languages provide the principal ingredients of urban Senegalese varieties. How is their relationship, and their role in urban talk, interpreted? From a rural perspective in 1970, there did not seem to be much sense that Wolof as spoken in Dakar or other cities was a special variety, only that there were a lot of French people in Dakar, as well as educated Senegalese who spoke French, still the language of school education, government, and international business. We have mentioned (Chapter 1) the disparagement with which high-caste townspeople at that time regarded French language, seeing it as griot-like and tending to imply moral laxity. They did contrast French (people and language) with Wolof, but their attention focused mainly on a local semiotic economy of social types and linguistic practices. Today the differences between urban and rural varieties of Wolof are much more noticeable, to urban and rural speakers alike. Although Senegalese people describe urban Wolof as incorporating a lot of French language – a distinction between the two languages is still drawn – nevertheless they see urban Wolof as a variety of Wolof. When compared with metropolitan French, it is Wolof; when compared with rural Wolof, it is "French-flavored Wolof" or "Wolof tainted with French" or "bastardized Wolof." (Notice the recursivity of these linguistic types.)

These expressions of "taint" and "bastardizing" suggest that something of the moral laxity rural speakers saw in French persists in urban views. We might notice, too, that for urban speakers to say they do not themselves speak the best Wolof resonates with the statements of those (non-griot) rural speakers who attribute the best Wolof to griots, that is, to others. Speaking "bad" or disfluent Wolof does not disqualify a person from high rank. Similarly, descriptions of a way of speaking as the most "deep," "old" (traditional), and "obscure," applied by city dwellers to the speech of rural peasants, could also be heard in rural areas as describing "griot speech." Moreover, both rural and urban informants apparently associate French with high pitch. In this connection Swigart (2001) and Thiam (1998) each report that urban speakers describe some urban varieties, such as the one called *cip-cip*, as "light[weight]" and "birdlike," as opposed to talk (and persons) that is serious and real. Those metapragmatic descriptions echo the rural regime of value that links seriousness, consequentiality, and stolidity with nobility, and connects high pitch, chatter, and volatility with low rank.

Yet, there are important changes too. The scale of vocal pitch, while relevant to both urban and rural speakers, does not line up with the same social metrics. For rural speakers high pitch coincides with low caste rank; for urban speakers, according to Thiam (1998), it indexes affectation and effeminacy – something rural speakers did not mention. It is also linked with other linguistic features deemed French, such as an exaggeratedly velar [r]. And the chronotopes contrasting an old-time rural Wolof with a new, modern, urban Wolof have taken over in urban and émigré descriptions, leaving caste distinctions behind. Nevertheless, a metric of cosmopolitanism and modernity does not simply translate into a scale of value. Émigrés' discussions of linguistic practices are ambivalent. French is called the language of education and modernity, but it is also the language of the colonizer. (Rural) Wolof is the language of roots and tradition, but it is also old – a language of backward people, hayseeds, people "just off the bus" (that brought them to Dakar).

All these scale-makings take part in their makers' ideologized projects. Wherever they live, Senegalese people must find their places in a world of social ranking and history; negotiate the encounter with French colonization and its aftermath; and, if émigrés, find their way in new environments and among new people.

Changes of Perspective: Uptakes and
Interdiscursivity in Scale-Making

The similarities – even if limited – between the rural contrasts of 1970 and the contrasts drawn by Senegalese in the United States in 2005 strongly suggest that the effects of scale-making – in this case the construction of the axis and its qualities – can long outlast the projects that gave rise to the scale-making originally. Such effects of scale-making, whether one's own or other people's, become part of the historical conditions of interconnection among communicative acts. Since interconnectedness can vary in extent, it is a dimension that may be scaled, though often not in conventional ways.

Among other things, previous connections between sites become available as background knowledge. All the stories in Gal's conversation with the husband and wife concerned Bóly as they remembered it, and with a farmer/artisan distinction. It was familiar to all of them, even Gal, who had heard about that era often. It grounded comparison and even situated their discourse in the particular event of speaking reported in that excerpt. Since such grounding must be familiar if it is to be persuasive, the social scope of familiarity matters, as Blommaert (2015) observes. He calls it the "scope of communicability of ... invocations." His discussion focuses on the availability of (images of) chunks of history – chronotopes – that can be invoked by some sociolinguistic range of speakers to frame their discourse.

Scale, in this sense, is a matter of the range of audiences for whom invoking this history will be meaningful – audiences who know enough about the chunk of history and its relevant interpretations to recognize how it contextualizes utterances in the here and now. This sense of communicability is useful for our purposes insofar as it calls attention to the effects of past scale-making. But there is a prior step. For history to be available as background knowledge, certain kinds of connections must have been made earlier among sites of discourse, connections necessarily involving perspective. This is the case because any bit of discourse, to become "communicable" – somehow relayed to another person, place, or time – requires uptake. Hence, so does any scaling of that "communicability."

How far discourse "travels," and among whom, depends on what happens in the uptake: who takes it up; what those who take it up do with it; and whether some chunk of discourse – for instance about a historical period and its interpretation – becomes institutionalized. Moreover, uptake always remakes, in some way, what it takes up, reflecting the projects and perspectives of those who do the uptaking. Contexts are constantly in the process of being made. So the relevance of chronotopes (or anything else) as tropes, as a means of understanding social relations in the present, depends on interdiscursive relations – connections among sites of discourse – and the ideological work that characterizes the interpretive frame.

In uptake, the interlocutor (potential uptaker) is also a social actor, who does something to the object that's taken up. What is done in uptake can itself expand or block the scope of the object's communicability. It therefore increases or blocks the degree of interconnectedness or extent of a discourse. In illustration, consider a genre of Wolof insult poetry called *xaxaar*. Uptake is an important aspect of this genre, which is much involved in the local politics of reputation. Ostensibly insulting the bride at a wedding – a *xaxaar* poem's immediate addressee – the poems can target any of her kin, or target the groom. The poems that are locally deemed most successful are those that poetically insult some prominent member of the bride's family, wording the insult so cleverly and memorably that the poem or some lines from it are repeated around town afterward, even years later, reaching audiences who were not present at the original performance (as the prominent insultee likely was not). That is, success in *xaxaar* performance is a scale-making effect, expanding the scope of the poem's audiences. Complicit interlocutors take up the poem and repeat it to others. One particular poem discussed by Irvine (1996) was one whose original performance she had not witnessed; instead, the griot performer's brother wrote it down and presented Irvine with a written text, a few months afterward. The brother was among the people who took up the poem, turning it into a written text as well as an oral rendering of his own (reading his text aloud). And when Irvine transcribed the poem and translated it in her text, she expanded the poem's audience to a transatlantic readership. All this created a scalar effect, involving uptake as a connection among sites.

Ideological Issues in Stabilized, Standardized Scales: Aperspectival Models

The modes of scaling we have just discussed involved, within the practice of the scaling itself, a presumption of changes in perspective and of its effects on the construed connection among sites. We call all these "perspectival models of scaling." However, the conventional models of scale-making that are most familiar in discussions of "scale" do not involve perspective in this way. Instead, there is an implied denial that the scales are matters of perspective. We call such models aperspectival (or nonperspectival) because their authorizing and empowering ideology claims that they are "objective," that they require and rely on no perspective at all. Instead, it is posited that the measurements and the differences the models produce would be the same no matter who did them, no matter when or for what purpose. They are presumed to be universally significant. This presumption is inherent to the model; it is not merely an attitude toward it. Examples are standard scales of length, weight or time, measured in meters, kilos, hours, and minutes (Galison 2003). One can argue about what to measure (or not) and what dimensions or units to choose, but if the model of measurement is aperspectival, the measures and scales themselves are assumed to be free of human interests. This presumption persists even when it is well known that such scales are historical products, perhaps resulting from international conflicts. Often they represent a state's-eye view (Scott 1998). So deeply are such models of scaling institutionalized and embedded in routine activities that for many people their measures no longer seem like a human construction at all. They seem merely to show the inherent and undeniable properties of the phenomena at issue.

Yet, construal of similarity and difference is always socially situated, and there is always more than one position from which construal might take place. Thus, despite a denial of perspective, these models too enact a point of view, a perspective – a line of sight – along which a scale is constructed. We ask: How are differences and similarities measured in supposedly nonperspectival models – by what metrics and practices? What projects give rise to such scaling? What point(s) of view govern the choice of one standard metric versus another? What semiotic moves are made necessary by the choice? Finally, what about approaches to comparison that deny scalar commensurability altogether?

Measuring is a crucial step in aperspectival models of scaling. And measuring has several forms. Psychologists some years ago proposed a typology of ways of measuring along any dimension (Stevens 1946).[5] A *nominal* measurement is a classification, sorting items into categories. A numerical code might be assigned to each category, but the numbers are just labels, and no calculations of numerical relationship can be made from them. Examples might be dog breeds, or parts of speech. An *ordinal* measurement imposes a ranking, but nothing more. There is nothing regular about the distance between ranks (the degree of difference between them). "Green/greener/greenest" might be an example. So are five-point opinion scales, since you cannot calculate whether a subject's assessment of the difference between "mostly agree" and "completely agree" is the same as the difference between "neutral" and "mostly disagree," let alone whether it is the same as any other subject's assessment. In *interval* ways of measuring, the degrees of difference are specified. Examples would include date (calendar year, i.e., number of years since some arbitrary moment such as the declaration of the French Republic), and temperature in Fahrenheit. You can measure the difference in years between, say, 1000 and 2000 CE, but it makes no sense to say that 2000 was twice as new as 1000. You could only say it was twice as many years from the arbitrary moment. Finally, *ratio* measures allow for calculating ratios among the values in a meaningful way, because ratio measures have a nonarbitrary zero point. For example, it makes sense to say one rod is twice as long as another. Thus interval and ratio measures are quantifiable in ways nominal and ordinal ones are not.

Psychologists' discussions of Stevens's typology and its later amendments have generally concerned what kinds of mathematical operations are permissible for a given type of measurement, and what empirical phenomena fit the types (see Michell 1986, 1999). The debates mainly focus on whether, and when, scalar metrics permit drawing valid inferences about the empirical world. Our own concerns are different.

We focus on the *practices* of scaling with aperspectival models. These start with the assertion of commensurability. A would-be scale-maker must first identify what is to be compared – two or more sites of attention – in a mere juxtaposition, perhaps naming the two differently. A next step would be to construe a particular quality or dimension on which the two are to be compared. Many dimensions are available: physical size, or number and type of personnel, or geographical scope, or duration, or intensity of color ("greenness"). A third step is to ask what kind of metric could or should measure that dimension. If the scale-making involves only juxtaposition, two things can be judged as the same or different. But any further connection between the sites in aperspectival models requires making a unit for the constructed dimension or property, and this unit is often standardized in some way. Then, anything to be measured is first compared to the standard unit and is then scalable (as more or less) with respect to other items measured in the same way. Unlike inclusions and encompassments, which compare sites directly, in aperspectival models there is a three-way practice with the standard unit acting as a means of commensuration.

Beauty is a handy example. If there is merely a nominal measure, providing a juxtaposition, then we have categories of sites perhaps labeled as beautiful and ugly. In an ideological move, any such juxtaposition can be turned into qualities. Out of one or more of those qualities, a dimension (or several) can be proposed and the compared sites ranked along the dimension of comparison: for example, more versus less beautiful, with various measures determining the ranking. One can think of beauty contests that create such rankings. If the scaling involves quantification, the sites compared may be lined up in relation to an abstract numerical scale. An example is the humorous idea of a "milli-Helen": if the beauty of Helen of Troy could launch a thousand ships, a milli-Helen would be the quantity of beauty that could launch one ship. The example shows how dimensions can be created out of contrast, and can be measured and thus scaled in various ways. In fact, part of ideological work – in many circumstances – is transforming one kind of measure (nominal, ordinal, interval, ratio) into another, since they and their entailments often serve diverse or even opposed ideological projects and values.

Quantification is one of the procedures that presumes one can create appropriate units relating to the properties of the things that are to be compared, so that these may be counted. For example, if people allege – as illustrated later in this chapter – that languages progress by increasing the vocabulary, they imply that a measure of linguistic progress compares two languages (or, one language in different historical eras) according to the number of words in each. Such a measure presupposes a definition of the "word" such that words can be counted. Is the countable "word" a lexical stem? Stem plus derivational affixes? What about compounds, infixes, word-creation patterns, and the like?

For another example of a scaling project – and the various steps of arguing about dimensions to be created and then the metric to be used – consider the debates on congressional representation in the US Constitutional Convention of 1787. On the one hand, the thirteen original states might be considered equal, simply juxtaposed, not measured on any metric. On this basis, each state would have the same number of representatives. On the other hand, the states might be ranked according to some measure, such as population, and then one would have to decide how exactly population would be measured and what the units of population would be. That the scale of population of a social unit should determine the scale of resources – political representation, among other things – to which that unit gets access, is itself a matter of ideology and political contestation. In the early republic, the Constitutional Convention saw rancorous debate over whether representation in the national legislature should be based on a population scale (proportional representation), or simply juxta-posed, representing each state equally. With the less populous states deeply discontented and threatening to withdraw, weeks of discord elapsed before a compromise could be found. In what was later called the Great Compromise of 1787, a bicameral legislature was created in which each state would be equally represented by two seats in the upper house (Senate), while seats in the lower house (House of Representatives) would be scaled by population.

This familiar example shows how a project of scale-making – lining up units according to population – had political entailments that transparently advan-taged some units over others. At the time, it was not altogether obvious that any ranking of states vis-à-vis each other was necessary at all; hence the discord. The example also shows how projects of scale-making can select a particular metric as the relevant one, more important for some project than some other measure that might have been adduced. A state's territorial size, for instance, might have been selected as the relevant metric, rather than its population. Finally, the example shows that the identification of quantifiable units is also subject to ideological work. Delegates to the 1787 convention debated who counted as a unit – a politically relevant person – for measuring a state's pop-ulation. As is well known, and now infamous, the population scale required an additional compromise concerning how slaves were to be counted, before it could be accepted by all the states.

Regimenting and Universalizing Scales
in the First French Republic

There can scarcely be a more conspicuously ideological scale-making project than the effort undertaken by the National Convention in the first French Republic. Begun in the years immediately following the 1789 Revolution, the aim was not only to rationalize and standardize but also to universalize all measures and institutions: weights and measures, units of space and time, even language and its constituent forms. Sites of the regime's attention covered a vast range of human activities, all to be connected through rationally organized systems of scaling. The scale-making was thoroughly enmeshed with nation-making, centralization, and a global ambition of standardization.

In planning how to construct these systems and their interconnections, the regime sponsored the creation of the metric system. The first step was to measure the distance determined by a portion of the meridian arc running through Paris and extending between Dunkerque and Barcelona. This distance, when calculated precisely, could predict the exact distance from the North Pole to the Equator, on which basis "natural" measures of length could be derived. The resulting new measure, the meter, was set at one ten-millionth of the length of this portion of this distance around the globe. Rendered as a bar of pure platinum, the meter was deposited in the National Archives in Paris as the original reference point for a universal standard of measurement (Alder 1995, 2003). All measures of length and distance were to be based on the meter and calculated decimally.

Time, as well, was to be measured in a more rational, therefore decimalized, way. The new Republican calendar was to replace the seven-day week with a ten-day *décade*, regularize all months to thirty days (with a special festival period occupying the remaining five days out of 365), and start with a new year I, the date France was declared a Republic. Measures of weight and volume were also unified and aligned metrically – more successfully in the long run than the measures of time, for the Revolutionary calendar did not survive its year XIV. (The Gregorian calendar and seven-day week returned to France on January 1, 1806.)[6]

Measures already existed for space, time, weight, and volume of various kinds of materials and goods. What was different in the Revolutionary project was the centralization and standardization, the reliance on a decimal system, and the appeal to a nonhuman "nature" as the basis of measurement rather than human anatomy or social relations. With its homogenized and coordinated units based on a universal geography, the metric system would depart from the measures used in the Ancien Régime, which were local and particular. Under the Ancien Régime, even when one region had the same terminology for measures as another region had, the referents – the units measured by those terms – were not the same.

Local variability in measures had not just been a random effect. It had distinct advantages as a response to local conditions (Kula 1986). For example, local practice could respond to the variability in agricultural fields' labor requirements – differences in soil richness, stoniness, hilliness, and so on – by avoiding global (acreage) measures in favor of local human practices and negotiations, such as the number of workdays the fields needed. For the Enlightenment-enthused leadership of the Revolution, however, all such particularities were due to feudalism and its tyrannies, and must be abolished. The Republic and the globe were the only appropriate reference points for weights and measures.

The same principles applied to language. On the 16th of the month of Prairial, in the year II of the French Republic, Citizen (formerly *abbé*) Henri Grégoire presented the National Convention with a report on the "Necessity and the Means of Abolishing the Patois and Universalizing the Usage of the French Language." He wrote:

The French language has conquered Europe's esteem. ... In its clear and methodical course, thoughts easily unfold; that is what gives it the characteristics of reason, of integrity. ... One can state without exaggeration that at least six million French people, especially in rural areas, are ignorant of the national language; that an equal number are nearly incapable of maintaining a sustained conversation; that in the last analysis, the number of those who speak it is not more than three millions and probably the number of those who write it correctly is still less. Thus, with thirty different patois, we are still, in regard to language, at the Tower of Babel, while in regard to liberty, we are the most advanced of nations.

... A universal language is, in its genre, what the philosopher's stone is in chemistry. But at least one can standardize [*uniformer*, make uniform] the language of a great nation, in such a way that all the citizens who constitute it [the nation] can communicate their thoughts to one another without hindrance. This enterprise, which has never been fully undertaken for any people, is worthy of the French people, who are centralizing all branches of social organization and who should jealously, as soon as possible, in a Republic one and indivisible, consecrate the unique and invariable usage of the language of liberty.

Language is always the measure of the genius of a people; words only accumulate with the progress of ideas and needs. ... Throughout the Republic, so many jargons are as so many barriers impeding the movement of commerce and attenuating social relations. (Grégoire 1975 [1794a]:300, 302, our translation)

In another speech a few months later, Grégoire (1794b) explicitly linked "the project of standardizing speech, and giving to the language of liberty the character it deserves," with the legislators' efforts at "invigorating" – rationalizing and widely distributing – the sciences, the arts, and military technology. As with weights and measures, so with language: the regional dialects (patois) were remnants of feudal divisions and ought to be eradicated in favor of a "rational" (and rationalized) standard French, the language of the nation and, potentially, of the world. Such a language, he proposed, would grow, enlarging itself and its inventory of words along with the progress of ideas.

Grégoire's texts from year II invoke various metrics, some quantified and some not: measures of population, and of the numbers of people controlling the French language in various ways (those ways also scaled); the number of dialects, and of words; a scale of national "genius," ideas, and needs; a ranking of nations according to their progress and liberty. Notice, moreover, that the kinds of sites Grégoire lined up and connected were themselves products of the ideological project. Some of what he took to be scalable might not previously have been considered amenable to comparison and scaling, such as the number of patois or the number of their words, or the rank of nations with respect to liberty.[7] Some might not now be considered measurable at all, such as the genius of a people – at least, not considered measurable by most social scientists today. As we have argued, scale-making is perspectival, subject to social and historical differences in point of view.[8] This is the case even when, as in Grégoire's texts, it posits external measures for comparison (and thus posits an objective, aperspectival process). And inversely: what you consider measurable is a sign of what your perspective is – who you are, how you are positioned, and what you value.

Most conspicuous in the Revolutionary project is the effort at commensuration across the board, along with standardization and regimentation through state institutions. To replace the local measures and linguistic forms, the metropolitan *savants* established exemplary objects (such as the platinum meter) and exemplary linguistic forms (a standard French), located in Paris and to be disseminated throughout the country via facsimiles and educational reforms. As much as possible, the scales along which things were measured were to be calibrated according to a decimal system. The decimal calibration could not perfectly fit the calendar, since the earth persisted in requiring 365 days to travel around the sun. Nevertheless, there remained an ideal of a universal language for describing and measuring all things, and an ideal of mathematical schemata for systematizing the products of human thought.[9] Commensuration was focused on the activities of citizens of the nation-state, where it was also supposed to be linked to national character and enforcement. And beyond the state, the world: these writers also imagined a global order of nations, a universal human fraternity led by France – just as the many regions of France would be centered on Paris. The conceptual model for all this was clearly centrist, with Paris the exemplar, reference point, and regimenter.

If the Revolution's disruption of the institutions of the Ancien Régime provided the historical conditions under which such a model might be imagined and translated into action, the Revolutionary *savants*' point of view was not unquestioned. Other perspectives differed, and these as well as practical problems interfered with the standardization project's success. Peasants were not so easily dislodged from their accustomed ways, and it was impossible to replace all older tools with metrically calibrated equivalents, reorganize artisan workshops, and homogenize materials. Many of the Revolutionary government's standardization projects collapsed in the face of such difficulties and were abandoned by Napoleon when he came to power (Weber 1976; Alder 1997, 2003). "Rationalized" military technology, for example, requires mechanics trained in its production, materials that are consistent and reliable, and machine parts that are in fact interchangeable; such was not the case for the artillery on which Napoleon relied for his military agenda. Moreover, Napoleon turned against the Revolutionary *savants* and their vision of an enlightened, free, egalitarian citizenry produced by a new language of scales. Though seizing upon the principle of centralized power, he revoked many of the National Convention's other scalar reforms.

Like other ideological projects, then, scale-making is vulnerable to historical forces and contingencies. Attempts to institutionalize scaling and commensuration, if they succeed, may endow scaling with a persistence that masks its human construction; but institutionalizations can also fail.

Denying Commensurability

Some models deny commensurability altogether, or deny it for certain kinds of sites or systems. We call these "models" because they invoke complex frameworks for understanding a site – whether an ethnographic case, a sociological construct, a set of grammatical forms, or a personal problem – in order to posit that it is incommensurable with some other site. What might it mean to claim, contra the Revolutionary *savants*, that a vineyard's *terroir*, a pasture, and a forest are incommensurable – that they should not all be described in terms of hectares? To argue, as did working mothers in an example offered by Espeland and Stevens (1998), that "quality time" with one's children is incommensurable with the amount of time the children spend in daycare? To assert that the postpositions of Turkish nouns are not the same kind of thing as the inflectional endings of Latin nouns? Arguments like these might be seen as arguments against comparison itself. But they, or some of them, might also be seen as arguments against the use of a particular metric, or a type of scaling, as opposed to another. That is, *all* comparison might be rejected, or a particular metric of comparison might be rejected because it picks out an inappropriate value.

Commensuration is not just a matter of describing facts about the world. As Espeland and Stevens point out, it is a social process, with social and political effects. Yet, its background in social projects and perspectives may become invisible, because those origins and background are naturalized and taken for granted. In seeking a common metric, commensuration may transform one kind of value into another; or it may neglect a quality that is highly valued by some people, in favor of a quality valued by others – such as the people who have the most to gain from the commensuration. In the case of working mothers, to distinguish "quality time" from daycare time is a claim of incommensurability that might assuage the worker's anxiety about spending workday time away from her children, Espeland and Stevens suggest. But stay-at-home mothers may scoff at "quality time," asserting that time is time, and measurable in the same way (1998:314). At issue is a tension between values, expressed in a language of commensuration. The commensurability of sites, then, requires selective attention to the sites' qualities; and selection among potential metrics might involve selection among competing values. The effort to commensurate the sites might succeed, but the metrics that might be employed to do so may have very different social values and implications.

Some models go further, however, claiming that in some cases commensuration is logically impossible. One such model could be characterized as a *Gestalt or holistic model*. The site cannot be understood in itself; it is part of a whole – an inclusion – whose integrity makes any particular part meaningless without the rest. No single metric can be picked out for comparison with another site, without doing violence to its role in the site at hand. Turkish postpositions, for instance, have only a superficial resemblance to Latin inflectional endings. Linguistic forms in a given language are bound together in patterns and systems; it makes no sense to pull out some particular form without considering its relation with others, in the overall patterning. We quite agree about Turkish postpositions. Yet, if the argument about incommensurability rests on assuming a rigid boundary to the "whole" object of analysis, problems arise. Even linguistic systems are not sealed off like that, as Edward Sapir pointed out long ago when commenting, "all grammars leak" (Sapir 1921:38).

Another model of sites' incommensurability involves a concept of *singularities*. A singularity is something that does not repeat, and has no true analogue; hence it is unmeasurable.[10] This model emphasizes context too, but now in terms of the site's emergence as product of particular circumstances. The concept of singularity emphasizes the new, unique, and concrete. Since the circumstances giving rise to the site are contingent and unrepeatable, owing much to accident, coincidence, and ephemera, they are not accommodated in any universal "laws" of social organization. Instead, the site ruptures any such regularities. Because abstract measures must move analysis away from the circumstances that brought a site into being, such measures and the comparisons that rely on them would not be useful. They would miss the point. When extreme, this approach may refuse comparison or any sort of explanation.

As Espeland and Stevens point out, denial of commensurability is itself an ideological move, with assumptions that are vulnerable to ideological critique. Moreover, the models we have explored in this section are focused on the activity of analysts who are positioned outside the site they study – or who so position themselves, in order to gain "objectivity," even if they ultimately conclude that objectivity is impossible. Meanwhile, the people under social analysis compare things and scale things, or deny their commensurability, without regard to academic strictures. These actors' moves derive from their projects. To deny that the social grouping with which you identify is comparable, according to some scalar measure (say, household income), with some other grouping is a sociopolitical move whose rationale is linked to that measure's perceived benefits and risks. Perhaps, for example, you are laying claim to rights distributed by the state according to ethnicity, not according to income.

Finally, an important anthropological argument about the limits to comparability comes from Elizabeth Povinelli's discussion of "radical worlds" (Povinelli 2001). Comparability, she argues, is linked to relations of power. A researcher, positioned in liberal Western civil society, may try to study social groups deemed radically divergent, morally and/or epistemologically; but the world of an oppressed population remains hidden, because of the power relation obtaining between them and the researcher. The onus is always on the oppressed people to make themselves comparable – to make some aspect of their world of experience visible to dominant outsiders. Such groups present the liberal subject with an intractable impasse, insofar as the liberal perspective, convinced of its own rightness, is unable or unwilling to envision a different point of view. Commensuration is impossible if there is no common moral or epistemological ground for it. One might say, in terms of our approach, that the powerful outsider can never share the perspective of oppressed people. Indeed, one could say this about any two people who are differently positioned. You can never fully enter into another person's mind. And power – although needing to be further specified – makes for different social positionings.

The example entails comparison along the important scale of power, as a dimension precluding any other dimension of comparison. Power relations are central in many other projects concerning scale too, whether scale-making or scale-denying. One would want to ask: In what does the power consist? How does it affect people? What are the aims of the comparison – who is doing it, what are their projects, and what are they trying to know? These questions are not just about scale-denying. They go to the heart of the ideological work involved in making scales and comparing sites.

Part IV

Pasts

The discussion of scaling demonstrated the ambition of some states to occupy an impossible "view from nowhere." That ambition to encompass everything in an objective view was matched by the universalist goals of science in the nineteenth century. For the study of language, comparative grammar was its great scientific achievement. Comparison in its various forms underlies our own scholarly practices too, although we are far from the presumptions of nineteenth-century linguistics. Indeed, practices of comparison that simultaneously communicate and make new knowledge are also characteristic of the everyday lives of villagers in Senegal and Hungary, as we showed in Part I and of nineteenth-century Americans, as we demonstrated in Part II. At first these juxtapositions and comparisons may have seemed a stretch. But we have followed our own advice in Part III to search for ever more proliferating connections among sites, linkages as well as comparisons across time and space – interdiscursivities as well as differentiations. And we found, to our surprise, that Senegal and Hungary were connected even in the nineteenth century, at least in the imaginations of language scholars. Thus the concepts developed in earlier chapters have contributed to our understanding of the past.

As we widened our view to include ourselves, our field sites, our illustrative examples, and then also nineteenth-century practitioners of linguistic research, we saw how linguists of the past did ideological work. And new connections appeared. We found some nineteenth-century scholars were distantly linked to our field sites and also variously in contact with each other. One of the Hungarian linguists, Pál Hunfalvy, was a German-Hungarian bilingual, interested in the history of Hungarian and the Finno-Ugric languages of Siberia. One of the early linguists in Africa was Samuel Ajayi Crowther, a missionary and an African. Robert Needham Cust, a former British colonial officer mapped South Asian and African languages and personally knew both Hunfalvy and Crowther. Sitting in his study in provincial Austria, Hugo Schuchardt – also acquainted with Hunfalvy – studied the Romance dialects of Europe as well as far-flung African and Caribbean languages. But none of these students of language occupied a central position in the philological world of nineteenth-century Europe. Nevertheless, it was through marginal scholars such as these that a good part of the globe was opened to the analytical and comparative gaze of the increasingly academic and professionalizing linguistics of the nineteenth century.

Instead of a history that focuses on the institutional hubs of scholarship, we glimpse the story of linguistic knowledge at an angle, taking problems of evidence as our centerpiece concerns. Scholars, wherever they were located, were united by a methodological puzzle: how to study the unwritten languages and dialects of denigrated populations in Asia, Africa, and rural Europe with modes of analysis based on the philological study of ancient, highly valorized written texts. Unwritten linguistic differences were also one of our interests in this book. Chapter 9 turns to the diverse pasts of studying such forms. Their inclusion as evidence in linguistic research in the nineteenth century satisfied the ambition to expand linguistic knowledge to a global and conceptually universalizing scale. The deep problems of method and theory that this brought into view were long left unattended and are still often obscured by disciplinary and subdisciplinary divisions.

9 Library to Field: Ideologies in Nineteenth-Century Linguistic Research

During a chilly week at the end of summer in 1881, the International Orientalist Congress met in Berlin. The plenary sessions were held in the splendidly gilded Great Hall of the University of Berlin, and scholars retired to chandeliered lecture rooms for section meetings. Berlin was a newer and rougher capital than the cities of the four previous congresses: Paris, London, Saint Petersburg, and Florence. But its university, founded by philosopher and linguist Wilhelm von Humboldt, was housed in an eighteenth-century palace and was home to the most illustrious orientalists. About 180 scholars of language and antiquities arrived from all over Europe. That week, the kaiser celebrated the tenth anniversary of his victory in the Franco-Prussian War and the resulting unification of Germany. Meanwhile, the congress celebrated its own achievements at the luxurious Central-Hotel, known for its spectacular Wintergarten, a glass-roofed atrium three stories high, with palm trees, hanging plants, and dozens of tables for conversation. The congress had reserved it for informal "evening gatherings." This was doubtless where – perhaps on Tuesday – Robert Needham Cust (1821–1909) from London and Pál Hunfalvy (1810–1891) from Budapest, veterans of earlier congresses, renewed their acquaintance. Cust gave a paper that day "On What We Know about the Languages of Africa" and Hunfalvy gave one on languages – Hungarian and other Finno-Ugric forms – as "The Formative Principle of Nations."[1]

From opposite ends of Europe, writing about different continents and languages, these two men had much in common. When we learned of their copresence in Berlin, we saw that the juxtaposition of West Africa and Eastern Europe has an intriguing past. Gal had written about Hunfalvy, Irvine about Cust. Thinking about the two men *together* – their methods, networks, politics, projects – provides our starting point for exploring the continuities and unravelings of linguists' ideologies in nineteenth-century Europe. These scholars are not the usual heroes of disciplinary histories. In following their contributions – along with those of many others – we highlight the discipline's changing perspectives and social exclusions. We move from libraries full of ancient texts to transcriptions of unwritten languages; from stories or proverbs dictated and recited in the field to presentations at glittering orientalist congresses.

In this way, we follow some of the scalar transformations of what scholars took for granted as "data." The values of scholars also existed in a variety of scaled realms: What was self-evidently patriotic and true about language in one venue and time was seen as betrayal and denied in another; what seemed patriotic to some, for a time, was revealed as racist by others.

In one sense, scholars and other language experts are like everyone else, swept up in ideologized interpretation of everyday life. Unlike others, however, they also select and foreground for special attention some communicative practices, using methods for analyses that are evaluated by others with similar, institutionally defined interests. Such experts might be scholars, missionaries, explorers, geographers, politicians, travelers, or administrators in colonies or in the academy. Their focus on linguistic materials is important but often only one aspect of their political or religious engagement. We ourselves could well be objects of such a study, but it is easier to discern the presumptions of others, at a temporal and social distance.[2]

To do so, we examine the ideologies and semiotics of differentiation that shape how language experts represent the social and linguistic materials they study. Their approaches and representations have consequences for the linguistic practices and relationships of those they observe. At the same time, the ways experts represent their objects of study are themselves *registers of expertise* that locate the perspective of the expert within discursive fields. Thus, we distinguish analytically (1) how experts formulate their images of others and (2) what the modes of analysis that produce those images signal about experts' positions in the networks, sites, and scales of their social and professional lives. While never losing sight of the images they create, we wish to examine as well this second aspect of the differentiation process: how experts' approaches to their "objects" are co-constituted in dialogical relationship with other viewpoints. Participants have much at stake – personal advance, institutional power, value commitments – as they oppose or align with other perspectives in the world of language studies. We wish to show that through their representations, experts define themselves on axes of differentiation in broader fields of discourse. Selecting a few aspects of those discourses, we trace some of their transformations and consequences.

Philological Assumptions

Hunfalvy and Cust were not much appreciated as "orientalists" at the Berlin Congress.[3] Cust was formerly a civil servant, having spent twenty-five years as a colonial administrator in British India. While there, he grew increasingly interested in the languages of the region and their relevance for administrative policy. On retiring to London he focused on linguistic pursuits and became an active member of scholarly associations and Anglican missionary societies.

Hunfalvy was a member of the Hungarian Academy of Sciences, a lawyer from a German-speaking family in Hungary (though not from the region of Bóly). He was a committed Hungarian citizen, having been in the government of the failed Hungarian revolution against Habsburg rule. Later, he studied Finnish and organized the first linguistic and ethnographic societies in Hungary. Near contemporaries, these two men – talented administrators and systematizers – were among the last of the passionate autodidacts in philology. Perhaps this was one way they felt marginalized. There were also more telling ways: they were devoted to unwritten languages of denigrated populations; they were – in different ways – outsiders to philology; and though they operated within *some* of its assumptions, they also participated in challenging others. We shall return to discuss how such challenges changed the methods and presumptions of nineteenth-century philology.

But first let us consider the centers of attention at such meetings: Indo-European and Semitic languages. Great interest was inspired by an intellectual search for European "civilization" through excavation of the deep past as a starting point for an imagined scale of human progress. It was a way for European elites to posit alternative genealogies for Christianity, posit their own racial, religious, and national superiority, and think about human origins. The method was philological: deciphering textual materials and artifacts that were obtained through European conquest of the Near East, Asia, and the Far East. The British in eighteenth-century India, relying on Indian scholars, compared Sanskrit to European languages, which inspired the idea of a primordial Indo-European language. French colonial efforts in North Africa and critical study of the Bible continued the search for a pre-Babel, universal language, while some scholars found ideals and origins in classical Greece. Further imperial efforts inspired more research. Soon after the orientalists' meeting in Berlin, the Berlin Conference (1884) divided the interior of Africa among the European empires. This intensification of existing military and economic incursions, along with Christian missionizing, entailed further study of African languages.

Up to the 1870s, the main European powers pursuing military, economic, and missionary interests in the Near East, Far East, and the interior of Africa were Britain, France, and Portugal. Yet, it was German-speakers who made some of the key analytical innovations. Some worked in libraries, poring over texts. For them, the study of what they called the Indo-*Germanic* languages evoked the image of a desired national unity not actually achieved till 1871. Others ventured abroad. In Africa, German missionaries – devoted to pietistic Protestantism more than to their small, pre-unification states – worked for British missionary societies, writing African grammars and dictionaries. Work "in the field" was not a new role for educated German-speakers in this period. Already in the eighteenth century, Russian monarchs had invited German scientists to document the human and natural wealth of Siberia. They provided some of the first descriptions of that region's Finno-Ugric-speaking peoples.

By the last quarter of the nineteenth century, comparative linguistics had become "the science of language," professionalized and somewhat distinct from literary studies of classical, eastern, and biblical texts, even if those texts remained important sources of data. The new approach attended to comparisons among linguistic forms rather than to the content of texts. Certain ideological commitments were taken for granted by practitioners: the new science's empirical basis; the autonomy of languages as natural objects, "out there" to be discovered, with delimited boundaries; the relevance of language classifications for plotting the histories and relations among the peoples who spoke them.

Enlightenment theorists like Locke had argued that an autonomous language, purified of links to social life, was an ideal vehicle for reasoned participation in a polity. Condillac, Herder, and their Romantic descendants in the early nineteenth century turned that thesis on its head, reconnecting language to social life by positing that languages are natural repositories of their speakers' particular "spirit" and keys to reconstructing their history. If linguistic differences are "natural" in this sense, not man-made, then they could be independent warrants for political independence. Accordingly, in 1808, as Berlin chafed under French rule, German philosopher Johann Gottlieb Fichte declared, "Wherever a particular language is found, there exists also a particular nation which has the right to run its own affairs and to govern itself" (2008 [1808]:161). The link among language, people, and territory was now firmly established in ideology and connected, in principle, to political ambitions.

Philological Practices, Unwritten Languages

These philosophical notions, we suggest, shaped the methods of late nineteenth-century linguistics as an evidence-based discipline. The methods, in turn, emboldened practitioners by making the presumptions seem matters of self-evident fact. Comparative philology derived temporal relationships among languages by juxtaposing surviving literary texts from ancient high cultures and, presumptively, among speakers. Working with such necessarily limited, written materials surely reinforced – if it did not actually produce – understandings about the boundedness of what counted as distinct "languages." African linguistic forms and those of most Finno-Ugric-speakers we will discuss were unwritten, or believed by Europeans to be unwritten. Thus, describing such unwritten linguistic practices with philological methods was a formidable challenge, provoking further ideological work and dramatic methodological innovations.

Looking at the work of language experts who tried to meet that challenge, three questions are of particular interest. First, what were considered appropriate sources of evidence for unwritten languages, and how did the social conditions and sites of early fieldwork – given the ideological assumptions we have outlined – shape the representations of languages and peoples? Second, what were the conventional genres for *presenting* linguistic materials to scholarly, missionary, or broader publics? Finally, how did semiotic principles organize the representation of language materials; how were these principles embedded in the scholarly arguments practitioners made?

Word lists were early sources of evidence that attempted to include material from unwritten languages along with written ones. Both in coastal Africa and in western Siberia – where speakers of many Finno-Ugric languages were found – great compilations of word lists juxtaposed linguistic materials from many presumably different languages. The German scholars invited to Siberia in the eighteenth century advised their colleagues that inquiries should be posed to "experienced" old people, preferably those who knew Russian, so as to avoid the mediation of hostile or unreliable interpreters (Vermeulen 2015:175). Consulting "priests and elders" was an early tactic in Senegal too (Dard 1826), as in Nigeria and elsewhere in Africa. Impressive lists resulted from the various German expeditions, each with an atlas to roughly adumbrate the presumed languages in newly mapped geographical space. The *Vocabularium Sibiricum*, compiled around 1760, had 307 words for each of forty languages, and comments in Russian and German.[4] Julius Klaproth's *Asia Polyglotta* in 1823 was even larger. *Polyglotta Africana*, the 1854 work of German-born missionary linguist Sigismund Koelle (1820–1902), with its 250-word vocabularies of more than one hundred languages, was a high point of this genre.

Yet word lists were insufficient for the generalizing, pattern-finding work of writing grammars. Koelle, working on a grammar of Kanuri, proposed a novel and more effective response to the evidence-dilemma:

Two or three weeks after the commencement of my Kanuri studies, I at once entered upon this plan of forming a literature, as the best way of becoming acquainted with the language and the surest foundation of grammatical investigations. (1854a:ix)

His interpreter dictated to him "a manuscript literature" of eight hundred quarto pages consisting of "stories, fables, romances, historical sketches." Similarly, Samuel Ajayi Crowther offered proverbs as the stand-in for literary sources in his *Yoruba Vocabulary* (1852). These genres, though oral, were taken to be analogous to European literature, in that they seemed bounded, decontextualizable, and "collectible," far from the pragmatic indexes and styles of everyday speech. Christian prayers and Bible chapters, translated by missionaries or native converts, also contributed to supplying the "missing" literary canon. As in Africa, so in Siberia, research trips in the nineteenth century searched for "songs, proverbs, tales, traditions about origins" or material from "ritual contexts" (Lukin 2017). As Matthias Alexander Castrén (1813–1852), the Finnish linguist/ethnographer of Siberia, explained, he needed

more abundant and reliable material than the ones available in written form and for this I was compelled to carry out expeditions in different parts of Europe and Asia. (1853:3)

What counted as a genre of the unwritten language was a result of collaboration between linguists and performers. Genres were omitted if they were improvised and therefore difficult to transcribe, or seemed too complex for the supposedly "simple" speakers of Africa and Siberia.

By the 1860s, the conventional format for grammars and dictionaries regularly included texts of oral literature or examples drawn from them.[5] Earlier presentational modes had been less regimented and had different aims. For instance, Jacques-François Roger (1787–1849), a French lawyer who served as governor of the colony at Saint-Louis-du-Sénégal, wrote a grammar of Wolof in the form of a philosophical essay and published a collection of Wolof tales as fables in French verse, as well as a novel about Senegalese history (Roger 1828). At that early date, before philology was professionalized, he was aiming to reach a popular literate audience, with a message inviting them to enjoy the Wolof tales as literature rather than as objectified data, and to accept their tellers as equals. He was not averse to including his own rearrangement of these materials. The authors of the later grammars also participated in forming texts, but effaced their own contributions.

Mapping was another presentational form of great importance. Early topographical maps were often matched with ethnographic and linguistic entities. Languages were cartographically imagined. The Germans in Siberia made maps of languages and human settlements; so did Castrén and Koelle. Hunfalvy began each of his grammatical sketches with careful delineation of the physical and ethnic "boundaries" of the language described. Decades later, faith in the language-people-territory manifold was so firm that Cust, in mapping African languages, declared, "Unless he [the cartographer] can find a place in his Map for the tribe, the Language can find no place in my Schedule" (1883:8). Both mapping and the collection of delimited genres buttressed the image of linguistic boundedness.

Yet, there were problems. Koelle's (1854b) word list was based on information gathered in Freetown, Sierra Leone, a colony of liberated slaves and a refuge for slaves liberated from many parts of Africa during the abolition campaigns that had accelerated since Britain outlawed the slave trade in 1807. Migrants were fleeing massive social disruption and chaotic conditions due to slave raiding, internal warfare, and an intensified European drive to expand commerce and missionizing into the interior. As the center of British abolitionist efforts in West Africa, Freetown became the base of Anglican missionary operations and of linguistic work, Bible translation, and religious conversion. In this chaos, attempts to ascertain and map the "core areas" of the refugees' languages were necessarily based on incomplete accounts, often from single interviews. In the refugee circumstances of Freetown and other such settlements, earlier patterns of variation and specialist vocabularies were likely to be lost; so were rhetorical styles indexical of social relations that no longer prevailed. For information, linguists often relied on children, or others who had never fully learned the language in question or had not used it in many years. The situation was ripe for register loss, dialect leveling, language mixing, multilingualism, and language shift.

Although French colonies operated on different principles and in a different framework for doing linguistic work, they also faced limitations. French Catholics were less invested than their British missionary counterparts in providing Africans with direct contact with the Bible. When Catholic missionaries did linguistic work, it was mainly for their own use, not to teach Africans literacy in their own languages. To the extent that a Western-style education was provided for Africans in French colonies, it was mostly secular and state run, as was increasingly the case in France itself. After a brief experiment in indigenous-language education, Africans too, like pupils in France, were to learn French – the only question being whether it should be metropolitan literary French or *français fondamental*, a deliberately simplified variety. Much linguistic research in the French colonies was done by colonial officers, both military and political. They also often turned to single informants – military captives or children – for information about far-flung languages. Yet, in both French and British colonial contexts, researchers ignored the limitations of their sources, representing languages in reduced versions, matching language, group, and territory.

Mediating these descriptions, in all the European colonies, were European ideologies about Africans. The situation the French encountered among the languages spoken in the region between the Senegal and Gambia rivers – part of today's Senegal – was probably a complex system of religious and political differences signaled by linguistic practices. The major languages in this region were Wolof, Fula, and "Sereer" – this last label conflating two sets of languages, very different from each other, but whose speakers were lumped together as "Sereer" by their Wolof-speaking neighbors. Among these languages, Wolof was the language of the politically powerful coastal kingdoms and was used, in the nineteenth century, for high-level political purposes even in areas where Sereer (either kind) was the language of the home. Thus Sereerspeakers were often bilingual. They were also associated with resistance to Islam, officially the religion of state in the Wolof kingdoms although its practice was highly variable. Arabic was the language of that religion, but among sub-Saharan African languages Fula (aka Peul, Pulaar) had the strongest

connection to Islamic orthodoxy because Fula-speakers had been early converts. This regional situation was interpreted, by European observers, in terms
of a supposed history of race relations, migrations, and conquests.

Accordingly, and assuming that black Africans were essentially simple-
minded people who knew no social organization more complex than the family
group, Europeans explained social hierarchy, multilingualism, and conversions
to Islam in terms of conquering races from the north who supposedly brought
social complexity with them, along with language, intellectual superiority and
an admixture of Caucasian blood. Fula-speakers, some of whom are lighter
skinned than their Wolof neighbors, were deemed "higher" in race and intelligence. They were thought to have brought from Egypt their "superior" religion,
hierarchical social organization, and language as influences upon the Wolof,
who in turn supposedly influenced the "simple" Sereer. This narrative of conquest and conversion fractally reiterates – inside Africa – the European conquest: white over black, complex over simple, and dominant over subordinate.

If Sereer were to represent African simplicity, there was ideological work
to be done. Since the social organization of people labeled "Sereer" varied
between small independent communities (speakers of one set of "Sereer" languages) and complex states (speakers of the other set), the small-community
set was picked out as best exemplar of the whole category. The other set, with
its states and hierarchy, was construed in terms of conquest: the same fractal
reiteration, this time inside "Sereer." Moreover, the language was expected to
be simple too, compared to Wolof and Fula. It was a variety of Sereer spoken
in the kingdom of Siin, rather than a language spoken in the small communities, that was taken to be the linguistic exemplar. Siin was a site of resistance
to Islam, and the location of a Catholic missionary settlement. The missionary
Père Lamoise, who wrote the first full-scale Sereer grammar (Lamoise 1873),
looked there for the "pure" Sereer language he supposed God had placed in its
speakers: a language whose forms would have the fewest traces of Wolof or
the influences of Islam. But this required stripping away overlaps with Wolof,
Wolof-influenced registers, and bilingualism between the two languages.
It also required downplaying Sereer's complex morphology. Thus, rhematization produced the posited "simplicity" and separateness of Sereer. Not only
indexical values but also the contents of a language – materials assigned to
it, rather than to another from which it "borrowed" them – seem to have been
rearranged.

The sharp boundary between Wolof and Sereer that was drawn in these
linguistic works was similarly drawn between their speakers and territories.
In 1865, General Louis Faidherbe (1818–1889), the military officer and
later governor responsible for effective conquest of the interior of Senegal,
produced a map in which boundary lines demarcate borders between Wolof
(people), Sereer, Fula, and territories ruled directly by France. His representation

of these languages as territorially separate was influential. So, too, was his linguistic work lining up these languages in parallel word lists and phrases (Faidherbe 1887). Thus the image of separate language-people-territory was as powerful for the French colonizers as for other European language experts, even while the goal of the *mission civilisatrice* ("civilizing mission") was to supplant African languages and customs.

A British example comes from Freetown. Some speakers there were called "Ibo" by others, leading Koelle and his fellow Protestant missionaries to presume that they must be from a group with that name and to posit a territory in eastern Nigeria as their homeland. Although the speakers so named said they had never heard the name before arriving in Freetown, missionary linguists presumed that the name had simply been lost. However, when linguists actually went to the area they had presumed to be "Iboland," the linguistic situation turned out to be different and more diverse than what they had seen in Freetown. Speakers in "Iboland" failed to recognize the language the missionaries had learned from "Ibos" in Freetown, or to agree that they all belonged to any sort of social unity. Nevertheless, whatever the term "Ibo" had once meant in Nigeria itself – it seems to have been mainly a geographical designator meaning "upland," and only became applied as a distinctive term for people among African slaves in the Caribbean – in Freetown it had become an ethnonym.

Moreover, the variation the linguists noted in "Iboland" was interpreted as excessive or "unruly," a diversity and individuality of dialects that matched what some even characterized as the disunion in their government. Ibos not only failed to speak in a homogeneous way, but also failed to form the coherent, homogeneous ethnic group the missionaries expected. This unruliness was even taken to be an essential part of Ibo personality – their national character. Disunity in speech, evidenced in spatial variation, and absence of a common government or social organization were taken as signs of Ibo quarrelsomeness – a case of naming and rhematization constructing a group and its character.

In Siberian investigations, the same European philological assumptions equating language, people and territory were in play. And, there were similar erasures of variation as well as similarity in the way the semiotics of differentiation shaped descriptions and presentations of Siberian languages. However, different theories motivated the projected distinctions. In Siberia, theories of developmental stages in subsistence – such as nomadic or agricultural – dominated the making of language borders and attribution of qualities to speakers and their languages. In addition, the political positions and goals of European linguists in Siberia – and therefore their relationship to speakers – also differed from those in Africa during the same period. In "civilizing missions" and Christian conversion, linguists in Africa created orthographies and bible translations that were supposed to "fix" (stabilize and improve) African languages and thereby provide "compensation for the woes of Africa" caused by the slave trade, as one missionary noted. By contrast, the linguists, ethnographers and travelers who trekked to northwestern Siberia in mid-nineteenth century had little part in Russian colonization efforts in the region, nor in improvement of indigenous lives, nor the proselytizing of the Russian Orthodox Church. In the eighteenth century it had been Germans who explored Siberia. In the nineteenth century it was Finnish and Hungarian scholars who did so. Unlike Europeans in Africa, they were looking for useable pasts for their national projects in Finland and Hungary.

Russian elites, for most of the nineteenth century, saw Siberia merely as an administrative problem and source of wealth. Russia had conquered it in the seventeenth century, and the many indigenous hunting, fishing, and reindeer herding populations of its northwest were long treated as "foreigners" in an occupied territory. They paid tribute in furs – "soft gold" – until animal populations were depleted. The Orthodox Church won nominal Christian converts, but was not notably successful.[6] The eighteenth-century German research expeditions had classified Siberian peoples according to linguistic differences (Vermeulen 2015:186–194). But Russian administration divided the great diversity of "aliens" into just three ranked subsistence categories: nomads, wanderers, and settled. On the presumed developmental scale, they were all in "childhood." When, in late nineteenth century, Siberia was redefined as Russia's colony, it was likened to the American frontier: a difficult but rich environment, in which Russian settlers had to deal with primitive "red men," backward eaters of raw fish, who had no writing or poetry and whose languages showed "relative simplicity and limited vocabulary" (Slezkine 1994:134; Bassin 1991).

In contrast to Russian neglect, Hungarian and Finnish elites, in the mid-nineteenth century, were eager to study the languages of northwestern Siberia. This interest had a long history. Leibniz (1646–1716) was among those who noted that Finnish, Lapp, and Hungarian resembled each other; the Siberian word lists suggested this too. Early on, two Hungarians – Sajnovics in 1770 and Gyarmathi in 1799 – found "affinities" among languages classified as Finno-Ugric (today more often termed Uralic). They pointed to lexical parallels, distinctive grammatical features in declension, comparison and conjugation, and in ways of using suffixes and affixes (Wickman 1988). This work was contemporaneous with William Jones's reports on Sanskrit in 1786 and Bopp's influential thesis in 1816, on parallels in verb conjugation patterns among some European and Asian languages. As Indo-European studies extended the pasts of Europe, Hungarian and Finnish elites, trying to build national consciousness and independence movements, but lacking ancient written sources, embarked on a search for (living) linguistic "kin" that took them, in the 1840s, to Siberia. M. A. Castrén was first to describe many of what are now considered the Finnic and Permian groupings of Uralic languages, and the Nenets (Samoyed) group. The Hungarian scholar and explorer Antal Reguly (1819–1858) returned from Siberia with materials from the Khanty and Mansi (Ostyak and Vogul), languages which are now counted, with Hungarian, as the Ugric group of Uralic (Abondolo 1998). Reguly died young, so Hunfalvy and his colleague József Budenz analyzed his materials. Bernát Munkácsi (1860–1937) completed the task, supplemented with his own fieldwork in Siberia.[7]

The far northern town of Obdorsk was a center of Siberian linguistic work. Located on the bend of the Ob river before it empties into the Arctic Ocean, Obdorsk was a frontier market town, a gathering place: Russian state servitors and peasants, Orthodox missionaries, Cossack guides, Polish craftsmen, Tatar, Udmurt (Votyak), and Komi (Zyrian) traders. Indeed, thousands of indigenous people came to Obdorsk's annual market, from December to February, to pay the required fur tax and exchange pelts for alcohol, metal equipment, and ornaments. With their reindeer herds, tents, and huts, they camped around the core Russian colony. Those not Christianized celebrated bear ceremonies and shamanic rites.

One can only guess about the complex social and linguistic relations in Obdorsk. As in Africa, ideologies about indigenous people shaped linguistic descriptions. Accordingly, European observers assumed that subsistence-mode matched language, territory, and name: Nenets were reindeer herders in the mountains; Khanty and Mansi were hunters and fishers along rivers; settled farmers were assumed to be Russian peasants. Yet travelers noted patterns that diverged from these expectations: children with Russian fathers were fluent in their mothers' Khanty. Many people spoke some Russian; many post-drivers – usually Cossacks – knew Khanty. Bilingualisms and borrowings must have been commonplace. Categories, groups, and subsistence mode did not always match Europeans' stereotypes: Some Khanty had reindeer herds. Some adopted Nenets customs; and still other Khanty with herds were said to know Nenets language "better than their own." In such circumstances registers related to practices no longer performed were bound to be lost and novel forms created: "[A] jargon has grown up in intercourse between [Khanty] and [Nenets] of the coast and mountains," reported one observer (Erman 1850:58). The indigenous categories of people – Khanty, Mansi, Nenets – were all organized into named, exogamous clans. But languages across the clan categories were not mutually intelligible. It is tempting to speculate that – as in aboriginal Australia or the Colombian Amazon – linguistic exogamy was paired with multilingualism.

Despite this diversity, the grammars and dictionaries that emerged from European research in Obdorsk were of single languages, territorially defined. Descriptions were based on single speakers. Castrén (1853:213) complained about the difficulty of finding "language masters" who had patience and knowledge enough to recite in the repetitive way needed for longhand transcription.

Reguly wrote to his colleagues that he had finally found a shaman who agreed to sing the traditional songs, but the shaman had trouble remembering what some of it meant (cited in Munkácsi 1892). Topographical names – especially of rivers where people were thought to regularly fish, hunt, or herd – were treated as names of ethnolinguistic groups. Time was as important as place. For instance, Castrén assumed that languages near Obdorsk would be especially pure, because of the town's longstanding isolation in the extreme north. Rhematization produced the languages' presumed purity, which he assumed would be recursive, allowing him to distinguish, when comparing languages, what "is original and what was added later" (Stammler-Gossmann 2009:200). Analysis of Khanty-Mansi myths similarly relied on fractally recursive chronotopes. This was in keeping with philological principles of what might be called purification, now applied to unwritten languages and genres. It was assumed that by stripping away layers of supposed borrowings – the results of presumed territorial contact with Turkish and Russian – one could get to the oldest language and religious practices (Munkácsi 1892).

Recursivity of time/place allowed Siberian peoples to be projected as ancestors of *specific* categories of Europeans. Traveling in 1845 among Udmurt (Votyak)-speakers in Siberia, Carstén's rhematizing narrative found qualitative similarities between peoples and landscapes that, he wrote, were not just "philological correspondences":

They [Finns and Votyaks] correspond to each other in having a quiet, civilized, and work-filled life, far removed from what one sees in other countries. ... That is how I find the Votyaks – devout, simple and innocent, like our Finnish peasants ... [and like] the genius of Spring [here] with its mild air, soft breezes and gentle butterflies. (cited in Hirnsperger 2013:98–99)

Elsewhere he mentioned that the Siberians are just like Finns of an earlier time, casting them as contemporary ancestors. Reguly's vision was similarly fractal, but importantly different in the qualities he noticed. Like many others, he believed the Mansi (Vogul) to be the closest kin of Hungarians and described, in an 1844 letter from the Obdorsk region, the themes of Mansi epic song:

[T]hey [Voguls, i.e., Mansi] recount with enthusiasm war-like acts of their past heroes and champions, some of whom are gods, fighting external enemies – the Zirjens and Samoyeds – others are princes who struggle with their brothers and neighbors to rule over territories. Their songs tell of military victories and mournful defeats. (cited in Munkácsi 1892:viii–ix)

Reguly himself made explicit the contrast evident in the comparison of his description with Castrén's: The Voguls' (Mansi's) aggressive spirit of sociality, Reguly wrote, directly contrasts with the spirit of other Finnic peoples whose poetry tells of the inner, individual life. Not coincidentally, Reguly's image of Vogul epics matched contemporary self-stereotypes by Hungarian elites. The implied comparisons within the language "family" opposed Voguls and Votyaks in the putative past, as rhematized, fractally recursive analogues to their supposed contemporary descendants, Hungarians and Finns in the present.

Europeans' ideologized images – via a semiotics of differentiation – shaped the descriptions of both Siberian and African languages, though with differing presumptions and through quite different social relations between the language specialists and the peoples observed. In one case the goal was the spread of empire and Christianity, in the other a search for a self-stereotyping, nation-making past. Considering these together highlights the circumstances of encounter and some of the effects of these different relations between Europeans and their "objects" of study who, to some extent, co-produced the images made by Europeans.

African and Finno-Ugric Linguistics, Upscaled

We turn now to a closer look at the way language scholars' representations of their analytical objects worked as expert registers with which the scholars differentiated among themselves. By inventing new methods for gathering unwritten materials to make them amenable to philological argumentation, scholars of African and Siberian languages were able to maintain the ideologized notion of languages as inherently divided into bounded units of language-people-territory. That presumption was fundamental to Siberian and African linguistic work, yet the work itself contributed to challenging this unity. Expert registers were organized into axes of differentiation that located contrasting positions with respect to controversies in the worlds of linguistics and in the political projects to which linguistic research contributed. Specifically: Scientific research was contrasted to vague, shoddy or humanistic work; images of the nation as unified and monolingual were contrasted with polyglot, liberal nationalisms. We illustrate this with three controversies: first, the role of unwritten languages; second, the links among language, *Volk* and race. As third, in a final section, we take up controversies about boundaries between languages, both territorial and linguistic. No less than the other categories of speakers analyzed in previous chapters, linguistic experts enacted the semiotics of differentiation among themselves. Sometimes they responded to conflicting demands at different scales of social life. In the process, they transformed to some extent the discursive field that was the study of language in the late nineteenth century.

What was the place of unwritten languages in the European scholarly world of language studies? At sites like the International Orientalist Congresses, we can observe alignments and oppositions among linguists. The congresses were prestigious events recognized by governments, funded by cities, universities and scholarly societies. In Berlin, the sparkling palace, the high-end hotel, and the presence of many academic celebrities confirmed and reproduced this prestige. So did the exclusions and absences. In contrast to the crowded, attention-getting Indo-European and Semitic sessions, the Finno-Ugric report was shoehorned into the tiny East Asia session. The so-called Africa session considered only ancient Egypt. These exclusions and marginalizations were taken for granted because entailed by established theories.

An example comes from the writings of F. Max Müller (1823–1900), one of Europe's most respected orientalists. Müller's expertise in Sanskrit, Indo-European philology and comparative religion along with his entertaining style attracted large audiences. Born in the German city of Dessau, trained in Berlin, he became the first professor of comparative philology at Oxford. At the Berlin Congress, his high status was underlined: he delivered not one but two papers. In his famous book *Lectures on the Science of Language* he had declared, "Genealogical classification ... applies properly only to ... languages in which grammatical growth has been arrested, through the influence of literary cultivation" (1866:174). In his view, the practices that "arrested" a language's structures, protecting them against uncontrolled variation and change were just what Africans lacked: written traditions, public forums, and orderly family life. In the same book, Müller expounded on a "Turanian [language] family" that included every language in Europe and Asia that was neither Indo-European nor Semitic. Finno-Ugric languages would therefore be classified as Turanian. For Müller, these were "nomad" languages of "empires [that] were no sooner formed than they scattered again like sand-clouds in the desert" and therefore, in contrast to "state and political languages," no "nucleus of political, social or literary character has ever been formed" in them (1866:324). These also supposedly lacked the family life and other institutions required for linguistic stability: genealogical method would simply not apply.

If the languages were irrelevant to cutting-edge science, small wonder that their analysts were marginalized. Very few of the major experts working on African languages, for example, attended the Orientalist Congresses at all. Crowther, the Nigeria-born, mission-educated author of important works on Nigerian languages, remained in Africa, as did other missionaries. Faidherbe, after his retirement from colonial service in Senegal and North Africa, mainly attended local meetings in Lille, his hometown. Koelle had been posted to Turkey. These scholars were not actively excluded (as women were, from the congress in Florence). They were simply absent; their networks did not intersect with those at the congresses.[8]

Yet, by the time of Müller's book and its multiple editions, much philological work had been done on unwritten languages in colonial, academic and military realms. The hypothesis of a Finno-Ugric family was a century old; linguists working with African languages increasingly grouped them into families in accordance with comparative philological methods. The issue, therefore, was not method but *scale*, on several differently imagined dimensions. Conceptually, analyses of these languages would be scaled up by inclusion in encompassing comparisons with other "families" in the theory and method that defined science. And socially: African work that had been made and circulated mainly in missionary and colonial networks or in local scholarly organizations would be scaled up if accepted in the rarefied world of academic comparative philology. Similarly, it would be a scalar jump if work motivated by the obsessions of small elites in peripheral, eastern parts of Europe and pursued in their scholarly academies were recognized by international congresses in the imperial capitals of London, Paris, and Berlin.

In the course of the century, that upscaling did occur, with some unexpected consequences. We can catch a glimpse of this upscaling in reactions from Cust and Hunfalvy to the reception they received at the congresses. Cust knew that his paper delivered at the Berlin Congress, his large map, and later his book-length schedule that included all African languages then identified were based on the most up-to-date linguistic science, linking languages to their classifications. He complained in his post-congress report that the work of missionary linguists was unfairly demeaned by ignoring sub-Saharan Africa, a populous region that would soon be politically and commercially important. Nor did Cust – the Englishman – approve of Müller, who had criticized Oxford at the Berlin congress and entertained the audience by bringing along an Indian pandit to display his religious rituals, evoking the "hilarity and ridicule of a ... crowd who neither understood the words uttered in Sanskrit, nor the solemn nature of the intended worship." In his report, Cust – the former Indian colonial officer – admonished Müller, noting, "All Religions are sacred," and added, with bitter irony, "When I read my paper [on Africa] it fell flat, because I had unwisely not taken the precaution of bringing with me a Negro ... to illustrate my statements" (1887:412, 415). Perhaps he thought of bringing Crowther, whom he admired – but he would have meant Crowther to illustrate Africans' intellectual capabilities, not to serve as a scientific specimen or an object of ridicule. Cust's angry reproach hints that he thought Müller was not a proper Englishman or Christian – an accusation made by others too.

Hunfalvy was even angrier. When Müller's *Lectures* were published in Hungarian in 1874, Hunfalvy added a chapter that tore apart the discussion of Turanian. That year, he went to the London Orientalist Congress, where he said,

The notion of the Turanian languages generally accepted by the linguistic literature of this country [i.e., England] is as ill-defined as its results are in the whole of negative character. But, I believe, a description of any of those languages, showing clearly the relations existing between that and other ones belonging to the same group ... will be of great value in the classification of languages. (1876a:64)

In what was surely an upscaling tactic, Hunfalvy challenged Müller, showing the applicability of genealogical methods to Hungarian, Finnish, Ostjak,
and Vogul (i.e., the Finno-Ugric family). Dismissing Müller's distinction
between "nomadic" and "settled" languages, he used the methods of the time
to show that the ancestors of Finno-Ugric peoples – supposedly nomadic –
had social hierarchy, religion, myths, songs, and "an established order of
family life" (1876a:87).

This upscaling, however, involved Hunfalvy and his allies in disputes at other
sites and scales. The relationship of Hungarian to the languages of Siberia was
not unanimously welcomed in Budapest. Hunfalvy understood his intervention
at the London Congress as a patriotic act in keeping with the dictates of science: "Hungarian science owes it to the Hungarian reader to correct the famous
writer [Müller] if he is wrong about languages to which Hungarian belongs"
(1874:395). But in Budapest other linguists disputed the relation of Hungarian to
the languages of Siberian fishers – "blubber-eating kin" (*halzsíros atyafiság*) –
and instead claimed kinship with Turkic languages. Budapest's illustrated
weeklies avidly followed this scholarly debate. The Hungarian public preferred
the Turks. Turkic languages evoked glorious warriors and political power, at a
time when linguistic minorities were challenging the hegemony of Hungarian
elites.[9] Instead of defending national honor as he had intended, Hunfalvy was
accused at home of betraying it. In what was for him a particularly painful
aspect of the dispute, his suitability for analyzing Hungarian was questioned,
citing his German family origins. Hunfalvy and his allies, in response, accused
the Turkic camp of shoddy science and pandering to popular views.

Race and its relation to language and *Volk* was a further dimension of this
dispute. It is the second controversy we take up. In the years of the Turkic
debate, impresarios were bringing "exotic" peoples for exhibition to European
cities. A Nenets (Samoyed) family and several Sami people from Lappland
arrived in Budapest. To great popular interest, they were displayed in the zoo.
Magazines wrote in ironic condescension about the "visiting relatives," and
about their physical features of diminutive height, flat faces and narrow eyes.
Implied was the question: are we really kin? In response, the Turkic camp
accepted the notion of racial kinship, but not with these visitors, and claimed
that "[t]he seed of the Magyar [Hungarian] race and language is Turkic"
(cited in Pusztay 1977:96). At the Berlin congress Hunfalvy responded in the
most general, conceptual terms, denying any link between language and race:
"Does language stand in any imaginable relation to the physical constitution of
humans? To this we must answer with a decisive no" (1882:52).[10] Earlier, in his
monumental ethnographic survey of Hungary, Hunfalvy had carefully detailed
the various physical measures that "race science" used to sort people, and then
declared that bodily descent (*származás*) does not make the human being nor
the nation, only language does (1876b:47).

The bruising debate on these issues in Hungary lasted several years and has been memorialized as the "Ugric-Turkic war." It established an axis of differentiation that distinguished scholars according to their description of the "object of analysis" (as Ugric versus Turkic); their views on the nature of language (as linked to nation only, or to race), and located the scholar either as a scientist or as a dabbler, and as either disloyal to the nation or a proper patriot. The distinctions on this axis were disputed by scholarly as well as popular audiences. Hunfalvy occupied one side: a scientist, accepting Ugric connection, rejecting race, and thought by many to be disloyal.

In a fractal reiteration of that set of distinctions, Hunfalvy differed even from some of his allies who accepted the linguistic definition of nationhood via the notion of linguistic "spirit," not race. Hunfalvy rejected even the notion of spirit, saying there was no objective measure of it. Acknowledging that language carries a nation's experiences, sufferings and hopes, he nevertheless added, "[I]n addition to one's so-called mother tongue, learned in childhood, one can learn another language, many other languages, and in that way step into other societies, be a member of other nations, as one wills" (1876b:47). This positivist version of philology was identified in 1880s Budapest as the truly scientific one, and this political view reflected the early, liberal policies of the 1848 revolution in which Hunfalvy had participated (Békés 1997). Hunfalvy's views also implied advocacy for a polyglot nationalism against nativist linguists and against the state's monoglot nationalizing policies.

Hunfalvy in Berlin – denying a link between language and race – was reacting against a powerful intellectual turn. Across Europe and the United States, scholars were giving linguistic genealogy a biological interpretation, casting it as a physical relation instead of a philological metaphor. Comparative philology had taught that language expresses the spirit of a group, but in 1869, the German linguist August Schleicher posited a stronger connection between language and biology. Although languages had long been thought "organic," Schleicher termed them "organisms of nature," making linguistics a *natural* science. Language was independent of speakers' thoughts, but subject to the same kinds of evolutionary forces as their bodies. His "family tree" of languages was supposed to parallel Darwin's image of evolution. Pushing this line of "family tree" reasoning further and tying languages to the particular physiologies of speakers' bodies, some linguists – whether accepting Darwin or not – combined linguistics with racial hierarchies, sorting speakers' bodies by hair texture, skull shape, face shape, and/or skin color.

Ironically, this adoption of racial classification contributed to the conceptual upscaling of African languages.[11] European linguists grouped African languages into families which, in turn, could be linked to a worldwide, racialized genealogy of all humankind. Among biologizing positions that linguists took up, there was a further subdivision according to the priority given race versus language. Friedrich Müller (no relation to Max), who had studied at Göttingen before becoming professor of comparative philology in Vienna, was one of those who distinguished groups on racial lines before dividing them by linguistic relationships. Since races (in his view) differed by hair form, he organized the language families of the world according to their speakers' hair: woolly, straight, curly, or tufted. Further racial distinctions applied within these groups, before the groups would then be divided into language families. As some contemporaries pointed out, hair form might not be the crucial marker of racial difference, so although Müller was widely cited, he was opposed by those who started with groupings according to linguistic facts, and then accorded these facts racial interpretations.

For example, in the second half of the century, Richard Lepsius (1810–1884), famed for his writings about ancient Egypt, and Wilhelm Bleek (1827–1875), who was a cousin of the biologist Ernst Haeckel, both embraced Darwinian theory and its implications for linguistics. They studied African systems of noun morphology with a biological twist that hinged – as had Max Müller's reasoning – on speakers' family form. Bleek compared noun classification systems based on sex distinction with systems based on other principles, or those lacking noun classification. Mentality, poetry, and religion of speakers were derived, he argued, from the group's handling of sexual and family relations, as evidenced in their language's noun classes:

[N]ations speaking sex-denoting languages [most European ones] are distinguished by a higher poetical conception ... forming the origin of almost all mythological legends. This faculty is not developed in the Kafir [i.e., Bantu speakers'] mind, because not suggested by the forms of their language. (Bleek [1867] 1869:ix-x)

Languages lacking sex-gender systems – such as most sub-Saharan African languages – revealed, to these scholars, the lack of a proper family life, "no moral ordering and [sexual] opposition in marriage" (Lepsius 1880:xxvi). Therefore, speakers were supposedly not yet able to recognize social hierarchy or assert independence. Lepsius and a younger scholar, Carl Meinhof (1857–1944), interpreted African linguistic genealogies in terms of racial essences and racial histories. Describing "mixtures" between northern and southern languages in Africa, they slipped into explaining them by reference to matings among their supposedly racially different speakers. And as his magnum opus on the "Hamitic" languages makes clear, Meinhof (1912) collaborated in research and writing with the Austrian physical anthropologist Felix Luschan, whose classifications of skin color contributed to the medicalized and racialized understanding of human differences that was specifically targeted against the humanistic scholarship of philology (Zimmerman 2001). For linguists too, adopting race categories was a claim to science, more so than positivist views in linguistics.

The alignments of science, nation and various linguistic views were not the same everywhere. One can detect an axis of differentiation among German-speaking scholars, who differed in how and how much they aligned race science with support for the state. After unification, German linguistics was no longer primarily a missionary effort. Like German anthropology, and sometimes in close cooperation and co-authorship with it, some perspectives in linguistics became a self-described auxiliary to Germany's colonial projects. For a cadre of professionals, practicing "race science" was a patriotic gesture that often brought career advancement.[12]

Among German-trained scholars, the contrasting position, in linguistics as in views of national politics, argued directly against these biologizing visions. For instance, Hugo Schuchardt, a young linguist at a provincial university in Austria, wrote a scathing review of a book by Lepsius, the eminent Egyptologist in Berlin. Ignoring academic hierarchy, Schuchardt demolished Lepsius's *Nubische Grammatik* (1880), especially its implication that language mixing was a result of racial mixing. It ridiculed Lepsius for conflating "genealogy" as a grammatical connection with its meaning as a blood relation. Schuchardt instead asserted, "The source of language mixing is always social, never physiological" (1882:868). Thirty years later, he wrote another devastating review about similar conflations and circular reasoning in Meinhof's "Hamitic" book. Schuchardt was a Romance specialist, but because linguistics now embraced a global range of languages, his particular interest in language "mixture" extended to Africa in search of evidence about the possible permeability of linguistic boundaries.

Boundary Controversies

Boundaries – both territorial and linguistic – define the final controversy we shall discuss. Language boundaries were fundamental for Cust and Hunfalvy, and so were maps as the way of representing them. But these men were of an elder generation at the 1881 Congress, having been born in the early decades of the century. For those like Schuchardt (1842–1927), born around midcentury and academically trained, boundaries – linguistic and territorial – became contentious issues. This is evident in efforts made late in the century to extend the methods of historical and comparative linguistics to yet more unwritten practices: this time to the rural dialects of Europe. This too was a scalar form of disciplinary ambition, in the opposite direction from the upscaling and inclusion of unwritten languages, for dialects were conceptualized as "smaller," downscaled versions of a language. Though meant to extend and sharpen the existing forms of analysis, this turn to spoken language undermined assumptions about the unity and boundedness of languages that had defined nineteenth-century language scholarship. In this controversy too, registers of expertise – different ways of mapping language and its boundaries – also distinguished between professional perspectives toward scientific work versus amateur dabblings, and distinguished contrasting views of what the nation should be, as a political form.

For most of the nineteenth century, language mappers presumed that languages were internally unified, evenly spread over territory and with firm boundaries, each one with its own spot on the map. Cust's method is a good example. He never doubted that African languages could be definitively identified and mapped, or that they corresponded to separate peoples inhabiting discrete territories. His map provided boundary lines between languages and language families, even if the descriptive text for a particular language noted that its exact boundaries were hard to define. In his map of India, he omitted languages of elites in favor of those who worked the land: "language field" had a quite literal sense for him. He sympathized with the farmers whose disputes he arbitrated as colonial administrator in a newly conquered province. Similarly, Cust's map of Africa displayed an imperial perspective for ruling without local political elites. It showed no African states. German nationalists, defining language much as Cust did, had a whole vocabulary to describe such linguistic territorialization: the *Sprachgebiet*, language area; the *Sprachgrenzen*, borders. They made aspirational maps that similarly showed no state boundaries, only the supposed limits of the Germanic languages (Dunlop 2015:75–77).

After midcentury, states also mapped languages, countering nationalists who wanted to break up states – or constitute bigger ones – using linguistic arguments. Often, states erased multilingualism and ignored linguistic variation. But unlike Cust and the German nationalists, they pictured languages only within state borders. Using the recently established state census bureaus, they attempted to apply to language the same individualized, positivist methods that worked well for demographic matters. But they ran into difficulties: Was language really a measure of nationality? What would count as a measure of "language"? International Statistical Congresses tried to forge agreements on census questions to assure comparability, but state ideologies differed wildly. Insistence on a single language had been German nationalists' means of opposing the political divisions among dynastic princedoms. After unification, nationalists continued to argue that "mother tongue" was an inherited, quasi-biological endowment, and the *only* possible measure of nationality. France refused to ask a language question at all: citizenship alone defined nationality. Austria, faced with eleven spoken languages, suggested *Umgangsprache* (community language), which was deemed unscientific because not individual. Hungary's chief statistician, faced with the state's policy of assimilating to Hungarian the many speakers of other languages, argued that language, like nationality, was a matter of choice.[13]

Also sharing the view of language as uniform, territorial and firmly bounded were German linguists who came to professional maturity in the 1870s.

Among them, the Neogrammarians were a group of historical and comparative scholars at the University of Leipzig who became interested in spoken language. They expected that the study of living dialects would allow greater phonetic sophistication and yield a clearer view of sound change – their special interest – than did written materials. Early in the century, Jakob Grimm had demonstrated how systems of sounds/letters in medieval texts were different from recent systems, but the new could be matched to the old with rules of astonishing regularity, suggesting systematic change. This work, soon called "Grimm's law," was hugely influential. "Indeed," as Morpurgo Davies (1992:144) remarks, "a detailed history of the various formulations and reanalyses of [Grimm's] law is exemplary for an understanding of the way in which the methodology of 19th century linguistics developed." The Neogrammarians, while rejecting Grimm's Romantic ideals, built on his technical innovations to show that even the exceptions to his regularities were systematic. They expected more such discoveries of regularity among the remaining irregularities, in a kind of "method of residues."[14] They continued text-based studies of Germanic and Indo-European. But in their famed 1870s manifesto they cited recent studies of provincial dialects as models for future work.

In one sense, the provinces were well known to be linguistically diverse. The genre of the provincial dictionary (*Idiotikon*), popular since the eighteenth century, alerted readers to the contrasts between dialect words and written German. Its format assumed unified, self-contained dialects, distinct from each other. This is just what the Neogrammarians explicitly envisioned: coherent dialects, described through self-analysis by single native researchers – a uniform language, writ small. Later, the dialects would be compared to each other and to medieval forms to make sound laws more precise. The writing of sound laws could continue unchanged. So could the fundamental understanding, traditional by this time, that just as Germanic diverged from other Indo-European languages, so current languages and dialects diverged from Germanic, and were separated and isolated, spread across the countryside in the image of the early Teutonic migrations. In many cases, the speech of a region was, in fact, named for the tribe presumed to have been its early settlers: *Schwäbisch, Fränkisch, Sächsisch.*[15]

Thus, for Georg Wenker (1852–1911), who became the author of the first dialect atlas of Germany, it must have been an easy switch from his 1876 dissertation on historical sound shifts in Germanic to studying dialects.[16] His teacher had written dialect dictionaries and encouraged students to study their own dialect speech. Wenker's first booklet, amusingly written and meant for a popular audience, was full of affectionate regard for dialects. It detailed their boundaries as widely presumed to exist in his home province, along the northern Rhine river. Wenker gave dialects and languages parallel treatment as bounded wholes. Near the Belgian border, he wrote, there are some French villages only a quarter hour from German villages, and "one finds absolutely no mixing between the two languages; one village is entirely German the other entirely French" (1877:4). These were commonplace ideas. But perspectives on borders were changing, especially regarding matters of scale.

Wenker had fought in the 1870–1871 war in which Prussia annexed Alsace and Lorraine and unified the German states. But his viewpoint remained provincial. It was to school principals in his province that he sent the forty sample sentences that teachers were asked to translate into local forms. This is how he transformed speech into mappable written symbols. Wenker did the painstaking work of processing the enormous amount of data, and even extended his sample geographically. But over ten years of requests, the national Academy of Sciences in Berlin refused to fund his work. His comments at a local Philological Society in 1885, some years after German unification, are revealing:

In 1876 I started with the idea of finding boundaries. ... I was under the impression that the various characteristics would wholly or almost wholly go in concert, giving a clear dialect border. ... This was entirely mistaken. The borders of the various characteristics each ran in their own route, and often crossed each other. ... The further the work went in the Rhine district the more confused the lines got. ... The old naïve idea of dialect boundaries had to be rejected.

The image he started with did not fit the data; but the political perspective no longer fit either:

Now the idea is to follow the developing changes in vowels and consonants and morphology historically. Not only the big, rough sweeping differences. Now my idea is that this research is the investigation of our *Stammesgeschichte* [tribal history], the mixture and the mutual influence of many ancient tribes. ... [With] the advantage of living materials from the Fatherland ... I have the hope that my work will extend to the whole of Germany ... and will be a monument to the unity of our *Volk* and our Fatherland. (1886)

Unity was the new key word. The historical aspects of his program were sympathetic to the Neogrammarian project. Indeed, it was Wilhelm Braune of the Neogrammarian circle who had invited Wenker to speak at that meeting; Hermann Paul was also present. The society voted its support and Braune wrote to Berlin, where the Neogrammarians were evidently well connected, urging the work's extension to the whole country. With this help, Wenker's change of political perspective, and a new education minister, the project was fully funded by the German state in 1888, apparently with Bismarck's intercession and from a fund at the Kaiser's personal disposal. The German dialect atlas has since been centrally organized. In the twentieth century, when Germany's political ambitions reached into Hungary, the atlas was extended to German-speakers in Hungary, including even Bóly.[17]

Wenker's opinions in the nineteenth century show how he serially embodied two different ideological stances. In one, dialects have boundaries, in the other they do not. The change reflected his new perspective on the materials, simultaneously encompassing a larger scale of territory and a smaller scale or closer view of the linguistic facts. Wenker's expert register, his way of approaching the "object" he was describing (dialects vis-à-vis territory), depended in part on the object, on his rescaled view of it, but also on his new alignment with Germany as a centralized, national state.

A parallel example from the other side of the 1871 Franco-Prussian War shows that there were contemporaneous perspectives that did not assent to centralization. As David Hoyt (2006) recounts, elites who were amateur philologists in the south of France, in Montpellier, argued that southern dialects derived from medieval Provençal were linguistically quite separate from northern dialects linked to Paris. Southern dialects ought to be taught in schools, they argued. Outdoing Wenker, the Montpellier researchers did fieldwork, talking to villagers across virtually all of central France. In 1876 they published the *Study of the Geographical Limits of Langue d'Oc and Langue d'Oïl* showing a line separating these two dialects. But Parisian scholars, professionally trained and active in government, were fearful of separatist politics. In the wake of the military defeat and the loss of Alsace-Lorraine to Germany, they were eager to unify the country, especially its educational system. They argued that there was no line dividing northern and southern dialects. And indeed, the scientific and "atomizing method of linguistic geography," used by their student Jules Gilliéron in his great dialect survey of France published a few years later, shows no such line (Hoyt 2006:102). The specifics of the two expert registers in French dialect study run parallel to those in Germany. In France, however, the two positions were not only in contrast but politically opposed.

Yet another view of boundaries was more radical, claimed to be *less* scientific and was aligned with another politics. It further undermined the methodology of mapping and, indeed, of comparative-historical linguistics. Hugo Schuchardt, the critic of the Africanists, also studied Caribbean Creoles and in later years attended the Orientalist Congress. He had trained at Leipzig just when the Neogrammarian group was forming. Later they invited him to return to teach at Leipzig, but he preferred to stay in provincial Austria. In 1870, at his dissertation defense, he rejected the "family tree" model, that is, the repeated divergence of daughter languages from a single ancestor. If divergence was followed by contact, he noted, then the theory fell apart. And empirically, neither dialects nor languages were ever isolated or self-contained units. After all, he asked, where does Italian end and French begin along the Mediterranean dialect continuum? This depends, he noted, on "centrifugal and centripetal forces." The first differentiates, the second unifies through political, religious, and literary communication (1928 [1870]:171).

Later, to Max Müller's credo that there are "no mixed languages," Schuchardt responded that there are no entirely *unmixed* languages. He saw bilingualism as a source of language mixing. "Two languages are not mixed like two dissimilar liquids, but rather like two different activities of one and the same acting subject" (1882:868). The implication is that speakers, not languages, ought to be studied. Texts, census questions, and sample sentences flatten what speakers do and erase diversity that exists even for one individual. Schuchardt recommended a different method. One must attend to the everyday speech of many kinds of people, to a linguist's own strategies when he does not know a language well, to caricatures of speech in jokes, theatrical imitations of different kinds of persons, and the "jargon" of various social groups. This made linguistics into the study of social practices. As he put it, "Language is not an object, it is the product of an acting subject" (1882:868).[18]

An interest in language mixture was not simply a scholarly issue for Schuchardt. Styria, the province of Austria-Hungary in which he lived, had a sizable Slovenian population. Language politics flared into violence in the 1880s when Pan-German and Pan-Slavic activists started their agitation, usually arriving from elsewhere. They tried to recruit people to linguistic nationalism in bilingual villages that had been living peaceably for centuries. The activists claimed to be defending "language frontiers" that they imagined with the help of language maps produced by states and nationalist movements (Judson 2006:100–141). They demanded monolingual states. Schuchardt was against purism and considered mixture both inevitable and beneficial; he was an advocate for multilingualism, citing cognitive and social advantages. His prize-winning book, *Slawo-deutsches und Slawo-italienisches* (1884), described in great detail the mutual linguistic effects of those languages. It "provincialized Europe," as we would now say, by showing that language mixing was as much a European phenomenon as an African or Creole process.[19] The book was also a passionate call for a polyglot nationalism. It recommended retaining German for administration, but encouraged education and civil society in all the languages of Austria-Hungary, which he characterized as a unique "experimental station" for liberal brotherhood. Predictably, he was attacked from all sides.

Conclusion

We have described nineteenth-century linguistics at a slant. Our two main characters – Hunfalvy and Cust – were important mostly in their limited time and place, which underlines the spatiotemporal locatedness of their, and our, knowledge. Choosing them highlighted perspectival changes of the discipline: on one hand, its social exclusions; on the other, the ambition for universality that led to the study of unwritten languages and dialects in Africa, Asia, and Europe. Tracking scholars from libraries and scriptoria to expeditions and field sites, we followed the scalar transformations of what counted as "evidence" in linguistic research. Scholarly values lived in a variety of realms, from international congresses to provincial workshops. They too were scaled and comparative: what was evident, true, and loyal for one venue was seen as false betrayal in another; what seemed patriotic to some was revealed as racist by others.

Our story was selective and illustrative. We focused on the last decades of the nineteenth century but colonialism and European Great Power struggles were only in the background, as were the usual large categories of intellectual and cultural history, Enlightenment, Romanticism, positivism. At the center of attention, instead, was a question about method and its ideological interpretation: how a scholarship based on written texts adapted those methods repeatedly, as its ambitions to be a universal science encouraged the consideration of unwritten linguistic forms from political peripheries and denigrated populations. A certain continuity was apparent: oral genres, sample sentences, and individual intuitions were analogized to ancient texts, so that similar analyses could be applied. These were productive analogies for a time, changing the forms of analysis. But they also involved enormous erasures of variation in speaker practices and in social forms that differed from European expectations.

Those expectations – the ideologies of linguistic research – were our main concerns. We showed that the semiotic principles detailed in earlier chapters shaped the way linguists defined, compared, and represented their objects of study: the languages and social groups they envisioned. Equally important was the comparison among positions within the study of language. The forms of description and analysis that linguists used to represent others were themselves the means of differentiating among scholars of language.

Modes of linguistic analysis – issues of genres, variation, and boundaries – were lined up with ideologies about race, nation, and science; together they came to organize and eventually transform the study of language. The ideological manifold of language-people-territory that, we argued, was questioned in one part of nineteenth-century linguistics, nevertheless gathered force elsewhere: it became ever stronger as a legitimation for nation-states in the twentieth century, creating difficulties for states that failed to match this image of modernity. In linguistics, the intuition of unified, homogeneous languages and communities was shifted by many scholars to the more abstract plane of structure. But the controversies we have described – about the boundedness of languages, the relationship of peoples to linguistic practices, and especially about methods for studying and defining "language" – are still very much on the scholarly agenda. These debates continue, if in different forms, making the discipline open-ended, its knowledge transforming and transformative.

Coda: Avenues of Inquiry

Where might one go from here, to inquire into ideologies and social difference? What we have offered in this book are conceptual tools and ways of exploring empirical materials, whatever those materials might be. The kinds of evidence we have exemplified here include ethnographic observations and recordings, historical information, linguistic analyses, legal cases, and various genres of literary texts, but there are others. We have no crystal ball to tell us what the research problems of the future may be, but we can suggest some ways of looking at whatever substantive issues arise. These are avenues; they are not destinations.

Unbounding Semiosis

The first part of this research strategy takes something potentially interesting as a *centerpiece*. One tracks connections outward from it in many directions. We have illustrated this approach through the notion of a site of ideological work as a focus of joint attention, the various gazes that attend to it, and the many kinds of connections there may be to other sites. *Anything* can be a starting point for this strategy. Although our examples started from material objects (glass panes and bus-stop benches), the springboard could be, instead – and with interesting results – an activity, an event, pieces of language, or anything else. In addition to our own work, there are precedents for this kind of approach. For instance, recall Vigouroux's (2009) study of the many languages, social actors, scripts, and long-distance connections that coincide in a South African internet café and could be tracked from there. A much earlier precedent is the "case method" of ethnographic inquiry recommended in the so-called Manchester school of social anthropology, deriving from casework in the law. The idea was to focus on some moment of contestation – a "social drama," in their terms – as an event whose history, participants, and consequences could be tracked, wherever the tracking might lead (Gluckman 1940, 1972). Legal cases and the detective stories that fictionalize crimes and their associated drama take this form.

Important in this strategy is that there is no intrinsic boundary to a site, including a research site; so one does not start by delimiting some social group, or place, or data set (of transcripts, say, or of social media threads), as a universe of social forms containing everything relevant to the research. To be sure, there can be reasons to look at distributions, to sample populations, to impose a stopping point on one's inquiry. But it is important to remember that even when studying the people who live on an island, there will be connections elsewhere in time and place. This is not a new strategy. Besides the "case method" approach, one might look to Malinowski as an ethnographer who did not stay put on the island of Kiriwina, but followed the Trobrianders as they traveled to other islands, where they exchanged kula valuables with people who otherwise differed from them in various ways. And there is also the example of Fredrik Barth, who advocated an approach that looked across ethnic boundaries, the better to understand how and why they were constructed and maintained. Our own ethnographic work cannot be characterized as "bounded" village or town studies. On the contrary: each analysis looked "out" onto other towns as comparisons, into local and regional histories, and into the ways one place was connected to another as remembered "homeland," or as where the versions of social life and/or language were ideologized as "real" or most "authentic" compared with somewhere else. In short, it is the connections, and the ideological work of drawing them, that are central to the research strategy.

Equally, the centerpiece could be a recognized contrast or actively invoked comparison, as in many of our examples. How is that contrast – its axis and qualities – evident as a focus of attention? What happens to that attention when the comparison is projected onto narrower or more encompassing contrasts? Just as the drawing of connections between sites is, in principle, without boundaries, so is the semiotic creation of fission and fusion. For instance, Kopytoff (1987) argued that African frontiers – where emigrants establish new settlements – are re-creations, ideologized and idealized visions of social relations in the old settlement. What we now call diasporas often work this way, in a fissioning and recursive process, as the naming of new settlements after old ones suggests (Anderson 1991). For the seventeenth-century migrants who established Massachusetts a pure/impure comparison was crucially at issue, with the Puritans understanding themselves to be breaking away as the virtuous "elect" of England, only to "find" or project sin, pollution, and impurity within their own American settlements (Bercovitch 1978). In quite another example, one can analyze the growth of knowledge by looking for the reiterated, fractal distinctions among scholarly theories (Abbott 2000), and at the same time attending to theories (as sites) and to the authorizing connections researchers draw among them, for instance seeing them as "continuing a tradition," or breaking away in a "scientific revolution" (Kuhn 1962). The unboundedness of semiosis implies that the investigator's strategy may consider the ideological work both of fractally proliferating distinctions (as sites) and of connecting them.

Notice in regard to the strategy of starting with a site of ideological work and tracking uptakes that there are (at least) two ways to do the tracking, which might turn up interestingly different results. One way is to follow how a single person takes up various perspectives and interprets the ongoing, and changing, scenes and conditions she or he experiences. In Part II we tracked Anne Royall in this way. The other way is to track successive uptakes by very differently located people of what seems initially like a single distinction but which often turns out to change over time and space, as we did with "Yankee." Part III also offered examples of this kind of tracking, and one could go on to follow up on more implications of changes in Baltimore slogans and mayoral campaigns, or those in the university departments where personnel changed and glass panes were covered over by more and more faculty members.

Social Organizations

Differentiation relies on contrast and creates comparison. As we have seen, comparisons often result in categories that can be bounded by participants to various degrees and in diverse ways. Further inquiry can reveal when and how bounded categories at one or more levels of encompassment or extent are made the basis of differential practices, sometimes even constituting identities and social groups that can act in concerted ways. Under what historical circumstances is some version of such a continuum of social process attempted? How does it succeed or fail? Brubaker (2004) emphasized the distinction between category and group for the case of ethnic categories, which are sometimes mobilized, but often are quiescent. Inspired by Foucault, Hacking (1999) tracked how differential diagnostic categories of illness create boundaries out of mere contrast, via systems of classification. It is worth asking, in this line of inquiry, what social group or institution creates the classifications, how and with what agenda, and how it affects the afflicted (Fleck 1979 [1935]). Often people have turned diagnostic categories into their forms of identity. If widely adopted, patient categories can be mobilized in social activism. Action may aim to destigmatize the category in public discourse. Alternatively or additionally, action may focus on lobbying for government and private funding to support research that would find a cure. Much of this line of inquiry has been in a medical realm.

But the implication of this book is that social action can be created around any category-contrast. By noting it, making it salient, creating a boundary out of the mere contrast, one can introduce distinctive practices that convey and reproduce the differentiation. This works in semiotically organized ways, regardless of what the contrasts are. Research in this direction has precedents and is worthy of further work. For example, musical, literary and/or artistic styles, so commonly associated with registers of speech, clothing, and other signs, allow fans and practitioners to recognize each other, and categorize each other. Their recognition opens the possibility of social organizing, if only to show support for the aesthetics of the artistic style, but often for wider-reaching goals. Or, think of the emergence of contrasting subdivisions of activity created within a single larger realm, for instance in eating (say: vegan versus farm to fork), alcohol consumption, hiking, or sexual activity. The distinctions seem to "grow" stereotypes of identity. Forms of expertise, rankings, and discourses of ethical conduct or aesthetics emerge. They often produce disputes and partake in politics. Power of various kinds moves along the social connections and tributaries created in this way, perhaps in the hope of rerouting power from previous directions of flow. Commercial organizations also form in order to supply the material for practicing the ideologized distinctions.

The process is evident in conceptual distinctions in the academy, for instance when a way of analyzing or collecting data coalesces for its practitioners as recognizably different from other methods. These practitioners may form factions in departments, but whether there are factions or not, invariably the "new" practice gets named in contrast with other parallel practices. An "interest group" may emerge at national meetings, ultimately perhaps even a separate subdiscipline that any self-respecting university would not be without. Of course, most such initiatives are blocked early on. We merely wish to draw attention to the semiotic aspects. There is always potential for transformation of contrasts into categories and boundaries; and the consequent possibility of making practices and organizations along a dimension of increasing regimentation and institutionalization.

Boundary Makers, Crossers, and Breakers

To the extent that social actors erect boundaries around contrasts – turning difference into categories – there will be people engaged in making the boundaries, in guarding and policing them if they are already established, or crossing them, or trying to erase them. Any performer or genre that is characterized as a "crossover" is involved in such activity; so are joint appointments across departments in universities, as are centers of interdisciplinary study.

Ironically, both crossing a boundary and policing it actually create what they cross. For example, in the usual understanding, linguistic translation is a practice that assumes a language difference great enough to be a barrier to comprehension. Some special effort, perhaps also a specialist, is required to cross the boundary, and create equivalences between the language of a source text and the target language of the destination text. But the metaphor of translation is now being used in anthropology and other disciplines to characterize a very wide range of such creations of boundaries along with their crossings (Gal 2015a). Note how ideological work is essential to any such endeavor, from the construal of what and "where" a boundary exists between categories and practices, to what sort of expertise it takes to make or cross it, to what the crossing creates as effect. Indeed, one of the crucial ideological questions for the broader sense of translation is what constitutes "equivalence." Propositional equivalence is by no means the only way of creating what will count as a parallel, especially when the arena is no longer linguistic translation but, say, the "translation" of choreography to music, or the translation of a bit of soil from the Amazon into evidence of (de)forestation. Commensuration is another way of characterizing the creation of such parallels, and contestation is always an option. Connecting sites is at issue in all such cases.

If we consider only the narrowly linguistic aspects of translation, many kinds of expertise are required: dictionary and grammar writers, orthographic experts, language standardizers of all kinds, publishing houses with their best practices, film and video dubbers, committees to decide what linguistic forms can be used where. Economic and political issues are centrally involved in the dissemination of texts in all media. The list goes on and is worth exploring in particular locations. But there is always more involved. Mertz (2007) showed how colloquial, morally weighted arguments in the US legal system are "translated" through protocols of reading and procedure into a dispassionate register of dispute settlement. In Bible translation, literal semantic equivalence is often not the goal; instead, the translator tries to find analogies and examples from the target social scene and region that will be both familiar (if details of Middle Eastern foods, flora, and fauna would not be) and spiritually inspiring. The assumptions about conduct and relationships that are embedded in the Bible are not always easily transferred; translation often requires quite striking transformations even of the grammar of the receiving language (Schieffelin 2014).

Looking for the unmaking of differences, the breaking of boundaries, is another avenue of inquiry. Encompassments in fractal processes routinely accomplish this, as we have shown. In Bóly, for instance, whether a speaker identified as Hungarian or German depended on the scale at which the comparison was drawn. Or, when "Yankees" are taken to be simply "North Americans," distinctions between residents of northern and southern states are ignored in favor of the encompassing unity. Such cases in fractal processes may not mean that the ignored distinction goes away forever. Perhaps it is ignored only until such time as it is again relevant to the situation at hand. Yet, some efforts at unmaking difference are meant to do something else. One kind of example would be the French colonial effort to unmake the boundaries between indigenous kingdoms in Senegal, and reorganize the colony in a new administrative system. The reorganization was an attempt to create permanent change, dissolving indigenous administrations and armies. Another kind of example would be the effort to create a new category, which, without deliberately destroying the old differentiation, aims to override it. The emergence of a "gender nonbinary" category illustrates this process, since the differentiation into male and female is still available for other people. Perhaps in some cases the people proposing a new, encompassing category simply lack the power or sufficient persuasiveness to create permanent change. Proposing the address form "Ms." for women, overriding a distinction between the married and the unmarried, did not do away with "Mrs." and "Miss" except in limited circumstances. Instead, it just added a new dimension of differentiation, based on adherence (or not) to feminist politics. Thus the unmaking of differences can end with making more categories, not fewer. In all these cases a semiotic approach to ideological work deepens the analysis.

Narratives of Rhematization and Essence

This strategy investigates the stories that explain whatever difference is created, and – more than that – expand on the qualities attributed to signs and objects. The range of possible qualities depends on frameworks of knowledge, including ideas about causation. The stories justify and authorize the distinction among signs and the similarity between sign and object. It has been a great question in the history of Western philosophy and science if and how one might distinguish between similarity, correlation, and causation. But this question is equally a problem for the practical conduct of everyday life. Ethical issues in many contexts hinge on attributions of cause and therefore on identifying the proper objects of blame and responsibility. Claims of mere correlation and similarity have their own implications for thought and moral action. The relations among these – to the extent that they appear in a sociocultural context – are closely related to narratives of rhematization, that is, explanations of differentiation.

We have shown that attributing the similarity of sign and object, and differences among signs, to something "inside" (or inherent to) the occupiers of the category, is a very common explanatory strategy, whether the category is people or objects or territories or something else. The inherent "something" is usually invisible, a posited essence (Gelman 2003, McIntosh 2005). How these explanatory stories arise, and when they are told, merits inquiry. Similarly, Just So stories deserve closer investigation, distinguishing logics of cause, their historicity, their effects and patterns of invocation in particular situations. One should also consider their role in social change. An example would be the stories that account for the origin of Wolof griots – stories that are actually accounts of the onset of their differentiation from nobles. Such stories show up in collections of narratives, but it is seldom clear when and why they might be told, or to what effect.

Another kind of story, however, is the kind that "explains" anomalous members of a category. Sometimes the anomaly is simply erased or denied. Anne Royall, on a rare occasion when she met a self-identified Yankee during one of her trips, simply would not believe him, because he was far too well dressed and well spoken to fit her stereotype. Intriguing cases of explanation for apparent anomalies pertain to categorization of "natural kinds." An example is the seven-legged spider, whose lack of the eighth leg – deemed crucial to spiderhood – must be accounted for; or the kind of story that explains how tadpoles, so different in appearance from the frogs they will become, nevertheless share froggy essence. Psychologists investigating children's cognitive development have found that youngsters operate with a widespread assumption that things in "natural kinds" categories share an essence that determines their external appearance. Some of this research also investigates practical reasoning by adults, suggesting how widespread is the strategy of hypothesizing an essence that purports to explain similarities as well as anomalies within a category. As Gelman and her colleagues also showed, an essence is most likely to be posited for a category if there is already a lexical label for it (Gelman 2003). Something our approach might add to this line of research concerns "field effects" in categorization processes: the ways a category, and the reasoning that relates to it, are affected by other categories in some larger system, perhaps a fractal one. There is a link here between (linguistic) anthropology and cognitive psychology that merits follow-up.

In sum, we urge our readers to explore: to find further implications and entailments, hidden patterns and colors, or unnoticed seams and folds in the approach to ideologizing and differentiation presented here. There are surely more connections to be found and made, more contrasts and distinctions, at which point revisions and transformations in analytic concepts will emerge, along with new avenues of inquiry.

Notes

Introduction

1. See, for example, Eagleton (2007), Freeden (1996, 2003), and Woolard (2019), among many others. See also the many authors in the influential collections on language ideology, such as Blommaert (1999), Woolard and Schieffelin (1994), Schieffelin, Woolard and Kroskrity (1998), and Kroskrity (2000).
2. Some of Peirce's more accessible writings include Peirce (1877, 1998 [1895], 1955). Parmentier's (1994) interpretation is indispensable. See also Buchler's (1955) introduction to a collection of Peirce's essays. Morris (1970) places Peirce among the other American pragmatist philosophers at the turn of the century; Menand (2001) adds a good deal of their sociohistorical context. Note that this approach is not the kind of "structuralism" that has been attributed to Saussure (1959 [1916]) by others.
3. Keane (2003, 2018) has argued for a semiotic ideology, while also noting the very problems addressed here; see also the essays in Cavanaugh and Shankar (2017).
4. The analysis of interaction and Goffmanian participation frameworks have long been at the center of linguistic anthropology. Gumperz (1982) initiated one direction; see also the chapters in the now-classic collection of Duranti and Goodwin (1992). Silverstein (1976, 1993) marks another thread; see the essays collected in Lucy (1993) and Agha (2007). Many ethnographies unfold through interactional analysis within a frame of language ideology: Richland (2008), Mertz (2007), Lempert (2012), Lemon (2018), Meek (2010), Kuipers (1998). Others link interaction to local politics: Schieffelin (1990), Duranti (1994), Graan (2016), and Eisenlohr (2006), among others. Sociolinguists have written about person-types and their characteristic ways of speaking, e.g., Eckert (2000), Coupland (2007), Bucholtz (2010).
5. Jane Hill (1986) brought anthropology's attention to Bakhtin, and he has since been an inspiration to many: see the essays in Hill and Irvine (1993), Wortham (2001), Bauman (2004).
6. In each of our examples throughout the book, we locate semiotic processes in the specificities of such background discursive materials.
7. Bourdieu (1984) too wrote influentially about "distinction" but approached it largely as a form of specifically class domination. He did not propose an ideological mediation for language. For more varied views on authoritative genres, see the essays in Gal and Woolard (2014 [2001]).
8. We return in Chapter 5 to ways in which our analysis resembles segmentary systems, especially Evans-Pritchard's (1969 [1940]) classic description of Nuer segmentary lineages, and in what ways the two differ.

9. Since even picking out a figure from the ground requires erasure, this part of the process may be an aspect of all perception and category formation. Erasure can also be likened to what Bruno Latour (1993) has called the work of purification.

10. Other examples farther afield that have inspired us include Georg Simmel's (1971 [1908]) discussion of relational switches among social dyads and triads and Michael Polányi's (1966) insistence that rigorous science actually builds on the "tacit knowledge" that was supposedly only for everyday life. Consider also Foucault's discussions of capillary power and his essay (1977) suggesting that in writing genealogy the author's own perspective is destabilized. Donna Haraway (1991) similarly proposed "situated knowledges" as what is critically observed not only in others' science but also for herself, the feminist investigator. Ethnographies have done this in various admirable ways: Herzfeld (1987) compared Greek comparisons to those of anthropology; Basso, in *Portraits of the "Whiteman"* (1979), looked at white stereotyping of Apache through Apache stereotyping of whites.

1 Wolof in Senegal

1. For some materials in this chapter we have drawn upon the following previously published works: Irvine (1990, 2001c, 2011, 2018). For the Wolof examples in this chapter and elsewhere, we follow the roman-script system developed by Senegalese linguists and officially adopted by the Republic of Senegal in 1971. The system is laid out in works such as the *Dictionnaire wolof-français* by Fal, Santos, and Doneux (1990). One peculiarity concerns vowel length. Although length of a vowel (or of a consonant) is represented by repeating its symbol, any diacritic is represented only on the first symbol. Thus, for example, the vowel é, when lengthened, is represented as ée, not éé.

2. In recent years, many young urban speakers in Dakar and in the Wolof diaspora declare that they find rural speech difficult to understand because of its "old" Wolof vocabulary and its relative lack of French insertions (see Chapter 8). The tutor here did not come from Dakar, however, and the differentiation of rural and urban speech patterns was less stark in 1970, when the conversation between Irvine and the tutor took place.

3. Administratively, this community was termed (in French) a *village*. To write "village" here, however, would overly connote smallness and primitiveness, compared to the next chapter's Hungarian-German community.

4. Strictly speaking, the *gewel* are only one subcategory of "griot," albeit the unmarked one and the most conspicuous.

5. See also Sine (1974).

6. Although the term "caste" has been applied to the societies of this Sahelian region for centuries, much of the literature has restricted its use to the *nyenyo* category – as if only the low ranks were "casted" (out? down?). Some recent works have argued, however (and in parallel with the use of the term for South Asian social systems), that "caste" – if appropriate as an analytical term at all – must apply to a larger social system, not just to its lower ranks. Here we do not enter into debates as to the applicability of the term "caste" outside India, although we do in fact believe it is appropriate for these Sahelian societies. We recognize, however, that the *jaam* category, especially in relation to the historical slave trade, complicates

the analogy with South Asia. Some authors argue, therefore, that the West African systems have a dual organizational principle, combining castes and orders. See A. B. Diop (1981).

7. Besides aristocrats, the "noble" caste includes many families of nonroyal farmers and Muslim clerics. Clerics' position in the *géer* category is complicated; see Irvine (1990) and Colvin (1974).

8. The status of "slaves" in Wolof society, both pre- and post-emancipation, must be understood in this light and linked with other obligations concerned with agriculture and manual labor.

9. See McLaughlin and Villalón (2011) for an account, with transcripts, of a *jotilékat* ('transmitter') relaying the words of a religious leader for the benefit of a large audience. In this case the transmitter is a cousin, assisted by a griot.

10. Although Irvine usually spoke Wolof with this griot, the particular conversation – which had started out with his explaining some obscure vocabulary – happened to be in French.

11. Apparently, many *jaam*, not sharing the whole of the ideology described here, had moved away from communities like the one we describe.

2 German-Hungarians in Hungary

1. In the examples from Bóly in this chapter and throughout the book, German forms are in *italics*, Hungarian forms in ***bold italics***. G = German, H = Hungarian. When examples include both Hungarian and German, the English text mirrors the fonts of the original. Unless the linguistic details are of analytical interest in the example, standard orthography is used for ease of reading. When necessary, a broad transcription system is used, as is conventional in German and Hungarian dialect studies in Hungary (see, e.g., Wild 2003). When necessary to distinguish Handwerkerisch from Bäuerisch in an example, the former is underlined. Ellipses in transcripts signal pauses. Speakers' names are pseudonyms.

2. The ancestors of this German-speaking population came to Hungary from German territories in mid-eighteenth century as land-hungry migrants. They were officially invited to farm a southwestern region depopulated in the seventeenth century's Ottoman wars, a region soon (ironically) labeled *Schwäbische Türkei* (Swabian Turkey). The expulsions and confiscation of property after the Second World War were justified by accusations that Hungary's German-speakers had been members of Nazi organizations. Such organizations had been entirely legal, since Hungary was allied with Nazi Germany during the war. For a history of this period and the organizations, see Spannenberger (2005). There were certainly some Nazi organizers, sympathizers, and SS volunteers amid Bóly's population. Most of those fled before the expulsions; claims about memberships were never systematically investigated or substantiated. Many people were deported merely for having claimed "German mother tongue" in the 1941 census. Hungarian farmers from southern Slovakia were settled in place of German-speakers, as per the Allies' agreements on population transfers. Some Bólyi returned later, in secret, but they did not regain their possessions. The Hungarians stayed; the town lost its earlier linguistic unity. See further discussion later in this chapter and also Gal (1994), Füzes (1986), Beer and Dahlmann (1999), and Seewann (2000).

3. Gal's field trips lasted three to six months in 1987, 1990, and 1997, with several shorter subsequent trips; many thanks to Katalin Kovács and Erzsébet Varga for their indispensable help and to Mónika Mária Váradi for her assistance in several interviews. Gal (1994) is an ethnographic account; earlier discussion of some of these materials appeared in Gal (2012, 2013, 2016b). Compare this particular ethnolinguistic minority with others in Europe (Gal 1987) and elsewhere (Gal 2017b).

4. Knowledge of Hungarian also relied on child exchange, here as in other regions. This was a matter of an informal though systematic organization between families acquainted through regional marketing. A boy of a rich farm family in Bóly would work for a family in a nearby Hungarian-speaking village to learn Hungarian; a boy from a Hungarian-speaking village would be sent to Bóly to learn German (Gal 2011a).

5. Table 2.4 is meant to be suggestive; it is based on four minutes of talk from each speaker, telling in their own words the familiar children's story of Little Red Riding Hood. This worked well because of the frequency of verbs in several central variables (e.g., *kann fressen*) and the diminutive. The frequency of occurrence of each variant was divided by the total number of possible occurrences to get the percentages displayed in the table. The patterns are robust: even though some Ns are small, the variation noted ethnographically is evident quantitatively.

6. Some linguistic descriptions allude uncritically to such origins. Dialectologists may have heard these origin stories in the region. The artisan/farmer social distinction existed in other German-speaking regions of Hungary, but the linguistic distinctions were different from those observed in Bóly. The cities that apprentices visited were likely the same (e.g., Vienna), regardless of region, but the linguistic materials that marked the category difference between farmers and artisans in northern Hungary as opposed to the south were different, and so were aspects of language ideology (Manherz 1977).

7. Yet, Just-So stories of origins appear in books published in Hungary and especially Germany by organizations funded by the German government, established by the deported groups or their children. They can be found in the living rooms of Bóly or of educated adults from Bóly living elsewhere.

8. Hutterer (1991) and Schirmunski (1962) – major theorists of German dialectology in Hungary – demonstrated that one cannot determine through linguistic evidence alone the origins of speakers in language islands formed by migration from numerous regions. As Hutterer famously showed, all Hungarian-German dialects are "mixtures" of many regional forms. Despite the scholarly acceptance of this analysis, German dialectology continues to characterize these dialects with the traditional system of regional, "tribal" classification: Hessian, Swabian (Auer 2005); we discuss this further in Chapter 9.

9. The artisans' association started to keep its minutes in Hungarian several years before the farmers followed suit. It is worth emphasizing the social embeddedness of the qualitative contrasts discussed throughout this chapter to stress that "refined" and "authentic" are complementary in this value system, but not necessarily in any other.

10. For some lexical differences, and in the case of the two diminutives, the form identified as the farmers' in Bóly is conventionally categorized by dialectologists as western Hessisch-Fränkisch, while the artisans' is identified as eastern Bavarian.

11. The titles **bácsi** and **néni** are Hungarian honorifics (derived from kinterms) for elderly men and women that are also old borrowings into local German. So are the discourse markers **hát** (well), **ugye** and **ugyis**, in (2.6) and (2.7). Mariperi/Marienberg is a section of the town's fields in which Marika's family had a vineyard.

12. Rosina was presenting herself in a favorable light; in a strictly standardizing worldview she might well be judged to speak neither language well.

13. See Szelényi (2007) for discussions of these differences in the twentieth century. Culturally important German-speaking intellectuals who assimilated include Ferenc Herczeg and Jenő Rákósi (Gal 2013). See Szelényi (2003) for Hunfalvy's region, the Zips. For more general views of ideologies of language and German in particular in Hungary in the nineteenth century, see Gal (2006, 2011a, 2015b) and Maitz (2008).

14. O'Donnell, Bridenthal, and Reagin (2005) and Seewann and Hösch (1991) provide different historical perspectives on these developments; on *Volksdeutsche* in eastern Europe, see Reagin (2005).

15. The census that had such disastrous consequences for the German-speaking population of Hungary has received much attention in recent years; for further literature, see the citations in Note 2.

16. Some scholarly works try to explain the basis of these stereotypes sociologically (Andrásfalvy 1978). See Swanson (2017) for a recent ethnographic discussion and Fata (1997) for brief, closer views of several villages in the region.

17. For discussions of these current issues of language and identity, see Bindorffer (2001), Erb (2012), and Erb and Knipf-Komlósi (2007), among others.

3 Ingredients: Signs, Conjectures, Perspectives

1. Peirce remarked, "We live in two worlds, a world of fact and a world of fancy." The "inner world" of "fancies" (ideas) interacts with an "outer world" of observables apprehended through ideas manifest as signs. The inner world is relatively malleable. The outer world is full of "irresistable compulsions" that are modified only with considerable physical effort (1955a:87; 1955c:283). See also Vygotsky (1978).

2. See Peirce's "The Fixation of Belief" (1877) and Buchler (1955:xiv). In his scientific attitude Peirce resembles a scholar a century earlier: Destutt de Tracy.

3. For the quote, see Peirce (1877:10). Goodman's teacher C. I. Lewis was part of the American school of pragmatism that considered itself descended from Peirce (Morris 1970; Elgin 2000).

4. What we are calling "tokens" (embodiments and instantiations) Peirce called "replicas" (1906). In Peirce's complex intersecting terminology, "types" are called "legisigns," i.e., signs by law. Nontypified real-time signs he called "sinsigns," single occurrences. Posited causes would be indexical relations that are Seconds (real-time events). And hypothesizing was "abduction." For more detail, see Parmentier (1994). See also the partly parallel work on typification by phenomenologists (e.g., Schütz 1970) and see also Bakhtin (1981).

5. The notion of qualia was introduced in Peirce (1998 [1903]:272), developed further by Munn (1986), and most recently by Chumley and Harkness (2013). See also others in the special issue on qualia of *Anthropological Theory*. Qualisigns are qualia taken to be signs.

6. The crucial effects of naming have been considered by many; see a penetrating discussion in Sapir (1921).
7. Peirce specified four kinds of iconic/similarity relation: *replicas* (tokens) are linked to types by posited similarity; in *images* the sign and object are taken to share qualities; *diagrammatic* icons depict resemblance of form (see Chapters 4 and 5); and *metaphor* is similarity construed in the symbolic realm.
8. Take the example of a tree observed outside one's window. It may instantiate the type-level category of "living thing," or be the token of a particular species of tree, which is a type, but also may betoken the concept of "shade" or even "suburb."
9. These interactional iconicities/similarities are also called "stances" in addition to alignments; see contributions in Jaffe (2009) and Coupland (2007, 2016). Bakhtin's (1981) discussion of stereotyped voices is a parallel; see its development in Agha (2005b). The points in the previous paragraphs draw on the work of the last few decades in the analysis of interaction; see the early essays in Duranti and Goodwin (1992).

4 Comparison: The Semiotics of Differentiation

1. A large literature on standard US English, its ideological underpinnings, and its history includes Simpson (1986), Baron (1982), Cmiel (1990), and Bonfiglio (2002), and early observations of US English in Mathews (1931).
2. See Clapp's biographies for these details and further discussion (2003, 2016).
3. "The icon's great distinguishing property ... is that by the direct observation of it other truths concerning its object can be discovered than those which suffice to determine its construction" (Peirce 1955a:106).
4. This is yet another turn in the development of the concept of qualia (qualisigns); see Note 5 in Chapter 3. Gal (2013, 2017a) discussed qualia in relation to axes of differentiation.
5. The quotations in this paragraph were culled by Smith (1960) and Justus (2004) from literary works of the 1810–1850 period, i.e., contemporaneous with Royall's observations. The last one is Justus's summary of many such passages.
6. Registers have long been discussed in studies of language; see work by Reid and others in the 1950s, more recently developed in Irvine (1990, 2001c); for "enregisterment" see Silverstein (1998 [1992]) and Agha (2005b). For a closer look at the processes that make up enregisterment, see Gal (2018).
7. Philosophers note that scientists of all stripes also need narratives as explanatory support to understand abstract schemas and equations (Morgan 2001).
8. As Woolard (2019) reminds us, such circularity is characteristic of ideologies' logic.
9. Contrasting qualities, seen here as opposites or poles, are transformable through ideological work into dimensions and into measurable gradients, as in projects of scaling; see Chapter 8.
10. This scene is presented by Royall in paragraph form; we reformatted it as dialogue, with her characterizations of utterances also inserted.
11. European and Canadian cases of standardization as an axis of anonymity versus authenticity have been widely discussed and are changing currently in interesting ways, especially for minoritized languages (Gal and Woolard 2014 [2001];

Woolard 2016; Gal 2006; Heller 2011; Heller and Duchene 2012; Urla 2012). For parallel processes of standardization and its dangers in other minority languages, see Gal (2012, 2017b).

12. Royall's life spanned two eras: from the Enlightenment years of the Revolution to Jacksonian populism when rude, illiterate speech signaled Western values in politics and was newly and widely accepted (Cmiel 1990; Appleby 1992, 2000).

13. The use of person labels for some dialects (Yankee, Tuckahoe) as distinct from place names for others is further explored in Chapter 5.

5 Dynamics of Change in Differentiation

1. For earlier studies of political distinctions (and aesthetics) enregistered in this way, see Gal (1991, 2002, 2005), Gal, Kowalski, and Moore (2015), Gal and Kligman (2000).

2. Derrida's "différance" (with an a) made the same point in philosophy: "an opposition of metaphysical concepts (speech/writing, presence/absence) is never the confrontation of two terms but a hierarchy and the order of subordination" (1988:21, see also Derrida 1976). Différance was the *making* of such a contrast, not simply noticing it, and revealed the "violence" of domination hidden by such contrasts.

3. A further encompassing development of this axis, for instance, is the unification of man/woman as cisgender in contrast to transgender people. Markedness can be a sign of subordination but may also lead to transformative projects.

4. Some anthropological studies of fractals consider whole societies as unities of fractal form (Mosko and Damon 2005); by contrast, Otto and Bubandt (2010) usefully reopen the question of holism.

5. A southerner in the nineteenth century told an English lady that he was *not* a Yankee. She responded, "Aye, a proud Virginian. To us you are all Yankees, rascals who cheat the whole world" (quoted in Taylor 1961:47).

6. Grimes's was a very early autobiography, written without the involvement of the abolitionist movement. See Andrews (1986) and comparisons in Davis and Gates (1985).

7. For instance, gender difference may be a contrast on an axis, but it can also be made salient as anchor of an axis. See Kramer (2011) for an internet case of rhematization in gender differentiation, and Butler's (1991) evidence about recursivity in butch and femme identities. Sociolinguistic change is often characterizable as a shifting salience in the dimension that linguistic forms index, whether place, time (old/new), and/or person type is most evident. See analyses by Johnstone (2013), Rosa (2018), Woolard (2016).

8. Strathern (1988:13) called this phenomenon the "dividual." See Havel (1985) for a discussion of individuals' internal political divisions.

9. Recall the case of blockage in Chapter 2, where the elderly woman's puzzled frustration, described in her narration, resulted in tears as a response to blockage.

10. Sources for blackface minstrelsy were mixed, not only African American (Smith 2013). Biting caricature was also appropriation; blackface minstrelsy has been called "love and theft" (Lott 2013 [1993]) and became central to American performing arts (Rogin 1992). Blacks certainly parodied whites too in closed social circles in the eighteenth and nineteenth centuries, but without the profit and publicity of blackface minstrelsy. Only in the 1890s did a black actor turn the tables somewhat, performing a "lovable loser" in whiteface (McAllister 2011:3).

11. Brubaker (2004, 2015) has emphasized this distinction between category and group and led a sociological approach to issues of categorization.

12. In campaigns for language purification, determinations of what is "native," not "foreign," are drawn increasingly tightly, as the judgment is applied to whatever is left in the "native" category after the previous wave. Erasure is a characteristic of purification more broadly, as in Latour (1993).

6 Situating Ideological Work

1. See, e.g., Heidegger (1996 [1978]).

2. To do him justice, Schatzki (2002, 2005) does not stay wedded to Heidegger's formulation either. Instead, he defines a site as the nexus of (social) practices.

3. See Silverstein (1998) on this metaphor/pun.

4. Our discussion of this matter is complicated by the fact that Peirce himself – as well as the literature in our field that draws on his vocabulary – used the term "sign" in two ways: sometimes "sign" is the representamen (that which stands for something to an interpretant), and sometimes "sign" is the whole package (the representamen, its object, and the interpretant). If a site is *like* a Peircean sign, it is in the latter sense – the whole package.

5. For more detail, see Yates (1966) on Cicero and Quintilian and the sixteenth-century "memory theater" of Giulio Camillo.

6. The contrast between these two positions is less stark than it has sometimes been made to appear. Both positions assume that some ideas may be articulated explicitly while others are not; notice Silverstein's reference to "*perceived* language structure and use" (emphasis ours). His discussion relies on comparing "rationalizations" with the linguistic patterns and (especially) indexical relationships that speakers must be drawing upon, i.e., must have internalized, in order to engage in goal-oriented action that creates indexical effects in discourse. Meanwhile, those who emphasize the implicit, such as Verschueren (1995:142), acknowledge that "ideology is also a combination of implicit and explicit views."

7. Arguing along similar lines, Jean and John Comaroff (1991:24) have called the implicit, naturalized conceptions "hegemony," reserving "ideology" for the explicitly articulated ones. We do not find, however, that separating the labels for explicit and implicit forms of knowledge resolves the issues in their relationship.

8. See also Eagleton's useful exposition of Bourdieu's *doxa* (Eagleton 2007:157).

9. Of course, it is not only in Soviet regimes that political opposition cannot easily be expressed openly, Cold War ideologies of discourse to the contrary (see Gal 1991). Consider, therefore, a piece of humor journalism titled "I Should Not Be Allowed to Say the Following Things about America." The article begins, "As Americans, we have a right to question our government and its actions. However, while there is a time to criticize, there is also a time to follow in complacent silence. And that time is now" (*Onion* 2004:104).

10. Barth (1969: 36) does offer a brief discussion of the "rather special situation of colonial peace and external administration." However, he focuses on the newly proliferating contacts between members of different ethnic groups, contacts made possible by the colonial pacification. He does not consider the colonial administration's power to impose ethnic identifications or regulate those contacts in other ways.

11. Although we discuss a recent example, there are older ones as well. The "case method" of the Manchester school of ethnography, modeled on legal cases, proceeded similarly. The idea was to identify an important event – often a conflict – and investigate its background, participants, and unfolding. See also the Coda.

12. E.g., Brown and Gilman (1960), Silverstein (2003), Errington (1985), and Paulston (1976) on Swedish, Morford (1997) on French, and Simpson (1997) on Thai, to name only a few.

13. Bóly usage thus resembles other cases, discussed in Silverstein (2003), of second-order indexicality: a kind of relational usage (relation of speaker to addressee) becomes interpreted in terms of characteristics internal to the speaker (greater refinement, concern for elaboration). See also Chapter 4.

14. These two forms are both second-person plural nominatives. Which one is used depends on verbal aspect and syntactic construction, not on any social distinction.

15. See Irvine (2018).

7 Among and Between Sites

1. E.g., Silverstein and Urban (1996), Inoue (2004), Agha and Wortham (2005), as well as more recent works such as Agha (2007), Silverstein (2013b), Carr and Lempert (2016), and Gal (2018).

2. See, for example, the benches in photographs such as those at http://farm3. static.flickr.com/2033/2048575489_6f67e19726.jpg and http://farm7.static.flickr. com/6214/6337991488_5b441601fd.jpg. Even the bench in Figure 7.3, though located in an upscale neighborhood, has a broken plank that looks hazardous to the health of anyone sitting on it.

3. In 1999, Schmoke declined to seek another term. O'Malley won votes from both white and black voters, although many black leaders favored one or another of his black opponents.

4. See, for example, comments by Linder & Associates (2003) in their Progress Report on the Believe campaign.

5. As a friend residing in Baltimore recently wrote to us, "We hope you will consider a visit to see us and the sites [*sic*] of Baltimore. Do not believe the television images of 'Charm City' (the local name for 'Ball-mer'). It is not all *Homicide* and *The Wire*. There are many cultural attractions here."

6. See Silverstein (2005) and Irvine (2005).

7. Philips is the scholar in our field who has worked the most, heretofore, to develop a rigorous notion of types of sites as scenes of cultural activity. We reformulate her analysis somewhat for our purposes here.

8. Special contexts of dictionary use can complicate this matter. Players of the word game *Scrabble* are advised by the game's producers to settle on a particular dictionary as authoritative – and certain dictionaries are recommended – because dictionaries of English vary in the words they list.

9. See, e.g., Philips (1998, 2016) and other works.

10. The Bóly example is one in which an important site of language ideology – a town, in this case – is not a piece of language. Moreover, the Bóly linguistic practices we focused on in Chapter 2, the registers differentiating artisans from farmers, were swept up in institutionalization processes that were not themselves conceived as part of a linguistic project. Many linguistic practices and artifacts

would have been involved all along, however, in constituting the clubs as institutions (speeches, meetings, by-laws, lists, books, educational lectures, etc.) and presumably contributing, therefore, to the institutionalization of the two varieties by concretizing the identities of their speakers.

11. For an extended discussion of such discursive entanglements, see Lempert and Silverstein (2012).

8 Scales and Scale-Making: Connecting Sites

1. Passages in this chapter are drawn from previously published essays: Gal (2016b), Irvine (2016).

2. In a work accorded a prize by the Académie Française, Xavier Deniau (2001) counts as speakers of "French" all residents of France as well as various other regions, such as parts of Belgium and Luxembourg; he also counts the francophone populations of Québec, "l'Acadie" (New Brunswick and Nova Scotia), and Louisiana. These are counted without regard for linguistic differences.

3. The example recalls Althusser's discussion of interpellation, as in "that very precise operation ... which can be imagined along the lines of the most commonplace everyday police (or other) hailing: 'Hey, you there!' " (Althusser 1994 [1970]:130–131). Through interpellation, concrete individuals are ideologically made subjects – "recognized" (or misrecognized) as socially positioned in specific relationships, such as a person of interest to the police.

4. Sonia Das (2016) describes a particularly complex diasporan situation in Montréal: Tamil-speakers from Sri Lanka contrast not only with Francophone and Anglophone neighbors, but also with Tamils from India. Competing versions of the "heritage language" and its global connections ensue.

5. Stevens's typology has been both amended and critiqued in the years since it was first proposed. See Michell (1986).

6. Napoleon effectively revoked the metric system altogether in 1812, adopting the "ordinary measures" – older nonmetric measures – for workaday purposes (Alder 2002:316). The metric system was not officially reinstated in France until 1837.

7. Rankings of nations with respect to "freedom" do exist today, although the criteria for the comparison are not always obvious.

8. Coen (2016) offers a similar argument.

9. The mathematician and philosopher Condorcet explored such a mathematical scheme in detail (in Granger 1954; and see Alder 2002:136).

10. Although there are concepts of "singularity" in other fields, especially mathematics and physics, use of this term in (philosophy of) social science comes mainly from Foucault. See Foucault (1990 [1978], 1996 [1978]).

9 Library to Field: Ideologies in Nineteenth-Century Linguistic Research

1. The congress proceedings are informative about these arrangements, see: *Verhandlungen des fünften internationalen Orientalisten-Congresses, gehalten zu Berlin im September 1881. Erster Theil: Bericht über die Verhandlungen.* The *Berliner Börsen-Zeitung* of September 13 reported on the week's weather.

2. We rely on many kinds of historiography – internalist descriptions of philology and linguistics, externalist and institutional histories, surveys of intellectual trends, regional schools and biographies, and mainly our own earlier work in archival and primary sources: Gal (2001, 2011a, 2011b, 2012, 2015b), Irvine (1993, 2001a, 2001b, 2008, 2009, 2011, 2015). General works on which we relied include Amsterdamska (1987), Olender (1992), Trautmann (1997), Benes (2008), Morpurgo Davies (1992), Vermeulen (2015), Aarsleff (1982), and Bauman and Briggs (2003). Translations are our own, unless otherwise noted.

3. We use "orientalist" not in Said's (1978) expanded sense, but as those in the nineteenth century used it; that is, not as a general image about a region, but as the practices of those who studied the texts and histories of Asia and the classical world, and later of Africa as well, and often called themselves "orientalists." Although early on the distinction between *Kulturvölker* and *Naturvölker* was important (Marchand 2009:xxii–xxiii), it is the breakdown of this distinction that we track.

4. See Vermeulen (2015:186–194) and Gulya (1974).

5. Invariably the grammars discuss the group, its location, then sounds, words, sentences, and text, often with a dictionary. Compare three different ones in this period: Steinthal (1867), *Die Mande-Neger-Sprachen*; Hunfalvy (1875), *Az éjszaki osztják nyelv*; and Kobès (1869), *Grammaire de la langue volofe*, where the dictionary and texts are interspersed.

6. Priests wrote some of the first prayer and Bible translations and may have had deeper influence, possibly unifying the diverse forms of Khanty (discussed later in this section) into one purported language, as with Buryat in eastern Siberia (Graber and Murray 2015). See also Forsythe (1992) and Werth (2002) for proselytizing in nineteenth-century Siberia.

7. Expeditions were funded by the Russian Academy of Sciences, the Hungarian Academy, and private donors. Each of the Siberian groups has an older appellation, derived from the name given to them by neighboring groups, and a newer one that is their self-label, now the official one. We use the old label, which is somewhat stigmatizing, only for clarity and in quotations from earlier sources.

8. The congresses welcomed works in German, English, and French, languages in which Castrén, Hunfalvy, Cust, the missionaries, and military linguists published. All the more striking that the networks were markedly separate.

9. Nineteenth-century Hungary's political situation was complex. It had its own minorities – Slovak, Romanian, Serbian, and German-speakers – and was part of the Habsburg (Austrian) Empire, revolted against the Empire in 1848, but failed to gain independence. In 1867, a weakened Austria shared some power, creating the Austro-Hungarian Monarchy. The two states were separate for internal matters, united for military and foreign policy until 1918.

10. Hunfalvy's comment in Berlin, rejecting race as a factor – "there are no racial differences in Europe" – was doubtless his reaction to racial anti-Semitism at that time, in Germany and Hungary. Later, Finno-Ugric studies also declared, "the origins of the language and the people are not the same" (Pusztay 1977:93). For Hunfalvy's scholarly context and background, see Zsigmond (1977) and Békés (1997).

11. There were also ways of upscaling that were not race-based. Motivated by Protestant missionary projects of bible translation, an international conference on script and orthography for all languages resulted in a model of articulatory phonetics (Lepsius 1981 [1863]), aspects of which are still used today. But the proposed universal orthography went nowhere. See Irvine (forthcoming).

12. For the history of German-speaking anthropology, see Gingrich (2005), Penny and Bunzl (2003), and Massin (1996). See Conrad (2012) for an overview of German colonialism. For German-speaking African linguistics, see Pugach (2012). The "Hamitic hypothesis" that inspired Lepsius's and Meinhof's racial histories was also dismissed by Whitney and Sapir but was not rejected more generally till the 1950s, if then. The Turkic origin of Hungarians continued in popular media throughout the twentieth century and in right-wing circles today (Laakso 2005:17).

13. Brix (1982) discusses these census debates; Keleti (1882) presents the Hungarian view; see Hansen (2015) on Prussia and more generally Anderson (1991) on censuses and maps.

14. Silverstein (2013a) argues for a long-term methodological continuity.

15. Wegener (1880) outlined the strategy and goals of the Neogrammarians in the study of dialects, in an article that was much like a research proposal; Murray (2010) provides a useful review of Neogrammarian dialect work; Schrambke (2010) tracks traditional dialectology; and Morpurgo Davies (1992) gives an excellent overview of the era.

16. Andreas Schmeller had made an early atlas of Bavarian dialects in 1820; like state maps of languages, it stopped at Bavaria's borders (Benes 2008).

17. See Schilling (1942). Even Austrian-German dialects were outside the early German dialect atlas. Boundedness of dialects was disputed in the twentieth century (Gauchat 1903) and continues to be so in the twenty-first (see review and alternative proposals in Auer 2005; Auer and Schmidt 2010).

18. Schuchardt is known for his opposition to the Neogrammarians on the regularity of sound change. We believe his views on boundaries are more important. The usual charge that he lacked a theory of linguistic structure is contested (Baggioni 1989); but we are less interested in that issue than in his novel methodologies.

19. Chakrabarty (2000) introduced this useful turn of phrase.

References

Aarsleff, Hans. 1982. *From Locke to Saussure: Essays on the Study of Language and Intellectual History*. Minneapolis: University of Minnesota Press.

Abbott, Andrew. 2000. *Chaos of Disciplines*. Chicago: University of Chicago Press.

Abondolo, Daniel, ed. 1998. *The Uralic Languages*. London: Routledge.

Abrams, Floyd. 2017. *The Soul of the First Amendment*. New Haven, CT: Yale University Press.

Agha, Asif. 2005a. "Introduction: Semiosis across encounters." *Journal of Linguistic Anthropology* 15(1):1–5.

    2005b. "Voice, footing, enregisterment." *Journal of Linguistic Anthropology* 15(1):38–59.

    2007. *Language and Social Relations*. Cambridge: Cambridge University Press.

Agha, Asif, and Stanton Wortham, eds. 2005. "Discourse across speech events: Intertextuality and interdiscursivity in social life." Special issue of *Journal of Linguistic Anthropology* 15(1).

Alden, John Richard. 1961. *The First South*. Baton Rouge: Louisiana State University Press.

Alder, Ken. 1995. "A revolution to measure: The political economy of the metric system in France." In *The Values of Precision*, ed. M. N. Wise, 39–71. Princeton: Princeton University Press.

    1997. *Engineering the Revolution: Arms and Enlightenment in France, 1763–1815*. Princeton: Princeton University Press.

    2002. *The Measure of All Things: The Seven-Year Odyssey and Hidden Error That Transformed the World*. London: Little, Brown.

    2003. *The Measure of the World*. Dibner Library Lecture. Washington, DC: Smithsonian Institution.

Althusser, Louis. 1994 [1970]. "Ideology and ideological state apparatuses (Notes toward an investigation)." In *Mapping Ideology*, ed. Slavoj Žižek, 100–140. London: Verso.

Amsterdamska, Olga. 1987. *Schools of Thought: The Development of Linguistics from Bopp to Saussure*. Dordrecht: D. Reidel.

Anburey, Thomas. 1789. *Travels through the Interior Parts of America in a Series of Letters*. Vol. 2. London: William Lane.

Anderson, Benedict. 1991. *Imagined Communities: Reflections on the Origin and Spread of Nationalism*. Rev. ed. London: Verso.

Andrásfalvy, Bertalan. 1978. "A táji munkamegosztás néprajzi vizsgálata." *Ethnographia* 2:231–243.

Andrews, William L. 1986. *To Tell a Free Story: The First Century of Afro-American Autobiography, 1760–1865*. Urbana: University of Illinois Press.

Appleby, Joyce O. 1992. "The 'agrarian myth' in the early Republic." In *Liberalism and Republicanism in the Historical Imagination*, 253–276. Cambridge, MA: Harvard University Press.

2000. *Inheriting the Revolution: The First Generation of Americans*. Cambridge, MA: Harvard University Press.

Auer, Peter. 2005. "The construction of linguistic borders and the linguistic construction of borders." *Current Issues in Linguistic Theory* 273:3–30.

Auer, Peter, and Jürgen Erich Schmidt, eds. 2010. *Language and Space: An International Handbook of Linguistic Variation*. Vol. 1. *Theories and Methods*. New York: Walter de Gruyter.

Ayers, Edward A., and Peter S. Onuf, eds. 1996. *All over the Map: Rethinking American Regions*. Baltimore: Johns Hopkins University Press.

Baggioni, Daniel. 1989. "Hugo Schuchardts Beitrag zur allgemeinen Sprachwissenschaft." *Historiographia Linguistica* 16(3):327–350.

Bakhtin, M. M. 1981. *Discourse in the Novel*. Austin: University of Texas Press.

1984. *Problems of Dostoevsky's Poetics*. Minneapolis: University of Minnesota Press.

Ball, Christopher. 2014. "On dicentization." *Journal of Linguistic Anthropology* 24(2):151–173.

Baron, Dennis E. 1982. *Grammar and Good Taste: Reforming the American Language*. New Haven, CT: Yale University Press.

Barrie, James. 1904. *Peter Pan*. Play produced at Duke of York's Theatre, London.

Barth, Fredrik. 1969. "Introduction." In *Ethnic Groups and Boundaries: The Social Organization of Culture Difference*, ed. Fredrik Barth, 9–38. Boston: Little, Brown.

Bassin, Mark. 1991. "Inventing Siberia: Visions of the Russian East in the early nineteenth century." *American Historical Review* 96(3):763–794.

Basso, Keith. 1979. *Portraits of the "Whiteman."* Cambridge: Cambridge University Press.

Bateson, Gregory. 1935. "Culture contact and schismogenesis." *Man* 35:178–183.

1958 [1936]. *Naven: The Culture of the Iatmul People of New Guinea as Revealed through a Study of the "Naven" Ceremonial*. Stanford: Stanford University Press.

Bauman, Richard. 2004. *A World of Others' Words*. Malden, MA: Blackwell.

Bauman, Richard, and Charles Briggs. 2003. *Voices of Modernity: Language Ideologies and the Politics of Inequality*. New York: Cambridge University Press.

Beer, Mathias, and Dittmar Dahlmann, eds. 1999. *Migration nach Ost- und Südosteuropa von 18. bis zum Beginn des19. Jahrhunderts*. Stuttgart: Jan Thorbecke Verlag.

Békés, Vera. 1997. *A hiányzó paradigma*. Debrecen: Latin Betűk.

Benes, Tuska. 2008. *In Babel's Shadow: Language, Philology and the Nation in Nineteenth Century Germany*. Detroit: Wayne State University Press.

Bercovitch, Sacvan. 1978. *The American Jeremiad*. Madison: University of Wisconsin Press.

Bindorffer, Györgyi. 2001. *Kettős identitás: Etnikai és nemzeti azonosságtudat Dunabogdányban*. Budapest: Új Mandátum Könyvkiadó.

Bleek, Wilhelm. 1869 [1867]. *On the Origin of Language*. ed. Ernst Haeckel, trans. Thomas Davidson. New York: L.W. Schmidt.

Blommaert, Jan, ed. 1999. *Language Ideological Debates*. Berlin: de Gruyter.

2015. "Chronotopes, scales, and complexity in the study of language." *Annual Review of Anthropology* 44:105–116.

Bonfiglio, Thomas. 2002. *Race and the Rise of Standard American*. Berlin: Mouton de Gruyter.

Bourdieu, Pierre. 1977. *Outline of a Theory of Practice*. Trans. Richard Nice. Cambridge: Cambridge University Press.

  1984. *Distinction: A Social Critique of the Judgement of Taste*. Cambridge, MA: Harvard University Press.

  1991. *Language and Symbolic Power*. Trans. G. Raymond and M. Adamson, ed. John Thompson. Cambridge, MA: Harvard University Press.

Boyd, Julian, ed. 1950. *The Papers of Thomas Jefferson*. Princeton: Princeton University Press.

Briggs, Charles. 1986. *Learning How to Ask*. Cambridge: Cambridge University Press.

Brisard, Frank. 2002. *Grounding: The Epistemic Footing of Deixis and Reference*. Berlin: de Gruyter.

Brix, Emil. 1982. *Umgangsprache in Altösterreich zwischen Agitation und Assimilation*. Vienna: Böhlau.

Brown, Peter H., and Daniel G. Abel. 2003. *Outgunned: Up Against the NRA*. New York: Free Press.

Brown, Roger, and Albert Gilman. 1960. "The pronouns of power and solidarity." In *Style in Language*, ed. Thomas Sebeok, 253–276. Cambridge, MA: MIT Press.

Brubaker, Rogers. 2004. *Ethnicity without Groups*. Cambridge, MA: Harvard University Press.

  2015. *Grounds for Difference*. Cambridge, MA: Harvard University Press.

Buchler, Justus. 1955. "Introduction." In *Philosophical Writings of Peirce*, ed. Justus Buchler, ix–xvi. New York: Dover.

Bucholtz, Mary. 2010. *White Kids: Language, Youth and Style in Youth Identity*. New York: Cambridge University Press.

Bushman, Richard L. 1992. *The Refinement of America: Persons, Houses, Cities*. New York: Vintage Books.

Butler, Judith. 1991. "Imitation and gender insubordination." In *Inside/Out: Lesbian Themes, Gay Themes*, ed. Diana Fuss, 13–31. New York: Routledge.

Byron, George Gordon, Lord. 1814. *The Corsair*. London: John Murray.

Carr, E. Summerson. 2011. *Scripting Addiction*. Princeton: Princeton University Press.

Carr, E. Summerson, and Michael Lempert, eds. 2016. *Scale: Discourse and Dimensions of Social Life*. Berkeley: University of California Press.

Caruthers, William Alexander. 1834. *The Kentuckian in New-York; or, The Adventures of Three Southerners by a Virginian*. New York: Harper.

Castrén, M. Alexander. 1853. *Reiseerinnerungen aus den Jahren 1838–1844*, ed. A. Schiefner. Saint Petersburg: Buchdrückerei der Kaiserlichen Akademie der Wissenschaft.

Cavanaugh, Jillian R., and Shalini Shankar, eds. 2017. *Language and Materiality: Ethnographic and Theoretical Explorations*. New York: Cambridge University Press.

Chakrabarty, Dipesh. 2000. *Provincializing Europe: Postcolonial Thought and Historical Difference*. Princeton: Princeton University Press.

Chumley, Lily, and Nicholas Harkness. 2013. "Introduction: Qualia." *Anthropological Theory* 13(1–2):3–11.

City of Baltimore, Department of Transportation. 2004. "City benches to get a face-lift." *Transportation News*, September 1.

Clapp, Elizabeth J. 2003. "The boundaries of femininity: The travels and writings of Mrs. Anne Royall, 1823–31." *American Nineteenth Century History* 4:1–28.
  2016. *A Notorious Woman: Anne Royall in Jacksonian America.* Charlottesville: University of Virginia Press.
Cmiel, Kenneth. 1990. *Democratic Eloquence: The Fight over Popular Speech in Nineteenth Century America.* Berkeley: University of California Press.
Coen, Deborah R. 2016. "Big is a thing of the past: Climate change and methodology in the history of ideas." *Journal of the History of Ideas* 77(2):305–321.
Cole, David. 2016. "The terror of our guns." *New York Review of Books* 63(July 14):12.
Colvin, Lucie. 1974. "Islam and the state of Kajoor: A case of successful resistance to jihad." *Journal of African History* 4:587–607.
Comaroff, Jean, and John Comaroff. 1991. *Of Revelation and Revolution: Christianity, Colonialism, and Consciousness in South Africa.* Chicago: University of Chicago Press.
Conforti, Joseph A. 2001. *Imagining New England: Explorations of Regional Identity from the Pilgrims to the Mid-Twentieth Century.* Chapel Hill: University of North Carolina Press.
Conrad, Sebastien. 2012. *German Colonialism: A Short History.* New York: Cambridge University Press.
Coupland, Nikolas. 2007. *Style: Language Variation and Identity.* Cambridge: Cambridge University Press.
  ed. 2016. *Sociolinguistics: Theoretical Debates.* Cambridge: Cambridge University Press.
Crowley, Tony. 1997. "Uniform, excellent, common: Reflections on standards in language." *Language Sciences* 19(1):15–21.
Crowther, Samuel Ajayi. 1852. *Vocabulary of the Yoruba Language.* London: Seeleys.
Cust, Robert Needham. 1883. *A Sketch of the Modern Languages of Africa, Accompanied by a Language Map.* London: Trübner.
  1887. *Linguistic and Oriental Essays*, Second Series. London: Trübner.
Dard, Jean. 1826. *Grammaire wolofe.* Paris: Imprimerie Royale.
Das, Sonia. 2016. *Linguistic Rivalries: Tamil Migrants and Anglo-Franco Conflicts.* New York: Oxford University Press.
Davis, Charles T., and Henry Louis Gates, Jr. eds. 1985. *The Slave's Narrative.* Oxford: Oxford University Press.
de Beauvoir, Simone. 1968. *The Second Sex.* New York: Modern Library.
de Certeau, Michel, Dominique Julia, and Jacques Revel, eds. 1975. *Une politique de la langue: La révolution française et les patois.* Paris: Gallimard.
Defoe, Daniel. 1720. *The Life, Adventures, and Pyracies, of the Famous Captain Singleton.* London: Brotherton.
  1999 [1724]. *A General History of the Robberies and Murders of the Most Notorious Pirates.* New York: Carroll & Graf.
Deniau, Xavier. 2001. *La Francophonie.* 5th ed. Paris: Presses Universitaires de France.
Derrida, Jacques. 1976. *Of Grammatology.* Baltimore: Johns Hopkins University Press.
  1988. *Limited Inc.* Evanston, IL: Northwestern University Press.
Diop, Abdoulaye-Bara. 1981. *La société wolof: Tradition et changement.* Paris: Karthala.
Diouf, Mamadou. 1990. *Le Kajoor au XIXe siècle: Pouvoir ceddo et conquête coloniale.* Paris: Karthala.

2000. *Histoire du Sénégal*. Paris: Maisonneuve et Larose.

Dlamini, Sibusisiwe Nombuso. 2005. *Youth and Identity Politics in South Africa 1990–1994*. Toronto: University of Toronto Press.

Douglass, Frederick. 1950–1975 [1849]. "Gavitt's original Ethiopian serenaders." *North Star,* June 29. Reprinted in *The Life and Writings of Frederick Douglass*, 5 vols., ed. Philip S. Foner, 1:141–142. New York: International.

Du Bois, W. E. B. 1896. *The Suppression of the African Slave Trade to the United States of America*. Oxford: Oxford University Press.

1903. *The Souls of Black Folk*. Chicago: McClurg.

Dumont, Louis. 1980 [1979]. *Homo Hierarchicus: The Caste System and Its Implications*. Chicago: University of Chicago Press.

Dunlop, Catherine Tatiana. 2015. *Cartophilia: Maps and the Search for Identity in the French-German Borderland*. Chicago: University of Chicago Press.

Duranti, Alessandro. 1994. *From Grammar to Politics*. Berkeley: University of California Press.

Duranti, Alessandro, and Charles Goodwin, eds. 1992. *Rethinking Context: Language as an Interactive Phenomenon*. Cambridge: Cambridge University Press.

Dworkin, Ronald. 2010. "The decision that threatens democracy." *New York Review of Books*, May 31.

Eagleton, Terry. 2007. *Ideology: An Introduction*. 2nd ed. London: Verso.

Eckert, Penelope. 2000. *Linguistic Variation as Social Practice*. Oxford: Blackwell.

Eisenlohr, Patrick. 2006. *Little India: Diaspora, Time and Ethnolinguistic Belonging in Hindu Mauritius*. Berkeley: University of California Press.

Elgin, Catherine Z. 2000. "Worldmaker: Nelson Goodman, 1906–1998." *Journal of General Philosophy* 31:1–18.

Erb, Mária. 2012. "Sprachgebrauch der Ungarndeutschen: Tendenzen und Perspektiven." In *Traditionspflege und Erneuerung: Perspektiven der deutschen Nationalität in Ungarn im 21. Jahrhundert*, ed. Marta Müller and Kerekes Gábor, 35–57. Budapest: Ad Librum.

Erb, Mária, and Elizabeth Knipf-Komlósi, eds. 2007. *Tradition und Innovation: Beiträge zu neueren ungarndeutschen Forschungen*. Budapest: ELTE Universität Germanistisches Institut.

Erman, Adolph. 1850. *Travels in Siberia: Down the Obi, to the Polar Circle*. Vols. 1–2. Trans. W. D. Cooley. Philadelphia: Lea and Blanchard.

Errington, Joseph. 1985. "On the nature of the sociolinguistic sign: Describing the Javanese speech levels." In *Semiotic Mediation*, ed. Elizabeth Mertz and Richard Parmentier, 287–310. Orlando, FL: Academic.

Espeland, Wendy, and Mitchell L. Stevens. 1998. "Commensuration as a social process." *Annual Review of Sociology* 24:313–343.

Evans-Pritchard, E. E. 1969 [1940]. *The Nuer: A Description of the Modes of Livelihood and Political Institutions of a Nilotic People*. Oxford: Clarendon.

1976 [1936]. *Witchcraft, Oracles and Magic among the Azande*. Oxford: Clarendon.

Faidherbe, Louis. 1887. *Langues sénégalaises: Wolof, arabe-hassania, soninké, sérère*. Paris: Leroux.

Fal, Arame, Rosine Santos, and Jean Léonce Doneux. 1990. *Dictionnaire wolof-français, suivi d'un index français-wolof*. Paris: Karthala.

Fanon, Frantz. 1967 [1952]. *Black Skin, White Masks*. Trans. Charles Lam Markmann. New York: Grove Press.

Fata, Márta, ed. 1997. *Die Schwäbische Türkei: Lebensformen der Ethnien in Südwestungarn.* Sigmaringen: Jan Thorbecke Verlag.

Faust, Drew Gilpin. 1988. *Confederate Nationalism: Ideology and Identity in the Civil War South.* Baton Rouge: Louisiana University Press.

Ferguson, Charles. 1983. "Sports announcer talk: Syntactic aspects of register variation." *Language in Society* 12:153–172.

Fernandes, Valentim. 1940 [1509]. *O Manuscrito "Valentim Fernandes," oferecido à Academia por Joaquim Bensaúde.* Lisbon: Academia Portuguesa da História.

Fichte, Johann Gottlieb. 2008 [1808]. *Addresses to the German Nation,* ed. and trans. Gregory Moore. Cambridge: Cambridge University Press.

Fleck, Ludwig. 1979 [1935]. *Genesis and Development of a Scientific Fact.* Chicago: University of Chicago Press.

Fliegelman, Jay. 1993. *Declaring Independence: Jefferson. Natural Language and the Cult of Performance.* Palo Alto, CA: Stanford University Press.

Floan, Howard Russell. 1958. *The South in Northern Eyes.* Austin: University of Texas Press.

Florusbosch, J. Henrike. 2011. "The powers of observation: Ideologies and practices of paying attention among rural Malian Muslims in Mande." PhD dissertation, University of Michigan.

Foner, Eric. 1995 [1970]. *Free Soil, Free Labor, Free Men: The Ideology of the Republican Party before the Civil War.* New York: Oxford University Press.

1998. *The Story of American Freedom.* New York: Norton.

Formisano, Ronald P. 2008. *For the People: American Populist Movements from the Revolution to the 1850s.* Chapel Hill: University of North Carolina Press.

Forsythe, James. 1992. *A History of the Peoples of Siberia: Russian's North Asian Colony, 1581–1990.* New York: Cambridge University Press.

Foucault, Michel. 1972. *The Archaeology of Knowledge.* Trans. Sheridan Smith. New York: Pantheon.

1977. "Nietzsche, genealogy, history." In *Language, Counter-Memory, Practice,* ed. D. F. Bouchard, 139–164. Ithaca, NY: Cornell University Press.

1990 [1978]. "Qu'est-ce que la critique?" *Bulletin de la Société française de philosophie* 84(2):35–63.

1996 [1978]. "The impossible prison." In *Foucault Live (Interviews, 1961–1984),* ed. Sylvère Lotringer, trans. Lysa Hochroth and John Johnston, 275–291. New York: Semiotext(e).

Fox, Dixon Ryan. 1940. *Yankees and Yorkers.* New York: New York University Press.

Fraser, Nancy, and Linda Gordon. 1994. "A genealogy of dependency: Tracing a keyword of the U.S. welfare state." *Signs* 19(2):309–336.

Freeden, Michael. 1996. *Ideologies and Political Theory: A Conceptual Approach.* Oxford: Clarendon.

2003. *Ideology: A Very Short Introduction.* New York: Oxford University Press.

Füzes, Miklós. 1986. "A népesség anyanyelv szerinti összetételét befolyásoló tényezők dél-kelet Dunántúlon 1941 és 1945 között." *Baranyai Helytörténetírás* 1985–1986:715–772.

Gal, Susan. 1987. "Codeswitching and consciousness in the European periphery." *American Ethnologist* 14(4):637–653.

1989. "Language and political economy." *Annual Review of Anthropology* 18:345–367.

1991. "Bartók's funeral: Representations of Europe in Hungarian political rhetoric." *American Ethnologist* 18(3):440–458.

1994. "Diversity and contestation in linguistic ideologies: German-speakers in Hungary." *Language in Society* 22:337–359.

2001. "Linguistic theories and national images in nineteenth century Hungary." In *Languages and Publics: The Making of Authority*, ed. Susan Gal and Kathryn A. Woolard, 30–45. Manchester: St. Jerome's Press.

2002. "A semiotics of the public/private distinction." *differences: A Journal of Feminist Cultural Studies* 13(1):77–95.

2005. "Language ideologies compared: Metaphors of public and private." *Journal of Linguistic Anthropology* 15(1):23–37.

2006. "Contradictions of standard language in Europe: Implications for the study of practices and publics." *Social Anthropology* 14:163–181.

2011a. "Polyglot nationalism: Alternative perspectives on language in 19th century Hungary." *Langage et société* 136:1–24.

2011b. "Language and political space." In *Language and Space*, ed. Peter Auer and Jürgen Erich Schmidt, 33–50. Berlin: de Gruyter.

2012. "Sociolinguistic regimes and the management of 'diversity.'" In *Language in Late Capitalism: Pride and Profit*, ed. Monica Heller and Alexandre Duchêne, 22–42. New York: Routledge.

2013. "Tastes of talk: Qualia and the moral flavor of signs." *Anthropological Theory* 31:31–48.

2015a. "Politics of translation." *Annual Review of Anthropology* 44:225–240.

2015b. "Imperial linguistics and polyglot nationalism in Austria-Hungary: Hunfalvy, Gumplowicz, Schuchardt." *Balkanistica* 28:151–174.

2016a. "Sociolinguistic differentiation." In *Sociolinguistics: Theoretical Debates*, ed. Nikolas Coupland, 115–135. New York: Cambridge University Press.

2016b. "Scale-making: Comparison and perspective as ideological projects." In *Scale: Discourse and Dimensions of Social Life*, ed. E. Summerson Carr and Michael Lempert, 91–111. Berkeley: University of California Press.

2017a. "Qualia as value and knowledge: Histories of European porcelain." *Signs and Society* 15(1):128–153.

2017b. "Visions and revisions of minority languages: Standardization and its dilemmas." In *Standardizing Minority Languages in the Global Periphery: Competing Ideologies of Authority and Authenticity*, ed. Pia Lane and James Costa, 222–242. New York: Routledge.

2018. "Registers in circulation: The social organization of interdiscursivity." *Signs and Society* 6(1):1–24.

Gal, Susan, and Judith T. Irvine. 1995. "The boundaries of languages and disciplines: How ideologies construct difference." *Social Research* 62(4):967–1001.

Gal, Susan, and Gail Kligman. 2000. *The Politics of Gender after Socialism*. Princeton: Princeton University Press.

Gal, Susan, Julia Kowalski, and Erin Moore. 2015. "Rethinking translation in feminist NGOs: Rights and empowerment across borders." *Social Politics* 22(4):610–635.

Gal, Susan, and Kathryn A. Woolard. 2014 [2001]. "Constructing languages and publics: Authority and representation." In *Languages and Publics: The Making of Authority*, ed. Susan Gal and Kathryn A. Woolard, 1–12. New York: Routledge.

eds. 2014 [2001]. *Languages and Publics: The Making of Authority*. New York: Routledge.

Galison, Peter. 2003. *Einstein's Clocks; Poincaré's Maps*. New York: Norton.

Gauchat, Louis. 1903. "Gibt es Mundartgrenzen?" *Archiv für das Studium der neueren Sprachen und Literaturen LVII, CXI*: 365–402.

Geertz, Clifford. 1973 [1964]. "Ideology as a cultural system." In *Interpretation of Cultures*, 193–233. New York: Basic Books.

Gelman, Susan. 2003. *The Essential Child: Origins of Essentialism in Everyday Thought*. New York: Oxford University Press.

Geraci, Robert P. 2001. *Window on the East: National and Imperial Identities in Late Tsarist Russia*. Ithaca, NY: Cornell University Press.

Gingrich, Andre. 2005. "The German-speaking countries." In *One Discipline Four Ways: British, German, French and American Anthropology*, ed. Fredrik Barth et al., 60–153. Chicago: University of Chicago Press.

Gleick, James. 1987. *Chaos: Making a New Science*. New York: Penguin.

Gluckman, Max. 1940. "Analysis of a social situation in modern Zululand." *Bantu Studies* 14:1–30.

1972. "Foreword." In Victor Turner, *Schism and Continuity in an African Society*, xv–xx. Manchester: Manchester University Press.

Goffman, Erving. 1981. *Forms of Talk*. Philadelphia: University of Pennsylvania Press.

Goodman, Nelson. 1972. "Seven strictures on similarity." In *Problems and Projects*, 437–446. Indianapolis: Bobbs-Merrill.

1978. *Ways of Worldmaking*. Indianapolis: Hackett.

Graan, Andrew 2016. "The nation brand regime: Nation branding and the semiotic regimentation of public communication in contemporary Macedonia." *Signs and Society* 4(1):S70–S105.

Graber, Kathryn, and Jesse D. Murray. 2015. "The local history of an imperial category: Language and religion in Russia's eastern borderlands, 1860–1930." *Slavic Review* 74(1):127–152.

Grabill, Jeffrey, and Stuart Blythe. 2010. "Citizens doing science in public spaces: Rhetorical invention, semiotic remediation, and simple little texts." In *Exploring Semiotic Remediation as Discourse Practice*, ed. Paul Prior and Julie Hengst, 184–205. New York: Palgrave Macmillan.

Gramsci, Antonio. 1985. *Selections from Cultural Writings*, ed. David Forgacs and Geoffrey Nowell-Smith. Cambridge, MA: Harvard University Press.

Grandgent, Charles. 1920. "The dog's letter." In Grandgent, Charles, *Old and New Sundry Papers*, 31–56. Cambridge, MA: Harvard University Press.

Granger, Gilles-Gaston. 1954. "Langage universelle et formalisation des sciences: Un fragment inédit de Condorcet." *Revue d'histoire des sciences* 7:197–219.

Grant, Bruce. 1993. "Siberia hot and cold: Reconstructing the image of Siberian indigenous peoples." In *Between Heaven and Hell: The Myth of Siberia in Russian Culture*, ed. Galya Diment and Yuri Slezkine, 227–254. New York: St. Martin's Press.

Grasso, Christopher. 1999. *A Speaking Democracy: Transforming Public Discourse in Eighteenth Century Connecticut*. Chapel Hill: University of North Carolina Press.

Grégoire, Henri. 1975 [1794a]. *Rapport sur la nécessité et les moyens d'anéantir les patois et d'universaliser l'usage de la langue française*. Reprinted in *Une politique de la langue: La révolution française et les patois*, ed. Michel de Certeau, Dominique Julia, and Jacques Revel, 300–317. Paris: Gallimard.

1794b. *Rapport sur les destructions opérées par le Vandalisme, et sur les moyens de le réprimer*. Paris: Convention Nationale. Imprimerie Nationale.

Grimes, William. 2008 [1826]. *Life of William Grimes, the Runaway Slave*. New York: Oxford University Press.

Gulya, János. 1974. "Some eighteenth century antecedents of nineteenth century linguistics: The discovery of Finno-Ugrian." In *Studies in the History of Linguistics: Traditions and Paradigms*, ed. Dell Hymes, 258–276. Bloomington: University of Indiana Press.

Gumperz, John J. 1982. *Discourse Strategies*. New York: Cambridge University Press.

Gumperz, John J., and Dell Hymes, eds. 1972. *Directions in Sociolinguistics: The Ethnography of Communication*. New York: Holt.

Gupta, Akhil, and James Ferguson. 1997. "Discipline and practice: 'The field' as site, method, and location in anthropology." In *Anthropological Locations: Boundaries and Grounds of a Field Science*, ed. A. Gupta and J. Ferguson, 1–46. Berkeley: University of California Press.

Gustafson, Thomas. 2012. *Representative Words: Politics, Literature and the American Language, 1776–1865*. New York: Cambridge University Press.

Guyer, Jane. 2004. *Marginal Gains: Monetary Transaction in Atlantic Africa*. Chicago: University of Chicago Press.

Habermas, Jürgen. 1998. *The Structural Transformation of the Public Sphere*. Cambridge, MA: MIT Press.

Hacking, Ian. 1999. *The Social Construction of What?* Cambridge, MA: Harvard University Press.

Hagège, Claude. 1990. *The Dialogic Species: A Linguistic Contribution to the Social Sciences*. Trans. Sharon Shelly. New York: Columbia University Press.

Hall, Basil. 1828. *Travels in North America in the Years 1827–1828*. Philadelphia: Carey, Lea and Carey.

Hansen, Janson D. 2015. *Mapping the Germans: Statistical Science, Cartography, and the Visualization of the German Nation, 1848–1914*. Oxford: Oxford University Press.

Haraway, Donna. 1991. "Situated knowledges." In *Simians, Cyborgs and Women*, 183–201. New York: Routledge.

Havel, Vaclav. 1985. "The power of the powerless." In *The Power of the Powerless*, ed. Vaclav Havel, 23–96. Armonk, NY: M.E. Sharpe.

Hebdige, Dick. 1979. *Subculture: The Meaning of Style*. London: Methuen.

Heidegger, Martin. 1996 [1978]. *Being and Time: A Translation of Sein und Zeit*. Trans. Joan Stambaugh. Albany: State University of New York Press.

Heller, Monica. 2011. *Paths to Post-nationalism: A Critical Ethnography of Language and Identity*. New York: Oxford University Press.

Heller, Monica, and Alexandre Duchêne, eds. 2012. *Language in Late Capitalism: Pride and Profit*. New York: Routledge.

Herzfeld, Michael. 1987. *Anthropology through the Looking Glass*. New York: Cambridge University Press.

Hill, Jane. 1986. "The refiguration of the anthropology of language." *Cultural Anthropology* 1(1):89–102.

2008. *The Everyday Language of White Racism*. Malden, MA: Wiley-Blackwell.

Hill, Jane, and Judith T. Irvine, eds. 1993. *Responsibility and Evidence in Oral Discourse*. New York: Cambridge University Press.

Hirnsperger, Markus. 2013. "Finno-ugrische Ethnologie und Nationalismus im 19. Jahrhundert: Sjögren, Castrén und Ahlqvist in Spannungsfeld nationaler Ideen." In *Wege zum Norden: Wiener Forschungen zu Arktis und Subarktis*, ed. Stefan Donecker, Igor Eberhard, and Markus Hirnsperger, 87–106. Vienna: Lit Verlag.

Hoyt, David L. 2006. "Dialects of modernization in France and Italy, 1865–1900." In *The Study of Language and the Politics of Community in Global Context*, ed. David L. Hoyt and Karen Oslund, 85–118. Lanham, MD: Lexington Books.

Hundley, Daniel R. 1860. *Social Relations in Our Southern States*. New York: H.B. Price.

Hunfalvy, Pál. 1874. "Észrevételek Müller Miksa nyelvtudományi felolvasásaira, különösen a nyolczadikra." In *Müller Miksa felolvasásai a nyelvtudományról*, ed. Zsigmond Simonyi, 395–413. Budapest: Akadémiai Kiadó.

1875. *Az éjszaki osztják nyelv*. Budapest: Magyar Tudományos Akadémia.

1876a. "On the study of Turanian languages." In *Transactions of the Second Session of the International Congress of Orientalists Held in London in September 1874*, ed. Robert K. Douglas, 64–97. London: Trübner.

1876b. *Magyarország ethnográphiája*. Budapest: A Magyar Tudományos Akadémia Könyvkiadó.

1882. "Ueber das bildende Princip der Nationen." In *Abhandlungen und Vortäge des fünften internationalen Orientalisten-Congresses gehalten zu Berlin im September 1881*, Zweite Hälfte. Berlin: A. Asher.

Hutterer, Carl. 1991. *Aufsätze zur deutschen Dialektologie*. Budapest: Tankönyvkiadó.

Ignatiev, Noel. 1995. *How the Irish Became White*. New York: Routledge.

Inoue, Miyako, ed. 2004. "The history of ideology and the ideology of history." Special issue of *Journal of Linguistic Anthropology* 14(1).

2006. *Vicarious Language: Gender and Linguistic Modernity in Japan*. Berkeley: University of California Press.

Irvine, Judith T. 1974. "Strategies of status manipulation in the Wolof greeting." In *Explorations in the Ethnography of Speaking*, ed. R. Bauman and J. Sherzer, 167–191. Cambridge: Cambridge University Press.

1978a. "When is genealogy history? Wolof genealogies in comparative perspective." *American Ethnologist* 5:651–674.

1978b. "Wolof noun classification: The social setting of divergent change." *Language in Society* 7:37–64.

1990. "Registering affect: Heteroglossia in the linguistic expression of emotion." In *Language and the Politics of Emotion*, ed. Catherine A. Lutz and Lila Abu-Lughod, 126–161. Cambridge: Cambridge University Press.

1993. "Mastering African languages: The politics of linguistics in nineteenth century Senegal." *Social Analysis* 33:27–45.

1996. "Shadow conversations: The indeterminacy of participant roles." In *Natural Histories of Discourse*, ed. Michael Silverstein and Greg Urban, 131–159. Chicago: University of Chicago Press.

2001a. "Genres of conquest: From literature to science in colonial African linguistics." In *Verbal Art across Cultures: The Aesthetics and Proto-Aesthetics of Communication*, ed. Hubert Knoblauch and Helga Kotthoff, 63–90. Tübingen: Gunter Narr Verlag.

2001b. "The family romance of colonial linguistics: Gender and family in nineteenth century representations of African languages." In *Languages and Publics: The Making of Authority*, ed. Susan Gal and Kathryn A. Woolard, 13–29. Manchester: St. Jerome's Press.

2001c. "'Style' as distinctiveness: The culture and ideology of linguistic differentiation." In *Style and Sociolinguistic Variation*, ed. Penelope Eckert and John R. Rickford, 21–43. Cambridge: Cambridge University Press.

2005. "Commentary: Knots and tears in the interdiscursive fabric." *Journal of Linguistic Anthropology* 15:72–80.

2008. "Subjected words: African linguistics and the colonial encounter." *Language & Communication* 28:323–343.

2009. "Stance in a colonial encounter: How Mr. Taylor lost his footing." In *Stance: Sociolinguistic Perspectives*, ed. Alexandra Jaffe, 53–71. New York: Oxford University Press.

2011. "Language fields: Robert Needham Cust's language map of South Asia, 1878." In *Knowing India: Colonial and Modern Constructions of the Past, Essays in Honor of Thomas R. Trautmann*, ed. Cynthia Talbot, 31–54. New Delhi: Yoda Press.

2012. "Keeping ethnography in the study of communication." *Langage et Société* 139:47–66.

2015. "Language as cultural 'heritage.'" In *The Politics of Heritage in Africa: Economies, Histories and Infrastructures*, ed. Derek R. Peterson, Kodzo Gavua, and Ciraj Rassool, 191–208. Cambridge: Cambridge University Press.

2016. "Going upscale: Scales and scale-climbing as ideological projects." In *Scale: Discourse and Dimensions of Social Life*, ed. E. Summerson Carr and Michael Lempert, 213–231. Berkeley: University of California Press.

2018. "Divided values, shadow languages: Positioning and perspective in linguistic ideologies." *Signs and Society* 6(1):25–44.

Forthcoming. "Minerva's orthography: Early colonial projects for print literacy in African languages." *Social Dynamics*.

Irvine, Judith T., and Susan Gal. 2000. "Language ideology and linguistic differentiation." In *Regimes of Language*, ed. Paul Kroskrity, 35–83. Santa Fe: School of Advanced Research Press.

Irvine, Judith T., and Liz Gunner. 2018. "With respect to Zulu: Revisiting ukuHlonipha." *Anthropological Quarterly* 91(1):173–208.

Jaffe, Alexandra, ed. 2009. *Stance: Sociolinguistic Perspectives*. Oxford: Oxford University Press.

Jakobson, Roman. 1960. "Linguistics and poetics." In *Style in Language*, ed. Thomas Sebeok, 350–378. Cambridge, MA: MIT Press.

1990 [1956]. "Two aspects of language and two types of aphasic disorders." In *On Language*, ed. Linda R. Waugh and Monique Monville-Burston, 115–133. Cambridge, MA: Harvard University Press.

Jakobson, Roman, and Krystyna Pomorska. 1990 [1980]. "The concept of mark." In *On Language*, ed. Linda R. Waugh and Monique Monville-Burston, 134–140. Cambridge, MA: Harvard University Press.

Janson, Charles William. 1807. *The Stranger in America*. London: J. Cundee.

Johnson, Walter. 2013. *River of Dark Dreams: Slavery and Empire in the Cotton Kingdom*. Cambridge, MA: Harvard University Press.

Johnstone, Barbara. 2013. *Speaking Pittsburghese: The Story of a Dialect*. New York: Oxford University Press.

Joseph, John, and Talbot J. Taylor, eds. 1990. *Ideologies of Language*. Cambridge: Cambridge University Press.

Judson, Pieter. 2006. *Guardians of the Nation: Activists on the Language Frontiers of Imperial Austria*. Cambridge, MA: Harvard University Press.

Justus, James H. 2004. *Fetching the Old Southwest: Humorous Writing from Longstreet to Twain*. Columbia: University of Missouri Press.

Kairys, David. 2010. "Money isn't speech and corporations aren't people." *Slate: Jurisprudence, Law, Lawyers and the Court*, January 20.

Keane, Webb. 2003. "Semiotics and the social analysis of material things." *Language & Communication* 23:409–425.

    2018. "On semiotic ideology." *Signs and Society* 6(1):64–87.

Keil, Frank C., and Robert A. Wilson. 2000. *Explanation and Cognition*. Cambridge, MA: MIT Press.

Keleti, Károly. 1882. *Magyarország nemzetiségei az 1880 népszámlálás alapján*. Magyar Tudományos Akadémia.

Kelly, Aileen. 2005. "A great Russian prophet." Review of Anna Akhmatova's *The Word That Causes Death's Defeat: Poems of Memory*, trans. Nancy Anderson. *New York Review of Books*, November 3, 63–66.

Kennard, James K., Jr. 1845. "Who are our national poets?" *Knickerbocker* 26(4):331–341.

Kerber, Linda K. 1970. *Federalists in Dissent: Imagery and Ideology in Jeffersonian America*. Ithaca, NY: Cornell University Press.

    1992. "The paradox of women's citizenship in the early republic." *American Historical Review* 97(2):349–378.

Kobès, Alois. 1869. *Grammaire de la langue volofe*. Saint-Joseph de Ngasobil: Imprimerie de la Mission.

Koelle, Sigismund W. 1854a. *Grammar of the Bornu or Kanuri Language*. London: Church Missionary House.

    1854b. *Polyglotta Africana*. London: Church Missionary House.

Kopytoff, Igor. 1987. "Introduction." In *The African Frontier*, ed. Igor Kopytoff, 3–86. Bloomington: Indiana University Press.

Kovács, Katalin. 1990. "Polgárok egy sváb faluban." *Tér és Társadalom* 1:33–76.

Kramer, Elise. 2011. "The playful is political: The metapragmatics of internet rape-joke arguments." *Language in Society* 40:137–168.

Krige, Eileen. 1950. *The Social System of the Zulus*. Pietermaritzburg: Shuter and Shooter.

Kroskrity, Paul, ed. 2000. *Regimes of Language: Ideologies, Polities and Identities*. Santa Fe, NM: School of American Research Press.

Kuhn, Thomas. 1962. *The Structure of Scientific Revolutions*. Chicago: University of Chicago Press.

Kuipers, Joel. 1998. *Language, Identity and Marginality in Indonesia*. New York: Cambridge University Press.

Kula, Witold. 1986. *Measures and Men*. Princeton: Princeton University Press.

Laakso, Johanna. 2005. *Our Otherness: Finno-Ugrian Approaches to Women's Studies or Vice-Versa*. Vienna: Lit Verlag.

Lamoise, Paul. 1873. *Grammaire de la langue sérère avec des exemples et des exercices renfermant des documents très-utiles*. Saint-Joseph de Ngasobil (Sénégambie): Imprimerie de la mission.

Latour, Bruno. 1993. *We Have Never Been Modern*. Cambridge, MA: Harvard University Press.

   2005. *Reassembling the Social: An Introduction to Actor-Network Theory*. Oxford: Oxford University Press.

Lemon, Alaina. 2018. *Technologies for Intuition: Cold War Circles and Telepathic Rays*. Berkeley: University of California Press.

Lempert, Michael. 2012. *Discipline and Debate: The Language of Violence in a Tibetan Buddhist Monastery*. Berkeley: University of California Press.

Lempert, Michael, and Michael Silverstein. 2012. *Creatures of Politics: Media, Message, and the American Presidency*. Bloomington: Indiana University Press.

Lepsius, Carl Richard. 1880. *Nubische Grammatik mit einer Einleitung über die Völker und Sprachen Afrikas*. Berlin: W. Herty.

   1981 [1863]. *Standard Alphabet for Reducing Unwritten Languages and Foreign Graphic Systems to a Uniform Orthography in European Letters*. 2nd rev. ed. London: Trübner.

Linder & Associates. 2003. *Baltimore Believe: Progress Report: Phase 1*. New York: Linder & Associates.

Looby, Christopher. 1996. *Voicing America: Language, Literary Form and the Origins of the United States*. Chicago: University of Chicago Press.

Lott, Eric. 2013 [1993]. *Love and Theft: Blackface Minstrelsy and the American Working Class*. New York: Oxford University Press.

Lowell, James Russell. 1977 [1848]. "Introduction." In *The Biglow Papers: A Critical Edition*, ed. Thomas Wortham, 27–46. DeKalb: Northern Illinois University Press.

Lucy, John, ed. 1993. *Reflexive Language: Reported Speech and Metapragmatics*. New York: Cambridge University Press.

Lukin, Karina. 2017. "Matthias Alexander Castrén's notes on Nenets folklore." *Journal de la Société Finno-Ougrienne (Suomalais-Ugrilaisen Seuran Aikakauskirja)* 96:169–211.

Ly, Boubacar. 1967. "L'honneur dans les sociétés Ouolof et Toucouleur du Sénégal." *Présence Africaine* 61:32–67.

Maitz, Péter. 2008. "Linguistic nationalism in 19th century Hungary." *Journal of Historical Pragmatics* 9(1):20–47.

Malinowski, Bronislaw. 1978 [1935]. *Coral Gardens and Their Magic*. Vol. 2. *The Language of Magic and Gardening*. New York: Dover.

Manherz, Karl. 1977. *Sprachgeographie und Sprachsoziologie der deutschen Mundarten in Westungarn*. Budapest: Akadémiai Kiadó.

Marchand, Suzanne. 2009. *German Orientalism in the Age of Empire: Religion, Race and Scholarship*. New York: Cambridge University Press.

Marcus, George. 1995. "Ethnography in/of the world system: The emergence of multi-sited ethnography." *Annual Review of Anthropology* 24:95–117.

Marone, Oumar. 1969. "Essai sur les fondements de l'éducation sénégalaise à la lumière des métaphores aqueuses de la langue wolof." *Bulletin de l'Institut Fondamental d'Afrique Noire, sér. B* 31:787–852.

Marriott, McKim. 1959. "Interactional and attributional theories of caste ranking." *Man in India* 39:92–107.

Martin, Bernhard. 1933. "Georg Wenkers Kampf um seinen Sprachatlas (1875–1889)." In *Von Wenker zu Wrede*, ed. Luise Berthold, Berhard Martin, Heinz Dützmann, and Hans Kuhn, 1–37. Marburg: N.G. Elwert'sche Verlagsbuchhandlung.

Massin, Benoit. 1996. "From Virchow to Fischer: Physical anthropology and 'modern race theories' in Wilhelmine Germany." In *Volksgeist as Method and Ethic: Essays on Boasian Ethnography and the German Anthropological Tradition*, ed. George W. Stocking, 79–184. Madison: University of Wisconsin Press.

Mathews, Mitford McLeod, ed. 1931. *The Beginnings of American English: Essays and Comments*. Chicago: University of Chicago Press.

McAllister, Marvin. 2011. *Whiting Up: Whiteface Minstrels and Stage Europeans in African American Performance*. Durham: University of North Carolina Press.

McIntosh, Janet. 2005. "Language essentialism and social hierarchies among Giriama and Swahili." *Journal of Pragmatics* 3(7):1919–1944.

McLaughlin, Fiona, and Leonardo Villalón. 2011. "Mettre en scène la légitimité: Un discours du feu Xalifa Abdoul Aziz Sy et de son jottalikat." In *Communication wolof et société sénégalaise: Héritage et création*, ed. Anna Diagne, Sascha Kesseler, and Christian Meyer, 323–344. Paris: L'Harmattan.

Meek, Barbra. 2010. *We Are Our Language*. Tucson: University of Arizona Press.

Meinhof, Carl. 1912. *Die Sprachen der Hamiten*. Berlin: L. Friedrichsen.

Melish, Joanne Pope. 1998. *Disowning Slavery: Gradual Emancipation and "Race" in New England, 1780–1860*. Ithaca, NY: Cornell University Press.

Melzer, Scott. 2009. *Gun Crusaders: The NRA's Culture War*. New York: New York University Press.

Menand, Louis. 2001. *The Metaphysical Club*. New York: Farrar, Straus and Giroux.

Mertz, Elizabeth. 2007. *The Language of Law School*. New York: Oxford University Press.

Michell, Joel. 1986. "Measurement scales and statistics: A clash of paradigms." *Psychological Bulletin* 100(3):398–407.

1999. *An Introduction to the Logic of Psychological Measurement*. Hillsdale, NJ: Lawrence Erlbaum.

Minor, Lucian. 1834–1835. "Letters from New England, #1, 2, 3, 4, 5." *Southern Literary Messenger*, November, 84–88; December, 166–169; July, 217–219; February, 273–276; April, 421–426.

Moore, Adam. 2008. "Rethinking scale as a geographical category: From analysis to practice." *Progress in Human Geography* 32(2):203–225.

Morford, Janet. 1997. "Social indexicality in French pronominal address." *Journal of Linguistic Anthropology* 7(1):3–37.

Morgan, Mary S. 2001. "Models, stories and the economic world." *Journal of Economic Methodology* 8(3):361–384.

Morpurgo Davies, Anna. 1992. *History of Linguistics*. Vol. 4. *Nineteenth Century Linguistics*. New York: Routledge.

Morris, Charles. 1970. *The Pragmatic Movement in American Philosophy*. New York: George Braziller.

Mosko, Mark S., and Frederick H. Damon, eds. 2005. *On the Order of Chaos: Social Anthropology and the Science of Chaos*. New York: Berghahn Books.

Moyn, Samuel. 2010. *The Last Utopia: Human Rights in History*. Cambridge, MA: Harvard University Press.

Mugglestone, Lynda. 1997. *"Talking Proper": The Rise of Accent as Social Symbol*. New York: Oxford University Press.

Müller, F. Max. 1866. *Lectures on the Science of Language*. London: Longmans, Green.

Munkácsi, Bernát. 1892. "A vogul-osztják népköltés irodalma." In *Regék és énekek a világ teremtéséről, vogul szövegek és forditásaik*. Budapest: Magyar Tudományos Akadémia.

Munn, Nancy D. 1986. *The Fame of Gawa: A Symbolic Study of Value Transformation in a Massim Society*. Durham, NC: Duke University Press.

Murray, Robert W. 2010. "Language and space: The neogrammarian tradition." In *Language and Space: An International Handbook of Linguistic Variation*, ed. Peter Auer and Jürgen Erich Schmidt, 70–87. Berlin: de Gruyter.

Németh, Béla. 1900. *Geschichte der Grossgemeinde Németh-Bóly*. Pécs: Literarische und Buchdruckerei.

Nickels, Cameron C. 1993. *New England Humor: From the Revolution to the Civil War*. Knoxville: University of Tennessee Press.

North American Review. 1837. "An oration delivered on the anniversary of the New England Society." January, 237–261.

Nyelv és Tudomány. 2014. "Látogassa meg rokonait az állatkertben!" January 17. http//in.nyest.hu/renhirek/latogassa-meg-rokonait-az-allatkertben.

O'Brien, Michael. 2010. *Intellectual Life in the American South, 1810–1860*. Chapel Hill: University of North Carolina Press.

Ochs, Elinor. 2004. "Narrative lessons." In *A Companion to Linguistic Anthropology*, ed. Alessandro Duranti, 269–289. Oxford: Blackwell.

O'Donnell, Krista, Renata Bridenthal, and Nancy R. Reagin, eds. 2005. *The Heimat Abroad: The Boundaries of Germanness*. Ann Arbor: University of Michigan Press.

Olender, Maurice. 1992. *The Languages of Paradise: Race, Religion and Philology in the Nineteenth Century*. Cambridge, MA: Harvard University Press.

Onion. 2004. *The Onion ad Nauseam (Complete News Archives)* 15.

Onuf, Peter S. 1996. "Federalism, republicanism and the origins of American sectionalism." In *All over the Map: Rethinking American Regions*, ed. Edward A. Ayers and Peter Onuf, 11–37. Baltimore: Johns Hopkins University Press.

Osnos, Evan. 2016. "Making a killing: The business and politics of selling guns." *New Yorker* 92(June 27):36–45.

Otto, Ton, and Nils Bubandt, eds. 2010. *Experiments in Holism: Theory and Practice in Contemporary Anthropology*. Malden, MA: Wiley.

Parmentier, Richard. 1994. *Signs in Society: Studies in Semiotic Anthropology*. Bloomington: University of Indiana Press.

Paulding, James Kirke. 1817. *Letters from the South*. New York: James Eastburn.

Paulston, Christina. 1976. "Pronouns of address in Swedish: Social class semantics and a changing system." *Language in Society* 5(3):359–386.

Peirce, Charles Sanders. 1877. "The fixation of belief." *Popular Science Monthly* 12:1–15.

    1906. "Prolegomena to an Apology for Pragmaticism." *Monist* 16(4):492–546.

    1955a. "Logic as semiotic: The theory of signs." In *Philosophical Writings of Peirce*, ed. Justus Buchler, 98–119. New York: Dover.

    1955b. "Perceptual judgments." In *Philosophical Writings of Peirce*, ed. Justus Buchler, 302–305. New York: Dover.

    1955c. "Pragmatism in retrospect: A last formulation." In *The Philosophy of Peirce: Selected Writings*, ed. Justus Buchler, 269–289. London: Routledge, Kegan Paul.

1998 [1895]. "Of reasoning in general." In *The Essential Peirce*, vol. 2, ed. Peirce Edition Project Staff, 11–26. Bloomington: Indiana University Press.

1998 [1903]. "Sundry logical conceptions." In *The Essential Peirce: Selected Philosophical Writings*, vol. 2, ed. Peirce Edition Project, 267–288. Bloomington: Indiana University Press.

Penny, H. Glenn, and Matti Bunzl, eds. 2003. *Worldly Provincialism: German Anthropology in the Age of Empire*. Ann Arbor: University of Michigan Press.

Philips, Susan U. 1998. "Language ideologies in institutions of power." In *Language Ideologies: Practice and Theory*, ed. Bambi Schieffelin, Kathryn Woolard, and Paul Kroskrity, 211–225. New York: Oxford University Press.

2000. "Constructing a Tongan nation-state through language ideology in the courtroom." In *Regimes of Language: Ideologies, Polities, and Identities*, ed. Paul Kroskrity, 229–257. Santa Fe, NM: School of Advanced Research.

2016. "Balancing the scales of justice in Tonga." In *Scale: Discourse and Dimensions of Social Life*, ed. E. Summerson Carr and Michael Lempert, 112–132. Berkeley: University of California Press.

Polányi, Michael. 1966. *The Tacit Dimension*. New York: Doubleday.

Porter, Theodore M. 1995. *Trust in Numbers: The Pursuit of Objectivity in Science and Public Life*. Princeton: Princeton University Press.

Post, Robert C. 2014. *Citizens Divided: Campaign Finance Reform and the Constitution*. Cambridge, MA: Harvard University Press.

Povinelli, Elizabeth. 2001. "Radical worlds: The anthropology of incommensurability and inconceivability." *Annual Review of Anthropology* 30:319–334.

Pugach, Sara. 2012. *Africa in Translation: A History of Colonial Linguistics in Germany and Beyond, 1814–1945*. Ann Arbor: University of Michigan Press.

Pukánszky, Béla. 2000 [1940]. *Német polgár magyar földön*. Budapest: Lucidus.

Pusztay, János. 1977. *Az 'ugor-török háború' után: Fejezetek a magyar nyelvhasonlítás történetéből*. Budapest: Magvető.

Reagin, Nancy R. 2005. "German Brigadoon? Domesticity and metropolitan Germans' perceptions of Auslandsdeutschen in Southwest Africa and Eastern Europe." In *The Heimat Abroad: The Boundaries of Germanness*, ed. Krista O'Donnell, Renate Bridenthal, and Nancy Reagin, 248–266. Ann Arbor: University of Michigan Press.

Richland, Justin. 2008. *Arguing with Tradition*. Chicago: University of Chicago Press.

Rivarol, Antoine de. 1784. *De l'universalité de la langue française; discours qui a remporté le prix à l'académie de Berlin*. Ed. H. Juin. Paris: Belfond.

Rodgers, Daniel T. 1987. *Contested Truths: Keywords in American Politics since Independence*. New York: Basic Books.

Rodgers, Daniel T., and Sean Wilentz. 1991. "Languages of power in the United States." In *Language, History and Class*, ed. Penelope J. Corfield, 240–263. Oxford: Blackwell.

Roediger, David. 1999. "Race, labor and gender in the languages of antebellum social protest." In *Terms of Labor: Slavery, Serfdom and Free Labor*, ed. Stanley L. Engerman, 168–187. Stanford: Stanford University Press.

Roger, Jacques-François. 1828. *Fables sénégalaises; recueillies de l'Ouolof, et mises en vers français*. Paris: Nepveu.

Rogin, Michael. 1992. "Blackface, white noise: The Jewish jazz singer finds his voice." *Critical Inquiry* 18(3):417–453.

Rosa, Jonathan. 2018. *Looking Like a Language, Sounding Like a Race*. New York: Oxford University Press.

Rosslyn, Wendy. 1995. "Poem without a hero: Overview." In *Reference Guide to World Literature*, 2nd ed., ed. Lesley Henderson. Detroit, MI: St James Press.

Royall, Anne Newport. 1826. *Sketches of History, Life and Manners in the United States, by a Traveller*. New Haven, CT: Printed for the Author.

1969 [1830]. *Letters from Alabama, 1817–1822, with Biographical Notes and Introduction by Lucille Griffith*. University: University of Alabama Press.

Said, Edward. 1978. *Orientalism*. New York: Pantheon Books.

Sapir, Edward. 1921. *Language*. New York: Harcourt, Brace, & World.

1949 [1938]. "Why cultural anthropology needs the psychiatrist." *Psychiatry* 1:7–12. Reprinted in *Selected Writings of Edward Sapir*, ed. David Mandelbaum, 569–577. Berkeley: University of California Press.

Sarfaty, Galit. 2012. *Values in Translation: Human Rights and the Culture of the World Bank*. Stanford: Stanford University Press.

Saussure, Ferdinand de. 1959 [1916]. *Course in General Linguistics*. Trans. Wade Baskin. New York: Columbia University Press.

1967 [1916]. *Cours de linguistique générale. Édition critique préparé par Tullio Mauro*. Paris: Payot.

Schatzki, Theodore. 2002. *The Site of the Social: A Philosophical Account of the Constitution of Social Life and Change*. University Park: Pennsylvania State University Press.

2005. "Peripheral vision: The site of organizations." *Organization Studies* 26:465–483.

Scheffler, Israel. 2001. "My quarrels with Goodman." *Philosophy and Phenomenological Research* 62(3):665–677.

Scheuringer, Hermann. 2010. "Mapping the German language." In *Language and Space: An International Handbook of Linguistic Variation*, Vol. 2: *Language Mapping*, pt. 1, ed. Alfred Lameli, Roland Kehrein, and Stefan Rabanus, 158–179. Berlin: Walter de Gruyter Mouton.

Schieffelin, Bambi. 1990. *The Give and Take of Everyday Life*. New York: Cambridge University Press.

2014. "Christianizing language and the dis-placement of culture in Bosavi, Papua New Guinea." *Current Anthropology* 55(S10):226–237.

Schieffelin, Bambi, Kathryn A. Woolard, and Paul Kroskrity, eds. 1998. *Language Ideologies: Theory and Practice*. New York: Oxford University Press.

Schilling, Roger. 1942. *A német nyelvatlasz Magyarországon*. Budapest: Akadémiai Kiadó.

Schirmunski, Viktor M. 1962. *Deutsche Mundartkunde: Vergleichende Laut- und Formlehre der deutschen Mundarten*. Berlin: Akademie-Verlag.

Schmidt, Robert, and Jörg Volbers. 2011. "Siting praxeology: The methodological significance of 'public' in theories of social practices." *Journal for the Theory of Social Behavior* 41(4):419–440.

Schrambke, Renate. 2010. "Language and space: Traditional dialectology." In *Language and Space: An International Handbook of Linguistic Variation*, ed. Peter Auer and Jürgen Erich Schmidt, 87–106. Berlin: de Gruyter.

Schuchardt, Hugo. 1882. "Zur afrikanischen Sprachmischung." *Das Ausland: Wochenschrift für Länder und Völkerkunde* 25:867–869.

1884. *Slawo-deutsches und Slawo-italienisches*. Graz: Leuschner und Lubensky k.k. Universitäts-Buchhandlung.

1928 [1870]. "Über die Klassifikation der romanischen Mundarten." Leipziger Probevorlesung von 1870. Reprinted in *Schuchardt Brevier: Ein Vademekum der allgemeinen Sprachwissenschaft*, ed. Leo Spitzer, 166–188. Halle: Max Niemeyer Verlag.

Schütz, Alfred. 1970. *On Phenomenology and Social Relations: Selected Writings*. Ed. Helmut R. Wagner. Chicago: University of Chicago Press.

Scott, James C. 1998. *Seeing Like a State: How Certain Schemes to Improve the Human Condition Have Failed*. New Haven, CT: Yale University Press.

Scott, Walter. 1822. *The Pirate*. Edinburgh: Archibald Constable.

Seewann, Gerhard. 2000. *Ungarndeutsche und Ethnopolitik*. Budapest: Osiris.

Seewann, Gerhard, and Edgar Hösch, eds. 1991. *Aspekte ethnischer Identität: Ergebnisse des Forschungsprojekts "Deutsche und Magyaren als nationale Minderheiten in Donauraum."* Munich: Oldenbourg Wissenschaftsverlag.

Segal, Daniel. n.d. "Translation effects in historical writing."

Shapero, Natalie. 2001. "The city that reads now the greatest city in America." *Johns Hopkins News-Letter*, February 15.

Silverstein, Michael. 1976. "Shifters, linguistic categories and cultural description." In *Meaning in Anthropology*, ed. Keith H. Basso and Henry A. Selby, 11–55. Albuquerque: University of New Mexico Press.

1979. "Language structure and linguistic ideology." In *The Elements: A Parasession on Linguistic Units and Levels*, ed. Paul R. Clyne, William F. Hanks, and Carol L. Hofbauer, 193–247. Chicago: Chicago Linguistic Society.

1993. "Metapragmatic discourse and metapragmatic function." In *Reflexive Language: Reported Speech and Metapragmatics*, ed. John Lucy, 33–58. New York: Cambridge University Press.

1998 [1992]. "The uses and utility of ideology." In *Language Ideologies: Practice and Theory*, ed. Bambi Schieffelin, Kathryn Woolard, and Paul Kroskrity, 123–145. New York: Oxford University Press.

2001 [1981]. "The limits of awareness." Sociolinguistic Working Paper 84. Reprinted in *Linguistic Anthropology: A Reader*, ed. Alessandro Duranti, 382–401. Oxford: Blackwell.

2003. "Indexical order and the dialectics of sociolinguistic life." *Language and Communication* 23 (3–4):193–229.

2005. "Axes of evals: Token versus type interdiscursivity." *Journal of Linguistic Anthropology* 15(1):6–22.

2013a. "From inductivism to structuralism: The 'method of residues' goes to the field." *History and Philosophy of the Language Sciences*. https://hipilangsci.net/2013/09/11/from-inductivism-to-structuralism-the-method-of-residues-goes-to-the-field.

2013b. "Discourse and the no-thing-ness of culture." *Signs and Society* 1(2):327–366.

Silverstein, Michael, and Greg Urban, eds. 1996. *Natural Histories of Discourse*. Chicago: University of Chicago Press.

Simmel, Georg. 1971 [1908]. *On Individuality and Social Forms*. Ed. Donald Levine. Chicago: University of Chicago Press.

Simpson, David R. 1986. *The Politics of American English, 1776–1850*. New York: Oxford University Press.

Simpson, Rita. 1997. "Metapragmatic discourse and the ideology of impolite pronouns in Thai." *Journal of Linguistic Anthropology* 7(1):38–62.

Sine, Babacar. 1974. "Esquisse d'un réflexion autour de quelques éléments de philosophie wolof." *Présence Africaine* 1974(3):26–40.

Slezkine, Yuri. 1994. *Arctic Mirrors: Russia and the Small Peoples of the North*. Ithaca, NY: Cornell University Press.

Smith, Christopher. 2013. *The Creolization of American Culture*. Carbondale: University of Illinois Press.

Smith, Henry Ash. 1960. *Virgin Land: The American West as Symbol and Myth*. Cambridge, MA: Harvard University Press.

Smith, Van, and Fred Siegel. 2001. "Can Mayor O'Malley save ailing Baltimore?" *City Journal* 11(1). http://www.city-journal.org/html/issue_11_1.html.

Smith-Rosenberg, Carroll. 1992. "Dis-covering the subject of the 'Great Constitutional Discussion,' 1786–1789." *Journal of American History* 79(3):841–873.

Sonneck, Oscar G. 1909. *Report on Star Spangled Banner, Hail Columbia, America and Yankee Doodle*. Washington, DC: Government Printing Office.

Southern Literary Messenger. 1837. "The New England character." July:412–416.

      1842. "Eloquence in New England: Scraps from the diary of a Virginian sojourning in Boston." 8(1):68–71.

      1860. "The difference of race between the Northern and Southern people." 30(26):401–409.

      1861. "A true question: A contest for the supremacy of race, as between the Saxon Puritan of the North and the Norman of the South." 33(1):19–25.

Spannenberger, Norbert. 2005. *A magyarországi Volksbund: Berlin és Budapest között*. Budapest: Lucidus Kiadó.

Spitzmüller, Jürgen. 2007. "Staking the claims of identity: Purism, linguistics and the media in post-1990 Germany." *Journal of Sociolinguistics* 11:261–285.

Stammler-Gossmann, Anna. 2009. "A life for an ideal: Matthias Alexander Castrén." *Polar Record* 45(234):193–206.

Stein, Roger, B. 1965. "Royall Tyler and the question of our speech." *New England Quarterly* 38:454–474.

Steinthal, Heymann. 1867. *Die Mande-Neger-Sprachen: Psychologisch und phonetisch betrachtet*. Berlin: F. Dümmler.

Stevens, S. S. [Stanley Smith]. 1946. "On the theory of scales of measurement." *Science* 103:667–680.

Stevenson, Robert Louis. 1993 [1883]. *Treasure Island*. New York: Dover.

Stone, Geoffrey. 2004. *Perilous Times: Free Speech in Wartime*. New York: Norton.

Storing, Herbert. 2008. *What the Anti-Federalists Were For: The Political Thought of the Opponents of the Constitution*. Chicago: University of Chicago Press.

Strathern, Marilyn. 1988. *The Gender of the Gift*. Berkeley: University of California Press.

Swanson, John. 2017. *Tangible Belonging: Negotiating Germanness in Twentieth Century Hungary*. Pittsburgh: University of Pittsburgh Press.

Swigart, Leigh. 2001. "The limits of legitimacy: Language ideology and shift in contemporary Senegal." *Journal of Linguistic Anthropology* 10(1):90–130.

Swiggers, Pierre. 1990. "Ideology and the 'clarity' of French." In *Ideologies of Language*, ed. John Joseph and Talbot Taylor, 112–130. Cambridge: Cambridge University Press.

Sylla, Assane. 1978. *La philosophie morale des Wolof*. Dakar: Sankoré.

Szelényi, Balázs A. 2003. "Enlightenment from below: German-Hungarian patriots in eighteenth century Hungary." *Austrian History Yearbook* 34:111–143.

2007. "From minority to Übermensch: The social roots of ethnic conflict in the German diaspora of Hungary, Romania and Slovakia." *Past and Present* 196(1):215–251.

Taylor, William Robert. 1961. *Cavalier and Yankee: The Old South and American National Character.* New York: G. Braziller.

Teachout, Zephyr. 2014. *Corruption in America: From Benjamin Franklin's Snuff Box to Citizens United.* Cambridge, MA: Harvard University Press.

Thacher, James. 1823. *A Military Journal during the American Revolutionary War, 1775–1783.* Boston: Cottons and Barnard.

Thiam, Ndiassé. 1998. "Catégorisations de locuteurs et representations sur le mélange wolof-français à Dakar." In *Imaginaires linguistiques en Afrique*, ed. Cécile Canut, 91–105. Paris: L'Harmattan.

Timberlake, Phil. 2003. "'A voice so cruel, and cold, and ugly': In search of the pirate accent." *Voice and Speech Review* 3(1):85–97.

Tomb, Howard. 1989. *Wicked French for the Traveler.* New York: Workman.

Toobin, Jeffrey. 2012. "Money unlimited: How Chief Justice John Roberts orchestrated the Citizens United decision." *New Yorker*, May 21, 36–47.

Trautmann, Thomas R. 1997. *Aryans and British India.* Berkeley: University of California Press.

Tsitsipis, Lukas. 2003. "Implicit linguistic ideology and the erasure of Arvanitika (Greek-Albanian) discourse." *Journal of Pragmatics* 35:539–558.

Tyler, Royall. 1970 [1887]. *The Contrast: A Comedy.* New York: Burt Franklin. (First performed in 1787).

Urciuoli, Bonnie. 1996. *Exposing Prejudice: Puerto Rican Experiences of Language, Race and Class.* Boulder, CO: Westview.

Urla, Jacqueline. 2012. *Reclaiming Basque: Language, Nation and Cultural Activism.* Reno: University of Nevada Press.

Vermeulen, Hans F. 2015. *Before Boas: The Genesis of Ethnography and Ethnology in the German Enlightenment.* Lincoln: University of Nebraska Press.

Verschueren, Jef. 1995. "The pragmatic return to meaning: Notes on the dynamics of communication, degrees of salience, and communicative transparency." *Journal of Linguistic Anthropology* 5(2):127–156.

Vigouroux, Cécile. 2009. "A relational understanding of language practice: Interacting timespaces in a single ethnographic site." In *Globalization and Language in Contact: Scale, Migration and Communicative Practices*, ed. James Collins, S. Slembrouck, and M. Baynham, 62–84. London: Continuum.

Vygotsky, L. S. 1978. *Mind in Society: The Development of Higher Psychological Processes*, ed. Michael Cole. Cambridge, MA: Harvard University Press.

Waldstreicher, David. 1997. *In the Midst of Perpetual Fetes: The Making of American Nationalism, 1776–1820.* Chapel Hill: University of North Carolina Press.

Waugh, Linda. 1982. "Marked and unmarked: A choice between unequals in semiotic structure." *Semiotica* 38(3–4):299–318.

Weber, Eugen. 1976. *Peasants into Frenchmen: The Modernization of Rural France, 1870–1914.* Stanford: Stanford University Press.

Webster, Noah. 1967 [1789]. *Dissertations on the English Language.* Boston: Isaiah Thomas and Co.

Wegener, Philip. 1880. "Über deutsche Dialektforschung." *Zeitschrift für deutsche Philologie* 11:450–480.

Weiner, Annette. 1984. "From words to objects to magic: 'Hard words' and the boundaries of social interaction." In *Dangerous Words: Language and Politics in the Pacific*, ed. Donald Brenneis and Fred Myers, 161–191. Prospect Heights, IL: Waveland.

Weinreich, Uriel, William Labov, and Marvin I. Herzog. 1968. "Empirical foundations for a theory of language change." In *Directions for Historical Linguistics: A Symposium*, ed. W. P. Lehmann and Yakov Malkiel, 97–195. Austin: University of Texas Press.

Weinrib, Laura. 2016. *The Taming of Free Speech: America's Civil Liberties Compromise*. Cambridge, MA: Harvard University Press.

Wenker, Georg. 1877. *Das rheinische Platt*. Düsseldorf: Im Selbstverlage des Verfassers.
1886. "Vortrag." *Verhandlungen der 38. Versammlung deutscher Philologen und Schulmänner in Gießen vom 30. Sept. bis 3. Okt. 1885*, 187–194. Leipzig.

Werth, Paul, W. 2002. *On the Margins of Orthodoxy: Mission, Governance and Confessional Politics in Russia's Volga Kama Region, 1827–1905*. Ithaca, NY: Cornell University Press.

Wickman, Bo. 1988. "The history of Uralic linguistics." In *The Uralic Languages: Description, History and Foreign Influences*, ed. Denis Sinor, 792–818. New York: Brill.

Wild, Katharina. 2003. *Zur komplexen Analyze der 'Fuldauer' deutschen Mundarten Südungarns*. Ungarndeutsches Archiv 6. Budapest: ELTE Germanistisches Institut.

Williams, Raymond. 1977. *Marxism and Literature*. Oxford: Oxford University Press.

Willson, Beckles. 1909. *The Life and Letters of James Wolfe*. New York: Dodd Mead.

Winkler, Adam. 2018. *We the Corporations: How American Businesses Won Their Civil Rights*. New York: Liveright.

Woolard, Kathryn A. 2016. *Singular and Plural: Ideologies of Linguistic Authority in 21st Century Catalonia*. New York: Oxford University Press.
2019. "Language ideologies." In *International Encyclopedia of Linguistic Anthropology*, ed. J. M. Stanlaw. New York: Wiley-Blackwell.

Woolard, Kathryn A., and Bambi B. Schieffelin. 1994. "Language ideology." *Annual Review of Anthropology* 23:55–82.

Wortham, Stanton. 2001. *Narratives in Action*. New York: Teachers College Press.

Wright, J. Skelly. 1976. "Politics and the constitution: Is money speech?" *Yale Law Journal* 85:1001–1021.

Wright, Robert. 1864. *The Life and Letters of Major General James Wolfe*. London: Chapman and Hall.

Yates, Frances. 1966. *The Art of Memory*. Chicago: University of Chicago Press.

Zahan, Dominique. 1970. *Religion, spiritualité et pensée africaine*. Paris: Payot.

Zimmerman, Andrew. 2001. *Anthropology and Antihumanism in Imperial Germany*. Chicago: University of Chicago Press.

Zsigmond, Gábor. 1977. "Hunfalvy Pál útja az embertudománytól az etnográfiáig." In *Népi kultúra – népi társadalom*, ed. Gyula Ortutay, 207–251. Budapest: Akadémiai Kiadó.

Index

314   Index